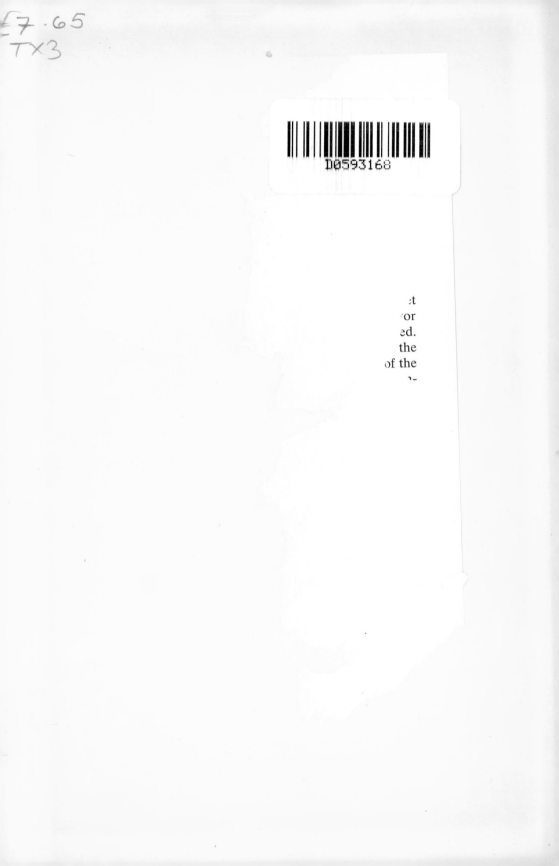

D0593168

ːt
ʹor
ed.
the
of the
ˈ⌐

Political integration:
The formation of theory and its problems

New Babylon

Studies in the behavioral sciences

10

Mouton
The Hague - Paris
mcmlxxii

Political integration:
The formation of theory
and its problems

Johan K. De Vree

Mouton
The Hague - Paris
mcmlxxii

This book was printed with financial support of the Netherlands Organization for the Advancement of Pure Research (Z.W.O.)

Library of Congress Catalog Card Number: 72-80002 √
© 1972 Mouton & Co
Printed in the Netherlands

Voor Anneke

FOREWORD

Political as well as social science today shows a distinct preference for publications presenting factual studies based on new empirical research; that is, for studies which add directly to our knowledge of the political and social environment.

This marks a reaction to an earlier tradition of books being written about books, in which frequently general speculations and descriptions by others were merely rephrased, in a manner of presentation not seldom less attractive than that of the originals.

Our present-day preference for case studies – factual descriptions and studies of concrete situations – is justified, since there are now so many workers who can professionally engage in the political and social sciences. Using modern techniques, these researchers collect many valuable data and thus carry out the routine labours which according to Thomas Kuhn are typical of 'normal' science. All the same, no discipline can do without the books about books, since these include not only publications rephrasing the expositions of others but also studies that contribute to the debate on theory formation, from which criteria for the design and setup of new empirical research are to be derived. Books of this kind will often be born of the desire to impose some sort of order on earlier research by analysing real or fancied contradictions in studies by different authors and by explicitly spelling out hitherto implicit assumptions.

De Vree's starting point was the question of whether different views of international integration contain elements that can be used for a general theory of integration. His efforts to answer this question inevitably produced a snowball effect. He had to sift through large amounts of material in his quest for arguments and assumptions which, combined with statements sometimes derived from entirely different contexts in the substantial writings of various authors, could lead to a reconstruction of their basic principles. But before he could start out on this methodical search, he himself had to construct the 'sieve' needed to tease out the elements of theoretical analysis frequently hidden in lengthy disquisitions. This aspect of his work is reflected in the extensive and penetrating methodico-philosophical discussion of Chapter II.

The snowball grew; even as De Vree analysed the various views of integration, the perspective of his chosen problem widened further. For it appeared meaningful to regard international integration, defined as the 'institutionalization of the political process among a group of states' as only one special case of political integration, defined as the 'process of the formation and development of institutions through which certain values are authoritatively allocated for a certain group of political actors or units'. Thus the way was opened for a study of those views of the political process in general which appear to underlie the modes of reasoning which the various authors adopt with regard to the integration phenomenon. For, while at first sight one gets the impression that there are a number of different contemporary theories of integration, closer scrutiny reveals that the modes of reasoning are identical in certain central aspects regarding the functioning of the politcal process. To explain this functioning, De Vree formulates twelve postulates which are seen to form the frequently implicit basis of the various integration theories dealt with.

Early on the emphasis already shifts from international integration to the general issue of institutionalization, while in the framing of the postulates it is suggested that integration be defined as 'any increase of a political system's decision-making capacity'. As a result, it is possible to direct attention to the important role that physical violence can play in the integration process, and which is not reduced until integration has reached that phase in which institutionalization takes place. De Vree points out that in the literature, remarkably, attention is focussed on integration as a peaceful process, in spite of the fact that in so many historical cases of integration physical violence has been a central factor.

This type of penetrating analysis of studies by other authors entails immense risks. Not least among these is the danger that the analyst, prompted by a desire to prove his own views right, does but scant justice to the theories under scrutiny and lets himself be lured into adopting a hypercritical stance. De Vree has avoided this trap by diligently searching for any clues, no matter how small, in the literature studied, as well as by consistently so interpreting any ambiguous passages as to give the authors, fully and unreservedly, the benefit of the doubt. As a result, his criticisms are invariably constructive, in the literal sense of the word: he always assumes fully worked out conceptual structures where frequently only a few elements are explicitly worded.

A a time when political science is often under attack for its alleged 'irrelevance' as falling short in social concern and responsibility, De Vree shows that an entirely different critical attack on many activities in the political science domain is possible and worthwhile: a critical attack directed at inadequate theorization. This proves to be an extremely relevant undertaking.

Hans Daudt
Professor of Political Science,
University of Amsterdam

TABLE OF CONTENTS

PREFACE

To a large extent this book deals with political integration in an indirect way. Rather than dealing directly with that phenomenon, the book is concerned primarily with theorizing about it; it is thus one step removed from the phenomenon itself. Accordingly, the book is to a large extent concerned with problems of a more general nature, such as those of the nature and structure of scientific theories, their relation to their subject-matter, and their development and historical growth.

From this perspective theorizing about integration merely serves as one domain among others in which to apply, test, and illustrate the more general, meta-scientific notions developed. Specifically, it is sought to demonstrate *how*, in the domain selected, such meta-scientific notions can be put to use, *how* crucial they are for a proper understanding of the theorizing discussed, and *how* they aid the development of insight into the domain's subject-matter (political integration) itself. In short, the book may be read as a case-study or exercise in the philosophy of science.

However, it is not only that.

The fact that the book is, to an important degree, indirectly concerned with political integration does not mean that this phenomenon would be unimportant here. On the contrary, theorizing about integration has been chosen as the subject for analysis precisely in order to deepen our understanding of that phenomenon. Against the background of the history of thinking about integration, the more important contemporary efforts at theory construction are subjected to a rather intensive and detailed analysis applying the meta-scientific theory developed in chapter two. Here my aim is to isolate, preserve, and reconstruct what appeared to be the strong points in current thinking and research, what seemed to contribute to the formation of a theory of political integration. And although this analysis does involve a certain amount of critique of the authors discussed, criticism is *not* the purpose of the present book. Rather than being a mere critical description and appraisal of existing literature in the field of political integration, the book is meant to be thoroughly constructive in that it seeks to use existing literature in the development of an adequate integration theory. Consequently, the analysis always opts for what seems to be the best possible interpretation of an author's writings.

Political integration turns out to be a phenomenon of central significance in the field of political science. It soon becomes apparent that any theory of political integration sharply poses the need for and the problems of general political theory and most, if not all, of its many aspects and elements.

Accordingly, in its several chapters the present book is to a significant extent concerned with general political theory. And it becomes clear, from the last chapter in particular, that no advance in the theory of political integration may be expected without considerable advances in political theory generally. Or that a much more advanced general political theory than is at present available is a prerequisite for the further development of a theory of integration. Although the development of such theory is difficult indeed, and although the theorizing discussed in this book shows many defects and weaknesses and still is of a relatively weak, loose and informal kind, yet a considerable body of rather tightly integrated and relatively plausible knowledge, the beginnings of a theory, can be seen to emerge from the literature. This provides a convenient starting-point for the development of stronger, i.e. more consistent, strict and precise, and empirically better testable theory. This may induce some sense of optimism as to the progressive and cumulative development of knowledge concerning politics and integration.

The book has been written as a doctoral dissertation under the guidance of Professor H. Daudt of the University of Amsterdam. During the entire course of the enterprise he has freely given me of his time and energy. His interest, advice, and criticism have greatly stimulated me and have considerably improved the book's quality. For all this I thank him very much. I also thank Professors P. R. Baehr and R. J. Mokken, equally from the University of Amsterdam, for having read the manuscript and for their many remarks on it.

It remains to be mentioned that, having finished my investigations for this book in the autumn of 1970, I was not able to discuss any literature published after that time.

INTRODUCTION

1. THEORY FORMATION AND POLITICAL INTEGRATION

Since the Second World War the phenomenon of international integration as manifested in the creation and development of such organizations as the European Communities, and the Latin American Free Trade Association, has received a good deal of attention from political scientists. Often their investigations have been of a rather limited scope. They deal with relatively small segments of the problem of international integration, with details of the structure and functioning of some particular institutional set-up, or with the historical circumstances of its inception and growth. In many cases, too, these investigations do not go much beyond what is immediately and empirically given, while no attempt is made to link them with knowledge of a more general character concerning the problems of integration and of politics. Frequently their character is more that of historical narration than of theoretical analysis and explanation.

In the work of some scholars, however, notably in that of Ernst B. Haas, Karl W. Deutsch, Amitai Etzioni, and Leon N. Lindberg, attempts are made to investigate the phenomenon of international integration in a more comprehensive and theoretical fashion. Dealing with the phenomenon in its entirety, these authors try to discover the mechanisms and processes which underlie its occurrence or non-occurrence and which determine its form and evolution. They attempt to transcend the immediately given in that they seek to acquire knowledge of general validity and applicability. In so far as particular cases of international integration are investigated, this is generally done in order to discover the principles that rule the integrative process, or to test insights concerning these already gained in some other way.

It is this contemporary theorizing in the field of international integration which constitutes the main theme of this book. This theme, however, involves two different ranges of problems that go beyond the comparatively narrow field of international integration. The first of these relates specifically to the term 'theorizing'. Here my aim is the development and application of certain methodological, or rather 'meta-theoretical', principles. In this respect the book may be viewed as an exercise in 'applied philosophy of science'. In the second place, with regard to the expression 'international integration', I have sought to find out whether and to what extent the authors mentioned have developed a scientific theory about that phenomenon. Although the analysis which follows will inevitably be critical at times, criticism and polemics have not been the reasons for which I have undertaken the analysis and written the book. Rather, I have been interested in what seemed to be the strong points in the reasoning of the scholars concerned, in what seemed to be of use for the construction of a scientific theory and as a starting point for further research. In so doing, it is hoped some contribution has been made to our knowledge of a process which, in my view, is of central significance both in the international and in the national political setting.

In the next two sections I will briefly deal with each of the two problems mentioned separately.

2. META-THEORY AND THEORY

This being in large part a book *about* some particular instances of scientific theorizing, a somewhat special vocabulary is needed in which to write it. Discourse *about* scientific theories is of a 'higher' level or order than discourse *within* them; it does not consist of the things or phenomena, the processes or mechanisms which figure in these theories themselves, but it is concerned with the nature of the concepts with which and the way in which such theorizing proceeds. In other words, a *meta-theory* is required in which questions regarding the meaning of the term 'theory', the character of theory formation, the structure of a theory, the rules for its acceptance or non-acceptance, and so forth, are answered.

In the case of an already fully developed and explicitly formulated scientific theory such a second-order theory is necessary to judge the adequacy of the former, the extent to which it meets the formal requirements, and in what respects it could or should be modified. However, intimately related to the role which has just been indicated, a meta-theory can also play a much more active role in the generation of a scientific theory. But then it would seem indispensible that it be formulated as explicitly as possible. If so, it can serve as a guide for theorizing: it establishes the criteria to judge the relevance and necessity of empirical research, it makes it possible for disparate pieces of knowledge to be tightly integrated within larger structures, it indicates the measure of freedom the investigator enjoys with regard to the empirical reality he seeks to explain. Insight into the nature of scientific theory formation in general would thus lead the theorist to preceed in a conscious and economical fashion. For the analysis to be undertaken in this book it is this second role which is most relevant.

As yet the word 'theory' cannot be said to have acquired a completely unambiguous meaning in the social sciences. Rather, it would seem, the word is used in a number of different senses, and it covers a whole range of somewhat different meanings. At one end of this range 'theory' seems to designate any kind of abstract reasoning without regard to its formal structure or the function it fulfils. At the other end of the range the word is used in a much more specific and precise sense: that of a deductive-nomological piece of knowledge, with a well-defined structure, and satisfying certain very rigorous standards both with respect to its internal structure and the relation with its subject matter. In this latter sense (which will be defined more precisely in chapter two) the word is used in such disciplines as logic, mathematics, and the physical sciences. In this 'strong' sense, too, it will be used in the present book.

However, if interpreted in this fashion, this raises a problem of somewhat special character with important consequences for the character of this work. For a reading of the publications of the scholars under consideration (i.e., Haas, Deutsch, Etzioni, and Lindberg) makes it soon clear that none of them does develop a theory in the strong sense which has been indicated. What they do, in fact, falls somewhere in between the two extremes mentioned. Their writings generally show a mixture, difficult to analyse, of historical narrative and the description of minute details, interspersed with bits of theoretical analysis, sometimes on a very high level of abstraction. An added complication is the fact that some of the authors have written very much, while no single publication gives a full exposition of their argument. Elements of this are to be found scattered over many different publications, and in order to gain a full understanding of their line of reasoning such elements somehow have to be put together.

Thus there can be no question of finding the theories of the authors concerned by just consulting one or two of their publications and summarizing their contents. Neither can the present investigation be limited to the task of judging whether or not such theories meet the standards of scientific theorizing, whether or not they are true and fit the facts. Questions such as these will even play a decidedly secondary role. Especially with regard to the problem of their fitting or not fitting the facts, their truth or falsity, it appears that no decision can be made as yet.

In these circumstances the task of the following analyses consists primarily of the (re-)construction of some scientific theories of the process of international integration on the basis of the writings of a few authors. Starting from the phenomenon of international integration as this has been defined by the authors themselves, their work is investigated with the aim of finding the elements with which, and the structure within which, that phenomenon can be explained, that is, from which its occurrence or non-occurrence can be deduced. It can be easily seen that for such an analysis to succeed a fairly explicit meta-theory is indispensable. For we need criteria which allow us to choose the elements that are necessary, to decide what is relevant and what is not, and to what extent, to judge which elements fit in with which other elements, and what is their position within the structure as a whole.

This approach raises another problem, one regarding the relation of the present writer to his sources, i.e., the publications of the scholars analysed. For the decisive criterion which guides the investigation of these sources is the way in which they contribute to the formation of a scientific theory. As compared with this the intentions of the authors themselves, or the verbal expressions they use, are of secondary importance. Obviously this involves a certain amount of freedom with regard to the sources. Sometimes Occam's razor will have to be used in order to eliminate superfluous concepts; sometimes, too, things that have been left implicit by the authors themselves have to be rendered explicit; and in some cases it will be useful or necessary to introduce somewhat different terms. But, of course, the process of formulating explicitly what is presupposed implicitly in any kind of empirical-scientific argument could go on endlessy. As a general rule I have kept as closely as possible to the explicit formulations of the authors themselves, and I have refrained from developing arguments for which no clear support could be found in their writings.

Primarily this analysis is meant to serve as a contribution to the formation of an adequate theory of the integration process. However, it has also been undertaken for two reasons of a somewhat different kind. In the first place it is hoped that it will show, or make visible, the direct and 'practical' importance of basic epistomological and philosophical research for the development of political science. Secondly, it will be attempted to show that there is no reason to reject the possibility of rigorous theorizing in the field of political science. As a matter of fact, it will appear that with regard to the problem of integration the beginnings of such a form of theorizing are already visible.

The above also suggests what this book is not: a historical survey of the origins, evolution, and influence of the opinions of a few particular political scientists in the tradition of the current histories of political theories. But although I have emphasized analysis rather than history, the subject is not without some historical interest. For one thing, seen against the background of earlier thinking on international integration the theorizing dealt with in this book marks a particularly crucial phase in the development of political science. It clearly shows a break through pre-scientific modes of reasoning and research. To make this visible has been the principal reason for including a brief chapter on the history of the subject. To some extent this book is also an attempt to take stock of present knowledge with regard to the process of integration, to assess the distance which has been covered thus far in explaining it, and to see in what direction further progress might be expected.

3. PRELIMINARY NOTES ON POLITICAL INTEGRATION

3.1. *Introductory*

It has already been said that the subsequent analysis of integration
theories will be concerned with integration as conceived by the respective authors themselves. That is, the phenomenon of integration itself
is approached in a rather naive fashion. No previous knowledge about
it is really necessary. But although at the outset of my investigations
I had this naiveté to a fairly large extent, this has been lost by now,
of course. As there is no sense in pretending to an innocence which
one no longer has, it may even be positively useful to be somewhat
more explicit about the phenomenon of integration itself; some insight
of a general nature into the character of the problem concerned may
serve as an aid to the understanding of what follows. Thus, while
trying not to prejudge the results of the analyses proper, I will very
briefly go into the nature of the setting in which the problem of integration arises (3.2), and into that of the phenomenon itself (3.3).
Finally, in sub-section 3.4, the problem of the selection of the authors
to be analysed shall be dealt with.

3.2. *The setting*

The world political scene, it seems, has been and still is dominated by
national states. So much, at least, would seem to apply to the 'modern'
period of our history. More generally, and leaving out of consideration
the question of what exactly a national state is, the world always
seems to have consisted of a relatively large number of more or less
isolated and exclusive political units, limited both geographically and
in terms of population.

Within such entities the political process is regulated and controlled,
sometimes to a remarkably high degree. The political activities of the
population are channelled through elaborate networks of institutions
and procedures so that the political process as a whole is enacted in a
relatively orderly and reliable manner. This is not to say, of course,
that there are no important differences to be found between such
states or statelike entities, and that they are all equally effective in
regulating political life within their borders. The frequent occurrence

of phenomena such as revolution and civil war, sometimes leading to their complete breakdown, in many parts of the world, shows that even on this level the political order can be a very precarious thing indeed. But at least in some cases such states are remarkably stable and effective political organizations, showing a high measure of resilience and adaptibility, and capable of effectively mobilizing the energies and resources of the population in the pursuit of common ends. Generally speaking, the national level is the highest level on which, up to the present, man has been able to achieve a certain measure of control over the political process.

As compared with what can be found within the states, politics between them generally is characterized by a singularly rudimentary degree of organization and regulation. In the absence of more or less sophisticated provisions for the solution of the problems arising between them, they are, to a large extent, thrown on rather crude and unreliable methods – especially war and the threat of using physical violence. Lacking institutions capable of making sure that obligations which have been undertaken are indeed met, any common solution reached in the international sphere seems to rest only on a shaky and momentary balance between the parties' capabilities to contest it. If anywhere, it would seem to be here that a primeval state of nature still can be seen to exist. In this realm, rather than controlling it man often seems to be the helpless victim of forces which he does not even seem to understand very well, but that nonetheless easily drive him to extremely costly catastrophes.

This situation, in one form or another, seems to have prevailed during the entire course of human history. This may well lend it the character of an ineluctable necessity deeply rooted in an immutable nature of man or of human society. Merely to think about possible alternatives, or to conceive of a change in the situation described, is already tinged with utopianism – something to be left to unworldly idealists. It could be, however, that this discrepancy between the regulation of national and of international politics, or, rather, the limited extent to which such regulation has been attained thus far, merely reflects a situation in which the concerns of most people were of a geographically and socially limited kind. In circumstances in which most of man's activities and problems only affect a comparatively small group of people, while such groups themselves live in a relative isolation from each other, we would expect effective political organization to emerge earlier within such groups than among them. So long as the number and importance of the problems arising between these groups remain relatively restricted, and so long as the costs of occasional warfare are deemed to be tolerable, there will hardly be an impetus for the organization of their relations beyond the level of incidental diplomatic bargaining and alliance-formation.

However, such a situation is not necessarily permanent. It might change in that the amount and importance of the traffic going on between the originally more or less self-contained units increases. A point might conceivably be reached at which the traditional mechanism of diplomacy is unable to cope with those increases. The result could be warfare, of course. But it could also set in motion forces leading to the development of new institutions and procedures capable of handling more problems in a more reliable way and on a more durable basis.

Taking a longer view, such a development seems indeed to characterize the international arena during the last century or so. The Industrial Revolution, with its new methods of production requiring large markets and bringing about an increase in trade and monetary operations, the development of new means of communication and transport, the revolutionary developments in weaponry and military organization, all this led to a rapid shrinking of the world. It brought the different parts of the world into very much closer contact with each other. It led to a considerable increase in the amount and the range of the problems arising among the several states. To an increasing extent the single state appeared to be too restricted an organization for effectively solving its most pressing problems, such as economic development and security. In the new circumstances their solution was only possible on an international level and required a kind of international cooperation rather different from that for which traditional diplomacy was fit.

Among the most visible consequences of this state affairs in the recent past have been one economic depression and two World Wars, all three of an utter destructiveness, and all three involving a very substantial part of the world's population. Somewhat less visible and spectacular, however, has been the emergence of a growing number of all kinds of international organizations, ranging from such highly technical bodies as the International Telegraphic Union of 1865 to the more recent and much more general United Nations. Although such organizations may differ considerably in many important respects, there are also some common features. Generally, they are organized on a permanent basis, having their own staff which, in principle at least, is independent from the bureaucracies of the constituent states. They perform some weak governmental functions, attempting to solve the problems arising in some field on an international scale, and formulating common policies with regard to these. Representing an increasing measure of organization or institutionalization of the international political process with regard to certain kinds of problems, they can be viewed as the beginnings of some form of international government. They are the manifestations of processes of international integration as conceived in this book.

On the basis of the considerations outlined above, such a development in the direction of an increased institutionalization of international political life in the recent past was to be expected. The historical development thus would seem to confirm at least the possibility that the national state is *not* the definitive and final form in which man's political life will be organized. However, we should be extremely careful in extrapolating developments of which we have as yet only seen the first weak symptoms. In the first place, the formation and development of the national state represents anything but a completed phase in the history of mankind. In many parts of the world, indeed, this phase even seems to have only barely begun. And in the case of those states which have already been established for a long time, they seem to assume ever more and more important functions and responsibilities with regard to the life of their members. This would tend to give them a greater weight for the peoples concerned, and it might well make international cooperation or integration more difficult to achieve. Secondly, we lack insight into the processes involved, and into the direction they might take. Thus, it is not at all certain that international integration will result in a form of government, global or regional, of the same character as can be found in present-day national states. Neither do we know whether, and to what extent, the existence and functioning of those states will be incompatible with evolving forms of international government. Finally, there is not, up to the present, any international organization which can be considered a true form of international government as compared with government within the states. Even the European Economic Community, which probably is the most advanced form of integration at present, is an enterprise of a rather limited scope, not only with regard to its functions, but also with regard to the way it performs them. There is no question of its Commission acting as a really autonomous government even within its proper sphere of competence.

The fact remains, however, that during the recent past certain typically international integrative developments actually have been taking place. In itself this is interesting enough to merit the attention of political scientists. More significantly, from a scientific viewpoint, international integration is merely one particular manifestation of a process of much wider import playing an important role both in national and in international politics. Insight into international integration could well further our understanding of politics on lower levels. In order to make this clear it is necessary to deal with political integration in somewhat greater detail.

3.3. *The phenomenon*

Before going into the question of how political integration is to be conceived, it is necessary to deal briefly with the nature of politics. This is not simply for the reason that the word 'political' serves as an adjective in the expression 'political integration'. Rather, a description of what politics is is needed to arrive at a meaningful concept of integration; it defines the context within which we are to look for a proper definition of the latter term.

Politics, then, may be defined as the process through which values are allocated authoritatively for the participants in some interaction. This is an extremely wide definition. It equally covers ordinary law-making and decision-making by governments, phenomena such as war and diplomatic bargaining through which values are in fact allocated authoritatively but which cannot be conceived simply as decision-making. In the same fashion the character of the participants, or of the interaction, is unspecified. Depending upon the nature of the problem to be investigated, the participants may be states or governments, interest groups or political parties, or just individual people. With regard to the nature of the values concerned, this may be any thing, situation, or ideal which the participants wish to have allocated authoritatively, including for example the official religion or ideology of a state, the price of milk, the international protection of human rights, or a subsidy to some depressed industry. 'Authoritative', or 'binding', may equally mean many things, from a command backed by the sanction of physical elimination, to a resolution of an international parliamentary assembly.

Rather than a weakness, however, the extreme elasticity of the above definition of politics must be considered its strength. In a sufficiently precise manner it indicates what, in any particular situation or context, has to be considered its political elements, or, alternatively, what renders it interesting for the political scientist. The definition does not restrict politics to some one particular institutional or procedural setting such as the contemporary Western nation-state. This renders it all the more attractive for an investigation into the integration phenomenon, since it occurs in a milieu which is not so institutionalized.

International integration, so much will have become clear by now, is concerned with the institutionalization of the political process among a group of states. It apparently consists of the creation of new political entities superimposed on the previously independent states which they comprise, and having their own apparatus of institutions and procedures through which they perform some governmental functions with regard to their members. In terms of the above definition of politics, *integration* can be defined *as the process of the formation and development of institutions through which certain values are authoritatively allocated for a certain group of political actors or units.*

Thus conceived integration is one particular way in which the political process can be enacted. As such it can be juxtaposed to the other ways or methods of conducting politics. In the case of politics among states one can think of two of these: war and traditional diplomacy, or, in somewhat more general terms, the use and threat of violence or the inflicting of more or less severe deprivations, and occasional bargaining. For, basically, these, too, are methods by which values are authoritatively allocated in some interaction. But being of an essentially incidental character, their regulatory capacity is rather low. They tend to come into play when important problems have already arisen, that is, in a relatively late stage. They are not, in general, fit to deal with these problems in depth, to deal with the roots of conflict, and to control the developments that underlie it. In contradistinction to all this, integration is concerned with the development of ways and means through which the political process among a group of units can be enacted in a more reliable fashion, and problems can be dealt with in a more permanent and less superficial way, so that the costs and risks of the process will be reduced.

The provisional definition given above clearly brings out that integration should not be conceived as an all-or-nothing affair. It allows of innumerable gradations, shades, and nuances. Thus it may be differentiated according to the kind of institutions involved (e.g. intergovernmental or supranational), the character of the values allocated (e.g. agricultural prices or human rights), and the nature of the actors (e.g. states or other human groups), and the degree to which the value allocations are binding and are made effective (e.g. advisory opinions or legislation supported by supervision and sanctions). This also implies a dynamic, rather than a static, conception of the integration phenomenon. Instead of restricting it to one particular set of values for the variables mentioned, a great number of different sets, indicating different forms or levels of integration, are possible. Different situations can thus be compared in a disciplined way, rendering it possible to trace changes in the course of time, indicating growth or decay, and to fix the character of the process involved.

An added advantage of this definition and of the type of analysis to which it conduces is that it supersedes the very rough traditional categories, such as 'supranational', 'federal', or 'confederal'. Their vagueness and lack of specificity easily lead to endless terminological discussions as to whether X is, or is not, really 'supranational', or whether X is a 'federation' or a 'confederation'.

Nowadays the problem of political integration is probably most often thought of within the context of international relations. The above definition, however, is equally applicable to the national political milieu, and to the contemporary national state. To some extent it depends on how one conceives of politics. In the definition used here no *a priori* distinction is made between politics on the national level and international politics. As far as I can see, the political scientist is interested in essentially the same phenomenon on both levels. In so far as any distinction is to be made at all it should rest upon rather more pragmatic considerations: additional special problems occurring on the two levels, different competences required, the need for some division of labour. In the present state of development of the discipline, however, a more integrated approach is probably more fruitful. In the case of the subject under discussion in this book there is a special reason for such an approach, namely that the phenomenon of integration does not entirely fit in the traditional categories. To some degree it partakes of both fields. On the one hand, at the outset of some particular integrative development it is concerned with an important transformation of an *international* system. On the other hand, at some later point it may well be concerned with something which might better be called a *national* system.

After all, from a scientific viewpoint the national state can be conceived as merely one particular (that is strongly institutionalized) form of a political process among others. It, too, can be conceived as the outcome of certain processes of integration. Moreover, it does not seem very plausible that even this national state can be seen as a static thing, or as a fixed endpoint. There are rather obvious differences in the level of integration attained by, say, the Netherlands, or Nigeria. And similarly there are probably important differences in the measure of integration of, for example, the United States now and around the middle of the nineteenth century.

Besides, there are important historical reasons for operating with a broad definition of integration. For it appears that 'international' is only a relative and time-bound notion. The relations between Bavaria and Prussia, or between Burgundy and Normandy, which once were of an international character, now are those of the parts of one national state. Conversely, Turkey and Egypt, or the Netherlands and Belgium, while now being separate national states, once were parts of larger political entities. Rather than to speak in terms of national and international politics, the problem is to investigate how and why such processes of integration and disintegration took place.

Both the more or less distant past and the contemporary period show a wealth of different forms of political integration: National states in almost all conceivable phases of development, empires, federations and confederations, international organizations properly so called in a large variety of shapes, the sometimes very loose, but extremely interesting structures to be found in so-called stateless societies. Among such phenomena the form of international integration with which, for the most part, the theories to be analysed in this book are concerned, is of a rather special and comparatively recent kind. With some exceptions, it is mainly the international integration of already well established Western industrial states in which the respective authors are interested. This, of course, poses some special problems. Among these the most important one seems to be that this form of integration is a particular kind of what might be called 'second-order integration'. That is, it concerns the integration of units which are themselves already integrated to a fairly high degree, having evolved strong and generally effective political institutions of their own. Besides, these units are extremely complex, both with regard to the character of their political structures and the large number and variety of the groups and individuals that participate in their political life.

This leads to such problems as how the external policies of those units result from what kinds of processes within them, who participates in them, and how, and with what effect? Further, how do those units interact, under what circumstances will institutionalization of these interactions occur, and what are the conditions for its stability and effectiveness? And to come full circle: how do occurrences in the inter-unit sphere enter the political processes within the units, and how does inter-unit integration affect the structure and funtioning of the units? It has already been shown, moreover, how closely the problem of integration is linked to those of peace and war.

An investigation into the phenomenon of international integration can thus be seen to involve to a significant extent many of the most important things with which political science is normally concerned. This will also appear clearly in the theorizing to be discussed subsequently. As such links to other parts of the discipline are generally rather obvious, however, I have for the most part refrained from explicitly drawing the reader's attention to them, or to the relevant literature. Finally, it has appeared that integration is a complex phenomenon of a wide scope and of fundamental importance, practical as well as theoretical. From the point of view which has been advanced sometimes, namely that the formation of adequate theories can, for the time being, only succeed with regard to phenomena of a much more limited kind and on a much smaller scale, integration would hardly qualify as an appropriate research subject. Although it will appear that there is not, as yet, a satisfactory integration theory, the measure of progress which has in fact been attained in that direction seems to be large enough so as to induce grave doubts concerning the above point of view.

3.4. *The theorists*

Originally this study was intended as an investigation into existing theories of international integration. As may have appeared from the foregoing introductory remarks, however, it soon became clear that the relevance of such theories was not restricted to the international field proper. For, in principle, the theories concerned would equally seem to apply to different kinds of other phenomena not normally considered to be international. Somewhat paradoxically, and with some slight exaggeration, it might even be said that those theories themselves do not even offer sufficient criteria for separating the international variant from other forms of integration. And what emerges from their analysis seems to be of a much more general validity and applicability.

For one thing, this has led me to drop any reference to the field of international relations from the title of this book. On the other hand, it induced me to consider a radical broadening of its scope. Should not, more specifically, other theories, concerned with integration in other settings, be brought in for extensive analysis? Relevant literature is not entirely lacking. Thus, research has been done on nation-building, particularly in the developing areas, and there is much literature, though mainly of an anthropological character, on so-called non-state societies. But in general it is concerned only with specific aspects of the problem, or deals with the phenomenon in a purely descriptive fashion. In contradistinction to the efforts to be analysed in this book, it does not in general attempt the construction of a comprehensive and rigorous theory. This does not lend it to the type of analysis to be undertaken in this book.

The above testifies to the extent to which the contemporary Western nation-state is, or at least was, taken for granted in political science. The fact that the scientific attack on the problem of integration has been centred on its international variant, can probably be explained by the high visibility and the great urgency of the problem in the post-war international setting.

In any case, it is in this field that we find some efforts to develop a comprehensive explanation of the phenomenon of integration. And although, as has already been said, these efforts have not been completely successful thus far, yet it appears that enough has been achieved to render extensive analysis of them, as scientific theories in a comparatively rigorous sense, possible as well as worthwhile. Particularly this applies to the investigations done by Ernst B. Haas, Karl W. Deutsch, Amitai Etzioni, and Leon N. Lindberg. To each of these authors a separate chapter will be devoted. They are not the only scholars, however, having done research in the field of international integration. In so far as others have made contributions of a more partial character to knowledge of the phenomenon such as Joseph S. Nye, Johan Galtung, and Claude Ake, these will be included in the final chapter of the book. In that chapter I will make an attempt to synthesize the findings of the foregoing analysis. For reasons which will be made clear in sec. 4.1 of chapter two, I will not deal separately and explicitly with the existing (critical) literature on the theorists to be discussed.

4. OUTLINE OF THIS BOOK

The plan of this book is as follows. Chapter one is devoted to a brief discussion of the tradition of thinking about international integration. It is not meant to be a comprehensive historical survey of that tradition. Rather, it attempts to isolate some of its most important elements and characteristics against which contemporary theorizing can be judged. It is concerned with showing some of the continuities and discontinuities as to problems and approaches between contemporary theorizing and earlier thinking on international integration. Thus, present-day efforts are put in a wider perspective.

In chapter two much attention will be paid to some of the more fundamental philosophical and epistemological problems involved in the scientific enterprise. For our purposes the most important among these is the problem of theory formation. The results of this inquiry are to guide the analyses of the several authors in the subsequent chapters. At first sight this arrangement (the chapter on theory formation after that on the tradition of thinking about international integration) may seem somewhat curious. However, as it appears that the tradition is almost entirely of a pre-scientific character, elaborate and sophisticated analytical tools are of very little use here.

As has already been indicated, the final chapter will be concerned with an attempt to synthesize what has been found so far. Do the foregoing analyses enables us to construct a basis from which further research can be undertaken, and what are the questions that should be answered in order to make the cumulative growth of knowledge about integration possible? In this chapter, too, other contributions than those of the scholars mentioned above will be included.

Finally, some brief remarks on the bibliographic materials used are in order. First, as to the authors whose work is to be analysed extensively, I have consulted all publications I could lay my hands on. Although I dare not pretend to completeness in this respect, I trust to have included enough of the relevant publications so as to permit a satisfactory analysis of the thoughts of their authors. In the second place, the literature which has been used in the preparation of the several chapters generally differs considerably. For this reason I have refrained from including one common bibliography for the whole book. Instead, separate bibliographies are added to each of the individual chapters.

1 INTERNATIONALISM, FEDERALISM, AND FUNCTIONALISM

1. ON THE PREHISTORY OF THE SUBJECT

1.1. *Antiquity*

Even when conceived in a narrow international sense, political integration has been a very common process in the history of mankind. It is anything but a particularly new and contemporary phenomenon, but it has occurred in all times and under a wide variety of circumstances. Nowadays a heavy emphasis is laid on the peaceful character of the integration process; the contemporary literature is almost wholly concerned with this form of the process. There is thus a tendency to lose sight of other kinds of integrative processes, past as well as present, some of which involve a significant amount of violence and warfare. One of the most obvious examples of such a form of integration is that of empire. Empires have been recurring phenomena in human history from a very early stage down to the present. The history of empire, while not, perhaps, very venerable, is a very long one indeed.

Empires, not without some justification, have traditionally been associated strongly with violence, coercion, and military conquest. Exclusive preoccupation with this one aspect, however, might carry the phenomenon beyond the pale of integration theory or even of political science. However, as has been made particularly clear by *Eisenstadt* (1963) and *Fieldhouse* (1966), among others, there is much more to empire than military force and coercion. In particular, it does not seem very plausible that these alone would account for the remarkable stability and longevity of some of these empires.

But empire is not the only form of international integration to have occurred in history, and physical violence not the only means through which it has been achieved. Larger political entities have been formed through marriage of rulers and through inheritance, by means of purchase, and by voluntary union or federation. Besides, history knows a multitude of weaker forms of integration such as alliances or leagues with common political institutions, or limited-purpose confederacies. Thus, to mention only some of the better-known examples, marriage and inheritance played important roles in the formation of Spain and of the Habsburg Empire; some parts of the present United States (notably Louisiana and Alaska) were acquired by purchase; Switzerland, the United States, and the Netherlands were constituted by means of union or federation. Somewhat looser forms are exemplified by such organizations as the Hanseatic League, and by the many alliances, leagues, and confederacies that existed in ancient Greece.

The above is certainly not exhaustive. Nor have the different categories used been established in a sufficiently precise fashion. Indeed, they will often overlap. For example, the distinction between a loose type of confederation and a well-knit defence alliance will not always be easy to establish. Also they cannot be differentiated in a straightforward fashion according to their involving or not-involving military force. In all of the cases mentioned such force did probably play a role, though in some it might have remained in the background more than in others.

The foregoing observations in and by themselves do not purport to serve as a scientific analysis of the integration process, nor do they amount to a concise history of the phenomenon. They merely indicate that processes of integration, and of disintegration, of course, have occurred during the entire course of human history. Seen in this light, it is really remarkable that thinking and theorizing about it occur only at a relatively late point in history. That is, even when we do not insist upon its complying with scientific standards, such thinking, to all intents and purposes, only dates from the late European Middle Ages.

As so much of contemporary achievement in the cultural field has its roots in ancient Greek civilization, not least with regard to political science, one would expect some Greek precursors in the field of integration theory, too. For, at first sight the conditions for the development of thinking about international integration in Greece could hardly be more favorable. In the first place, a considerable advance in political science was made. And secondly, the phenomenon itself was certainly not unknown to the Greeks, and played a far from insignificant role in their political life.

It may well be that the ultimate destruction of the Greek political system was caused above all by the failure of the city-states to arrive at a stable and durable order among themselves. Lacking cohesion and the means for an efficient common use of their resources, the city-states ultimately proved to be incapable of effectively resisting the newly emerged outside powers, Macedonia and Rome in particular. This, however, does not imply that the Greek world only consisted of closed, self-consistent, and autarkic political units, living in a state of nature and continuously waging war on each other. On the contrary, a rich variety of political institutions and procedures had emerged through which the relations among generally limited numbers of units were regulated. These ranged all the way from the mainly religious, and politically rather insignificant, Amphictyonic Council of Delphi which comprised almost the whole of the Greek world, to the much more limited Achaian League which came close to being a full-fledged federation. In between we find a considerable number of alliances, leagues, or confederacies, with limited membership, to a greater or lesser extent institutionalized, and with limited functions, such as foreign policy or defence (see especially *Ténékidès*, 1956a and b; *Freeman*, 1893). While it remains true that the Greek peninsula as a whole did not succeed in attaining a sufficient measure of integration to withstand the pressure of the Roman and Macedonian empires, it cannot be said that the city-state system was ignorant of any process of integration.

In the contemporary political philosophy, however, these phenomena have gone largely unnoticed. Although they must have been of considerable concern to politicians and citizens, they have left almost no traces in the literature. Several reasons can be adduced to account for this striking neglect.

1. The most advanced forms of integration tended to occur in the relatively backward areas of the Greek world (*Freeman*, 1893: 112). In such areas there were no fully developed, powerful city-states which would have had to sacrifice their sovereign independence, and to swallow their hegemonial ambitions.

2. The greatest cultural advance took place in the city-states. This

more or less naturally led to a conception of the city-state as the most advanced political form, and to a rather exclusive preoccupation with this particular form among political thinkers.

3. Greek political thought has a distinctly moral character. It is concerned above all with such things as justice and the good life. Such problems, however, arise most directly, and are most pressing and visible, in man's immediate surroundings, especially when politically organized – the (city-)state. For here many of man's most important concerns are subject to political control and regulation; important rights and duties are created; people command other people; and common ends can be pursued. All this is much less the case in the sphere of international politics. Except for the few who are directly concerned, most people are linked to it only indirectly; lacking, for the most part, effective political institutions, rights and duties exist only to a minimal extent, and so do common ends; also there seems to be much less room here for the conscious control of man's fate and the realization of the good life. Consequently, it may be suspected, a typically moral attitude is not particularly conducive to the analysis of international integration. One may rather expect it to result in a more or less exclusive preoccupation with those forms in which man's political life is organized and regulated in a more direct and immediate fashion, the state in particular.

Greek political thought did not immediately develop into an empirical science of politics in the modern sense. Rather, it is moral concerns that came to dominate political thought to the virtual exclusion of empirical research and theorizing. No tools for the analysis of the phenomenon of international integration were fashioned. Besides, large-scale empires became the major forms in which political life was organized. The most important among them, the Roman Empire, seemed to be simply a matter of straightforward military conquest – something to be justified, rather than explained. As it proved to be extremely durable, it could be very easily taken for granted by political thinkers. After all, it has remained a major focus of attention for political thinkers, and a source of legitimacy for rulers, far into the European Middle Ages. This is not, perhaps, a very favorable situation for the growth of interest in, and the formation of theories about, international integration. In any case, both seem to be virtually non-existent before the end of the Middle Ages.

1.2. *Middle Ages*

Professor Brugmans (1958/61, Vol. II: 16-17) describes how, in the
10th and the 11th centuries A.D., the Church made some attempts
at regulating warfare in Europe. These attempts, however, were of a
very limited nature. Rather than with a fundamental attack on the
phenomenon of war through a radically different organization of political life, they were concerned with mitigating its harshest features,
and protecting the Church itself from damage to its possessions. Their
practical results have been insignificant. Apparently, they neither led
to further reflection upon international integration.

Since about the fourteenth century, however, there is a marked increase of interest in the phenomenon. From that time onwards there
is a steadily growing stream of publications on the subject. As has
already been said, I will not attempt to describe the history of this
thinking and writing, but will restrict myself to the isolation of some
tendencies and elements that are relevant to the understanding of
present-day theorizing. For this purpose I have distinguished, rather
roughly, to be honest, between 'internationalism', 'federalism', and
'functionalism'. The first of these three labels requires, perhaps, some
clarification. It is meant to designate the body of proposals, schemes,
pleas, and projects for some form of international integration that
have been formulated and advanced from the fourteenth century up to
the present day. Federalism and functionalism represent somewhat
later stages in the history of thinking about integration. They also involve more empirical research, and are more directly related to present-
day theorizing.

In this chapter a separate section will be devoted to each one of the
intellectual currents mentioned. In a final section I will attempt to
draw some more general conclusions from the foregoing discussion.

2. 'INTERNATIONALISM'

On internationalism, the oldest of the three currents, we can be relatively brief. As indicated above, it is made up of innumerable plans
and proposals for international integration in one form or another.
But it does not constitute, nor does it seem to be based upon, a definite

doctrine or theory about that phenomenon. Indeed, it is meant to guide action and policy rather than to explain integration. In the absence of an analysis as to when and how such integration can occur at all, internationalism has a somewhat utopian flavor. In retrospect it is really astonishing how long it took man merely to start asking questions concerning the character of integration, the conditions for its occurrence and development, etc. The problem is put almost exclusively within a normative context. Instead of asking such questions as 'what is it?', or 'how and why does it occur?', it is asked 'what do (or should) we want?', or 'how can we achieve it?'. Of course, these latter questions cannot really be answered without some kind of answers to the non-normative questions mentioned, without some insight into the conditions under which integration does or does not occur. On the other hand, any answer to a normative question will somehow imply some insight into the non-normative problems involved. But this latter need not be fully consciously and explicitly formulated. This, in fact, fully applies to internationalism.

This history of internationalism may be dated from the beginning of the fourteenth century (for this history, see *ter Meulen*, 1917, 1929, 1940; *Voyenne*, 1964; *Foerster*, 1967; *Brugmans*, 1965). At that time Dante wrote his *De Monarchia* (around 1313), and the French royal lawyer Pierre Dubois his *De recuperatione Terre Sancte* (around 1306). Both men are concerned with the organization of international political life in an important period of transition in European history. This period is characterized, on the one hand, by the emergence of strong national states, and, on the other hand, by the decline of the position of both pope and emperor. But whereas Dante, more strongly bound by the tradition, looks back towards the Roman empire which he seeks to universalize to some extent, Dubois politically is the more modern of the two in that he accepts the new national state as given. Rather than raising the matter of the national state in any fundamental fashion, he proposes a plan for the establishment of institutions through which the relations among the existing national states can be regulated in a more or less peaceful way, and common purposes can be realized.

As its title indicates, Dubois's pamphlet proposes a renewal of the crusades against the Turks. This was to be realized through the creation of a particularly close European alliance, highly institutionalized, with a representative council and a permanent court. It was to have fairly wide powers of arbitration, intervention, and sanctions. In short, it went rather far in the direction of a kind of European federation.

Probably, the plan is interesting less for the details of the specific institutional structure put forward than for the motives which underlie it. Like many later plans and proposals, this one, too, seems to serve a mixture of purposes. Thus, most conspicuously, it is aimed at the creation of the capacity to wage war on a powerful outside enemy. On the other hand it proposes the organization of an intra-European peace. At the same time, however, it is meant to secure a hegemonial position for France in Europe. And, finally, it is to serve the French king Philip the Fair, in his struggle against the pope, Boniface VIII, who was to be deprived of his secular power.

When we look at things from a larger historical perspective, it appears to be no accident that thinking about international integration, be it only in the form of formulating recommendations for policy, started in France and in the fourteenth century. As indicated above, it marks the transition from thinking in terms of empire to a conception in which the national state became the basic unit of the European political process (cf. *Rougemont*, 1961: 55). While the idea, or myth, of European unity under the two swords gradually lost its attractiveness and relevance, there emerged, on a lower level, powerful units of a more restricted kind: the national states, such as Spain, France, and England. But this also necessitated a different kind of organization of European political life. Somehow, common tasks, in particular the defence against the Turks, had to be fulfilled. Problems arising between independent states had to be solved, and war among them had to be limited as far as possible. These functions could no longer be fulfilled by pope or emperor. In other words, international organization had become a problem; and, one may argue, especially so for Frenchmen. For, at that time, France probably was the strongest and most ambitious state on the European continent. An institutionalization of international life could serve as a very convenient cloak for French hegemonial aspirations. It would have solidified the present French position; to some extent Dubois's plan can be interpreted as representing an attempt to claim for France the position formerly held by pope and emperor (*Foerster*, 1967: 73; see also *ter Meulen*, 1917: 82).

Although the internationalist tradition may be said to start with

Dubois's plan, and although international relations remained a problem ever since the fourteenth century, thinking about international integration progressed only very slowly. It took more than a century and a half before Antoine Marin's and George Podiebrad's *Traité d'alliance & confédération entre le Roy Louis XI George Roy de Bohéme & la Seigneurie de Venise, pour résister au Turc* (1462) was published. And between this scheme and Thomas Campanella's *Von der Spanischen Monarchy, . . .* (1620), again some 160 years elapsed. In the meantime the curiosity and energy of political thinkers seem to have been absorbed by the national state and its problems. After all, it is the period during which the European system of national states became firmly established, a development which was to be consolidated in the Peace Treaty of Westphalia (1648).

From the seventeenth century onwards, however, there is a steadily growing stream of schemes and proposals for some kind of international organization or another (see *Foerster*, 1967: 325-354, for a chronological list of such plans from 1306 until 1945). Thus, Crucé and Sully write in the seventeenth century, the Abbé de Saint-Pierre and Kant in the eighteenth, Saint-Simon and Proudhon in the nineteenth, and Coudenhove-Kalergi and Streit in the twentieth century – to mention only a very few of the better-known writers.

Although it is extremely difficult to generalize about this mass of writings, it would seem that after the seventeenth century more than before, the desire to abolish or contain war has inspired internationalism. Whereas, for instance, the plans by Dubois and by Podiebrad were largely power-political schemes, much of later internationalism seems to be motivated by an awareness that 'war does not pay' (as in Crucé's *Nouveau Cynée*, 1623), or that it is morally reprehensible (as, e.g., in Kant's *Zum ewigen Frieden*, 1795).

In so far as this is true, later internationalism would reflect a growing awareness of the material, political, and moral costs involved in the functioning of the system of national states. Moreover, to put the problem of international integration in terms of peace and justice, rather than in those of the more or less traditional power-political interests of some one of the states concerned, raises it to a more general level of discussion. The problem then becomes one of the state system as such, rather than one of the purposes and interests of any particular state therein. This is, of course, its proper location: it is concerned first of all with a transformation of a certain state *system*, and only secondarily with the individual states and their policies. Thus, conceiving the problem in such general terms as peace and justice might lead sooner to the development of an adequate insight into it. To some extent, therefore, later internationalism shows progress over its earlier manifestations. All this does not mean that a desire for peace and justice has been the sole motive underlying later internationalism. Especially in projects for the integration of a limited part of the world, Europe, for example, a desire for peace within that part may well be accompanied by a desire for aggression, or for more power, vis-à-vis the rest of the world.

As has been noted before, internationalism does hardly contain a scientific analysis of the phenomenon of international integration. The questions which are raised concerning it are almost entirely normative. Although the way in which the problem was conceived in much of internationalist thinking after the 17th century could have led more easily to a scientific analysis properly so called, this possibility has hardly been realized. As will appear from the section on functionalism, elements of scientific reasoning begin to appear only in a very recent past. With regard to the non-normative insights into international politics and integration underlying internationalism, a few common traits may be isolated.

1.   To begin with, the difference between national and international politics would seem to be conceived as consisting in the absence of common governmental institutions among the states. Thus, these states, or rather their rulers, can act out their greed, passions, and ambitions with relative impunity. Not inhibited by any sanction of a higher authority, they freely use armed force in order to further their designs. As such force can only be checked by counterforce, the result is endless warfare among the states. International society is in a state of nature.

2.   In general, internationalist thinking is focused on the actors in international politics. The ills of international society are explained in terms of the motives and conduct of the states, and more specifically of their rulers. There seems to be hardly an awareness of the processes going on *between* those actors, their dynamics and their influence upon the external actions and the internal developments of the states. Neither is there an analysis of the way in which the foreign

policies of the states are formed, and of the relationships between those policies and the political forces within the states.

3. Accordingly, international integration is conceived of as a rather simple problem. It is essentially one of convincing the rulers of the states that it is in their own best interest to submit to common institutions. This problem solved, integration then simply consists in the conclusion of a formal treaty between the participating states – more or less in the fashion of traditional contract theories. This conception is essentially static and not very convincing.

4. Internationalism is concerned with the framing of plans and proposals for practical policy. But in the absence of more rigorous analysis and research, it hardly rises above the level of utopian scheming. Therefore, it is no accident that its practical effects would seem to have been very limited. Probably its historical role has been that of sensitizing people to the problems involved, and of preparing them for alternatives to the national state, rather than to initiate and to guide the process of integration itself.

3. FEDERALISM

In practice the distinction between internationalism and federalism is not always easy to make. As in internationalism, many federalist thinkers make proposals for some kind of international integration; federalism, too, has a strong normative bent, and many federalist writers seem to be interested more in normative discourse than in scientific analysis. The subject of federalist thinking, however, seems to be somewhat more sharply delimited than that of internationalism. For, while in principle at least internationalism is interested in any kind of international organization, federalism is only concerned with a political organization which has two or more layers of semi-autonomous authorities. Federalism is a comparatively well-established concept in legal theory (cf. *Strong*, 1963: 103 ff.), whereas internationalism largely lacks such a convenient point of departure.

Federalist thinking is a somewhat more recent phenomenon than internationalism. In fact, it can be dated from Johannes Althusius's *Politica Methodice Digesta* (1603). It developed only slowly, however. The main body of federalist writing has been written since the eighteenth century, that is, since the foundation of the American federation. A detailed historical survey of this literature, however, would greatly exceed the scope of the present section (see *Mogi*, 1931). Instead, I will largely limit myself to the contemporary literature, in so far as it is of a political, rather than of a purely legal, nature.

Even when thus restricted, federalism cannot be said to constitute one well-defined political doctrine or theory. For it appears that in abandoning a purely legal approach, much of the precision and definition of the concept of federalism is lost too. Nevertheless a number of common elements do indeed emerge from the vast body of federalist literature.

1. In a general way, as has already been indicated, federalism is concerned with a form of goverment characterized by two or more layers of semi-autonomous political authority. In a unitary state all governmental functions are performed by one central government while the position and competencies of other bodies depend on, and are regulated by, the central government. In a federation, however, the constituent parts (the 'states') themselves are independent political entities whose status and competencies are not controlled and regulated by the central government. Both the centre and the parts have limited governmental tasks; in some fields decisions have to be made by the government of the federation as a whole, and in other fields it is the government of the constituent state that decides. The delimitation of these field is, in principle, a matter requiring the consent of the states themselves which is to be laid down in a constitution – the compact which brings the federation into being. Waiving all legal technicalities, it is this concept of federation which would seem to lie at the basis of federalist thinking.

2. Quite generally, too, a federation is conceived as a means toward an end, a fact which is important in so far as it shows the essentially normative nature of federalist thinking. A federation, then, is a political structure which allows for cooperation and common policies to be conducted by a number of territorially distinct political units in certain fields, whereas those units remain fully independent in other fields. The constituent states relinquish just so much of their 'sovereignty' that common problems can be solved in a regular and peaceful fashion, that tasks exceeding their individual capabilities can

be undertaken successfully. On the other hand, they retain their powers with regard to those problems which they are capable of solving, or that are of a more specific nature, deriving from the particular circumstances (e.g., the nature of the population, language, geography, climate, resources, etc.) existing in each of them individually. Federation, in other words, is a means for achieving unity where necessary, while allowing diversity where possible. This theme of unity in diversity runs through all of federalist thinking (cf. *Berger*, 1956: 28; *Brugmans* and *Duclos*, 1963; *Elazar*, 1966: 2; *Aron*, 1958a: 33; *Friedrich*, 1968: 7-8; *Wheare*, 1963: 244-245).

3. But federation is not only a means for integrating existing political units in larger wholes. It can also be conceived as an instrument for the dissolution of unitary states. The conscious application of the federalist principle at all levels of government would mean a cure for many of the ills associated with the large-scale centralized state. Thus, it would bring government much nearer to the people. That is, everybody would have a say in the affairs which most directly concern him in his immediate environment – village, city, county. But he would also have a voice in the 'foreign' policies of such bodies, in the way they would cooperate with other such bodies, and in the policies to be followed in common with them. Being consensual in nature, federalism would greatly limit the possibilities for oppression by powerful centralized states. Minorities would have their own limited government, and there would be no need to suppress them in a fully federalized world. Federalism, in short, would entail a maximum degree of political freedom for everybody.

This line of reasoning has been followed especially by continental European authors (cf. *Aron* and *Marc*, 1948: 7, 129 ff.; *Duclos*, 1968: 3; *Brugmans*, 1956: 11; *Proudhon*, 1921: 113ff.; *Bareth*, 1958: 158). It is extremely critical of the modern national state (see also *Aron* and *Marc*, 1948: 95) in which it is closely related to the thinking of Proudhon (see in particular *Chevallier*, 1956: 87-88, 105; *Proudhon*, 1921). It is directed against the unitary state, and it is probably no accident that it is especially the French authors in whom this 'anarchist' tendency seems to be most outspoken. At the same time, federalism is conceived in an extremely broad fashion. It is meant as a particularly fundamental and deep-going refashioning of man's entire political life. Politics would be put upon an entirely new basis: 'internally' the dis-

solution of the centralized state is meant to exclude oppression and
tyranny, 'externally' it should make war impossible (see especially
Aron, 1958b: 62). Accordingly, federalism is sometimes put forward
as a radically different 'way of life' (*Duclos*, 1968: 5 ff.), or as a new
mystique (*Marc*, 1961: 16) through which the great problems of contemporary man and his civilization are to be solved.

4. There is a strong tendency in federalist writing to conceive the
problems involved in extremely broad and elastic terms, to remain on
a very high level of abstraction, and to arrive at (normative) conclusions in a somewhat cavalier way. Thus, one may well doubt
whether political freedom will always be realized better, or more
securely, under a federation than in a more centralized state. More
specifically, it is not at all certain that any one individual would
enjoy more freedom within a small political community, even when
he has a voice in its affairs, than in a larger one, where his voice
would conceivably count for less. And that a federation as a whole
might be oppressive, is not to be excluded on a priori grounds. Consequently, the federalist thesis about the relationship between freedom
and federation has been contested (see in particular *Neumann*, 1955;
Riker, 1964: 139 ff.). Much the same considerations apply to the idea
that the establishment of a federation would mean an end to warfare,
or that a federation would be less war-minded than a unitary state. In
both cases the relationships posited would have to be spelled out in
much more detail than is actually done, and, especially, they should
be empirically investigated. As matters now stand, federalism leaves
us in the dark as to the precise nature of whose freedom, in what
respects and to what degree, in what kind of a federation (which
bodies have which competencies), will be realized under what conditions. Also it remains silent as to the kinds of violence which would
or would not occur in such a federation, and under what circumstances.

5. Nonetheless, by putting the problem in a broad and abstract
fashion federalist thought relativizes the concept of the national state.
To some extent it does indeed break through the more traditional
conceptions of national and international politics. It shows that political integration (although that term itself is seldom used in the federalist literature) constitutes a problem of a very general nature, whose
importance is not restricted to any one particular setting, be it national
or international. Instead of sanctifying, or ossifying, the national state

as the foreordained, ineluctable endpoint in the organization of man's political life, it rather conceives of that state as a momentary phase, as the momentary result of certain historical developments, developments which may, however, continue.

This insight is already implicit in such thinkers as Althusius and Proudhon; it has been expressed with particular clarity by Carl J. Friedrich. He conceives federalism as a process 'by which a number of separate political organizations, be they states or any other kind of association, enter into arrangements for working out solutions, adopting joint policies and making joint decisions on joint problems' (*Friedrich*, 1963a: 594). As such the phenomenon forms the middle range of a whole spectrum of political organization; at one end it shades into the unitary state, at the other end into the extreme of completely unrelated governments (*Friedrich*, 1963a: 599). Largely the same insight is expressed in what Dusan Sidjanski calls the 'amphictyonic' movement, or process, (*mouvement amphictyonique*. See *Sidjanski*, 1954: 6; *Sidjanski*, 1956: 4, 8), referring to the ancient Greek religio-political Amphictyonic Councils that represented some measure of international integration. This indicates a process in which political organization is attained at ever higher levels. As man's actions come to cover ever wider territories and touch ever wider circles of people, there may grow ever larger political organizations, covering more people and territories. Federalism is a particular manifestation of this process, in Sidjanski's view (*Sidjanski*, 1956: 55).

To repeat, the very general way in which the problem of political integration is put in federalist thinking represents an important advance over traditional internationalism. Less bound by any one particular political form, it operates within a larger historical perspective. It is much more congenial to ideas of process and development. Conceivably, all this could lead more easily to a dynamic approach of the phenomenon of integration, to investigations into the character of the processes underlying it. That is, federalist thinking is much closer to contemporary scientific conceptions of integration as a dynamic process than is internationalism.

However, it has already become clear with regard to the relationship between federalism and freedom or war, that the generality and abstraction of federalist thought are not wholly unmixed blessings. Indeed, these qualities rather seem to have kept it from detailed analysis, and from careful empirical research. Much the same thing seems to occur with regard to the formation of theory in this field. Most of the literature seems to be concerned more with conceptual analyses, or with definitions, than with the explanation of the phenomenon of federalism. But although such analyses are of course indispensable, they constitute only a first step. In federalist literature, however, much less attention is given to the necessary next steps – the analysis of the underlying processes, the generation of testable propositions or hypotheses, and the careful investigation of empirical cases. Consequently, the literature does not show the development of one coherent body of theoretical knowledge about federalism. And instead of a cumulative development of knowledge, we find scattered bits of insight and reasoning.

6.   For all that, federalist thought does show a greater awareness of the problems involved than traditional internationalism. Much more than the latter does, it pays attention to the role of human values, to the dynamics of the process, and to the development of general categories through which to understand the phenomenon. Thus Friedrich writes that 'if values, interests, and beliefs exhibit a stable and structured pattern in which the commonly shared values, interests, and beliefs are counterbalanced by values, interests and beliefs that are not shared, though territorially distributed, then a federal development becomes possible' (*Friedrich*, 1964: 127; see also *Friedrich*, 1955: 521). Now such a proposition is extremely vague. In the absence of further information concerning the specific nature of the values, interests, and beliefs involved, their distribution, and the circumstances under which they will, or will not, lead to federalism, the proposition might be easily dismissed as rhetoric. Nevertheless, it embodies the very important insight to link the process of federalism with the structure of values, beliefs, and interests obtaining in the participating units. And this, in its turn, might well lead to a closer investigation of the relation between the process of federalism and the political processes going on within these units.

Interestingly, Friedrich also hints at an important dynamic aspect of the federalizing process: the role which is, or can be, played by federal institutions once they have been established. While a federalizing process normally involves the establishment of executive institutions at a certain moment, these institutions, in their turn, tend 'to become the spearhead of the process itself' (*Friedrich*, 1955: 522).

'The trend is promoted not only by the vested interests growing up around such an executive (whether in the form of positions, prestige, or material advantages) but also by the greater insight into the objectives, interests, and needs of the inclusive community' (*Friedrich*, 1955: 522). This indicates that a certain transformation in a political system made up of a number of different units (i.e., the establishment of common political institutions) will lead to other transformations, both in the units involved and in the system as a whole. It points to important feedback processes which play a prominent role in the integration theories to be analysed subsequently.

7. In federalist thinking there is a fairly widespread insight that the contemporary national state is obsolete, or obsolescent. To a certain extent, of course, this insight is implied in the 'anarchist' tendency in federalism, as we have seen. There however it was rooted in a very general and largely moral rejection of the unitary or centralized state. Sometimes, however, it is expressed in a more clearcut and precise fashion, opening up important avenues to further research and analysis. Thus, it is maintained, in the present-day world with its developments in technology, communications, transport, industry, and weaponry, and the concomitant increase in the factual interdependency of the peoples of the world, or of very large areas, the national state is unable to perform the functions in response to which it developed. The national state has become too restricted a setting for the provision of such essential services as physical well-being and safety (cf. *Mark*, 1965: 1-3, 131 ff.; *Fischer*, 1955: 59; *Streit*, 1939: 62 ff.; *Schlesinger*, 1945: 3-4).

Whatever might be the plausibility of such a view, it evidently is still far from offering an adequate explanation of the phenomenon of federalism. But whatever may be its demerits, it points to some important relationships. In particular, it relates political institutions to the functions they perform. And although these functions themselves are not analysed in great detail, the problem is at least recognized. Through these functions political institutions can be related to people's expectations, values, and interests concerning them. Through the latter, in turn, institutions are related to developments, processes, and forces in such fields as technology, science, and the economy. This line of reasoning thus holds a potential for a rather sophisticated type of analysis of federalism, or integration. In the federalist literature, however, it is hardly elaborated; but it does play an important role in the theories to be dealt with in subsequent chapters.

8. When federalist literature deals with more specific factors or variables by which the process of federalizing is to be explained, it generally does so in a somewhat loose and untheoretical fashion. The general procedure would seem to be this: from an investigation into a certain number of historical cases of federation, the authors (see in particular *Watts*, 1966; *Wheare*, 1963) isolate certain motives or circumstances that were present in the successful cases or absent in the unsuccessful ones. Thus, Wheare enumerates such factors as military insecurity, a desire to be independent of foreign powers, a hope of economic advantage from union, some prior political association of the units concerned, geographical neighbourhood, and similarity of political institutions (*Wheare*, 1963: 37), to produce a desire for union. In the same vein, Watts produces a set of 11 factors, among which figure the desire for political independence, economic advantage, administrative convenience, defence and diplomatic influence, similarity of political, administrative, and legal institutions, and the role of an outside power (*Watts*, 1966: 43-62).

Now, the point is certainly *not* that these authors have been wrong in enumerating the factors mentioned, or that those factors would be the wrong ones. It seems highly plausible that they are relevant, and that they will play some role in any explanation of federalism or of integration. Such an explanation, however, requires more than this initial plausibility. In particular, it should be shown *why* these particular factors, rather than some others, are relevant, and *how* precisely they are related to the phenomenon of federalism. It is not just a matter of the categories used being rather vague and general, or that their empirical referents are not defined very clearly and precisely. This is important enough, of course. More fundamental is, however, the general absence of argument and reasoning. No criteria are established ruling the choice of variables; the reasoning through which the factors chosen are linked to the phenomenon of federalism generally remains implicit; and hardly an attempt is made to integrate the variables chosen in a larger network of relationships which would allow for the explixit derivation of the thing to be explained – federalism.

In the absence of such an explicit structure of reasoning, the results attained through an empirical study of cases of federation are at best plausible without being entirely convincing. For, even the observation that factor 'x' was present in all known cases of successful federation, while absent from all the unsuccessful ones, is not very enlightening in itself. For one thing, there is absolutely no guarantee that 'x' is at all relevant, that 'x' really had an influence upon the phenomenon. This relevance can only be established on the basis of some prior reasoning; and whether or not the factor involved was indeed influential, equally depends upon such a prior theoretical scheme in which it plays a certain role. Besides, the observation in itself does not say anything about the role of other factors that may well have been much more important. Thus, such an observation is something to be explained, rather than to use it in an explanation of something else.

Thus far, federalist thinking has not resulted in the development of a comprehensive scientific theory of the federalizing process. Nevertheless, it contains a good many starting points for further research and theoretical development. Its conception of federalism as a general problem of political organization, in which it breaks through the traditional national-international distinction; its awareness of the process character of the phenomenon which may conduce it to a dynamic, rather than a static and legal, approach; and its insight that the phenomenon is related to the functions of political institutions, to the values and interests of the participants, and to other social and political processes and phenomena; all these things mean an important advance over traditional internationalist scheming. Federalist thinking might thus be interpreted as an important preliminary to the formation of a scientific integration theory, be it only of one particular form of political integration.

However, this should not be conceived in a narrow chronological sense. It does not mean that federalist thinking is also chronologically prior to contemporary theorizing about integration. In fact, in the foregoing discussion of federalism I have largely ignored chronology. And while it is true that much of the federalist literature does date from a more distant past, much of it is strictly contemporaneous with the theorizing to be analysed extensively in subsequent chapters.

9. In view of this it is really striking how little use federalist thinking makes of the reasoning and findings of current integration theories. The relevant literature is only very rarely referred to. Federalist investigations, it would seem, are virtually unrelated to the efforts of

contemporary political scientists to understand the process of political integration.

It is difficult to give an adequate account of this remarkable situation. The reason can hardly be that the respective subjects are radically different, or totally unrelated. It would seem to be rather obvious to interpret a federation as a particular form of political integration. In both cases the problem is that of the formation of governmental institutions for a number of initially independent units. It is, perhaps, less a question of a fundamental difference as to subject-matter than of a somewhat different background from which federalist thought and current integration theories approach that subject-matter. Federalism generally proceeds on the basis of a relatively well-established legal conception of federal government. Much of the federalist literature remains wedded to a legal vocabulary, and to legal ways of thinking. Current integration theories, on the other hand, are primarily concerned with much looser forms of intergovernmental cooperation and with international institutions, such as the European Communities, which generally lack such a precise legal definition. To some extent these fall outside the traditional legal categories. They are not governments, neither of a federal, nor of any other kind – at least not in a formal legal sense. And to someone who approaches the subject of international integration from a formal legal perspective, such institutions and forms of cooperation might well be uninteresting. That is, he might well conceive them as particular manifestations of rather traditional alliances and leagues of states, but not as possible stages in the process of federalizing.

Besides, as has already been mentioned, federalism has a strong normative orientation. The problem is that of realizing the good life and the good society, to secure freedom and to abolish war. This tendency is particularly outspoken in continental European federalism (see especially: *Richard*, 1958; *Aron*, 1958a; *Marc*, 1961; *Brugmans*, 1956). Now, whatever may be the merits or demerits of a normative orientation in itself, it would seem that in the case of federalism it has tended to keep the authors concerned from the type of analysis which leads to the formation of scientific theories. And apparently this type of analysis, in so far as it occurs in the literature on integration, has neither seemed to be attractive nor relevant to those authors.

As a whole the federalist tradition belongs to a comparatively early phase in the development of scientific insight into the integration phenomenon. That much of it is contemporaneous with more advanced types of analysis and ways of thinking indicates that science does not necessarily progress in a neat linear fashion.

4. FUNCTIONALISM

The last intellectual current to be dealt with in this chapter is that designated by the name of 'functionalism'. As its name implies, functionalism represents an attempt to explain government, and politics generally, in terms of the functions it performs which, in their turn, are related to the needs and interests of the people being governed. Briefly, a government or governmental institution is an agency performing certain functions through which the needs of certain people, individuals or groups, are satisfied. Now, whatever the merits or demerits of functionalism itself, it will be clear that such an approach realizes, or conduces to, two things.

In the first place, it establishes certain analytical categories (functions and needs) through which politics can be meaningfully related to other aspects of human life and to other social processes. At the same time these categories would seem to be perfectly accessible to empirical research. For, in principle at least, it must be possible to establish empirically what functions a certain government, or a certain political process, performs, and what needs, of what groups or individuals, are satisfied through it. To some extent this approach destroys the notion of the state as a monolithic, sovereign body. Instead, it opens up the way for investigations into the precise character of the groups composing it, and into the processes through which these determine the 'how' and 'what' of governmental policies. Functionalism, in short, would thus conduce to a typically scientific analytical approach of politics.

In the second place, the functionalist analysis, through the categories it uses, conduces to a much more general study of politics. As it is not bound to any specific institutional setting, that of the contemporary national state in particular, it makes it possible to investigate political processes in settings which are much less structured and institutionalized. This renders it especially suitable for the analysis of international politics, and for the study of processes of political integration, both on a national and on an international level. Also, it makes it possible to develop alternatives to the national state, that is, other forms of organization of political life.

It must be admitted, though, that actual functionalist thought has not fully exhausted the potentialities, as indicated above, of its approach. In a number of cases the reasoning involved is defective, or the argument is not developed far enough. Instead of careful scientific research, policy recommendations are framed. As in internationalism and federalism, the jump from scientific theorizing to the solution of normative problems is made too quickly (for extensive critical discussions of the functionalist argument, see *Haas*, 1964, Ch. 1; *Foerster*, 1967: 344 ff.).

Functionalism is associated first and foremost with the work of David Mitrany. It is he who has elaborated the doctrine most fully, and who has formulated it most clearly. In this short exposition of the main ideas contained in that doctrine, I shall limit myself to Mitrany's writings. This is not to say, of course, that Mitrany is the only author to have expounded functionalist ideas, nor that his ideas have been developed in an intellectual vacuum, entirely unrelated to other currents of thought. Thus, Haas relates it to Guild Socialism, Marxism, Pragmatism, and Liberalism, while in some form or another functionalism can be found in such writers as Paul S. Reinsch, H. G. Wells, Leonard Woolf and G. D. H. Cole (see *Haas*, 1964: 8 ff., 19 ff.; *Sewell*, 1966: 4 ff.). Without delving very deeply into the precise nature of such relationships, or into questions of intellectual influence, it may be useful to view functionalism in a somewhat broader historical perspective. In particular, it would seem, the doctrine can be placed against the background of two broad historical developments which have occurred during the past hundred years or so.

The first of these is that of the gradually growing measure of international regulation in restricted, and relatively 'technical' fields of activity, as embodied in the Public International Unions of the nineteenth century, the Allied Maritime Transport Council in the First World War, the International Labor Organization, and the many technical committees associated with the League of Nations. Experience with such institutions suggested a new approach to international peace and integration. It seemed to be possible to achieve

these ends without a head-on attack upon sovereignty and the traditional prerogatives of the established states. In order to achieve international peace it did not seem necessary to have the states merge all
at once in a full-fledged federation – a remedy of rather dubious
feasibility. Rather, international cooperation in relatively restricted
fields, initially limited to the more technical aspects of social and
economic life, could easily be conceived as a method to circumvent
the difficult and delicate question of state sovereignty: it would gradually eat into that sovereignty and, ultimately, it would empty sovereignty and the state of their substance.

Traces of such an approach can already been found in certain ideas
propounded by Woolf and the Fabian Society during World War I.
These amount to a proposal to achieve international peace in a gradual
fashion through a generalization of the system of the Universal Postal
Union (*Zimmern*, 1936: 169-173). Experience with the technical committees of the League of Nations after the First World War equally
led to the development of typically functionalist ideas. As Sir Alfred
Zimmern relates,

Thus there emerged, in League circles, what may be described as a new
form of the old Fabian or gradualist doctrine, based upon the assimilative
power of the Geneva spirit and of the institutions which it was creating.
Little by little, so it began to be believed, the morass of 'high politics' would
dry up along its edges, as one issue after another was drained off to Geneva.
Thus eventually there would be a world-wide co-operative system held
together by a network of contacts between government departments (other
than Foreign Offices), professional organisations and individual experts. It
was, indeed, a curious combination of Fabianism and Cobdenism. The
Fabians had looked forward to a co-operative system resulting from public
ownership or control. The Cobdenites had expected to arrive at it through
the multiplication of individual commercial contacts guided by Adam
Smith's 'invisible hand'. Under the League, private and public agencies were
to work together with the same object in view (*Zimmern*, 1936: 322-323).

The second important historical development to which functionalism can be related and of which it represents a manifestion, is of a
more fundamental character. It concerns a rather important change in
the mode of thinking about politics and the state which seems to
characterize political thought in the nineteenth and twentieth centuries

(cf. *Wolin*, 1961: 352 ff.). I have already mentioned that to some extent functionalism dissolves the state into a number of functions through which certain needs of the population are satisfied. Instead of a monolithic state, with an undivided sovereign government caring for the general interest or expressing a general will, there is a system of agencies through which specific needs are translated into specific functional activities. The awe-inspiring abstract state is brought down to earth by conceiving it in terms of more or less trivial and earthly human needs and interests.

Of course, such a conception could also be derived without too much difficulty from earlier contract theories, such as those of Hobbes and Locke, or, more generally, from any theory which explains politics in terms of self-interest, such as that of Spinoza. It would seem, however, that it is only during the nineteenth century that the conception which has been sketched above begins to gain a wider currency. The trend is especially clear in Marx and in socialism generally. Here, as is well known, politics is approached in terms of social and economic forces and interests, and the state is proclaimed an executive agency for an exploitative bourgeoisie. Not only does this show an awareness of the political relevance of a variety of social and economic phenomena and processes, but it places the state in the context of a struggle between groups motivated by different and even antagonistic interests. Besides, the conditions in which industrialization proceeded, and the increasing political mobilization of the population (e.g. through the gradual extension of suffrage) resulted in an erosion of the liberal conception of a state limited to the functions of external and internal security. New political demands were effectively put forward which tended to have the state assume ever more functions in social and economic life. As Mitrany writes, the state suffered a 'complete metamorphosis'.

At the advent of parliamentary government the new middle-class was struggling essentially for two positions: individual freedom and economic freedom. In both respects it wanted to check the promiscuous interference of the autocratic State; or, to put it differently, it wanted power in order to keep the State under control in a negative way – to restrict its functions and activities in favour of *laisser-faire*. Now, on the contrary, every section of the community and every economic interest is imposing some new task upon the State. Hence the State is becoming increasingly a service State – an instrument of life and not merely of order – and that is in my view the present and very different reason why every section and interest is seeking to gain control of the State (*Mitrany*, 1933: 92-93).

To some extent, one might say, functionalism puts the seal of doctrine upon these developments.

After the foregoing discussion the gist of the functionalist argument may have become clear already to a certain extent. At its root is the idea that the activities with which states are concerned can be divided into 'political' and 'technical' matters. 'Political' matters directly involve the existence of the states in their current form and concern in particular the more intangible, 'irrational', and emotionally sensitive factors such as ideology, power, and prestige. This is the area of antagonism and contradiction, which, by their very irrationality and intangibility, are very difficult to bridge and to resolve. 'Technical' matters, on the other hand, mainly involve questions of material welfare concerning which most people are presumed to have the same ideas and needs, and on which consensus does generally exist or is relatively easy to arrive at, being primarily matters of technical and 'objective' ex· pertise.

In a world which is made up of a number of autonomous, sovereign states, war is endemic. In the present condition of the development of technology, industry, economic life, and of the means of communication and transport, the traditional state is unable to provide security and material well-being. It is too small to protect its citizens against the consequences of modern warfare; but it is equally too restricted a setting to secure welfare for its citizens. In modern conditions economic life is a global affair, and individual states only control relatively limited aspects of it. Effective solution of the problems arising in this sphere greatly exceeds the capacities of the individual states. In Sewell's words:

... the functionalist analysis traces the world's difficulties to a global pattern of overtaxed nation-state machinery. For the functionalists, society is innivator, but also society is a maker of claims. Expectations grow for the performance of services (functions), yet the state is no longer able to fulfil even its initially assigned function – the provision of security. Along with a general breakdown in security, linked to it and given a special status by the functionalist thesis, the state has proved itself impotent to satisfy the expanding non-security needs pressed upon it by society (Sewell, 1966: 33).

Mitrany is extremely sceptical about the success of a direct full-scale attack upon state sovereignty to remedy the ills of the present organization of political life. He doubts the feasibility of schemes which, by some neat constitutional arrangement, purport to achieve world government at one stroke (cf. *Mitrany*, 1966: 28 ff.). For such an approach would from the very start directly involve those 'political' problems which are most difficult to solve. In Mitrany's view political integration should not be conceived to consist in an immediate and complete abolition of the existing national states. His idea is, rather, to circumvent it, by initiating processes which will gradually, but none the less certainly, lead to its ultimate disappearance as the dominating form of political organization. Thus he writes, with regard to the problems of peaceful (territorial) change after the First World War:

The only sound sense of peaceful change is to do internationally what it does nationally: to make changes of frontiers unnecessary by making frontiers meaningless through the continuous development of common activities and interests across them (*Mitrany*, 1966: 62).

International integration should start in the area of the 'technical' problems. These are directly related to needs felt by all, the problems involved are clear to everyone, or at least they can be made so, their solution is a matter of scientific insight and technical expertise. Consequently, international government with respect to such problems can best be entrusted to bodies of experts in this field. Governments will the more readily consent to such a transference of their authority as the advantages involved are clear and can be easily calculated, while such a transference in itself only concerns an infinitesimal proportion of their authority and does not involve its 'political' substance.

Such a method also obviates the need for rigid constitutional schemes and for the arduous and delicate labor of precisely fixing the limits and divisions of power and authority. Indeed, such rigidity might well be positively harmful to the process of functional integration. For, 'technical' matters being what they are, it is the inherent scientific or technical nature of the problems involved that determine the scale on which they can most appropriately be solved, the character of the actions and institutions required, and the power needed by the international functional bodies (cf. *Mitrany*, 1966: 72-73). Fixed formal arrangements beyond those which originally define the nature of the function to be performed may block further growth and evolution, and adaptation to new developments. To a large extent such technical activities carried on by international expert bodies should be left to their own devices.

Functional integration, apparently, is a dynamic process. Once started,

... a personnel which would be largely technical and permanent is likely to develop both a professional pride and a vested interest in good performance (*Mitrany*, 1966: 78).

Furthermore, as such international government would concentrate on practical issues, directly related to concrete and tangible human interests and needs, such government would come to enjoy the support of the people (*Mitrany*, 1966: 79). This would tend to make it more difficult for the existing governments to break off their cooperation with, or to obstruct the functioning of, such international governing bodies. Besides, as the process gains momentum and ever more, and more important, activities are brought under the sway of international functional arrangements, the traditional territorial states increasingly loose their functions. Gradually they will loose control over more and more important activities. This will make it increasingly difficult for them to disengage from the growing network of international functional arrangements. And ultimately those states will find themselves to be empty shells, remnants of a primitive past. Thus will be achieved 'peace by pieces', or 'federalism by installments' (*Mitrany*, 1966: 83) – a kind of managerial revolution on a grand scale.

The above exposition of the outline of Mitrany's argument has been cast in a prescriptive mood – and so it is offered by the author himself. In so far as the argument contains a purely scientific, or at least a non-prescriptive, analysis, it calls forth a number of questions and it shows some important gaps and deficiencies. Most of these have already been dealt with more or less extensively by Haas (*Haas*, 1964, Ch. I), Sewell (*Sewell*, 1966, Ch. II), and Claude (*Claude*, 1964, Ch. 17). Accordingly, I will limit myself to two or three of the most fundamental elements of the argument.

1. In the first place, one may have grave doubts as to the distinction between 'technical' and 'political' matters. Of course, there is a difference between, say, a defence policy and policies concerning epidemic diseases. The former would seem to be much more 'important', and to be imbued with more or less vague 'ideological' reasoning to a much greater extent, while its effects are much less easily calculable, than it seems to be the case with regard to the latter. But it is far from easy to go beyond such a relatively impressionistic judgment and to fix such differences more precisely. Besides, it is not at all a priori certain that international cooperation and integration in the field of public health would really proceed more smoothly than in that of defence. Whether or not this is the case would require much more intensive analysis and empirical research.

Mitrany hardly deals with these questions. He does not establish independent criteria for the two categories 'technical' and 'political'. But in their absence much of the argument threatens to become vacuous. Specifically, it comes dangerously close to a conception in which 'technical' merely signifies what works in functional arrangements, and 'political' that which cannot be made to work thus. Obviously, this does not make for understanding the process of integration. Furthermore, Mitrany does not analyse in detail the circumstances under which integration in any one field will, or will not, proceed and through what mechanisms and processes. That, in the political realm, 'technical' problems could be solved by experts, rather than by politicians, on their own technical merits alone, seems to betray a grossly inadequate conception of politics. It overlooks the fact that such problems, once they have entered the political arena, become *political* problems, and are solved on the basis of *political* considerations – whatever be their status in the scientific, technological, or any other field. In particular, the fact – if fact it be – that in some respects all people have the same needs, does not imply that politically they also will have the same interests. And it is far from certain that people having the same political interests would, for that reason, more easily cooperate rather than fight.

2. Secondly, scant attention is paid to the dynamics of the process of functional integration. Apparently, it is assumed to take on ever growing proportions in the course of time. Apart from the fact that Mitrany only hints at the mechanism through which this would occur (see pp. 42-43), he seems to overlook the possibility that functional

integration once started, might also raise counterforces. Certain groups or interests could be affected adversely by the process; this could unchain actions aimed at its abrogation. In particular, one could hardly expect the existing governments, or the politicians, and all the interests which are bound up with the existing state of affairs, indefinitely to play the docile role which Mitrany seems to assign to them.

3. Finally, Mitrany's image of the future organization of international political relations is not entirely convincing. It is difficult to conceive of a world which is ruled by a network of autonomous functional agencies. For, many of the problems with which they deal will be closely interrelated; powers and competencies will intersect and clash; and measures taken in one field will have consequences in others. This poses the problem of the relations among the several functional agencies, and particularly that of the coordination of their activities. Would not some overarching institution or institutions be necessary in order to regulate the relations among the agencies, and to control their policies? If so, the structures which would emerge would probably resemble the present-day states, be it on a much larger scale. Mitrany does not go very deep into these problems. While he recognizes them, he apparently does not deem it worthwhile to deal with them at length for the present moment. Rather than to indulge in working out neat schemes for a future which in all probability is very far off, his is a more practical approach: to get things going in the first place, while trusting that problems emerging in a later stage will eventually find their proper solution. To be true, the absence of a detailed analysis of the problems mentioned does not in itself vitiate the functionalist argument as a whole. It means only that it has not yet been developed far enough.

The foregoing discussion shows that as a theory of the integration process functionalism leaves something to be desired. But, it would seem, functionalism at least contains the potential for a purely analytical and empirical approach of the problem of integration. At the same time it breaks through the traditional, and mainly legal, conceptions of the state and of sovereignty. In this fashion it attains to a level of generality and abstraction commensurate with the proper study of integration processes. Besides, it sharply poses the problem of the future organization of man's political life. It is clearly aware of the historical relativity and the shortcomings of the contemporary national state. And although, perhaps, the functionalist alternative is not viable, or is at least not sufficiently elaborated, at any rate the problem is recognized.

Functionalism as it has been discussed in this section is not yet a scientific theory of integration. In the way it conceives the problems involved, and in the direction in which it seeks their solution, however, it is already quite close to contemporary theorizing in the field of political integration.

5. THE TRADITION – PRE-SCIENTIFIC STAGE OF DEVELOPMENT

The last three sections of this chapter, those on internationalism, on federalism, and on functionalism respectively, cover a fairly long historical period. Of an integration theory we have as yet seen only the faintest beginnings. Much less than the formation of such a theory, the period discussed shows the slow development of the categories in which such a theory might eventually be framed. And rather than explaining the integration process, political thinkers grope for the proper concepts in which to define it. And although Althusius already clearly saw the need of a specifically *political* approach of political problems, as distinct from a legal, philosophical, or theological one (*Althusius*, 1603: 5 ff.), with regard to political integration such an approach has begun to develop rather late in history.

In fact, most of the literature on integration of the period discussed in this chapter is written in a vocabulary which is legal rather than political. Thinking is dominated by the traditional legal concepts: rights and obligations, contracts and treaties, constitutions and laws, competencies and sovereignty, and the state as an international legal entity. The reason is, probably, that already at a relatively early point in history law was a fairly developed discipline embodying an impressive common stock of rather refined and precise concepts relating to politics and public affairs. Moreover, this discipline (unlike early political philosophy which was of a more abstract, even metaphysical, and distinctly moral character) was immediately applicable and practically relevant. For a large proportion of the day-to-day activities in government and politics is cast in juridical forms – laws and decrees have to be formulated and applied, treaties and contracts have to be concluded, etc. Consequently, it is conceivable that people, especially educated people, came to see politics through the eyes of the law. Preoccupation with these outward forms and formalities might easily make one forget about the underlying political processes.

Another characteristic aspect of the three approaches which have been discussed thus far, is that they are predominantly prescriptive rather than descriptive. That is, they seek to realize certain ends, they frame proposals, and they recommend particular policies. Non-normative questions come to be asked only in a relatively late stage. In so far as theory formation is initiated by the recognition of important problems in extra-scientific spheres, in particular in that of everyday life and the world of practical action, and in so far as it is problems of a normative character which are most easily so recognized and are felt to be most urgent, this prescriptive preoccupation of the literature is understandable. And in fact there is nothing against, and much in favor of, undertaking such explicitly normative analyses. In the case of the literature on integration, however, these normative concerns seem to have kept political thinkers from the analysis of 'what is', as distinct from 'what should be'. The result has been both that we have not gained sufficient insight into the process of integration, and that the schemes which have been put forward are not wholly convincing, or that we do not know whether or not (and how) they can be realized.

But we have also seen that thinking showed a certain evolution. Both in federalism and in functionalism there seems to have developed an increasing awareness of the necessity of non-normative analysis and inquiry. And although often prescriptive intensions remain relatively near to the surface, elements of a purely descriptive analysis come to play a larger role.

Accordingly, the history of thinking on the subject of integration may be interpreted as an extremely slow, dual process of emancipation: from an established vocabulary and ways of thinking, on the one hand, and from the pressing normative concerns of practical life, on the other. In both cases there is an erosion of the categories and conceptual structures of immediate experience, or rather those in which and through which reality is most immediately experienced in a particular culture. Thus far, the process has been a very slow one. This places the theorizing of the period after the Second World War in a proper historical perspective: some 25 years of more or less scientific theorizing against some 600 years of pre-scientific efforts. This makes it better possible to judge the former; it may make for more modest expectations concerning the results of recent theorizing; and it may prevent an undue desperation as to the feasibility of theory formation on the basis of present-day achievements.

It is undoubtedly true that the theoretical inquiries to be dealt with in subsequent chapters represent a new and more strictly scientific stage of development. Accordingly, there is some justification for setting this post-World War II *scientific* stage against the previous *pre-scientific* one as it has been discussed thus far. However, such a rigid historical scheme should not be taken too seriously. As a matter of fact, there is much overlapping and historical continuity, while the differences between the two stages are sometimes relatively small.

Thus, we have already seen that much of the pre-scientific literature is strictly contemporaneous to that of the more scientific variety. Furthermore, certain elements of the earlier tradition are to recur in later developments. In particular this occurs with respect to the functionalist argument. Finally, even in contemporary inquiry scientific sophistication is not yet a solid achievement which could be taken for granted.

What, however, is a scientific approach, and what is a scientific theory? In the foregoing discussion it was not necessary to go deeply into these questions; thus far rather vague and more or less common general notions concerning these matters sufficed. But from now on much more precise and elaborated concepts are imperative. Without these, adequate analysis of the rather refined and involved constructions to be met with in contemporary theorizing is an impossibility. And this is surely an indication of progress.

BIBLIOGRAPHY

Note: In cases where I found particular contributions to books of readings especially useful, I have listed them separately.

ALTHUSIUS, Johannes, 1603. Grundbegriffe der Politik. *Politica methodice digesta.* Vittorio Klostermann, Frankfurt am Main, 1948.
ARON, Robert, 1958a. Qu'est-ce que le fédéralisme? In: *L'Ere des fédérations,* pp. 27–36. Plon, Paris.

ARON, Robert, 1958b. Actualité du fédéralisme. In: *L'Ere des fédérations*, pp. 54–73, Plon, Paris.
ARON, Robert & Alexandre MARC, 1948. Principes du fédéralisme. Le Portulan, Paris.

BARETH, Jean 1958. Le fédéralisme interne, la commune et l'Europe. *L'Ere des fédérations*, pp. 157–170, Plon, Paris.
BARKUN, Michael, 1968. *Law without sanctions – order in primitive societies and the world community*. Yale University Press, New Haven and London.
BENNETT, Walter Hartwell, 1964. *American theories of federalism*. University of Alabama Press, University Alabama.
BERGER, Gaston et al., 1956. *Le fédéralisme*. P.U.F., Paris.
BERGER, Gaston, 1956. Introduction psychologique et philosophique aux problèmes du fédéralisme. *Le fédéralisme*, pp. 11–29. P.U.F., Paris.
BERLE, Adolf A. Jr., 1955. Evolving capitalism and political federalism. In: Arthur W. Macmahon (Ed.), *Federalism mature and emergent*, pp. 68–82. Doubleday, Garden City (N.Y.).
BODENHEIMER, Susanne J., 1967a. *Political union – a microcosm of European politics*, 1960–66. Sijthoff, Leiden.
BODENHEIMER, Susanne J., 1967b. The 'political union' debate in Europe – a case study in intergovernmental diplomacy. *Int. Orgn 21 (1)*: 24–54.
BOWIE, Robert R. & Carl J. FRIEDRICH, 1960/62. *Etudes sur le fédéralisme*, 2 vols. R. Pichon et R. Durand-Auzias, Paris.
BRINTON, Crane, 1948. *From many one – the process of political integration, the problem of world government*. Harvard University Press, Cambridge (Mass.).
BRUGMANS, Henri, 1956. *Panorama de la pensée fédéraliste*. La Colombe, Paris.
BRUGMANS,, Henri, 1958/61. *Les origines de la civilisation européenne*, 2 vols. R. Pichon et R. Durand-Auzias, Paris.
BRUGMANS, Henri, 1958. Le fédéralisme et l'Europe. In: *L'Ere des fédérations*, pp. 98–114. Plon, Paris.
BRUGMANS, Henri, 1965. *L'idée Européenne 1918–1965*. De Tempel, Bruges.
BRUGMANS, Henri, 1968. *La pensée politique du fédéralisme*. Sijthoff, Leiden.
BRUGMANS, Henri & Pierre DUCLOS, 1963. *Le fédéralisme contemporain – critères, institutions, perspectives*. Sijthoff, Leiden.

CARDIS, François, 1963. *Fédéralisme et intégration européenne*. Centre de recherches européennes, Université de Lausanne.
CHEVALLIER, J.J., 1956. Le fédéralisme de Proudhon et de ses disciples. In: Gaston Berger et al., *Le fédéralisme*, pp. 87–127. P.U.F., Paris.
CLARK, Grenville & Louis B. SOHN, 1964. *World peace through world law*, 2nd revised ed. Harvard University Press, Cambrigde (Mass.) (1st ed. 1958).
CLAUDE, Inis L. Jr., 1964. *Swords into plowshares – the problems and progress of international organization*, 3rd revised ed. University of London Press, London (1st ed. 1956).

DEUTSCH, Karl W. & William J. FOLTZ (Ed.), 1963. *Nation-building*. Atherton Press, New York/Prentice Hall International, London.
DUCLOS, Pierre, 1964. L'Etat et le fédéralisme. *6th Wld Congr. IPSA* (Geneva, 1964).
DUCLOS, Pierre, 1968. *L'Etre fédéraliste*. R. Pichon et R. Durand-Auzias, Paris.

EISENSTADT, S.N., 1963. *The political system of empire – the rise and fall of the historical bureaucratic societies*. The Free Press of Glencoe, New York.
ELAZAR, Daniel J., 1966. *American federalism – a view from the states*. Crowell, New York.
L'Ere des fédérations, 1958. Plon, Paris.

FARRELL, R. Barry (Ed.), 1966. *Approaches to comparative and international politics*. Northwestern University Press, Evanston (Ill.).
FIELDHOUSE, D.K., 1966. *The colonial empires – a comparative survey from the eighteenth century*. Weidenfeld and Nicholson, London.
FISCHER, John, 1955. Prerequisites of balance. In: Arthur W. Macmahon (Ed.), *Federalism mature and emergent*. Doubleday, Garden City (N.Y.).
FOERSTER, Rolf Hellmut, 1967. *Europa – Geschichte einer politischen Idee*. Nymphenburger Verlagshandlung, München.
FRANCK, Thomas M. (Ed.), 1968. *Why federations fail – an inquiry into the requisites for successful federalism*. New York University Press, New York/London University Press, London.
FREEMAN, Edward A., 1893. *History of federal government in Greece and Italy*. 2nd ed., edited by J. B. Bury. MacMillan and Co., London/New York (1st ed. 1863).
FRIEDRICH, Carl J., 1950. *Constitutional government and democracy – theory and practice in Europe and America*. Ginn, Boston etc.
FRIEDRICH, Carl J., 1955. Federal constitutional theory and emergent proposals. In: Arthur W. Macmahon (Ed.), *Federalism mature and emergent*, pp. 510–533. Doubleday, Garden City (N.Y.).
FRIEDRICH, Carl J. (Ed.), 1962. *The public interest*. Nomos V. Atherton Press, New York.
FRIEDRICH, Carl J., 1963a. *Man and his government – an empirical theory of politics*. McGraw-Hill, New York.
FRIEDRICH, Carl J., 1963b. Nation-building? In: Karl W. Deutsch & William J. Foltz (Ed.), *Nation-building*, pp. 27–32. Atherton Press, New York/Prentice Hall International, London.
FRIEDRICH, Carl J., 1964. International federalism in theory and practice. In: Elmer Plischke (Ed.), *Systems of integrating the international community*, pp. 119-155. Van Nostrand, Princeton.
FRIEDRICH, Carl J., 1966a. International politics and foreign policy in developed (western) systems. In: R. Barry Farrell (Ed.), *Approaches to comparative and international politics*, pp. 97–119. Northwestern University Press, Evanston (Ill.).
FRIEDRICH, Carl J., 1966b. Some general theoretical reflections on the problems

of political data. In: Richard L. Merrit & Stein Rokkan, *Comparing nations – the use of quantitative data in cross-national research*, pp. 57-72. Yale University Press, New Haven/London.

FRIEDRICH, Carl J., 1968. *Trends of federalism in theory and practice*. Praeger, New York etc.

GEERTZ, Clifford (Ed.), 1963. *Old societies and new nations – the quest for modernity in Asia and Africa*. The Free Press of Glencoe, London.

GREGG, Robert W. (Ed.), 1968. *International organization in the Western hemisphere*. Syracuse University Press, Syracuse (N.Y.).

HAAS, Ernst B., 1964. *Beyond the nation-state – functionalism and international organization*. Stanford University Press, Stanford.

HAY, Peter, 1966. *Federalism and supranational organizations – patterns for new legal structures*. University of Illinois Press, Urbana (Ill.)/London.

MACMAHON, Arthur W. (Ed.), 1955. *Federalism mature and emergent*. Doubleday, Garden City (N.Y.).

MARC, Alexandre, 1956. Histoire des idées et des mouvements fédéralistes depuis la première guerre mondiale. In: Gaston Berger et al., *Le fédéralisme*, pp. 129–148. P.U.F., Paris.

MARC, Alexandre, 1961, *Dialectique du déchainement – fondements du fédéralisme*. La Colombe, Paris.

MARK, Max, 1965. *Beyond sovereignty*. Public Affairs Press, Washington (D.C.).

MERRIT, Richard L. & Stein ROKKAN, 1966. Comparing nations – the use of quantitative data in cross-national research. Yale University Press, New Haven/London.

MEULEN, Jacob ter, 1917. *Der Gedanke der internationalen Organisation in seiner Entwicklung*, Vol. I: 1300–1800. Martinus Nijhoff, Den Haag.

MEULEN, Jacob ter, 1929. *Der Gedanke der internationalen Organisation in seiner Entwicklung*, Vol. II: 1789–1870. Martinus Nijhoff, Den Haag.

MEULEN, Jacob ter, 1940. *Der Gedanke der internationalen Organisation in seiner Entwicklung*, Vol. III: 1867–1889. Martinus Nijhoff, Den Haag.

MITRANY, David, 1933. *The progress of international government*. Yale University Press, New Haven

MITRANY, David, 1966. *A working peace system*. Quadrangle Books, Chicago.

MOGI, Sobei, 1931. *The problem of federalism – a study in the history of political theory*, 2 vols. Allen and Unwin, London.

MONTESQUIEU, 1849. *Esprit des lois, avec les notes de l'auteur et un choix des observations de Dupin, Crevier, Voltaire, Mably, La Harpe, Servan, etc.* Firmin Didot Frères, Paris.

NEUMANN, Franz. L., 1955. Federalism and freedom – a critique. In: Arthur W. Macmahon (Ed.), *Federalism mature and emergent*, pp. 44–57. Doubleday, Garden City (N.Y.).

PLISCHKE, Elmer (Ed.), 1964. *Systems of integrating the international community.* Van Nostrand, Princeton.

PROUDHON, P.J., 1921. *Du principe fédératif et de la nécessité de reconstituer le parti de la révolution (1863).* Avec une introduction et des notes par Charles Brun. Editions Bossard, Paris.

RICHARD, Max, 1958. Principes et méthodes du fédéralisme. In: *L'Ere des fédérations*, pp. 40–53. Plon, Paris.

RIKER, William H., 1964. *Federalism – origin, operation, significance.* Little, Brown and Company, Boston/Toronto.

ROUGEMONT, Denis de, 1961, *Vingt-huit siècles d'Europe – la conscience européenne à travers les textes d'Hésiode à nos jours.* Payot, Paris.

ROUGEMONT, Denis de, 1965. *Die Schweiz – Modell Europas – der Schweizerische Bund als Vorbild für eine europäische Föderation.* Molden, Wien/München.

SCHLESINGER, Rudolf, 1945. *Federalism in central and eastern Europe.* Kegan Paul, Trench, Trubner and Co., London.

SCHÖNDUBE, Claus & Christel RUPPERT, 1964. *Eine Idee setzt sich durch – der Weg zum vereinigten Europa.* Warnecke, Hangelar bei Bonn.

SEWELL, James Patrick, 1966. *Functionalism and world politics – a study based on United Nations programs financing economic development.* Princeton University Press, Princeton.

SIDJANSKI, Dusan, 1954. *Du fédéralisme national au fédéralisme international.* Rouge, Lausanne.

SIDJANSKI, Dusan, 1956. *Fédéralisme amphictyonique – éléments de système et tendance internationale.* Rouge, Lausanne.

SIDJANSKI, Dusan, 1963. *Dimensions européennes de la science politique – questions méthodologiques et programmes de recherches.* R. Pichon et R. Durand-Auzias, Paris.

SIDJANSKI, Dusan, 1964. Aspects fédératifs de la Communauté Européenne. *6th Wld. Congr. IPSA* (Geneva).

SIDJANSKI, Dusan, 1969. Nouvelles orientations des recherches sur l'intégration européenne. *Politico 34 (4)*: 680–689.

SPEER, James P., 1968. Hans Morgenthau and the World state. *Wld. Polit. 20 (2)*: 207–227.

STRAYER, Joseph R., 1963. The historical experience of nation-building in Europe. In: Karl W. Deutsch & William J. Foltz (Ed.), *Nation-building*, pp. 17–26. Atherton Press, New York/Prentice Hall International, London.

STREIT, Clarence K., 1939. *Union now – a proposal for a federal union of the democracies of the North Atlantic.* Jonathan Cape, London.

STRONG, C.F., 1963. *Modern political constitutions – an introduction to the comparative study of their history and existing form*, 6th revised and enlarged edition. Sidgwick and Jackson, London (1st ed. 1930).

TARLTON, Charles D., 1965. Symmetry and asymmetry as elements of federalism – theoretical speculation. *J. Polit. 27 (4)*: 861–874.

TÉNÉKIDÈS, Georges, 1956a. Le fédéralisme grec du Ve au IIIe siècles avant J.C. In: Gaston Berger et al., *Le fédéralisme*, pp. 215–239. P.U.F., Paris.

TÉNÉKIDÈS, Georges, 1956b. Droit international et communautés fédérales dans la Grèce des Cités (Ve-IIIe siècles avant J.C.). *Recl Cours* 90: 471–652.

THOMSON, David, E. MEYER & A. BRIGGS, 1945. *Patterns of peace-making.* Kegan Paul, Trench, Trubner and Co., London.

THORNTON, A.P., 1965. *Doctrines of imperialism.* Wiley, New York.

VEDEL, Georges, 1956a. Les grands courants de la pensée politique et le fédéralisme. In: Gaston Berger et al., *Le fédéralisme*, pp. 31–86. P.U.F., Paris.

VOYENNE, Bernard, 1964. *Histoire de l'idée européenne.* Petite Bibliothèque Payot, Paris.

WATTS, R.L., 1964. Recent trends in federal economic policy and finance in the Commonwealth. *6th Wld Congr. IPSA* (Geneva).

WATTS, R.L., 1966. *New federations – experiments in the Commonwealth.* Clarendon Press, Oxford.

WHEARE, K.C., 1963. *Federal government*, 4th ed. Oxford University Press, London (1st ed. 1946).

WILDAVSKY, Aaron (Ed.), 1967. *American federalism in perspective.* Little, Brown and Company, Boston.

WOLIN, Sheldon S., 1961. *Politics and vision – continuity and innovation in Western political thought.* Allen and Unwin, London.

YALEM, Ronald J., 1965. *Regionalism and world order.* Public Affairs Press, Washington (D.C.).

ZIMMERN, Sir Alfred, 1936. *The League of Nations and the rule of law, 1818–1935.* McMillan, London.

2 SOME META-SCIENTIFIC PROBLEMS*

1. INTRODUCTION

It is very well possible to build a bridge without any precise knowledge of the physical laws involved. In fact, most of the bridges actually built in human history have presumably been built in just that fashion; intuition and common sense, rather than explicit scientific knowledge, guided their construction. Such a method has its limitations, however. To judge the quality of a bridge; to build better bridges, in difficult circumstances of terrain and of climate; and to do it in an economical way – all this requires much more than intuitive knowledge. And modern bridge-building is inconceivable and impossible without highly advanced scientific and technological knowledge.

Likewise, comparing scientific theorizing with the bridge-building mentioned above, it might be possible to develop an adequate scientific theory in the absence of anything more than the most rudimentary intuitive notions about what a theory is, what requirements it ought to meet, and what principles govern its formation. But although possible in principle, it does not seem very likely that scientific knowledge would develop very fast in such conditions. Rather, one would expect that without a clear insight into what one is doing, into the precise nature of the goal one tries to reach, and into the paths which lead, or do not lead, to it, science would be a hit-or-miss affair. Progress would occur only accidentally. Instead of growth and development through the emergence of new insights, and the occurrence of important breakthroughs, science could well remain for centuries incarcerated within the same (unsatisfactory) conceptual system. By and large, this is what

* This chapter is based upon two articles which have been published earlier, in Dutch (*De Vree*, 1968, 1969).

has happened with regard to the problem of political integration, and, one may fear, with regard to political science generally. By leaving the fundamentals of the scientific enterprise in the dark, traditional knowledge, its ways of thinking and conceptual systems, may easily come to be taken for granted. Its defects are ignored, science may easily degenerate into an empty word-play, and scientific excellence may well come to consist of the mere virtuosity with which the old categories are handled.

Insight into the nature of science and of theory formation, on the other hand, makes for a much more controlled and conscious pursuit of knowledge. Explicit meta-scientific or meta-theoretical knowledge acts as a kind of steering mechanism in scientific investigation and analysis. It points to inadequacies in existing knowledge, it guides the formation of new concepts and the development of new conceptual structures, and it indicates where empirical research is necessary, and of what kind. It thus enables the scientist to proceed economically and to overcome the limitations of existing knowledge somewhat more easily and earlier, even though, of course, such insight does not by itself generate any truths or fruitful ideas in some particular scientific field – its role is of a more formal nature. Besides, the development of really powerful theories, and the use of advanced mathematical and probabilistic techniques, or of computers, are hardly possible without a rather deep insight into the complicated logical and epistemological issues involved. Finally, such knowledge is indispensable for the analysis of particular pieces of scientific knowledge, or of specific theories. For in discussing particular scientific theories, we need a vocabulary in which, and rules and principles via which this may be done. And these are exactly the things a meta-theory provides.

Accordingly, in this chapter I shall deal briefly with the fundamental problems involved in science and theory formation in general. This will bring me into the fields of epistemology, logic, and the philosophy of science. These subjects are characterized by a very high degree of abstraction; they often seem to be removed very far from the more practical concerns of the working scientist. I have already indicated why I consider that to be a false impression. It is hoped that this will become clearer still as the fundamentals to be developed in this chapter are put to use with regard to the more mundane theory of political integration.

To begin with, I shall go into the problem of ontology (section 2). In section 3 the problem of scientific theory formation will be dealt with. Finally, section 4 is concerned with the problem of the analysis of integration theories.

2. ONTOLOGY

2.1. *Empirical reality is problematical*

Ontology is concerned with what is or exists, and it has a somewhat queer ring. It deals, or dealt, with such questions as do angels exist or not; is there, or has there been, phlogiston; and is the table at which I am at present writing real or not, or is it, for all its apparent solidity, only a mass of elementary particles separated by immense empty spaces? – to mention but a few relevant examples. Apparently, some of its problems do not make much sense; they could be solved, so it seems, in the same way as Dr. Johnson refuted bishop Berkeley's epistemological idealism: by kicking a stone. The resulting pain, apparently, provided sufficient proof of the external reality of that stone and of similar things.

However, not all ontological problems admit of such an easy solution, if solution it be. Things like states, integrative processes, political systems, and authority cannot simply be kicked at. In general, like almost everything with which the social sciences are concerned, politics and political phenomena are highly abstract and elusive things. They can neither be seen nor touched, nor are they in any other way accessible to direct sensory inspection. And, unlike many of the phenomena that form the subject-matter of the natural sciences, they cannot be isolated physically for observation and experimental manipulation. Political phenomena are closely interwoven with the fabric of social life from which they cannot be separated in a straightforward, physical or concrete fashion. That is, politics should be conceived as an 'aspect' of social life, along with other such aspects that are studied by other sciences such as psychology and economics, but from which it can only be separated in the abstract, or 'analytically'.

But terms such as 'aspect', 'abstracs', or 'analytically' do not, in themselves, provide much information. What exactly does it mean to separate 'analytically', in the 'abstract', some particular 'aspect' from something else? How is one to do that; does that 'aspect' acquire an independent status; from what precisely has it been separated; what remains; and what are the relationships between that 'aspect' and 'the rest'? An attempt to answer such questions leads to the heart of the ontological problem. It is concerned with the status and structure of reality, of the subject which is to be investigated, and our relation to it. It has important implications for the way in which concepts are formed, and for our conception of theorizing and empirical research. While it concentrates upon *what* is to be investigated, it is equally relevant as to *how* that is to be done. Ontology, indeed, is of central importance in the problems concerning empirical science. And in view of the difficulty and special nature of political and social reality, it is more than doubtful that a simple and common-sense solution to these problems will suffice.

2.2. *The ontology of common sense*

Everyday life does not normally offer us many occasions to question the nature of the real world. Mental disturbances and poetic licence apart, so it seems, it imposes itself on the human mind as something given and external. Its character and form are in all essential respects fixed and determined once and for all, and it is withdrawn, for better or worse, from human caprice. Apparently, it remains quite indifferent to our sublunary doings in all but rather trivial aspects. We learn to know it in long and continuous social processes of learning of which we are for the most part not even aware; indeed, we cannot even judge their effects by comparing them with a reality which is *not* thus learnt. Reality appears as an unassailable inevitability – something to be taken for granted.

Accordingly, science as the pursuit of knowledge about this outside world will be quite easily conceived as a process of *discovery*. Just like the explorer in the old days, the scientist is supposed to penetrate into reality as into something which in essence is already present and given, be it as yet unknown, and which he has to map out faithfully. But all these activities do not in the least interfere with the 'objective' existence of the territory to be explored. Truth is something the scientist may or may not find, but somewhere it is to be *found*.

La démarche première de l'esprit scientifique est *l'exploration du réel*; cette démarche, première dans l'ordre logique, est aussi l'essentielle: la méthode expérimentale reconnaît que le réel ne peut être identifié ni par la pensée spontanée, ni par la pensée rationnelle; le réel ne peut être découvert que par une information sensorielle méthodique; (...) (*Fourastié*, 1966: 133; see for analogous conceptions *Deutsch*, 1963: 5; *Singer*, 1961: 79; *Direnzo*, 1966b: 248 ff.; *Meehan*, 1967: 13-14; *Morgenthau*, 1967).

In such a conception the essential thing would seem to be that 'reality' and 'knowledge' are treated as two independent phenomena. Knowledge is viewed as some form of registration of reality, the result of which would be predetermined by the fixed nature of reality itself. The subject matter of a particular science would simply be a certain region in reality, to be delimited on the basis of certain specific characteristics that inhere in reality itself – its essence (cf. *Freund*, 1965: 1).

2.3. *Two assumptions about reality, knowledge, and perceptions*

2.3.1. *Reality involves knowledge*
But, what actually is reality?

In this rather general form, however, the question does not lend itself to an easy and clearcut answer. In what terms, or context, and with respect to what, should the concept be defined?

In order to arrive at a solution of this problem it appears to be first of all necessary to assume, or postulate, that man has or can obtain 'knowledge' about reality. In point of fact, it is difficult to see how else it would be possible merely to ask questions about it. We may not judge our present knowledge adequate or satisfactory; but there seems to be no way of escaping the fact that before any question can even arise and be formulated *some* prior knowledge, be it only of the most rudimentary and vague kind, must already exist.

This also means that our conception of reality ought to be related to man as a knowing and thinking creature. Only then can reality truly be said to constitute a problem. There is no sense at all in speaking about 'reality' with regard to non-thinking and non-knowing organisms. In other words, the reality with which we are, and only can be, concerned is one that is thought and known. That is, the 'phenomena' of which it consists are thought and known phenomena; these and reality as a whole are of a conceptual character. We do not know 'concrete things' as such, but as concepts, or, rather, 'concrete thing' is a specific concept or conceptual category (cf., for instance, *Lewis*, 1956: 14, 29; *Cassirer*, 1957: 13 ff., 313).

To conceive of reality as something external and independent, the 'world out there' may be entirely legitimate. Yet, even as such it would still remain a known and conceptual entity. After all, 'external', 'independent', or 'the world out there', are categories of our knowledge. Thus it would be somewhat misleading to conceive our known and conceptual world as a copy or reflection of such an 'outer world' external to and independent of our thinking. For, on the one hand, such a postulated 'outer world' would still be *known* in conceptual form. But, on the other hand, it would, by definition, remain outside of and inaccessible to our thinking. This is a rather obvious contradiction. And as it would never be known what it is that would be copied or reflected, there is hardly any sense in applying such a construction.

All this does not yet answer the question as to when to ascribe or deny reality to our concepts. Hallucinations, ghosts, phlogiston, etc., make it clear that not everything conceptual and known can be straightforwardly considered real and existing. Also it does not answer the question how reality is formed, or structured.

2.3.2. *The concept to be related to perceptions, but . . .*

At first sight the direction in which a solution for these problems is to be sought seems to be a matter of course. For, since we are concerned with empirical knowledge nothing would appear more obvious than to relate the concept of reality to our sensory perceptions. That is, reality could be defined in terms of sensory experiences as an independent datum. This is, indeed, the road I will take here. Specifically, I will assume that man does have sensory experiences which are essentially independent of his will, and that reality has to be conceived in terms of these.

Logically, this second preliminary step, too, is nothing more than a postulate and a matter of choice. But there is much in favor of it. For one thing, it is rather difficult to conceive of reality as a completely autonomous creation of the human mind operating in a vacuum. Because sensory impressions as such (but not necessarily their actual content) are assumed to be given, this would also go far to explain the apparently given character of reality. Furthermore, if we also make

the not unreasonable assumption that the mechanism of sensory perception is very much the same in all human beings, these perceptions
might help account for the possibility of 'intersubjectively transmissible
knowledge' (*Brecht*, 1959: 106, 114 ff.). Moreover, it would seem that
even the most metaphysically inclined thinkers are ultimately concerned
with understanding the world of appearances, empirical reality.

This is not to say, however, that the relationship between reality
and sensory perception is an altogether unproblematical one. In particular, it cannot be maintained that reality is made up simply of the
contents of these perceptions. In the first place, there are many things,
e.g., ghosts and hallucinations, of which it cannot simply be said that
they are *not* perceived. Nevertheless, they cannot be accepted straight-
away as real either. Moreover, it is not so easy for all kinds of 'abstract' phenomena, such as politics, the state, and motives, to be linked
directly and unambiguously to sensory perceptions. Generally, these
things are *not* perceived as such. Yet, we would hesitate to deny them
all claims to reality and existence. At any rate: to solve these difficulties
would already imply going rather considerably beyond any 'simple'
sensory perception.

But sensory observation itself is not so simple an affair as we normally take it to be. While the autonomous occurrence of perceptions
may be postulated, this does not mean that their specific content may
equally be taken for granted. Instead of a more or less passive reception of impressions from some 'outside world' on the part of the human
organism, perception appears to be molded to a significant extent by
the activities, needs, preferences, and purposes of that organism itself
(cf. *Duijker* et al., 1963: 102, 115-130; *Krech* et al., 1962: 20-65).

Even more fundamental, however, is that what is designated as
sensory perception is itself already known in a conceptual form. In
other words, the processes through which reality is to be formed, are
already presupposed in sensory experience. But this again implies that
perceptions *cannot* in a straightforward fashion be thought of as the
independently given building blocks of reality (see also *Nagel*, 1961:
121; *Frohock*, 1967: 56; *Maxwell*, 1962; *Wartofsky*, 1968: 111). At
this point it becomes imperative to go somewhat more deeply into the
character of knowledge.

2.4. *Knowledge*

2.4.1. *Its diversity*

In order not to fall victim to certain difficulties and inconsistencies when dealing with the phenomenon of knowledge and with the formation of reality, it is necessary to realize that we are now thinking *about* these things. That is, we operate on a level which is one step removed from that on which we usually know, and perceive, reality; in other words, we are talking in a meta-language, instead of in the language of ordinary scientific or everyday discourse. Further, the problem is *not* to investigate what is explicitly recognized as knowledge by people, or what they are aware of when they know and perceive reality. The problem is, rather, that of developing certain categories through which knowledge and reality formation can be understood, to investigate their formal properties, and to discover what underlies it. Thus, the fact that often knowledge is acquired in a more or less unconscious way, or that the 'decision' to ascribe or deny reality to something is not normally made explicitly, or that many things are perceived as matters of course, without further reflection – these things are hardly relevant here.

With respect to the phenomenon of knowledge, human culture, both historically and contemporary, shows a large variety of different forms. However striking the differences among them, phenomena such as myth and superstition, religion, 'common sense' and scientific theories with their definitions, functions, postulates and theorems, all embody knowledge of some kind or another.

Of course, it would be perfectly possible to choose the path taken by a large part of traditional western epistemology from the Greeks onwards, and to define knowledge exclusively as 'certain' knowledge, or as 'true opinion' (see *Ackermann* (1965) for a short introduction into the history of the subject). According to such an extremely restricted definition, only the scientific variety could possibly qualify as knowledge proper. By the same token, an insurmountable barrier would be erected between science and the other forms mentioned. But it is precisely herein that one of the basic limitations of any such epistemology lies. It is extremely doubtful whether 'certain' knowledge would be an attainable ideal at all; and it is even far from certain that such a certainty can be defined in a scientifically adequate way. Moreover, the creation of such a sharp distinction tends to hide from view the fundamental continuity which links the different forms (cf. *Nagel*, 1961: 2; *Wartofsky*, 1968: 3; *Popper*, 1963: 50). This is bound to obscure our insight, not only into the character of knowledge *per se*, but equally into that of reality and its formation.

For the problem which concerns us here it is not necessary to deal in detail with what distinguishes science from those other forms. Suffice it so say that it is bent upon arriving at more reliable and consistent knowledge of the world. Its methodology aims at breaking through certain limitations of the other forms, and to gain knowledge which is precise, consistent, and 'intersubjectively transmissible'.

2.4.2. *A common element*

More pertinent to the argument at this point is the common thread which runs through all the different manifestations of the phenomenon of knowledge. Each of them, in its distinctive fashion, seems to form the expression of man's continuing efforts to order and structure the experiences that confront him. In each of them knowledge consists in determining certain relationships between concepts. Things are known, that is to say, described, defined, understood, perceived, distinguished, explained, etc., as certain relationships between other things. Even the very fact of perceiving or designating something already means that it has been distinguished and isolated from among other things, i.e., that it has been located in some relational structure. Formally and most explicitly, these various denotations of knowledge can be rendered as answers given to such questions as 'what?', 'how?', 'when?', 'where?', and 'why?'; or alternatively as the solution of problems suggested by certain experiences. This is the form in which knowledge occurs most clearly in science. As a matter of fact, such explicit questions probably come to be asked only in a comparatively advanced stage of intellectual development. But this does not invalidate our constructing other forms of knowledge, too, as attempts to answer (implicit) questions, or to solve problems (though not explicitly thus recognized), originating from certain inadequacies or deficiencies in existing knowledge of reality.

To know something means that it has been located in some relational structure. Conversely, it is inconceivable to know something as an absolute, self-contained entity, existing only in and for itself in an otherwise empty space. Ultimately,

The nature of the concept as such is its internal (essential or definitive) relationship with other concepts (*Lewis*, 1956: 83; see also *Cassirer*, 1957: 298).

Without dealing in any detail with the nature of these relationships, it is important to note that they are basically of a logical character (in some cases in a mathematical, or a probabilistic form). They are so by virtue of the fact that it is fundamentally the science of logic which studies them and in which they are defined most explicitly and precisely. They cannot be juxtaposed to other kinds of relationships that would not conform to the canons of logic or of some specific logical system. Apart from the possibility that logic would not as yet have discovered and analysed such relationship, they simply could not be used validly and would lead to false arguments and contradictions. Also, there is no question of everyday discourse being a-logical in principle. Indeed, much of logic consists of formalizing ways of valid and invalid reasoning used in everyday discourse.

2.4.3. *Relational structures and their relativity*

It is easy to imagine how in practice the pursuit of knowledge will result in the construction of more or less lengthy chains of relationships. The questions posed by some initially problematic concept will easily lead to the formation of larger or smaller systems of concepts and the relationships among them. For, while initially A may be known in terms of x, y, and z, as soon as we turn our attention to these latter concepts, they, in turn, can be known as still other structures of still other concepts, and so *ad infinitum*. Consequently, human knowledge can be conceived as the construction of more or less comprehensive systems of interrelated concepts that derive their cohesion from the fact that together they answer our questions with regard to some initially problematic concept or group of these.

But we lack some Archimedian point to which such systems could be chained up once and for all, thus to acquire a fixed and unassailable status. The moment we direct our attention to the momentary foundations of our constructions, these always turn out to vanish and to escape us, as they dissolve into ever new structures of concepts and their relationships. Not only do we lack any fixed and unquestionable basis for our systems of knowledge, but our initially problematic concepts cannot be known as independent and self-contained entities either.

For both what is to be known and the concepts in terms of which it is to be known, can only be distinguished or perceived in relation to certain other concepts, as I have already shown. But what these latter concepts will be is again dependent upon our preliminary ideas, hunches, or insights, vague though they may be, concerning the character of the system in which they are eventually to be known. Hence, even the very fact of perceiving something as a problem already contains some answer to the question of how and in what terms it shall be known. And the same applies, though in a 'reverse' direction, to the primitives, i.e., the undefined basic concepts, of the system.

The foregoing is of an entirely general validity. It equally applies to the most sophisticated products of scientic creativity, as to the most crude 'common sense' of everyday life. In Karl Popper's words:

My point of view is, briefly, that our ordinary language is full of theories; that observation is always *observation in the light of theories*; and that it is only the inductivist prejudice which leads people to think that there could be a phenomenal language, free of theories, and distinguishable from a 'theoretical language'; ... (*Popper*, 1959: 59 note).

Nothing can be known otherwise than as certain nodal points in a network of relationships that mutually and reciprocally determine and condition each other. Nothing can be known in any other fashion than in so far as it fulfils a function, and plays a role, in some such system of relationships. Conversely, this principle plays a central role in the conscious formation of concepts, e.g., in a scientific theory. In the subsequent analyses of integration theories it will often appear that concepts are introduced, or applied, for the sole reason that they figure in common discourse on the subject, while it is not made clear why precisely such concepts are chosen at all. The above principle says, in fact, that concepts in a theory should be explicitly defined and elaborated in terms of, and only in terms of, their relevance for the problem of that theory. In other words, it is the theory in its entirety, and more specifically its primitives and postulates, which rules the formation of the concepts to be used and nothing else (but see also section 2.5.2).

2.4.4.   *Relational structures – interrelated and in isolation*
It goes without saying that man is not just confronted with merely

one problem, and that does not construct only one self-contained system. On the contrary, the many problems with which he meets will, in principle, lead him to form a number of different systems. But, although different, these are not totally unrelated and independent. Unless certain more or less artificial restraints are imposed, such systems will be interrelated in that concepts formed in one of them will constitute the problems of, or serve as the foundations for, another one. Quite naturally our concepts will thus come to constitute a seamless web.

It is this interrelatedness and comprehensiveness which is especially characteristic of the conceptual world of everyday life, whose formation does not, in general, proceed in a self-conscious and systematic fashion. This peculiarity tends to obscure the basic relativity which is inherent in all our knowledge of any concept. That is, since our everyday conceptual world is extremely extended, we tend to lose sight of the fact that ultimately all our concepts can only be known in terms of each other. There is, it might be said, a fundamental circularity involved in all our knowledge; in everyday life, however, the circle is so large that it can hardly be observed (cf. *Lewis*, 1956: 82).

In science, on the other hand, attention is focused upon just one problem or problem complex at one time, to be known within a much more determinate and restricted relational structure. What is thus lost in terms of the comprehensiveness of such structures, is to be won in greater depth and precision. But here, too, things can only be known within the specific structures constructed, in so far as they fulfil a function and occupy a position in them. Overlooking this may quite easily lead to grave misunderstandings. As conceptual systems of the scientific variety cannot be constructed from scratch, it is inevitable that concepts, or rather terms, will be used initially that also have a certain status in other relational systems – those of everyday discourse or those of other disciplines. Within any other particular scientific system, however, those statuses and roles in other systems are hardly irrelevant. The fact that certain concepts do sometimes have a traditional position within some particular relational structure does not mean that in using its name in a new structure we remain interested in it in terms of that antecedent position – we even cannot, if the new structure is indeed a new one.

2.5. The construction of reality

2.5.1. *To account for our perceptions*

In the preceding subsections (2.3.1-2; 2.4.1-4) it has been shown that reality cannot be conceived as something which is just given to us from the outside once and for all. Rather, both the phenomena which seem to be directly observed, and the more abstract and non-observable ones, have appeared to be constructions of man's knowing mind. I use the term 'construction' advisedly here. For, in the relational structures that make up human knowledge, nothing is completely predeterminated and fixed. Such systems are matters of choice and human decision. And were we even to decide that they were preordained by some fixed 'nature of things', this would still be *our* decision – and it could well be otherwise.

If it is realized that the reality, or the real things, with which we are, and only can be, concerned, are known and are of a conceptual character; if it is further realized that knowledge consists of the construction of systems of relationships within which 'things' are known in so far as they play a role in them; and if, finally, it is assumed that there exist sensory perceptions in terms of which reality is to be conceived; then, I think, the conclusion will be clear: *reality is a structure of concepts constructed in order to account for our sensory perceptions; and only if something does indeed fulfil this function, directly or indirectly, it can be called 'real' and does 'exist'* (see also *Leinfellner*, 1965: 194-195).

Thus, for instance, phlogiston, horror vacui, or ghosts are not, but electrons, quanta, states and governments are, real, as far as existing scientific knowledge goes, that is. But it also implies that we need not necessarily speak about just one reality as an immutable and determinate entity: rather, we must accept the existence of a plurality of realities depending upon the problems whose solution their construction is to serve, as well as upon the character of the relationships used (analogously: *Apostel*, 1965). By the same token, what is considered real at one time need not be so at another.

2.5.2. *A 'dialectical' process*

Yet, the foregoing applies with equal force to sensory experience itself. This seems to involve us in a vicious circle. But at this point, it is imperative to bear in mind that the acquisition of knowledge and the construction of reality are also historical processes.

While it is difficult to conceive of any fixed and definable starting-point of these processes which lose themselves in the obscure first stadia of human evolution, it *is* possible to imagine man's having at some time, somehow, some perceptions. This is also the sense in which these perceptions have been postulated, rather than derived from something else. We may imagine man's becoming aware in an early stage of his development of things like hunger, pain, and fear, as well as of those things by which they are caused, or which lead to their disappearance.

Once some such perceptions are assumed, however, it can be understood how man will form concepts and posit relationships in order to account for them. But this, in turn, will enable him to perceive more, again leading to the construction of ever more comprehensive and complex structures to account for this expanding universe. In principle this is a continuous process: what has been constructed in any one phase will pose the problems leading to the construction of new or modified reality in the next phase, and so *ad infinitum* (see also *Cassirer*, 1955: 31 ff.; *Popper*, 1963: 47; *Frey*, 1969; *Kuhn*, 1963: 108-109).

In this historical, or dialectical process empirical science, which may be said to be concerned with the construction of such relational structures as allow for the most explicit, logically determinate, and transparant accounting for sensory experience possible, represents the most advanced stage at any one moment. Although it must necessarily start from the existing conceptual structure, that is, generally that of our everyday life, and although its problems are inevitably those which *that* structure poses, this does not mean that it has to treat this existing world as something unassailable. Quite on the contrary. In order to attain a more precise and rigorous ordering of human experience science will form new concepts and new relational structures whose ambiguity, vagueness, and indeterminateness, both logically and empirically, are less than those whom they replace. But in doing this it will at the same time create a new reality, or new realities. These incidentally, may ultimately find their way into the common world, but initially they are bound to differ from the structure then in use. After all, science starts from the problems which that structure poses, that is, from the awareness that somehow it fails or is insufficient. It goes without saying that this may result from time to time in certain communication failures (witness, e.g. *Bull*, 1966; *Morgenthau*, 1967; see also *Cassirer*, 1957: 17; *Frank*, 1961: 291).

Thus, through the problems which provide the starting-points for scientific curiosity and inquiry, science is intimately related to the concerns of man's daily life. These concerns will often be of a normative kind: they relate to the decisions, choices, and judgments man must make. One might even argue that it is precisely in this normative sphere that man is confronted with his most urgent problems; and that it will be precisely such problems that will first provoke the need for further (scientific) knowledge, and lead him to expend the time, energy, and resources to gain it. By the same token, one may expect this initial quest for knowledge (or early science) to be easily dominated by such practical and normative problems and orientations, and that non-normative inquiry represents something of an emancipation not automatically and easily achieved (cf. p. 47 above; see further *De Vree*, 1970).

2.6.   *The definition of a discipline*

2.6.1.   *The nature of the problem*

In view of the fact that it is *political* theories that form the subject matter of subsequent chapters, it is necessary to deal with the question of what is implied by such an adjective. This requires a brief analysis of what it means to define and delimit some particular science, and what are the consequences of such a definition.

It has been shown that science generally springs from the problems posed by the reality of common experience. That is, the subject-matter of some science is first of all determined by some problem or complex of problems in reality as known at a certain moment (see also *Nagel*, 1961: 79; *Easton*, 1960: 105; *Oberndörfer*, 1966b: 11; and *Weber*, 1922: 166). Of course, the link may be an *indirect* one, in that (sub-) disciplines sometimes originate from the problems posed by an already existing discipline. While introducing some complications, this does not in any fundamental way affect the present argument; and at any rate it is not pertinent to the case of political science.

It is essential to see that this basic choice of a problem or problem area to form the starting point for the development of some discipline is not itself a matter to be decided by purely scientific or philosophical reasoning alone. For the problem to be designated can, at least initially, only be formulated in everyday language and derives its significance from that sphere only. Whether or not it is worthwhile to serve as the starting-point for a particular science, depends upon its being recognized or not as an important problem in the structure of the common reality, and on the basis of criteria accepted there, i.e., generally of an extra-scientific character. In a later stage of the development that problem may well come to be formulated in different, and purely scientific terms, while eventually this new terminology, in its turn, may find its way into everyday speech. Also, the progress of scientific knowledge may lead to new insights, or modify existing ones, into the importance and significance of particular problems. But at any particular moment in this process one can only start from what is available at that time; and this, ultimately, is the more or less common world.

Consequently, to define 'politics' as the central problematical phenomenon of political science is a problem of a somewhat special character. It comes to developing a scientifically useful and adequate formulation of what, by the name of 'politics', is understood as a significant problem in the world of everyday discourse. Accordingly, the definition to be given is one of a rather special kind – an *explication*, as Hempel writes,

Explication is concerned with expressions whose meaning in conversational language or even in scientific discourse is more or less vague (...) and aims at giving those expressions a new and precisely determined meaning, so as to render them more suitable for clear and rigorous discourse on the subject matter at hand (*Hempel*, 1952: 11).

2.6.2. *The discipline's field*
This basic problem once being formulated, the discipline further consists in the construction of a system of concepts and relationships such that its problem can be solved, the phenomenon in question can be known (on the notion of 'system', see also Section 3.5). In this way, a particular scientific reality is consciously constructed. In point of fact, this reality will consist of the union of a number of different (sub)-systems determined by different questions that may be posed concerning the original phenomenon in different settings. But however com-

plicated things may thus become in practice, this does not fundamentally affect the matter in either way.

This system will not be a completely isolated and closed one.
Through the use of certain terms and concepts it will be related to
other such systems, not only to that of the common reality, but also
to those of other disciplines; after all, it originates in the problems posed
by such other systems. Such terms or concepts may well have positions
that are traditionally firmly entrenched in those other systems (cf. section 2.4.4). But although inevitable, and although their original meanings will initially guide and shape thinking for some time, in the process
of developing the new system of knowledge or disciplines (which may
take a long time), they should increasingly be ignored as they gradually
become irrelevant. When one does not sufficiently disabuse one's mind
from them, one might well be led to conclude, with Raymond Aron,
that

Toute étude concrète des relations internationales est donc une étude
sociologique et historique . . .

because

La théorie des relations internationales diffère de la théorie économique
par le fait que la discrimination entre variables endogènes et variables exo-
gènes, même dans l'abstrait, est impossible (*Aron*, 1967: 851).

Or, as Vernon Van Dyke criticizes Easton's conceptions:

More generally, Easton's conceptual scheme does not do much to resolve
the question of the extent to which political scientists must also be econ-
omists, sociologists, psychologists, and military strategists (*Van Dyke*,
1966b: 13; but see also *Van Dyke*, 1962: 59).

It has been shown, however, that the character of such concepts is not
determined once and for all by some fixed 'nature of things', but by
the particular system within which they are known. There are no in-
trinsically 'sociological', 'economic', or 'political' facts – nor are there
'facts' without more ado. What 'facts' and their qualifications are, is
determined by the system within which they fulfil a role. When some
concepts also seem to have a status within other systems, it is not
these particular statuses which interest us, but only their role in the

particular system with which we are concerned for the moment. Thus, too, the political scientist, qua political scientist, can only deal with *political* integration, whatever may be his conception of politics. The term 'economic', for instance, in the expression 'economic integration' makes sense only in so far as it has a political scientific status – e.g., that of the specifically defined kind of value with regard to which integration occurs. More generally, it is the conception of the basic problem of the discipline which governs the way in which, what concepts are formed and applied (cf. p. 64 above).

3. THEORIES

3.1. *Introduction*

After the foregoing brief discussion of the general problems of knowledge and reality, I will now go into the problem of scientific theory formation. A theory may be said to represent a very advanced form of scientific knowledge. It commonly designates a particularly well integrated, coherent, and precisely articulated piece of knowledge. To have a scientific theory about a particular phenomenon seems to imply having found rather definite answers to the questions it raises. This tends to lend theory formation a rather special place in the pursuit of knowledge. But however justified this may be, it should be realized that from an epistemological point of view a theory represents 'only' a particular form of knowledge, a particular structure in which knowledge has been crystallized. Specifically, the foregoing considerations on knowledge and reality also apply to the formation of scientific theories.

3.2.1. *Explanation*

To begin with, the concept of theory can be related to the questions man may ask with respect to his experiences, and in which the quest for knowledge originates. There are a good many of such questions (cf. section 2.4.2). Among these the question 'why?' occupies a somewhat special position. It can be asked meaningfully when all those other questions have already been answered. Thus, it may be asked *why* X is what it is, how and when it occurs, or *why* it moves in this direction rather than in another. Conversely, the question 'why?' cannot be answered without first having answered one or more of the other questions. For, at least it should be known what it is about which we ask 'why?'

Accordingly, the question 'why?' may be said to represent the ultimate and most fundamental question which can be asked. And in general our thirst for knowledge will only be quenched after this particular question has been answered. In essence, this answer appears to consist in showing that the thing regarding which it is asked 'why?', should necessarily be what (how, when, where, etc.) it actually is. This answer represents, in other words, an *explanation* in which the thing to be explained (the *explanandum*) is derived as a necessary consequence from certain initial circumstances, facts, or occurrences (the *explanans*) (cf., for example, *Nagel*, 1961: 15; *Wartofski*, 1968: 32; *Hempel*, 1965: 245, 334).

In practice the term 'theory' would seem to be used primarily in relation with such explanation. Conversely, we would hesitate to apply the term to mere definitions, descriptions, or observations. Consequently, the function of a theory will here be conceived to be that of explaining, of giving answers to 'why?' questions.

3.2.2. *The structure of explanation*
The special character of the question 'why?' is also reflected in the more complicated structure of its answer. For, in order to explain something definitions or observations alone will not suffice. From a definition of what a revolution is, for example, no conclusions can be drawn. Neither does an enumeration of all the 'facts' of the political situation in a particular country, however complete, in and by itself allow any conclusion as to the occurrence or non-occurrence of a revolution there.

Explanation becomes possible only if and in so far as we have certain rules, 'laws', or 'hypotheses', that establish a certain connection between the explanandum and the things in terms of which it is to be explained. And only if it is also observed that the facts or circumstances figuring in these general rules do, or did, in fact occur, it can be said that the explanandum is explained. Thus, the Russian revolutions of 1917 can only be explained in so far as we know *both* the empirical facts and developments in terms of which we wish to

explain these revolutions, *and* the rules which connect the phenomenon
of revolution to such facts and developments.

Accordingly, the general structure of an explanation can be described
as follows (cf. *Hempel*, 1965: 174; *Popper*, 1959: 59; *Rudner*, 1966: 60):

$$\frac{L_1, \ldots \ldots L_n}{E}$$
$$C_1, \ldots \ldots C_n$$

Here $\{L_1, \ldots \ldots L_n\}$ represents a certain system of laws, or postulates, or general rules, in which particular relationships between certain
phenomena are established. $\{C_1, \ldots \ldots C_n\}$ is the set of observations
of the relevant phenomena figuring in $\{L_1, \ldots \ldots L_n\}$. Together,
these two elements, finally, lead to the conclusion 'E', where 'E' stands
for explanandum.

3.2.3. *Explanation, prediction, deduction, and induction*

Thus far we have spoken exclusively of the explanation of given facts.
That is, given E, the problem is that of finding such sets. $\{L_1, \ldots \ldots L_n\}$
and $\{C_1, \ldots \ldots C_n\}$ as allow the derivation of E. But we can also reverse this sequence. Given $\{L_1, \ldots \ldots L_n\}$ and $\{C_1, \ldots \ldots C_n\}$, it
can be concluded that E should occur. In this case we have a *predic-
tion*, whose structure is identical to that of an explanation. However,
this does not mean that this concept of prediction covers all meanings
normally associated with prediction. As a matter of fact, many of the
forecasts, or projections into the future of certain developments, both
in ordinary life and in certain parts of science, do not fit this scheme.
They are made without resting upon explicit reasoning or sufficient
empirical evidence (much the same applies to explanation, in fact). Of
course, this does not detract from the significance of the fact that disposing of suitable sets of $\{L_1, \ldots \ldots L_n\}$ and $\{C_1, \ldots \ldots C_n\}$ does
enable us to make predictions.

Also, in speaking about prediction we should not exclusively think
of forecasting the *future*. In principle it is equally possible to predict
phenomena that have occurred in the past. Actually, time is hardly
relevant here. It is much less a question of the course of time than
of the place where, in the structure described, investigation starts. Thus,
on the basis of certain general laws and knowledge of the facts about
the political situation in eighteenth-century France, the occurrence of

the French revolution might well be *predicted*. Such a prediction allows us to test our laws or hypotheses. It fulfils a function which is the same as that of experiment.

Prediction and explanation are thus two sides of the same thing: a structure in which certain (empirical) propositions are derived from others. This is of the essence of *deduction*; the relationship between *explanandum* and *explanans* is in fact a deductive one. Deduction, however, is frequently identified exclusively with such sciences as logic and mathematics. As against such 'deductive' sciences, the empirical sciences are often thought to be 'non-deductive', or 'inductive'. Approximately, induction could be described as the derivation of certain conclusions from 'the facts' – from empirical reality. Empirical laws would have to be conceived as generalizations of a certain restricted number of empirical observations. And this would be justified through some 'principle of induction', that is:

... the *belief that laws have a general validity if they have been tested in the limited realm of available observations*, but with the *proviso* that such laws can lose their validity under extreme circumstances which are strongly different from those under which they were tested (*Zanstra*, 1962: 16; see also *Reichenbach*, 1949a: 340; *Reichenbach*, 1949c).

But even when such an inductive conception were to be accepted, the *explanation* of reality would still remain a deductive process, in conformity with the structure described above. Induction is concerned with the generation of general rules from empirical observations. But explanation of reality in terms of such laws still has to proceed through deduction. And the principle of induction, in whatever formulation, does *not* give us a method to derive such laws more or less automatically and mechanically from our observations. It still presupposes such laws. The principle only justifies their generalization beyond the immediate domain for which they were formulated. Moreover, in view of the (necessary) restriction in the second part of the sentence quoted, it is doubtful whether such a justification is really necessary. At any rate, it is difficult to see what function it could perform.

In a certain sense induction is concerned with a problem which lies before that of deduction: whence and how do we get our laws and hypotheses? This question is, of course, entirely legitimate, e.g. from an historical or a psychological point of view. For a scientific theory itself, however, its answer is hardly relevant. The point is whether and to what extent a law helps to explain reality, not its origins. To qualify empirical science as 'deductive' actually means nothing more (nor less) than that the process in which certain propositions are derived from others is a deductive one. But it does *not* mean that the basic laws, the postulates, on the basis of which explanation proceeds are themselves arrived at deductively. From a logical point of view, to maintain this would even be an absurdity. Such laws or postulates are discovered or invented so as to render interesting, significant, or relevant explanations possible. This does not occur in some more or less mechanical fashion, i.e., by deduction or so-called induction, but, rather, it involves creativity and some good luck.

Ultimately, the inductivist position, the idea that our knowledge of the world is just a matter of observation and the application of some principles, probably rests upon a conception of empirical reality as some kind of given entity with a determinate structure independent of human thinking and knowledge. It has already been shown, however, that, instead, reality is throughout a construction of man's knowing mind, a process governed by principles whose formalization is undertaken mainly by the science of logic. Consequently, it is not surprising that it has appeared impossible to formulate rules of induction so as to derive mechanically laws from 'the facts'.

There are, then, no generally applicable 'rules of induction', by which hypotheses or theories can be mechanically derived or inferred from empirical data. The transition from data to theory requires creative imagination. Scientific hypotheses are not *derived* from observed facts, but *invented* in order to account for them. They constitute guesses at the connections that might obtain between the phenomena under study, at uniformities and patterns that might underlie their occurrence (*Hempel*, 1966: 15; see also *Hempel*, 1965: 5-6; *Popper*, 1959: 28; *Leinfellner*, 1965: 98-99, 119).

All this is not to deny the difference between the formal and the empirical sciences. But this difference does not concern deduction, but their relation to empirical reality. Both kinds of sciences are deductive; but whereas a logical or mathematical theory need not be interpreted empirically, an empirical theory should. This poses rather special problems, but it does not detract from the deductive character of empirical theories.

A somewhat different problem is constituted by the nature of the laws and concepts through which we seek to explain certain problematic phenomena. Explanation, one could say, consists in elucidating things that are unclear or unknown in terms of things that are themselves clear or known. Now, such a conception could easily lead to the conviction that, ultimately, it is the self-evidence of an explanation's basic laws or concepts, i.e., those which are not further explained or defined, that rules our choice of them; the basis of a theory, which itself is unexplained and undefined, would consist, then, of things that are clear, known, and self-evident. Waiving the question what it is that is denoted by terms as 'clarity', or 'self-evidence', such a criterion is entirely irrelevant. The only point is whether the basis of an explanation, its postulates and primitive concepts, allows us to deduce certain results; whether or not this basis is also evident, is rather uninteresting.

It is inessential whether A is self-evident, and whether B becomes self-evident by being derived from A. The important point is to demonstrate that B follows from A, that B can be derived from A in accordance with the rules of the system (*Kotarbiński*, 1966: 247; see also *Rosenkrantz*, 1969: 345).

Finally, it is important to see that the above is of an entirely general nature. That is, it covers logical and mathematical, as well as probabilistic explanations. This offers no great difficulties with respect to ordinary logical and mathematical explanation, but sometimes deductive and probabilistic explanations are opposed as two fundamentally different categories (e.g. *Meehan*, 1965: 97 ff.). However, what specific form the explanatory scheme adopted here will assume, depends entirely upon the particular formal system of reasoning (logical, mathematical, or probabilistic) which is chosen. This choice governs the way in which the relevant laws and concepts are to be formulated, and the rules through which inferences can be made from them. And this choice, in its turn, rests upon our insight into what system is most adequate to the problems with which we are concerned. Thus, a probabilistic system of reasoning might be chosen because, for example, we are less interested in the behavior of specific elements (people, facts, or occurrences) than in that of classes of elements that are similar in certain respects, but dissimilar in others. But such a probabilistic system is just as deductive as a conventional logical or mathematical one, although, of course, its rules of inference are different. It goes without saying that in such a calculus only probabilities can be derived; but this does not affect the deductive nature of the process.

3.3. *The structure of theories*

3.1.1. *Primitives, postulates, and theorems*
A theory is one of those systems of concepts and relationships which have been described in section 2.4.3. It differs from other such systems in that it gives a particularly tight and rigorous ordering of experience, that is, it explains it. Through this function its character and structure can be defined more precisely. This will be done in the next subsections (3.3.2 to 3.3.5) which will deal with the calculus, the problem of its empirical interpretation, and that of models generally while in the last subsection, by way summary, the different elements will be brought together.

To begin with, viewed from a somewhat different perspective than in section 3.2.2, an explanation basically contains two kinds of elements: concepts and laws linking such concepts. It has already appeared that knowledge has no definite end-point. Further questions can always be asked, and, in principle, things can always be defined, or explained in terms of still other things. Thus, starting from any one particular concept, we can, in principle, construct endless chains of definitions. The concepts used in the *definiens* in one stage can again be defined, in their turn, in terms of other concepts in the next stage. Similarly, the laws used in one stage can be explained in terms of ever different, mode general or more fundamental, laws in subsequent stages. In principle, then, there is infinite regress.

But such infinite regress cannot, of course, be tolerated in practice. Somewhere the process must end, if only momentarily. Consequently, the process of explanation has to end at some moment in a set of concepts that are not defined any further, and of laws that are not further explained in terms of other laws. These two constitute the basis of the explanation in the sense that everything else is derived from it. From the undefined *primitive* concepts the other concepts used are formed. And from the fundamental laws the other laws used are derived.

As to those laws, however, a somewhat different vocabulary than used thus far shall be introduced. Up to now I have used the common terms 'laws' and 'hypotheses' to denote the general rules figuring in explanations. In the first place, however, these terms do not contain any information as to their position within a theory. Thus, a law might be one of its most fundamental rules, serving in the basis of the theory, but it could equally be one which has been derived from that basis. Accordingly, I will subsequently use the term 'postulate' or 'axiom' for the former, i.e., for the basic propositions underlying the theory, and the term 'theorem' for those propositions to be derived from them. In the second place, the term 'law' has a strong metaphorical connotation of a command issued by some fixed nature or reality, a fixed principle governing nature, physical or social. As against such a 'law', a 'hypothesis' would merely be a potential law, one in the process of being discovered; it is an idea as to what the law could be, but the idea has not as yet been fully confirmed. It has appeared, however, that reality is essentially an intellectual construction, theory formation being one of the modes of constructing, and that as such its structure cannot be conceived as being predetermined by some 'nature of things', but that it is and remains hypothetical throughout. Rather than discovering the fixed, eternal laws ruling the universe, we continuously seek to formulate such propositions so as to organize experience more rigorously and, thus, more reliably. Both 'laws' and 'hypotheses' are hypothetical, they result from human choices that may always prove to be wrong. In so far as the terms 'axiom', or 'postulate', and 'theorem' are not appropriate, i.e., outside some relatively well-integrated body of knowledge, a theory, I shall apply the term 'hypothesis', only.

3.3.2. *The calculus – abstract core of a theory*

As a relational structure a theory presupposes logic (or mathematics, or a probabilistic system, as the case may be) which governs the way derivations are to be made, and in which the relationships to be applied are defined. We need not normally bother about this; most of the actual empirical social sciences (still) remain well within the bounds of ordinary logic as it is applied, usually without too much difficulty, in ordinary discourse. It should be noted, however, that here, too, is an area of choice. That is, in certain cases it might be necessary or useful to apply a system of reasoning which differs from that of common discourse – some special logical, mathematical, or probabilistic system. Such a choice entails important consequences for the character of the theory which will be constructed. These will not be dealt with here, however.

An empirical theory is to explain empirical reality. It is an intellectual construction dealing with an already existing conceptual structure known as empirical reality. Ultimately, it is to be formulated in terms having a status within, or related to, the latter. In other words, its concepts should have an empirical meaning or content. In order to analyse the structure of an empirical theory, however, it is necessary first to start by abstracting from the empirical content of the concepts used. What then remains is a completely abstract relational structure whose concepts are empty in that they do not mean anything empirical, and which can best be named by means of such symbols as the letters of the alphabet.

This abstract structure will be designated here as the theory's *calculus* (cf. *Rudner*, 1966: 16; *Wartofsky*, 1968: 131-132; *Bocheński*, 1965: 39; *Carnap*, 1960; *Rozeboom*, 1962: 282-283; *Meehan*, 1965: 137). It may be said to constitute the skeleton of an empirical theory – the structure of reasoning through which its explanandum is deduced from its basis. It consists of a set of primitives, whose use within the calculus is governed by the postulates and definitions, and from which further concepts and theorems are formed.

As has been said, these primitives and, consequently, all the other concepts figuring in the theory that have been formed from them, do not have any empirical content. They are, it might be said, empty and have no meaning. This, however, is too simplistic. For, actually, those concepts are anything but empty, and they do have a meaning. It has to be sought for, not outside the calculus, but within it. That is, their meaning consists of the relations they have with the other concepts of the calculus; it is defined by the function they play within it as governed by the postulates and the definitions. Instead of definition in terms of concepts outside the calculus, they are defined through the use which is made of them within it.

In this perspective, accordingly, the fundamental assumptions of a theory constitute a set of abstract or uninterpreted postulates, whose constituent non-logical terms have no meaning other than those accruing to them by virtue of their place in the postulates, so that the basic terms of the theory are 'implicitly defined' by the postulates of the theory (*Nagel*, 1961: 91; see also *Cassirer*, 1950: 26).

The primitives and the other concepts of the calculus determine each other reciprocally, governed by its formal structure. This procedure makes a strong impression of circularity. But it has already appeared in section 2.4.4 that such circularity is a quite general occurrence. Unless the circle is drawn very narrowly, such circularity in itself does not stand in the way of our gaining satisfactory and useful knowledge. Implicit definition of the primitives does mean that their meaning is fixed and determined to a lesser extent than in the case of a 'normal' definition. For any additional postulate will alter it. But far from constituting a defect, this may well be an advantage in so far as it makes for flexibility and easy manipulation and adaptation (cf. *Presley*, 1960: 216).

3.3.3. *Empirical interpretation*

A calculus as described does not and cannot convey any information about empirical reality. It is an axiomatic system which does not differ from those that are constructed in logic or mathematics. But if it is required that the calculus be more, i.e., that it does inform us about empirical reality, then the concepts which it employs must be known also in another conceptual structure, namely that which is known as 'empirical reality'. The concepts of the calculus should, in other words, acquire a meaning which can be determined empirically; they should be translated in terms of sensory experiences.

Thus, to give the calculus an *empirical interpretation* requires rules that connect it unambiguously with observable reality. Such rules are known under a variety of names, such as 'interpretative sentences', 'semantical rules', or 'correspondence rules', while in the social sciences they are most commonly known as 'operational definitions' (cf. *Hempel*, 1966: 88; *Rudner*, 1966: 18; *Popper*, 1959: 43; *Nagel*, 1961: 90; *de Groot*, 1966: 88). It is important to see, however, that it is not necessary to give each and every concept figuring in the calculus a distinctly empirical interpretation: some of them may be 'indirectly so interpreted, i.e., via others to which they are linked by definitions or postulates'.

The calculus when empirically interpreted and the empirical reality, or the observations, with which it is connected, are not two fundamentally different things. Essentially, as has been shown in section 2, both are relational structures constructed by man's knowing mind. This means, among other things, that the operationalization of an 'abstract' calculus consists of connecting two different structures of knowledge. And when such a calculus is called 'theoretical', it does not mean that the 'observational' basis with which it is linked is of a less 'theoretical' character. The line which would separate 'theoretical' from 'observational' concepts is difficult to draw, indeed (cf. *Maxwell*, 1962: 14-15).

Of course, such a calculus is developed in order to explain part of the existing structure known as empirical reality. That is, it should be developed in such a fashion that its concepts, interpreted in terms of observations, still satisfy its postulates and theorems. However, this is not an altogether unilateral affair. For, while initially observations are made and known within, and determined by the existing structure, the development of the calculus, through the formation of new concepts, can generate or lead to entirely different kinds of observations (cf. *Feyerabend*, 1962: 29; *Wartofsky*, 1968: 284-285). Theory formation, in fact, represents a particularly disciplined and rigorous form of reality construction.

The meaning of the concepts in the uninterpreted calculus is determined, as we have seen, by the role they play within it. They have no status, or content outside the calculus, and they cannot be isolated from it. In other words, it is the calculus as a whole which constitutes the relevant unit of thinking. But the same applies to the concepts when interpreted empirically, and to the empirical theory which results from such interpretation (cf. *Hempel*, 1965: 113; *Leinfellner*, 1965: 28-30; *Toulmin*, 1962: 82). In this case, too, it is the theory as a whole which determines the meaning of the concepts used, whether directly observed or not. Accordingly, it is somewhat inaccurate and misleading to speak of the operationalization of an individual concept. What is operationalized, actually, is a certain structure of relationships as determined by the calculus in its entirety. It consists in constructing such logical connections with propositions containing observables as to satisfy the rules prescribed by the calculus. To say that some concept has been defined operationally is a mere abbreviation – innocuous as long as it is realized that it stands for what is usually a quite complex structure of relationships not all of which will be definitions in a narrow sense. This is particularly important with regard to calculi of a high degree of generality, that aim at being interpretable in many more or less different domains – such as, for instance, those of a general theory of integration or even of the political process. In such cases, one might say, the 'distance' of the calculus to its empirical domain(s) is very great, and, consequently, to connect them will generally require complex and lengthy chains.

The empirical interpretation of a calculus enables us to test it. For, if the theory is right, and the relevant observations are actually made, then we should also be able to observe the things which the theory deduces from the initial observations. By referring unambiguously to sensory observations, empirically interpretative rules enable us to make decisions as to whether or not things do, or do not, occur. And since the distinction between 'theoretical' and 'observational' statements is only of a limited significance, Maxwell applies the expression 'quickly decidable sentence' in this context:

But we should take as its basis and its unit not the 'observational term', but, rather, the quickly decidable sentence. (. . .) A quickly decidable sentence (in the technical sense employed here) may be defined as a singular, nonanalytic sentence such that a reliable, reasonably sophisticated language user can very quickly decide whether to assert it or deny it when he is reporting on an occurrent situation (*Maxwell*, 1962: 13).

But what, actually, do such sentences decide with regard to the theory as a whole? Not that it would be 'true', and that it could be treated henceforward as a solidly established piece of knowledge which could be taken for granted. For, however often a theory may have been tested with positive results, this does not allow the conclusion that in future tests the theory will be equally confirmed. And when confirmation is conceived as the establishment, once and for all, of the definite truth of the theory, then such a conformation is impossible. What can be established, however, is that the theory does *not* fit the facts of experience, or that it is *un*true. For the theory predicts certain observations. If these do *not* occur in proper circumstances, it can at least be said that in that situation the theory is false. In the words of Blaise Pascal:

. . . pour faire qu'une hypothèse soit évidente, il ne suffit pas que tous les phénomènes s'en ensuivent, au lieu que, s'il s'ensuit quelque chose de contraire à un seul des phénomènes, cela suffit pour assurer de sa fausseté (quoted from *Popkin*, 1968: 14 note; see also *de Groot*, 1966: 105; *Popper*, 1959: 40 ff.).

Thus, empirical interpretation of a certain calculus makes it possible that it can be falsified rather than that its truth could be definitely established. And, it could be said, through empirical investigations we do not *discover* truth, but, rather, we *test* our ideas concerning it (cf. *Toulmin*, 1962: 44, 64). Probably, however, such falsification ought not to be conceived as an all-or-nothing affair. A theory which has as yet worked satisfactorily will not be rejected readily and completely on the basis of one contrary instance – theories are scarce goods. It will be attempted to adapt and revise it. Generally, too, the problem will involve some different and conflicting possible explanations of which one may be falsified, thus making a choice possible (cf. *Feyerabend*, 1962: 66; *Wartofsky*, 1968: 268; *de Groot*, 1966: 115). And in practice falsification should probably be thought of more in terms of more or less, of different degrees, than in those of the dichotomy accept-reject (see for a probabilistic account in terms of information *Rosenkrantz*, 1969). It should be noted, finally, that to speak in terms of 'falsification' does not necessarily rule out the use of the term 'confirmation'. For, of course, a theory that has withstood many attempts at falsification may be said to have been *confirmed*, in the sense that it has been shown to work thus far, and that it deserves our trust for the time being.

3.3.4. *Models – empirical and non-empirical*
The empirical interpretation of a calculus which has just been dealt with, appears to be 'only' a (very important) special case of a much more general phenomenon. It has been shown that such an empirical interpretation consists of connecting one particular relational structure (the uninterpreted calculus) with another one (that of empirical reality). However, we need not necessarily choose the latter. It is equally possible to connect the calculus with other such (as yet non-empirical) structures, for instance those developed in other disciplines. The set of operational definitions which has been discussed, then, constitutes a special category of what may be called, more generally, an 'interpretative system'.

Let T be a theory characterized by a set of postulates in terms of a finite *theoretical vocabulary* Vt, and let Vb be a second set of extralogical terms, to be called the *basic vocabulary* which shares no terms with Vt. By an *interpretative system* for T with the basis Vb we will then understand a set J of sentences which (i) is finite, (ii) is logically compatible with T, (iii) contains no extra-logical term that is not contained in Vt or Vb, (iv) contains every element of Vt and Vb essentially, i.e., is not logically equivalent to some set of sentences in which some term of Vt or Vb does not occur at all (*Hempel*, 1965: 208).

Such a system enables us to connect the elements of the calculus with those of other structures. The terms of the calculus (the 'theoretical vocabulary') acquire the meaning of terms from some other domain (the 'basic vocabulary'), such that they satisfy, or can be used according to, the rules of the original calculus; that is, when the two are *isomorphic*. The result of such an interpretation is a *model* of the calculus.

Every system of concepts which satisfies a system of axioms can be called a *model of that system of axioms* (*Popper*, 1959: 73; see also *Rudner*, 1966: 24).

Thus too, an *empirical* interpretation of a calculus results in an *empirical* model of that calculus.

A model closely resembles a metaphor. As Black observes, regarding the metaphor 'man is a wolf',

A speaker who says 'wolf' is normally taken to be implying in some sense of that word that he is referring to something fierce, carnivorous, treacherous, and so on. The idea of a wolf is part of a system of ideas, not sharply delineated, and yet sufficiently definite to admit of detailed enumeration. The effect, then, of (metaphorically) calling man a 'wolf' is to evoke the wolf-system of related common-places. If a man is a wolf, he preys upon other animals, is fierce, hungry, engaged in constant struggle, a scavenger, and so on. Each of these implied assertions has now to be made to fit the principal subject (the man) either in normal or in abnormal senses (*Black*, 1962: 40-41).

Thus, the metaphor, too, can be conceived as a particular alternative interpretation, be it of a somewhat loose kind, of a certain conceptual system.

The significance of *non-empirical* models (i.e., those not yet cast in terms of observables) for the development of an *empirical* science is not immediately clear. For here the ultimate problem is that of the development of *empirical* models. It might well be asked why it would be necessary to insert some other non-empirical model between the original calculus and its ultimate empirical interpretation. Why not directly construct and (empirically) interpret such a calculus?

The answer would be that in some cases it seems to be possible to apply some calculus which has been developed elsewhere and with regard to a different domain. In principle, too, it is perfectly possible to develop calculi which may be applied in a number of different fields, or can be interpreted in several disciplines. Thus, systems analysis and cybernetics claim to be isomorphic with a number of different domains (see section 3.5). The application of such calculi, however, in a particular discipline first requires their (non-empirical) interpretation in terms of that discipline, before an empirical model can be generated from them. The use of such a calculus from another discipline might, in principle, save us the labor of constructing an adequate calculus ourselves. And just like a well-chosen metaphor, it could stimulate new and fruitful insights. Besides, it is probably impossible to start scientific analysis on the basis of completely abstract and 'empty' calculi. Presumably, we will proceed initially on the basis of more familiar conceptual systems and metaphors performing the function of the calculus of a more developed theory (cf. *Nagel*, 1961: 90; *McClelland*, 1966: 11; *Reichenbach*, 1949a: 159).

Accordingly, there is no reason to reject the use of such calculi deriving from other disciplines in principle (as seems to be done in *Hoffmann*, 1960: 172). On several occasions in the foregoing discussions it has appeared that it is irrelevant how we arrive at the basic ideas, concepts or postulates, underlying the theory or whence the calculi we use originate.

Similarly, some purely mathematical calculus might be used. This requires, of course, its interpretation in abstractly political, and in empirical terms. However, it would seem that the more powerful the theory to be developed, the more constraints it imposes. In particular, the development of a mathematically formulated theory generally requires its empirical interpretation to meet the rigorous conditions of some numerical system. That is, it would require some form of measurement (cf. *Rapoport*, 1961: 48; *Leinfellner*, 1965: 48; *de Groot*, 1966: 230; *Nagel*, 1960; *Stevens*, 1960).

But there are also some dangers involved in the use of calculi from other disciplines. This is especially so when such calculi are not very well formulated, when they are networks of loosely connected concepts rather than calculi in the narrow sense employed here, and when they are equally loosely interpreted. In such circumstances such application may amount to nothing more than the introduction of a pompous vocabulary, which may be very technical and involved, but which does not clarify anything. And instead of leading to new insights and opening up new avenues for fruitful research, such calculi may, by the same token, introduce problems which are entirely irrelevant, and substitute a different obscurity for the old.

3.3.5. *Summary, and two conditions*

Summarizing the foregoing discussion, an empirical scientific theory may be described as a structure of postulates and primitives, formulated in a certain formal (logical, mathematical, or probabilistic) system, from which through definitions and theorems, certain concepts are deduced from others – the calculus –, and from which, through an interpretative system, one or more different models can, but an empirical model must, be generated.

Such a theory represents a particularly rigorous and conscious method of reality construction. Through its empirical interpretation its concepts acquire the quality of 'real things' as they thus meet the criterion for reality (cf. sections 2.5.1 and 3.3.3). The transparancy and explicitness of its logical structure together with its unambiguous connection with sensory perceptions maximize its intersubjective accessibility and transmissibility.

Such an empirical theory should satisfy two conditions. In the first place, it should be consistent. That is, it should not be possible to deduce contradictory results from it. In that case the theory would explain nothing, indeed. In the second place, it should contain an adequate empirical interpretation. Unless this is the case the theory would not really tell us anything about the real world, while it could not be falsified. As against these two requirements it does not seem very likely that criteria such as 'simplicity' or 'elegance' will come to play an important role in the social sciences in the near future, quite apart from the difficulty involved in determining what they mean (cf. *Popper*, 1959: 140 ff.; *Hempel*, 1966: 40-45).

3.4. *The possibility of theory formation*

It might be asked whether the formation of an empirical theory as it has been discussed above is at all feasible. One sometimes meets with grave doubts concerning this. For, it is observed, empirical reality is much too refractory to fit into the neat schemes devised by man's imagination.

Now, without discussing this problem in its entirety, one observation which is pertinent to it should certainly be made. However complicated and confusing empirical reality may appear to us, it is an intellectual construction, a product of our knowing mind, as has been shown in the preceding discussion. And although we are largely unable to control our actual sensory experiences, and have to accept them as given to a large extent, still they can only be known as constructions of our mind. In other words, reality itself presupposes or contains a certain order and structure. Accordingly, it is difficult to see why theory formation should be a priori impossible. For the problem is that of developing a new order on the basis of the existing one. And since the (logical) principles underlying both are not inherently and fundamentally different, the odds would seem to be on the possibility of theory formation (cf. *Lewis*, 1956: 345 ff.).

A related problem concerns the nature of the science in which theory formation is undertaken. Specifically, it has often been argued that rigorous theory formation, while possible in the natural sciences, is an impossibility in the social sciences. Implicitly this objection has already been answered in part by what has just been said. More generally, however, and without dealing extensively with that problem, it should be noted that there is nothing in the meta-theory which has been developed thus far, which is inherently restricted to any one particular field. Accordingly, it is difficult to see that there are really fundamental differences between the natural and the social sciences (cf. *de Groot*, 1966: 360 ff.). The former are obviously much more advanced than the latter at the present moment. It may well be that for man as a social being, who is intimately and emotionally concerned with the social reality which he is to investigate, it is much harder to extricate himself

from, and to transcend, the existing conceptual structure and its categories, than is the case with regard to physical reality (cf. sec 2.5.2).
This seems to be confirmed by the long history of thinking about international integration, as we have seen in the previous chapter. But, however difficult theorizing thus may be, it does not mean that this difficulty could not be overcome.

3.5.   *Some notes concerning systems analysis and cybernetics*

In connection with the discussion of models in section 3.3.4, it may be
useful, in view of the general nature of the problems concerned, to
deal briefly with systems analysis and cybernetics. Both play a certain role in the recent history of political science, and they also figure
in the integration theories of Haas, Deutsch, and Lindberg. They represent clear examples of attempts at a political application of calculi
that have been developed outside the discipline and that are of an extremely general nature.

In a general sense, the term 'system' refers to something (a 'thing',
a process, a mechanism, an organism, for instance) which can be conceived as a whole existing in an environment from which it can be
distinguished. From this environment it receives certain stimuli (the
input) which it processes, leading to certain actions of the system upon
the environment (its output). These in their turn may modify the environment thus leading to a changed input into the system, a process
which is termed 'feedback' (see *Friedrich*, 1963: 24 ff.; *Easton*, 1965:
21 ff.; *Kaplan*, 1957: 4; *Haas*, 1964: 52 ff.; *Kuhn*, 1963: 45 ff.; *Mesarović*, 1962: 10-11).

Now, it is imperative to bear in mind that like all our conceptual
constructions this one, too, is to serve our understanding of a certain
phenomenon. In other words, it is an analytical device. And it is not
necessary that it should be capable of identification with other such
constructions which have been defined in other terms and which may
be deeply embedded in traditional usage and ways of thinking. Specifically, the concept of system need not be identified with 'things' or
'entities' which are defined spatially, or which have a spatial dimension;
a political system is not necessarily a state in its geographical extension,
or a group of states occupying a certain geographical region. Indeed,
whether or not such an element enters into the definition of a particular

system depends entirely upon the problem which is to be analysed. Conversely, Luxemburg and China could be conceived as constituting one system if that would be useful in studying particular problems arising between them.

Strictly speaking, then, a system is merely a set of interrelated variables or statements through which some initially problematic phenomenon is known (cf. *Kaplan*, 1957: 4; *Kuhn*, 1963: 50; *Easton*, 1965: 21; *Mesarović*, 1962: 10; *Haas*, 1964: 53; see also sections 2.4.3 and 2.4.4). Accordingly, the environment of a system consists of those, and only of those, variables or statements (or, in colloquial terms, things, processes, etc.) that determine the values of the variables that define the system itself.

It now becomes clear why the concept of system, and systems analysis, are claimed to be of such a general applicability and validity – and justifiably so. They merely denote the structure of our knowledge: some phenomenon, X, is explained in terms of a set of variables $\{a, b, \ldots \ldots n\}$, together forming a system; the values of these variables are determined by another set of variables $\{x, y, z\}$, the environment, while X, in its turn, is related to these latter variables, through feedback relations. All this is perfectly general, of course. But the scheme is also rather empty. That is, it does not contain any information as to what variables to choose, and how they are interrelated. To make this choice and to discover those relationships is exactly what knowledge in general consists of, and the character of this problem is quite unaffected by the introduction of a systems vocabulary. These considerations are reinforced by the fact that in its political applications there is no question of a well formulated and developed systems-analytic calculus being interpreted politically. Rather than a formal system of reasoning in which theorems are derived from postulates, and whose concepts are given a political meaning, systems analysis in its political application is largely a set of terms, a vocabulary a conceptual scheme rather than a well formulated theory (see also *Kaplan*, 1969: 49; *Spiro*, 1967: 165; *Meehan*, 1967: 328 ff.).

Accordingly, the significance of systems analysis does not reside in the fact that it provides us with a ready-made calculus from which to generate a political and empirical model. The introduction of the systems-analytic vocabulary would rather seem to represent a step in the process of emancipation from the traditional political notions and the insights associated with these. Thus, instead of conceiving politics exclusively in terms of 'sovereign states' as fixed and rather static entities, geographically determined, systems analysis makes for a much wider conception of politics. It is inherently dynamical, and it forces us to choose variables which are relevant and to make explicit why they are so. To realize all this, systems analysis is not strictly necessary. Nevertheless, its boxes and arrows presumably represent a less misleading way of visualizing a political process than clockworks, mechanisms, or organisms (cf. *Deutsch*, 1951a).

Much the same observations apply to cybernetics as it figures especially in the work of Karl W. Deutsch. In point of fact, the distinction between systems analysis and cybernetics is often difficult to make in practice. For, cybernetics, too, uses a systems vocabulary, while, conversely, the social sciences are generally concerned with systems that are *steered* (i.e. capable of bringing about specific relationships with their environment, cf. *Deutsch*, 1963: 91), which is of the essence of cybernetics. Cybernetics, one might say, is concerned with a particular kind of system, namely one that is steered and that is conceived in terms of communication and information.

Like systems analysis cybernetics moves on an extremely high level of abstraction. It is concerned with things as diverse as brains and living cells, human bodies and industrial production, traffic regulation and machines, learning processes and computers, organizations and societies, etc. Accordingly, its concepts are of an extreme generality and they may not be identified with the meaning they acquire in any one particular system with which it may deal. First of all this pertains to the concepts communication and information.

Briefly, communication can be described as the transmission of messages. These messages, in their turn, convey information, which Deutsch defines as

... those aspects of the state description of each physical process which all these processes had in common (*Deutsch*, 1966: 94; see also *Deutsch*, 1963: 147).

Thus, photography can be conceived as a process of communication in which the messages which are transmitted in its several phases consist of certain optical, chemical, and often electrical, impulses. The information which is conveyed through this process is a certain structure of optical impulses, characterizing the object photographed, which remains invariant through its several transformations during the process. Messages are the vehicles of information; communication consists of the transmission of messages in general, while information is a narrower concept, referring only to what really comes through a certain chain of communication processes. These two things are not necessarily identical as is exemplified by what may happen to a message which is orally transmitted through a chain of people. While communication does occur here, it may well be that no information at all will be transmitted by the chain as a whole.

As already indicated, the concepts of information and communication have a very wide meaning in cybernetics. Depending upon the specific character of the system under study, they may concern electrical, chemical, mechanical, political, or economical impulses. The common element in all these and similar forms would seem to be that certain elements, units, components, or instances, emit certain impulses or complexes of impulses which, to the extent that they are in fact received by other units or instances, influence the conduct or behavior of the latter, specifically, the impulses which these in their turn will emit.

A cybernetic system is a set of communication processes through which certain impulses, information, which it receives from the environment, are processed into impulses which the system in its turn releases unto the environment. To do this the system needs detectors or receptors through which it can take in information from the environment. In the second place, it needs effectors which are capable of giving off certain impulses themselves. A cybernetic system, however, is one that is *steered*, i.e., one that is equipped to bring about a specific relationship with its environment. This relationship may be termed the 'goal' of the system (*Deutsch*, 1963: 91). However, as the environment is not completely static, but will change, the system, in order to reach its goal(s), must be capable of choosing or selecting the impulses which it is to give off. Thus, in addition to receptors and effectors, it needs a selector (cf. *Kuhn*, 1963: 45), or a decision area in Deutsch's terms (*Deutsch*, 1964: 62; also *Deutsch*, 1963: 258).

But choice and selection imply the system's capacity for the storage of information. It must dispose of alternative responses, and rules or criteria which govern their choice, as well as the facilities to combine this stored information with information it receives from the environment. In other words, the system needs *memory* (*Deutsch*, 1963: 85, 206).

Memory enables the system to *learn*, that is, to change its output in relation to changes in its input such that it still may realize its original goals (*Deutsch*, 1963: 92, 164). Such learning is a *feedback process* which Deutsch describes as follows:

In other words, by feedback – or, as it is often called, a servo-mechanism – is meant a communications network that produces action in response to an input of information, and *includes the results of its own actions in the new information by which it modifies its subsequent behavior* (*Deutsch*, 1963: 88).

It is important to note that in more developed systems feedback may also result in the system's changing its own initial goals and structure so as to render it better capable of survival in a changing environment (cf. *Deutsch*, 1963: 92-93).

At this stage of our inquiry it is not necessary to go any further into the details of the cybernetic scheme. Like systems analysis it offers a conceptual scheme rather than a well developed calculus in the strict sense of that word. Like systems analysis, too, its interpretation in political terms leaves the problems pretty much as they were before the introduction of that vocabulary. How political information is taken in from the environment, how it is transmitted, how it is combined with stored political information, how the environment in its turn receives information from a particular political system, all such questions are not answered by just giving a political meaning to the abstract cybernetic terms concerned. The use of such terms as 'communication' and 'information' may even be positively misleading. For these terms also play a certain role in everyday discourse, where they have a relatively established meaning. When no sufficient note is taken of the entirely different nature of these concepts in cybernetics and everyday language, respectively, very peculiar errors may occur. As will appear from chapter four, Deutsch largely fails to give an explicit political interpretation to the cybernetic terms 'communication' and 'information' himself. Ignoring this problem, he pays considerable attention to the measurement of 'communication' in terms of mail-flows, telephone traffic and so on, without being sufficiently aware, apparently, that he is no longer dealing with (political) cybernetics. Now, of course, mail-flows and similar things may play a role in a political, or even a political-cybernetic, theory, e.g. an 'environmental' variable. But their role is *not* that of communication politically interpreted, which, with Deutsch, can be better rendered in such terms as 'demands', 'support', and 'binding decision'. In this way, Deutsch is led to neglect the analysis of political communication proper while, incidentally, he also fails to make the political relevance of such things as mail-flows sufficiently clear.

In the political application of systems analysis and cybernetics we meet with rather early stages in the formation of political theories. It amounts to no more than the introduction of a somewhat different vocabulary, a 'calculus' of an extremely weak form, one might say. Its significance would seem to reside less in any direct and immediate contribution to our insights into political problems, than in its indirect role of breaking through an established and traditional conceptual scheme.

4. PRELIMINARY NOTES ON THE ANALYSIS OF INTEGRATION THEORIES

4.1. *Some general problems*

It should be noted, to begin with, that the foregoing analysis is *not* a recipe for theory formation or a description of how theories are actually formed. Rather, it is a 'rational reconstruction', in Reichenbach's terminology (*Reichenbach*, 1949a: 5-6). It describes how that particular structure of knowledge is to be organized and formulated for it to be called a theory, and to be counted as an acceptable piece of knowledge. But in its postulates and conceptualization creative imagination is presupposed. There being nothing which ineluctably prescribes them, or from which they are automatically and mechanically generated, they rather represent lucky hits, whose success is 'measured' by the capacity of the results deduced from them to withstand empirical falsification.

Also, in the historical process of the development of knowledge it is not to be expected that theory formation would start with the formulation of abstract calculi. Actually a theory will initially be formulated in terms which are anything but empty, but which will have referents (or are intended to have them) in the empirical reality as it is known at the time. The explicit formulation, or isolation, of the calculus of such a theory will occur only in a relatively advanced phase of development, that of its formalization, for instance, when it is attempted to formulate it in more precise mathematical language. In its turn, such a formalization increases the precision and rigorousness of the theory, but by the same token it will uncover its weak points and lead to new problems, thus conducing to its subsequent development.

To some extent such a formalization is what the analyses of the following chapters amount to. However, as has already been indicated (introduction, section 2) the theories to be analysed are of a rather weak variety. Generally, they are lacking in explicitness and deductive rigor; often, lines of reasoning are suggested rather than pursued to their logical conclusions; sometimes, inconsistencies occur. In these circumstances it does not seem useful or worthwhile to carry formalization to its limits, that is, to reconstruct calculi which really consist of empty symbols rather than more or less common names. Such formalization would involve going too far beyond the theories as originally formulated and published. As I have already said (introduction, section 2), in my reconstruction of these theories I will keep as closely as possible to the explicit formulations of their authors – even though, from a logical or empirical-scientific viewpoint, the result will not be entirely satisfactory.

Although such common names for the concepts in the calculi will be used and this may facilitate thinking, it should not be forgotten that so long as they have not been explicitly interpreted empirically (or operationalized), their status within the calculus remains essentially that of empty symbols. That is, while the use of such terms, precisely because they do already have *some*, usually vague, empirical referents, does have some pragmatic or heuristic advantage, it should constantly be borne in mind that in the calculus to be constructed such traditional empirical referents are not automatically relevant. They are so only when explicitly so formulated, or when it follows from the rules of the calculus; moreover, the (empirical) meaning of such common terms generally is much too vague and ambiguous as to allow for their use in the testing of the empirical propositions in which they figure. Operationalizing a calculus represents an extremely difficult problem, and as a general rule the use of common terms with their empirical referents should not lead us to take its solution for granted.

All this is not to deny that even in applying common names, without an explicit and precise empirical interpretation, theorizing may result in better and deeper understanding. For, after all, even in the absence of an explicit and sharp operationalization of the concept applied, theorizing may at least refine common sense. As will appear from the subsequent analyses such operationalization is the exception rather than the rule. Nevertheless, the theories concerned do represent a clear advance over unformed common sense; and at least they allow for a relatively precise location of problems for further research.

Except for very advanced theories which have been highly formalized, a rigid distinction between the abstract calculus and its operationalization is somewhat artificial. Normally, there will be a continuous chain of reasoning linking the abstract concepts of the calculus with observations. As to the theories under study, accordingly, the point at which the study of their calculi ends and that of their empirical interpretations begins, is to some extent arbitrary. As a general rule I have tried to develop these calculi as far as this seemed possible without having to deal with empirical matters. Empirical observations, and problems of measurement, since these are intimately bound up with observation, have been dealt with under 'operationalization'.

Finally, as I have already mentioned in section 3.4 of the introduction, I will not deal expressly with existing (critical) literature on the theorists to be discussed subsequently. Since this literature is written from a rather different angle than the present book, to discuss it would have necessitated a considerable amount of reformulation and elaboration without a concomitant increase in the understanding of the theories as developed here.

4.2. *The course of analysis*

The structure of the analyses to be undertaken in the chapters which follow is reflected in the way these chapters are organized.

In *section 1* of each chapter I will discuss the general character of the approach of the author concerned.

In view of the fundamental importance of how politics is conceived for subsequent research, a separate section (*section 2*) will be devoted to an analysis of the author's general conception of politics.

The way in which integration is defined by the author concerned will then be analysed in *section 3*.

In *section 4* I will investigate how the author explains the occurrence or non-occurrence of integration as defined by him. Here I will generally proceed as follows. First, the author's conception of the integration process as a whole will be investigated. In the second place, attention will be focused upon the separate elements which play a role in that process, both with regard to their function in that process itself and to those (environmental or background) factors which determine their behavior, 'from the outside' one might say. The precise arrangement of this section in any individual chapter, however, will also depend upon the way the author himself treats the subject.

While the foregoing sections deal with the author's thinking as an abstract, uninterpreted system or calculus, its empirical interpretation will be dealt with in *section 5*.

In *section 6*, finally, I will conclude with a brief appraisal of what has been found so far.

BIBLIOGRAPHY

ACKERMANN, Robert, 1965. *Theories of knowledge – a critical introduction.* McGraw-Hill, New York.

APOSTEL, Leo, 1960. Towards the formal study of models in the non-formal sciences. *Synthese 12 (2/3):* 125–161.

APOSTEL, Leo, 1965. The justification of set theories. In: Yehoshua Bar-Hillel (Ed.), *Logic, methodology and philosophy of science*, pp. 199–209. North Holland Publishing Co., Amsterdam.

ARON, Raymond, 1967. Qu'est-ce qu'une théorie des relations internationales? *Rev. fr. Sci. polit. 17 (5):* 838–61.

AYER, A.J., 1956. *The problem of knowledge.* MacMillan, London.

BAR-HILLEL, Yehoshua (Ed.), 1965. *Logic, methodology and philosophy of science.* North Holland Publishing Co., Amsterdam.

BARTLEY III, W.W., 1968. Theories of demarcation between science and metaphysics. In: Imre Lakatos & Alan Musgrave (Ed.), *Problems in the philosophy of science*, pp. 40–119. North Holland Publishing Co., Amsterdam.

BAYER, Raymond, 1954. *Epistémologie et logique depuis Kant jusqu'à nos jours.* Presses Universitaires de France, Paris.

BERGER, Joseph, Bernard COHEN, J. Laurie SNELL & Morris ZELDITCH Jr., 1962. *Types of formalization in small-group research.* Houghton Mifflin, Boston.

BERGER, Joseph, Morris ZELDITCH Jr. & Bo ANDERSON, 1966. *Sociological theories in progress.* Houghton Mifflin, Boston.

BERTELS, Kees & Doede NAUTA, 1969. *Inleiding tot het modelbegrip*. De Haan, Bussum.

BLACK, Max, 1962. *Models and metaphors – studies in language and philosophy*. Cornell University Press, Ithaca (N.Y.).

BLALOCK Jr., Hubert M., 1969. *Theory construction – from verbal to mathematical formulations*. Prentice-Hall, Englewood Cliffs (N.J.).

BOCHEŃSKI, I.M., 1965. *Die zeitgenössischen Denkmethoden*, 3. Aufl. Franke, Bern/München (1. Aufl. 1954).

BRECHT, Arnold, 1959. *Political theory – the foundations of twentieth-century political thought*. Princeton University Press, Princeton (N.J.).

BROAD, C.D., 1968. *Induction, probability, and causation*. Reidel, Dordrecht.

BRODBECK, May (Ed.), 1968. *Readings in the philosophy of the social sciences*. MacMillan, New York.

BRONOWSKI, J., 1956. *Science and human values*. Julian Messner, New York.

BRONOWSKI, J. & Bruce MAZLISH, 1960. *The Western intellectual tradition – from Leonardo to Hegel*. Hutchinson, London.

BUCKLEY, Walter (Ed.), 1968. *Modern systems research for the behavioral scientist – a sourcebook*. Aldine, Chicago.

BULL, Hedley, 1966. International theory – the case for a classical approach. *Wld Polit. 18 (3)*: 361–377.

BUNGE, Mario, 1967. *Scientific research*, 2 vols. Springer, Berlin.

BURNS, Arthur Lee, 1968. *Of powers and their politics – a critique of theoretical approaches*. Prentice Hall, Englewood Cliffs (N.J.).

BURTON, J.W., 1968. *Systems, states, diplomacy and rules*. Cambridge University Press, Cambridge.

CARNAP, Rudolf, 1960. Elementary and abstract terms. In: Arthur Danto & Sidney Morgenbesser (Ed.), *Philosophy of science*, pp. 150–158. The World, Cleveland/New York.

CASSIRER, Ernst, 1950. *The problem of knowledge, philosophy, science and history since Hegel*. Yale University Press, New Haven/London.

CASSIRER, Ernst, 1951. *The philosophy of the enlightenment*. Beacon Press, Boston.

CASSIRER, Ernst, 1953. *The philosophy of symbolic forms*, Vol. I. Yale University Press, New Haven/London.

CASSIRER, Ernst, 1955. *The philosophy of symbolic forms*, Vol. II. Yale University Press, New Haven/London.

CASSIRER, Ernst, 1957. *The philosophy of symbolic forms*, Vol. III, Yale University Press, New Haven/London.

CASSIRER, Ernst, 1962. *An essay on man – an introduction to a philosophy of human culture*. Yale University Press, New Haven/London.

CHARLESWORTH, James C. (Ed.), 1966. *A design for political science – scope, objectives, and methods*. American Academy of Political and Social Science, Philadelphia.

CHARLESWORTH, James C. (Ed.), 1967. *Contemporary political analysis*. Free Press, New York.

CHISHOLM, Roderick M., 1966. *Theory of knowledge.* Prentice Hall, Englewood Cliffs (N.J.).

CHURCHMAN, C. West & Philburn RATOOSH (Ed.), 1959. *Measurement – definition and theories.* Wiley, New York/London.

DAHL, Robert A., 1963. *Modern political analysis.* Prentice Hall, Englewood Cliffs (N.J.).

DANTO, Arthur C., 1968. *Analytical philosophy of knowledge.* Cambridge University Press, Cambridge.

DANTO, Arthur & Sidney MORGENBESSER (Ed.), 1960. *Philosophy of science.* The World, Cleveland/New York.

DEUTSCH, Karl W., 1951a. Mechanism, organism, and society – some models in natural and social science. *Phil. Sci. 18 (3):* 230–252.

DEUTSCH, Karl W., 1951b. Mechanism, teleology, and mind – the theory of communications and some problems in philosophy and social science. *Phil. phenomenol. Res. 12 (2):* 185–223.

DEUTSCH, Karl W., 1963. *The nerves of government – models of communication and control.* Free Press of Glencoe, London.

DEUTSCH, Karl W., 1964. Communication theory and political integration. In: Philip E. Jacob & James V. Toscano (Ed.), *The integration of political communities,* pp. 46–74. Lippincott, Philadelphia.

DEUTSCH, Karl W., 1966. *Nationalism and social communication – an inquiry into the foundations of nationality,* 2nd ed. MIT Press, Cambridge (Mass.) (1st ed. 1953).

DIRENZO, Gordon J. (Ed.), 1966a. *Concepts, theory and explanation in the behavioral sciences.* Random House, New York.

DIRENZO, Gordon J., 1966b. Toward explanation in the behavioral sciences. In: Gordon J. Direnzo (Ed.), *Concepts, theory and explanation in the behavioral sciences,* pp. 239–291. Random House, New York.

DOWSE, Robert E., 1966. A functionalist's logic. *Wld Polit. 18 (4):* 607–622.

DUIJKER, H.C.J., B.G. PALLAND & R. VUYK, 1963. *Leerboek der psychologie,* 3e druk. Wolters, Groningen (1e druk 1958).

EASTON, David, 1960. *The political system – an inquiry into the state of political science.* Alfred A. Knopf, New York (1st ed. 1953).

EASTON, David, 1965. *A systems analysis of political life.* Wiley, New York.

ECKSTEIN, Harry & David E. APTER (Ed.), 1963. *Comparative politics – a reader.* Free Press of Glencoe, New York.

ENRIQUES, F., 1938. La théorie de la connaissance scientifique de Kant à nos jours. Hermann, Paris.

EULAU, Heinz (Ed.), 1969. *Behavioralism in political science.* Atherton Press, New York.

FARRALL, R. Barry (Ed.), 1966. *Approaches to comparative and international politics.* Northwestern University Press, Evanston (Ill.).

FEIGL, Herbert & Grover MAXWELL (Ed.), 1962. *Scientific explanation, space, and time.* University of Minnesota Press, Minneapolis.

FEIGL, Herbert & Wilfrid SELLARS (Ed.), 1949. *Readings in philosophical analysis.* Appleton-Century-Crofts, New York.

FEYERABEND, P.K., 1962. Explanation, reduction, and empiricism. In: Herbert Feigl & Grover Maxwell (Ed.), *Scientific explanation, space, and time*, pp. 28–97. University of Minnesota Press, Minneapolis.

FLANIGAN, William & Edwin FOGELMAN, 1967. Functional analysis. In: James C. Charlesworth (Ed.), *Contemporary political analysis*, pp. 72–85. Free Press, New York.

FOURASTIÉ, Jean, 1966. *Les conditions de l'esprit scientifique.* Gallimard, Paris.

FRANK, Philipp, 1961. *Modern science and its philosophy.* Collier Books, New York.

FREY, Gerhard, 1969. Über die Gültigkeit genereller Sätze. *Synthese 20 (1):* 104–120.

FREUND, Julien, 1965. *L'Essence du politique.* Éditions Sirey, Paris.

FRIEDRICH, Carl Joachim, 1963. *Man and his government – an empirical theory of politics.* McGraw-Hill, New York.

FROHOCK, Fred M., 1967. *The nature of political inquiry.* Dorsey Press, Homewood (Ill.).

GARCEAU, Oliver (Ed.), 1968. *Political research and political theory.* Harvard University Press, Cambridge (Mass.).

GOLEMBIEWSKI, Robert T., William A. WELSH & William J. CROBLY, 1969. *A methodological primer for political scientists.* Rand McNally, Chicago.

GROOT, A.D. de, 1966. *Methodologie – grondslagen van onderzoek en denken in de gedragswetenschappen*, 3e druk. Mouton, The Hague (1e druk 1961).

HAAS, Ernst B., 1964. *Beyond the nation-state – functionalism and international organization.* Stanford University Press, Stanford.

HANSON, Norwood Russell, 1965. *Patterns of discovery – an inquiry into the conceptual foundations of science*, 2nd ed. Cambridge University Press, Cambridge (1st ed. 1958).

HEMPEL, Carl G., 1952. *Fundamentals of concept formation in the empirical sciences.* University of Chicago Press, Chicago.

HEMPEL, Carl, G., 1949. On the nature of mathematical truth. In: Herbert Feigl & Wilfrid Sellars (Ed.), *Readings in philosophical analysis*, pp. 222–237. Appleton-Century-Crofts, New York.

HEMPEL, Carl G., 1960. Operationism, observation, and theoretical terms. In: Arthur Danto & Sidney Morgenbesser (Ed.), *Philosophy of science*, pp. 101–120. The World, Cleveland/New York.

HEMPEL, Carl G., 1962. Deductive-nomological vs. statistical explanation. In: Herbert Feigl & Grover Maxwell (Ed.), *Scientific explanation, space, and time*, pp. 98–169. University of Minnesota Press, Minneapolis.

HEMPEL, Carl G., 1965. *Aspects of scientific explanation and other essays in the philosophy of science*. Free Press, New York.
HEMPEL, Carl G., 1966. *Philosophy of natural science*. Prentice Hall, Englewood Cliffs (N.J.).
HOFFMANN, Stanley (Ed.), 1960. *Contemporary theory in international relations*. Prentice Hall, Englewood Cliffs (N.J.).
HOFFMANN, Stanley, 1965. *The state of war – essays on the theory and practice of international politics*. Praeger, New York.
HOLSTI, K.J., 1967. *International politics – a framework for analysis*. Prentice Hall, Englewood Cliffs (N.J.).

JACOB, Philip E. & James V. TOSCANO (Ed.), 1964. *The integration of political communities*. Lippincott, Philadelphia.
JANSSON, Jan-Magnus, 1966. Defining political science – some basic reflections. *Scand. polit. Stud.* (yearbook): 13–24.

KAPLAN, Abraham, 1964. *The conduct of inquiry – methodology for behavioral science*. Chandler, San Francisco.
KAPLAN, Morton A., 1957. System and process in international politics. Wiley, New York.
KAPLAN, Morton A., 1961. Problems of theory building and theory confirmation in international politics. In: Klaus Knorr & Sidney Verba (Ed.), *The international system – theoretical essays*, pp. 6–24. Princeton University Press, Princeton (N.J.).
KAPLAN, Morton A., 1967. Systems theory. In: James C. Charlesworth (Ed.), *Contemporary political analysis*, pp. 150–163. Free Press, New York.
KAPLAN, Morton A. (Ed.), 1968a. *New approaches to international relations*. St. Martin's Press, New York.
KAPLAN, Morton A., 1968b. The systems approach to international politics. In: Morton A. Kaplan (Ed.), *New approaches to international relations*, pp. 381–404. St. Martin's Press, New York.
KAPLAN, Morton A., 1969. *Macropolitics – selected essays on the philosophy and science of politics*. Aldine, Chicago.
KEMENY, John G., 1960. A philosopher looks at political science. *J. Conflict Resolution 4 (3)*: 292–302.
KNORR, Klaus & James N. ROSENAU (Ed.), 1969. *Contending approaches to international politics*. Princeton University Press, Princeton (N.J.).
KNORR, Klaus & Sidney VERBA (Ed.), 1961. *The international system – theoretical essays*. Princeton University Press, Princeton (N.J.).
KÖRNER, Stephan, 1966. *Experience and theory – an essay in the philosophy of science*. Routledge and Kegan Paul, London.
KOTARBIŃSKI, Tadeusz, 1966. *Gnosiology – the scientific approach to the theory of knowledge*. Pergamon Press, Oxford.
KRECH, David, Richard S. CRUTCHFIELD & Egerton L. BALLACHEY, 1962. *Individual in society – a textbook of social psychology*. McGraw-Hill, New York.

KUHN, Alfred, 1963. *The study of society – a unified approach.* Richard D. Irwin and the Dorsey Press, Homewood (Ill.).

KUHN, Thomas S., 1968. *The structure of scientific revolutions.* University of Chicago Press, Chicago/London (1st ed. 1962).

LAKATOS, Imre & Alan MUSGRAVE (Ed.), 1968. *Problems in the philosophy of science.* North Holland Publishing Co., Amsterdam.

LASSWELL, Harold D. & Abraham KAPLAN, 1963. *Power and society – a framework for political inquiry.* Yale University Press, New York/London (1st ed. 1950).

LASSWELL, Harold D., 1964. *The future of political science.* Prentice Hall, New York.

LEINFELLNER, Werner, 1965. *Struktur und Aufbau wissenschaftlicher Theorien – eine wissenschaftstheoretisch-philosophische Untersuchung.* Physica Verlag, Wien/Würzburg.

LEWIS, Clarence Irving, 1956. *Mind and the world order – outline of a theory of knowledge.* Dover Publications, New York (1st ed. 1929).

LEWIS, Clarence Irving, 1949. Experience and meaning. In: Herbert Feigl & Wilfrid Sellars (Ed.), *Readings in philosophical analysis,* pp. 128–145. Appleton-Century-Crofts, New York.

LEYS, Colin, 1963. Models, theories, and the theory of political parties. In: Harry Eckstein & David E. Apter (Ed.), *Comparative politics – a reader,* pp. 305–314. Free Press of Glencoe, New York.

LOCKE, Don, 1967. *Perception and our knowledge of the external world.* Allen & Unwin, London/Humanities Press, New York.

McCLELLAND, Charles A., 1970. The function of theory in international relations. *J. Conflict Resolution 4 (3):* 303–336.

McCLELLAND, Charles A., 1966. *Theory and the international system.* Macmillan, New York.

McDONALD, Neil A., 1965. *Politics – a study of control behavior.* Rutgers University Press, New Brunswick (N.J.).

MACKENZIE, W.J.M., 1967. *Politics and social science.* Penguin Books, Harmondsworth.

MACKLIN, Ruth, 1969. Explanation and action – recent issues and controversies. *Synthese 20 (3):* 388-415.

MAXWELL, Grover, 1962. The ontological status of theoretical entities. In: Herbert Feigl & Grover Maxwell (Ed.), *Scientific explanation, space, and time,* pp. 3–27. University of Minnesota Press, Minneapolis.

MEAD, George H., 1967. *Mind, self, and society – from the standpoint of a social behaviorist* (edited and with an introduction by Charles W. Morris). University of Chicago Press, Chicago/London (1st ed. 1934).

MEEHAN, Eugene J., 1965. *The theory and method of political analysis.* Dorsey Press, Homewood (Ill.).

MEEHAN, Eugene J., 1967. *Contemporary political thought – a critical study*. Dorsey Press, Homewood (Ill.).

MESAROVIĆ, Mihaljo D., 1962. On self-organizational systems. In: Marshall C. Yovits, George T. Jacobi & Gordon D. Goldstein (Ed.), *Self-organizing systems*, pp. 9–36. Spartan Books, Washington (D.C.).

MESSELKEN, Karlheinz, 1968. *Politikbegriffe der modernen Soziologie – eine Kritik der Systemtheorie und Konflikttheorie, begründet aus ihren Implikationen für die gesellschaftliche Praxis*. Westdeutscher Verlag, Köln/Opladen.

MORGENTHAU, Hans J., 1967. Common sense and theories of international relations. *J. int. Affairs 21 (2)*: 207–214.

MUELLER, John E. (Ed.), 1969. *Approaches to measurement in international relations – a non-evangelical survey*. Appleton-Century-Crofts, New York.

NAGEL, Ernest, 1949. Logic without ontology. In: Herbert Feigl & Wilfrid Sellars (Ed.), *Readings in philosophical analysis*, pp. 191–210. Appleton-Century-Crofts, New York.

NAGEL, Ernest, 1960. Measurement. In: Arthur C. Danto & Sidney Morgenbesser (Ed.), *Philosophy of science*, pp. 121–140. The World, Cleveland/New York.

NAGEL, Ernest, 1961. *The structure of science – problems in the logic of scientific explanation*. Harcourt, Brace and World, New York.

NAUTA, Doede, 1970. *Logica en model*. W. de Haan, Bussum.

NUCHELMANS, G., 1969. *Overzicht van de analytische wijsbegeerte*. Spectrum, Utrecht/Antwerpen.

OBERNDÖRFER, Dieter (Hrsg.), 1966a. *Wissenschaftliche Politik – eine Einführung in Grundfragen ihrer Tradition und Theorie*, 2. Aufl. Rombach, Freiburg im Breisgau (1. Aufl. 1962).

OBERNDÖRFER, Dieter, 1966b. Politik als praktische Wissenschaft. In: Dieter Oberndörfer (Hrsg.), *Wissenschaftliche Politik – eine Einführung in Grundfragen ihrer Tradition und Theorie*, 2. Aufl., pp. 9–58. Rombach, Freiburg im Breisgau.

POPKIN, Richard H., 1968. Scepticism, theology and the scientific revolution in the seventeenth century. In: Imre Lakatos & Alan Musgrave (Ed.), *Problems in the philosophy of science*, pp. 1–39. North Holland Publishing Co., Amsterdam.

POPPER, Karl R., 1959. *The logic of scientific discovery*, Basic Books, New York.

POPPER, Karl R., 1962. *The open society and its enemies*, 2 vols, 4th ed. Routledge and Kegan Paul, London (1st ed. 1945).

POPPER, Karl R., 1963. *Conjectures and refutations – the growth of scientific knowledge*. Routledge and Kegan Paul, London.

PRESLEY, C.F., 1960. Laws and theories in the physical sciences. In: Arthur Danto & Sidney Morgenbesser (Ed.), *Philosophy of science*, pp. 205–225. The World, Cleveland/New York.

QUADE, E.S. & W.I. BOUCHER (Ed.), 1968. *Systems analysis and policy planning – applications in defense*. American Elsevier, New York.

QUINE, Willard Van Orman, 1964. *From a logical point of view*, 2nd ed. Harvard University Press, Cambridge (Mass.) (1st ed. 1953).

RAPOPORT, Anatol, 1961. Various meanings of 'theory'. In: James N. Rosenau (Ed.), *International politics and foreign policy – a reader in research and theory*, pp. 44–52. Free Press, New York.

REICHENBACH, Hans, 1949a. *Experience and prediction – an analysis of the foundations and the structure of knowledge*. University of Chicago Press, Chicago (1st ed. 1938).

REICHENBACH, Hans, 1949b. The logical foundations of the concept of probability. In: Herbert Feigl & Wilfrid Sellars (Ed.), *Readings in philosophical analysis*, pp. 305–323. Appleton-Century-Crofts, New York.

REICHENBACH, Hans, 1949c. On the justification of induction. In: Herbert Feigl & Wilfrid Sellars (Ed.), *Readings in philosophical analysis*, pp. 324–329. Appleton-Century-Crofts, New York.

ROSENAU, James N. (Ed.), 1961. *International politics and foreign policy – a reader in research and theory*. Free Press, New York.

ROSENAU, James N., 1966. Pre-theories and theories of foreign policy. In: R. Barry Farrell (Ed.), *Approaches to comparative and international politics*, pp. 27–92. Northwestern University Press, Evanston (Ill.).

ROSENAU, James N. (Ed.), 1969. *International politics and foreign policy – a reader in research and theory*, revised edition. Free Press, New York.

ROSENKRANTZ, Roger D., 1969. On explanation. *Synthese 20 (3)*: 335–370.

ROZEBOOM, William W., 1962. The factual content of theoretical concepts. In: Herbert Feigl & Grover Maxwell (Ed.), *Scientific explanation, space, and time*, pp. 273–356. University of Minnesota Press, Minneapolis.

RUDNER, Richard S., 1966. *Philosophy of social science*. Prentice Hall, Englewood Cliffs (N.J.).

RUSSELL, Bertrand, 1961. *History of western philosophy – and its connection with political and social circumstances from the earliest times to the present day*. Allen and Unwin, London (1st ed. 1946).

RUSSELL, Bertrand, 1964. *Human knowledge – its scope and limits*. Simon and Schuster, New York (1st ed. 1948).

SAID, Abdul A. (Ed.), 1968. *Theory of international relations – the crisis of relevance*. Prentice Hall, Englewood Cliffs (N.J.).

SAUER, Friedrich Otto, 1965. *Mathematisches Denken auf dem Wege zur Philosophie – eine Studie zur heutigen Wissenschaftslage*. Bayerischer Schulbuch-Verlag, München.

SCHLICK, Moritz, 1949. Meaning and verification. In: Herbert Feigl & Wilfrid Sellars (Ed.), *Readings in philosophical analysis*, pp. 146–170. Appleton-Century-Crofts, New York.

SINGER, J. David, 1961. The level-of-analysis problem in international relations. In: Klaus Knorr & Sidney Verba (Ed.), *The international system – theoretical essays*, pp. 77–92. Princeton University Press, Princeton (N.J.).

SINGER, J. David (Ed.), 1968. *Quantitative international politics – insights and evidence.* Free Press, New York.

SPIRO, Herbert J., 1966. An evaluation of systems theory. In: James C. Charlesworth (Ed.), *A design for political science – scope, objectives, and methods,* pp. 164–174. American Academy of Political and Social Science, Philadelphia.

STEBBING, L. Susan, 1960. Furniture of the earth. In: Arthur Danto & Sidney Morgenbesser (Ed.), *Philosophy of science,* pp. 69–81. The World, Cleveland/New York.

STEVENS, S. S., 1960. On the theory of scales of measurement. In: Arthur Danto & Sidney Morgenbesser (Ed.), *Philosophy of science,* pp. 141–149. The World, Cleveland/New York.

STINCHCOMBE, Arthur L., 1968. *Constructing social theories.* Harcourt Brace and World, New York.

STROLL, Evrum (Ed.), 1967. *Epistemology – new essays in the theory of knowledge.* Harper and Row, New York.

SUPPES, Patrick, 1960. A comparison of the meaning and uses of models in mathematics and the empirical sciences. *Synthese 12 (2/3):* 287–301.

TARSKI, Alfred, 1949. The semantic conception of truth and the foundations of semantics. In: Herbert Feigl & Wilfrid Sellars, *Readings in philosophical analysis,* pp. 52–84. Appleton-Century-Crofts, New York.

TIMASHEFF, Nicholas S., 1957. *Sociological theory – its nature and growth,* 2nd revised edition. Random House, New York (1st ed. 1955).

TOPISCH, Ernst (Hrsg.), 1968a. *Logik der Sozialwissenschaften,* 5. Aufl. Kiepenheuer und Witsch, Köln/Berlin (1st ed. 1965).

TOPISCH, Ernst, 1968b. Sprachlogische Probleme der sozialwissenschaftlichen Theoriebildung. In: Ernst Topisch (Hrsg.), *Logik der Sozialwissenschaften,* 5. Aufl., pp. 17–36. Kiepenheuer und Witsch, Köln/Berlin.

TOPISCH, Ernst, 1968c. Das Verhältnis zwischen Sozial- und Naturwissenschaften – eine methodologisch-ideologie-kritische Untersuchung. In: Ernst Topisch (Hrsg.), *Logik der Sozialwissenschaften,* 5. Aufl., pp. 57–71. Kiepenheuer und Witsch, Köln/Berlin.

TOULMIN, Stephan, 1962. *The philosophy of science – an introduction.* Arrow Books, London (1st ed. 1953).

TULLOCK, Gordon, 1967. *Toward a mathematics of politics.* University of Michigan Press, Ann Arbor.

VAN DYKE, Vernon, 1962. *Political science – a philosophical analysis.* Stanford University Press, Stanford.

VAN DYKE, Vernon, 1966a. *International politics,* 2nd ed. Appleton-Century-Crofts, New York (1st ed. 1957).

VAN DYKE, Vernon, 1966b. The optimum scope of political science. In: James C. Charlesworth (Ed.), *A design for political science – scope, objectives, and methods,* pp. 1–17. American Academy of Political and Social Science, Philadelphia.

VREE, J.K. De, 1968. De wetenschap der politiek – het vraagstuk van een definitie. *Acta polit. 4 (1)*: 55–81.

VREE, J.K. De, 1969. Over theorievorming. *Acta polit. 4 (3)*: 275–297.

VREE, J.K. De, 1970. Opmerkingen over 'theorie' en 'praktijk'. *Soc. Wet. 13 (1)*: 12–36.

WARTOFSKY, Marx W., 1968. *Conceptual foundations of scientific thought – an introduction to the philosophy of science.* MacMillan, New York.

WEBER, Max, 1922. *Gesammelte Aufsätze zur Wissenschaftslehre.* Mohr, Tübingen.

WIGHTMAN, W.P.D., 1951. *The growth of scientific ideas.* Yale University Press, New Haven/London.

YOVITS, Marshall C., George T. JACOBI & Gordon D. GOLDSTEIN (Ed.), 1962. *Self-organizing systems.* Spartan Books, Washington (D.C.).

ZANSTRA, Herman, 1962. *The construction of reality – lectures on the philosophy of science, theory of knowledge and the relation between body, mind and personality.* Pergamon Press, Oxford.

3   ERNST B. HAAS

1. INTRODUCTION

1.1. *Functionalism?*

Haas's thinking is akin to and influenced by Mitrany's functionalism
– so much so, indeed, that it might be described as a 'revised functionalism' (cf. *Haas*, 1964a: 140; see also *Haas*, 1964a, preface). Both
conceive politics and government in terms of functions which are fulfilled in relation to human needs and wishes. Like Mitrany, Haas is
concerned with a process of (peaceful) integration which starts in one
or more specific and relatively 'technical' sectors of social life. In Haas,
too, we meet with the idea of a dynamic and more or less automatic
integrative process gradually encompassing ever more and more important functional sectors, couched in such expressions as 'spill-over'
and 'the expansive logic of sector integration'.

But there are also some important differences. In the first place, as
will become clear hereafter, the argument upon which Haas bases his
conclusions differs considerably from that of Mitrany. It is more rigorous and elaborated, and, in particular, his conception of politics is
much more refined and sophisticated than Mitrany's. And whereas
Mitrany is concerned above all with recommendations for practical
political action, Haas's thinking represents an attempt to explain the
integration phenomenon in a non-normative way, irrespective of his
private opinions concerning its desirability. Accordingly, the label 'functionalism' or 'neo-functionalism' for Haas's theorizing should not be
understood too narrowly. The more so as it appears that it is also substantially similar to the thinking of Karl Deutsch whom we would
hesitate to call a 'functionalist', which throws some doubt on the sense
of using the label at all.

1.2. *The role of systems analysis in Haas's thinking*

For the most part Haas's thinking is of a purely political character. That is, his theorizing does not derive from some extra-political calculus or vocabulary. Interestingly, however, he does develop a systems analytic conception in his *Beyond the nation-state* . . . But in the context of his thinking in its totality, this systems analytic conception is of a decidedly minor importance. For, rather than systems analysis being the matrix from which his political conceptions emerge, it is these conceptions, already developed elsewhere and earlier, that are reinterpreted in systems analytic terms. This reinterpretation does not really add anything substantial to his political ideas; it is, we might say, a non-essential application of the systems analytic vocabulary. Consequently, no prior knowledge of it is needed for an understanding of Haas's thinking; I will discuss it briefly in the context of his general conception of the political process (section 2).

1.3. *A note on the literature*

Haas's theorizing is rendered difficultly accessible by the fact that none of his publications does contain a complete exposé of it. Besides, those publications generally consist of a complex mixture of history and political science, of pieces of quite abstract reasoning and of the narration of historical detail. In these circumstances some brief notes on the literature may be in order.

The main lines of Haas's thinking concerning politics and integration become visible in his *The uniting of Europe* which dates from 1958. His conception of a more or less automatic spill-over process, leading from integration in one particular sector to integration in ever more different sectors, which he developed in *The uniting of Europe*, is modified in the article 'International integration – the European and the universal process' (*Haas*, 1961) by the thesis that functional contexts are autonomous, which greatly limits the scope of the spill-over process. *Beyond the nation-state* . . . (*Haas*, 1964a) represents an extensive elaboration of Haas's earlier insights without fundamentally changing them. As already mentioned, it contains a systems analytic interpretation of his thinking, while it deals in detail with Mitrany's functionalism. Besides, it attempts to apply the conception developed in a different context – that of the International Labor Organization.

By 1967 Haas has come to the conclusion that European integration has not progressed as he thinks his theory predicts it. In his 'The uniting of Europe and the uniting of Latin America' (*Haas*, 1967) he limits the scope of the spill-over process still further by postulating that his conception of 'pragmatic interest politics' does not work in the sphere of, roughly, 'high politics'. His new Preface to the second impression of *The uniting of Europe* . . . (1968) contains a useful summary discussion of the modifications mentioned.

It has already become apparent that Haas's investigations into the process of integration are not concerned solely with just one of its manifestations – e.g. that in contemporary Europe. Apart from the publications already mentioned, it is especially in those written together with Philippe C. Schmitter that he deals more or less extensively with developments in Central and Latin America (*Schmitter & Haas*, 1964: *Haas & Schmitter*, 1965; 1966). While these investigations do not fundamentally affect the structure of the theory, they show at least that its applicability is not a priori limited to the setting for which it was first developed.

With regard to the quantitative operationalization of particular elements of the theory, it is especially his *Consensus formation in the Council of Europe* (*Haas*, 1960b), 'System and process in the International Labour Organization' (*Haas*, 1962b), and 'The operationalization of some variables related to regional integration' (*Barrera & Haas*, 1969) which are relevant.

His last book *Tangle of hopes* (1969), finally, is not expressly concerned with integration theory. The book is primarily an analysis of American foreign policy with regard to international organizations. And although it does contain some interesting evidence concerning a growing and unintended involvement in international organization on the part of the United States, which fits in with the theory, that theory itself is not systematically elaborated any further.

2. POLITICS

2.1. *Outline of this section*

In this section on Haas's general conception of the political process I will proceed in three steps. First I will deal with that conception in general terms (section 2.2). Next it will be related to international affairs (2.3), while, finally, his systems analytical interpretation of all this will be briefly discussed.

2.2. *Politics – demands, support, binding decisions, and two postulates*

Haas defines politics in the context of a political community, that is, a human group which is bound together by institutions capable of issuing commands to the group as a whole, or through which decisions binding upon all the members of the group can be achieved. Thus he writes:

Political community, therefore, is a condition in which specific groups and individuals show more loyalty to their central political institutions than to any other political authority, in a specific period of time and in a definable geographic space (Haas, 1958c: 5).

'Loyalty', in its turn, is described as follows:

A population may be said to be loyal to a set of symbols and institutions when it habitually and predictably over long periods obeys the injuctions of their authority and turns to them for the satisfaction of important expectations (*Haas*, 1958c: 5).

The concept of loyalty, and consequently that of political community, is defined in a rather restricted fashion. It is concerned with 'habitual' and 'predictable' behavior over 'long periods'. If anywhere, one may presume, this will occur mainly in communities which already are firmly established. Nevertheless, the above definitions enable us to reconstruct what Haas understands by 'politics'. The question is 'what makes loyalty a political phenomenon?'. To answer it, it is necessary to see that it is defined in relation to two other elements of a more general character which play an important role in the theory.

In the first place, loyalty consists of the obedience of the members of the group to its central institutions; that is, they obey and conform to the commands and injunctions of these institutions. Generalizing somewhat, this element can be suitably designated by the term 'support' – one, incidentally, that Haas also occasionally uses in the sense intended here without, however, defining it (see for example *Haas*, 1958c: 290; 1964a: 113 ff.; 127; 1964b: 73; *Haas & Merkl*, 1960: 44). Its meaning can be reconstructed, however, both from the above quotation and from the way Haas expressly applies the term in other contexts. Thus, the obedience of the members of a group to the decisions of its central institutions can be conceived as a form of support. But it may also consist in supporting, defending, or agreeing with, the decisions, policies, plans, or proposals, of other bodies, groups, or organizations. And it may concern both support which is rooted in long traditions and which is given habitually and unconditionally, and very ephemeral and conditional forms. Also, the term 'negative support' may be used to refer to such forms of behavior as disagreement with, disobedience to, or resistance against policies or demands.

But the members of a political community do not only *support* the decisions of its central institutions, they also turn to them for the satisfaction of 'important expectations'. This is the second constituent element of the concept of 'loyalty'. Here Haas generally applies the terms 'interests', or 'demands'.

I postulate a more extended meaning for the notion of interest, one that encompasses every kind of group – backed demand that enters the marketplace of political competition. *Any claim made upon the community on behalf of the values dear to some group represents an interest*, even though substantively it may refer to religious education, residential zoning, reforestation, or the prevention of cruelty to animals (*Haas*, 1964a: 34) (my italics).

Thus, while in common discourse the term 'loyalty' denotes such things as faithfulness and devotion, or, in political terms, a certain form of support behavior, it is important to see that in Haas's thinking it acquires a more complex meaning. That is, it covers both support and demands that are directed by the members of a certain political community at its central institutions which, in their turn, make them into decisions that are binding upon the whole community.

Regarding the extent to which those central institutions and their decisions are in fact supported, two somewhat different concepts are introduced by Haas – 'authority' and 'legitimacy'. 'Authority' is defined in an international context, as follows:

The indicator we label 'authority' means merely that member governments and voluntary groups accept the peaceful change procedures by implementing whatever is decided or recommended, *without necessarily agreeing that the decision or the recommendation is just and right*. In fact, they may denounce the organization as meddling in domestic matters and stepping outside its declared objectives. This does not matter for present purposes, as long as the protesting governments implement the decisions or recommendations anyway (*Haas*, 1964a: 132).

When we abstract from the international context within which the term is defined here, authority can be conceived as the measure of support which the central institution enjoys with regard to some particular decision, and regardless of the motives which inspire this support on the part of the members.

In addition to this concept, Haas introduces that of legitimacy. As follows:

The criterion of legitimacy is the regular invocation of UN Charter principles in advocacy and debate by those holding out for more UN action as well as by those who seek to block such action (the balancer and the agressor both invoke the Charter regularly), *plus* the demonstrated willingness to expand the UN's task in order to implement the Charter principles put forward (*Haas*, 1962a: 300).

Apparently, legitimacy must be conceived as the measure of consensus existing among the members of a community with regard to the desirability of certain political institutions or procedures. While authority is bound to specific binding decisions, legitimacy is concerned with support of a more formal character, a kind of second-order support. It concerns the existence and the functioning of the institutions themselves, regardless of the decisions produced by them. The second part of the sentence quoted indicates that this support ought not to be of a purely verbal nature. Rather, the members should be prepared to submit to its consequences: they should accept that the institutions concerned actually fulfil their functions. Probably legitimacy can best be conceived as the willingness of the members to accept the authority of decisions taken by a certain institution, or reached through a certain procedure (see also *Haas*, 1964a: 269).

Yet such support cannot be taken for granted. With regard to the international political milieu and the institutions functioning therein, this almost goes without saying. But it equally applies to the national milieu and to firmly established political communities. For it is an important element of Haas's thinking that he does not conceive of a political community as a monolithic bloc of people all demanding the same things of its central institutions and all having the same ideas about its 'general interests'. Rather, the essence of political life in such a community consists of conflict between the different groups and individuals of which it is made up. All these different actors will, in principle, make different demands. All will seek to have their particular values translated into binding decisions so as to have them imposed upon, and recognized by, the whole community. Accordingly, 'decision-making' and 'conflict-resolution' are treated as equivalent concepts.

Yet we know, following our assumptions about interest politics and group identification with perceived interests, that every major decision is a choice among conflicting demands and values, and therefore involves the relative victory of one group over another. Hence, in the focus of our concern, 'decision-making' and 'conflict-resolution' are one and the same process (*Haas*, 1964a: 104).

The members of a political community may differ considerably with regard to the specific decisions to be taken by the central institutions. But for such a community to exist at all it is necessary that its central institutions command a certain measure of general support which is *not* directly connected with specific decisions – that is, if we ignore, as Haas does, physical coercion as a means for generating such support. In other words, the institutions must have legitimacy (see also *Haas*, 1958c: 6; 1964a: 39).

   To explain such legitimacy, and political behavior in general, Haas uses two postulates. The first of these runs as follows: *Personal political loyalties are the result of satisfaction with the performance of crucial functions by an agency of government* (*Haas*, 1964a: 49; actually, he formulates this proposition in the context of his reconstruction of the functionalist doctrine of, mainly, Mitrany. But it appears to reflect rather accurately Haas's own conception of interest politics, so that it seems to be justified to consider it as Haas's own postulate; see, e.g., *Haas*, 1964a: 30 ff.). Now loyalties consist both of demands and support behavior. Generalizing somewhat, the propositions quoted may be interpreted as saying that the members of a group will address their support and demands to those institutions whose decisions they expect to conform most to their wishes. Conversely, if such institutions are to acquire authority and legitimacy they will have to take such decisions as to elicit sufficient support from among the members, and to assure that these members will continue to address their demands to them.

In the second place, Haas refers to the psychological principle of cognitive dissonance, as he writes, quoting Charles Osgood: *

When people are made to keep on behaving in ways that are inconsistent with their actual attitudes (e.g., as if they really trusted each other), their attitudes tend to shift into line with their behaviors (*Haas*, 1964a: 112).

Thus, even those members who, initially, do not positively support the institutions of the political community will tend to change their attitudes in the course of time when no alternatives are open to them. The mere fact of the functioning of such institutions, accordingly, would tend to lend them legitimacy after a certain period of time.

2.3. *Politics – national and international*

The foregoing discussion of the character of the political process proceeded largely within the context of a political community. Probably the most important form which such a political community assumes in practice, is that of a 'state', which is described in the following terms:

The state, in short, is the formal incorporation of the community into an entity which can formulate policy and make decisions, the government, and carry out its decisions by means of compulsory measures, the law (*Haas & Whiting*, 1956: 35-36).

A state is thus a highly developed political community whose central institutions dispose of special means of eliciting support for their decisions: they may even enforce it. And, more generally, a political community in its turn must be conceived as a particular kind of political process: namely, one that is enacted predictably and over long periods of time through specific institutions.

It would be wrong, however, to identify politics with the form it assumes in such a political community or a state. For the important thing is not that certain institutions dispose of particular means to generate support, or that they may function for a long time, but, much

* Charles E. Osgood: Suggestions for winning the real war with communism, in *Journal of Conflict Resolution 3* (1959): 321.

more generally, that they fulfil a particular function. This function is
to make demands and support into decisions binding upon the members of a certain group, or the participants in a certain interaction. It
can be fulfilled by institutions other than 'governments' in the narrow
sense of the word – by international organizations, for example. The
fact that generally the capacity for making binding decisions of international organizations is, as yet, much more limited than that of most
national governments, is of secondary importance. When institutions
exist which fulfil the function just mentioned, albeit in a very restricted
fashion, there is the beginning of a political community, which differs
only gradually from the more advanced forms such as states.

Haas's conception of the political process covers both national and
international politics. In both cases politics consist of the struggle
between groups and individuals seeking to have their values recognized
by and imposed upon their partners. In both cases demands and support are to be made into binding decisions. While in the national milieu
there have emerged institutions and procedures through which the
political process is regulated so that it can be enacted in a comparatively orderly and reliable fashion, this has not yet occurred to the same
extent in the international milieu. Consequently, here the process often
degenerates into open warfare. But warfare and the use of open violence and naked force to solve political problems are not exclusively
restricted to international life. Regarding this, too, the differences are
of a gradual rather than of a fundamental nature.

The groups participating in international life are primarily the several
national political communities. These communities act through their
governments – generally to the exclusion of other groups and organizations. Accordingly, from an international point of view these communities might easily be conceived as monolithic and closed bodies, with
governments as the sole international actors. Haas, however, rejects this
conception as too static. With regard to international politics, too, it is
necessary to be aware of the fact that such national communities consist
of a greater or lesser number of different groups. This conduces to a
dynamic rather than a static conception of international politics.

This approach to international relations regards individuals and groups
as basic constituent elements. It denies that the actors upon the world stage
are nations or states, conceived as monolithic units with fixed policies

dictated by immutable injunctions of geography, principle, and power. It focuses on the *dynamic* aspects of international relations, the ever-shifting aims and demands which flourish *within* nations and which cause recurrent conflict and compromise between them (*Haas & Whiting*, 1956: 21).

In the first place, the foreign policy of a community's central institutions itself is the outcome of the political processes going on within it, and must be understood in terms of the different demands and support of the various groups and individuals involved. But in the second place such groups and individuals may acquire, in some circumstances, a direct international significance. This is of fundamental importance in Haas's thinking. It is both an important consequence of, and a causal element in, a process of international integration.

2.4. *A systems-analytic reinterpretation*

As I have already mentioned, Haas, in his *Beyond the nation-state*, develops a systems analytic interpretation of his conception of the political process. After the general discussion of systems analysis in chapter two (section 3.5), we can be brief about Haas's application of it.

To begin with, Haas is clearly aware that the concept of system is a purely analytical device. It is an abstract relational structure which is constructed by outside observers in order to understand some particular problem. It may, but need not, be identified with some directly observable mechanism or organism, or with some political entity having a definite geographical or institutional referent (cf. *Haas*, 1964a: 53 ff.). It may be said that, whatever the actual significance of systems analysis for the theory may be, Haas's approach to some extent necessitates the introduction of such an abstract term like 'system'. For it has appeared that in his conception states and political communities merely represent particular subsets in a much larger set of phenomena. And whereas states and communities have a relatively definite status in terms of geographical location and institutional structure, and are comparatively easy to observe, Haas is especially concerned with political processes in contexts which are of a much more fluid and less definite character. With respect to such political configurations, then, the generic term 'system' seems to be more appropriate.

Accordingly, a political system is defined in a very general way:

The particular relationships which define a given system, then, are the patterns of inputs and outputs that prevail during a given epoch *(Haas, 1964a: 77).*

Inputs and outputs, in their turn, are defined as follows:

Governmental policies emanating from the environment are the inputs into the system; collective decisions are the outputs *(Haas, 1964a: 77).*

Now, Haas is here concerned with defining an *international* political system. It has been seen, however, that this restriction is quite inessential, and may be disregarded. Besides, as will appear subsequently, it is not only governmental policies that constitute the inputs into the (international) system. And rather than 'governments', Haas's more general term 'units' should be preferred.

The *unit* is whoever puts forth demands effectively, i.e. is in a position to be heard in the system's structures. This, for the most part, is a position held by governments, though for some items subject to functional analysis, national and international voluntary groups must be included *(Haas, 1964a: 84).*

It has already been noted that the international role of such non-governmental groups is very important in Haas's conception of the integration process. Further, in his definition of input, Haas only refers to demands and does not explicitly mention support. Support, however, has been seen to constitute an equally important aspect of the political behavior of units. Consequently, a political system should be conceived as a set of relationships through which demands and support (inputs) are made into collectively binding decisions (output).

A system has a structure which is defined as '. . . its body of law, its organizations, national, regional, and universal' *(Haas, 1964a: 77).* This structure regulates the political process within the system. It also has an environment.

Environments, in turn, are made up of the totality of policies, aims, expectations, fears, hopes, and hatreds funneled into the institutional structure and its political processes, the 'system' proper *(Haas, 1962a: 278; in the same sense 1964a: 77).*

It is, in short, everything which determines the character of the input (demands and support) into the system, and which, in its turn, is influenced by the binding decisions produced by the system.

Quite interestingly Haas's general conception of the political process shows a striking affinity to that of Easton, particularly as described in the latter's *A systems analysis of political life* (1965). Both speak in terms of demands and support. And while in Haas these categories are related to the 'binding decisions' of central institutions, Easton relates them to the 'authoritative allocation of values', a difference which does not seem to be great. This fundamental similarity is even more conspicuous as both authors develop a systems analytic vocabulary. Their conception of a (political) system appears to be basically the same although in Easton's thinking it is elaborated in more detail at first sight. Haas's conception is even more general than that of Easton. For whereas Easton defines a political system in relation to a 'society' (*Easton*, 1965: 21), which seems to indicate a definite and fixed human group, Haas does not. The difference may be more apparent than real, however. For Easton, too, extends the applicability of his systems analytic conception to the international political milieu (*Easton*, 1965: 484 ff.).

3. POLITICAL INTEGRATION – DEFINITION

The conception of the political process which has been analysed in the preceding section is of a very general and dynamical character. That is, it is not bound to any particular institutional or legal setting such as a 'state'. Rather, it is concerned with ongoing political processes in which particular institutional forms merely represent particular phases. Thus a state can be conceived as the outcome of certain political processes working during relatively extended periods of time. But the establishment of such a state does not thereby mean that the underlying processes have spent themselves, or that they would not occur in a larger area. Also we should not generally expect the establishment of such institutional structures to occur from one day to the next. This did not happen with regard to the national states of the present day, and it is not very likely that it will occur with regard to larger structures.

Accordingly, Haas conceives of political integration as a process (cf. *Haas*, 1964a: 29). In conformity with his conception of the political process in general, he defines it as

... the process whereby political actors in several distinct national settings are persuaded to shift their loyalties, expectations and political activities toward a new centre, whose institutions possess or demand jurisdiction over the pre-existing national states. The end result of a process of political integration is a new political community, superimposed over the pre-existing ones (*Haas*, 1958c: 16).

In this definition the expression 'possess *or demand* jurisdiction' may, perhaps, cause some surprise. It must be understood in the context of Haas's conception of the active role which the new institutions can play in the process of integration. In large part this role indeed consists in *demanding* jurisdiction or more powers. Also it must be kept in mind that Haas's 'loyalties' consist both of demands and support. Accordingly, the addition of the term 'expectations and political activities' is actually superfluous. It is hard to see what they would add to the concept of loyalty. At this level of analysis I have been unable to find in Haas's writings any 'expectation' or 'activity' which could not be transformed into the two basic categories 'demands' and 'support'.

Generalizing somewhat by abstracting from the specifically international context, the above definition may be interpreted as saying that political integration is the process through which, for a certain number of political units, institutions are developed which are capable of attracting the demands and support of those units, and of making these into decisions which are binding upon them. Political integration, in other words, consists of the institutionalization of a particular political process.

International political integration is concerned with a radical transformation of some particular international system. This transformation is the more difficult as the units involved in it are primarily autonomous states, i.e., groups which have already developed political institutions of their own. But integration implies a breakdown of, or interference with, the autonomy of these institutions in favor of new ones superimposed on the pre-existing institutions. On the other hand, the states concerned can act internationally only through their governments, that is, the very institutions that are to be the first victims of integration. Accordingly, such integration is not something to be taken for granted.

Nevertheless, governments do not control everything. Developments in the environment of some international political system (for instance, with respect to defence, technology, trade, communication, and economic development) might conceivably lead to problems which the states are unable to solve in isolation. More precisely, such developments might give rise to demands which the existing national institutions are unable to meet. This, in turn, would then lead to demands aiming at a certain measure of international integration. Assuming that some such integration, albeit of a very limited kind, would indeed be attained, this in itself might then set in motion processes which, to an increasing extent, are beyond the control of the existing national governments. That is, the process of integration may acquire its own dynamics and become independent of the initial purposes of the governments concerned (cf. *Haas*, 1964a: 35). It is this particular aspect of the problem of integration which has been elaborated most by Haas.

4. POLITICAL INTEGRATION – EXPLANATION

4.1. *Outline of this section*

As indicated in chapter two (section 4.2), the present section will deal consecutively with the nature of the integration process as a whole (section 4.2), the role and character of the international institutions concerned (4.3), and that of the units among which integration takes place (4.4).

4.2. *The mechanism of integration*

We have already seen that in Haas's opinion decision-making and conflict-resolution are one and the same thing. He identifies three different patterns.

The first of these is called 'accommodation on the basis of the minimum common denominator'. As its name indicates it consists of an exchange of concessions which does not go beyond what the least cooperative bargaining partner wishes to concede (*Haas*, 1964a: 111). It is typical of traditional diplomatic bargaining among autonomous and equally sovereign units.

The second pattern is 'accommodation by splitting the difference'. As Haas describes it, 'Conflict is resolved, not on the basis of the will of the least cooperative, but somewhere between the final bargaining positions' (*Haas*, 1964a: 111). Moreover, it differs from the first pattern in that here 'the mediatory services of a secretary-general, or an ad hoc international expert study group, may be admitted by the parties' (*Haas*, 1964a: 111).

Finally, conflicts may be resolved on the basis of 'deliberately or inadvertently upgrading the common interests of the parties'. This mode of conflict-resolution requires an 'institutionalized mediator, whether a single person or a board of experts, with an autonomous range of powers' (*Haas*, 1964a: 111; for these patterns, see also *Haas*, 1961: 95-96). Here the conflict is resolved by 'redefining' it 'so as to work out a solution at a higher level' (*Haas*, 1964a: 111).

For the theory these three patterns are interesting mainly in so far as they indicate an increasing measure of institutionalization of the setting in which politics is enacted. While in the first pattern a common decision is supported only if and in so far as it embodies the substance of the demands made by the bargaining units, in the second and the third patterns a somewhat different element is introduced. This involves support given to certain procedures and institutions concerning the decision-making process itself. This procedural support, which is of the essence of the concept 'legitimacy', can apparently compensate for a certain measure of dissensus with regard to the substance of the decision to be taken.

Accordingly, the growth of this legitimacy of the emerging international institutions and procedures would enable them to make ever more decisions with regard to a widening range of different and conflicting demands. In other words, the higher the legitimacy of the international institutions, the greater their capacity for decision-making and the more controversial the demands that can be accommodated through them. Conversely, the progress of integration requires a growth of legitimacy on the part of the new international institutions (cf. *Haas*, 1962a: 306).

At the outset of a process of integration, when no international institutions have yet emerged or fixed procedures have been decided upon, decision-making will have to proceed according to the first pattern mentioned. But if integration is to result, the minimum common denominator will have to include the establishment of new political institutions. And this procedural consensus also underlies the other two patterns of decision-making mentioned. In other words, for integration to proceed, integration itself must be, and continue to be, desirable for the units concerned (*Haas*, 1964b: 73).

It has been already mentioned (section 3) that initially, i.e., at the start of a process of international integration, the states concerned can act only through their governments. Consequently, it is these governments for whom the establishment of new institutions must be, and remain, desirable. But it has also appeared that the policies of these governments, in their turn, are the outcomes of political processes that are enacted within the respective states. And in order to explain integration we may not limit ourselves to the level of governmental policies by simply taking them as given. Instead, we should delve deeper, and relate integration to the political processes going on within the states concerned. Thus integration is not merely an affair between a limited number of governments but through these it involves a greater or lesser number of different units, such as political parties and interest groups, in different settings.

This has important implications with regard to the conception of the consensus, the common demands or interests, that may lead to integration. Whereas the establishment of new international institutions can only occur on the basis of a common demand made by the governments concerned, this does not mean that they seek to realize identical values through it. In view of the variety of units involved and the different settings in which they operate, such identity is extremely unlikely. Accordingly, the common demand for the establishment of new international institutions will normally be based upon a pattern of more or less different demands which at some moment converges in a demand for integration and which will be supported in so far as such integration will meet the particular interests of the units concerned. Thus Haas writes, with regard to the European Coal and Steel Community:

Our basic finding was that the acceptance of ECSC is best explained by the convergence of demands within and among the nations concerned, not by a pattern of identical demands and hopes (*Haas*, 1958c: 286; see also *Haas*, 1964a: 276).

This conception does not a priori rule out the possibility of a complete consensus, of course. In principle it might well be that in certain circumstances integration would result from the common pursuit of an ideal shared by all. It would merely be a degenerate instance of the more general conception described above. And the more political units are involved, the less likely it will occur. But the fact that there is a variety of different interests rather than complete consensus does not necessarily mean that integration is thereby rendered more difficult. On the contrary, it may well be a positive advantage, as is indicated by Haas:

In the absence of the initial agreement of all parties to integration on the precise motives for working toward political community, the fact that a variety of motives are dominant in each national unit actually facilitates the emergence of supranational ideologies at a later stage (. . .). If a uniform consensus within each national unit had existed at the outset of the integration step, ideological realignments would be made more difficult because of the pre-existing rigidities in outlook and expectations, some of which are bound to be disappointed as integration goes forward (*Haas*, 1958c: 158; see also *Haas*, 1958c: 290, 312).

The fundamental mechanism via which decisions are taken in such a setting is as follows. To begin with, a decision which is binding is so to the extent that it is supported (see section 2.2). That is, such a decision can be taken only if sufficient support for it is available, if enough units are disposed to abide by it. According to Haas's first postulate the units will give such support to the extent that the decisions to be taken are in conformity with their demands. Consequently, to have a binding decision taken it will have to be formulated so as to meet the demands of a sufficiently strong group or coalition of units. The composition of such a coalition need not be the same for all decisions. In fact, it may rest upon a convergence of demands which is limited to only one occasion. The fact that in the case of the establishment of new international institutions this coalition will have to include the governments concerned does not affect the matter in a fundamental way.

The support for given steps rests on the convergence of expectations of the participants; competing expectations and goals can be compromised on the basis of swapping concessions from a variety of sectors, all under the generalized purview of supranational institutions and processes (*Haas*, 1964b: 73).

When new international institutions with a certain decision-making capacity (albeit, perhaps, a very limited one) have been established, this does not represent an end-point to a process of integration. On the contrary. For Haas makes it clear that, on the one hand, the mere existence and functioning of an international organization will have certain independent effects, while, on the other hand, the organization may use the mechanism described above to its own profit – to increase its own competencies. Thus a process of integration may acquire its own dynamics.

To some extent the effect of the functioning of new international institutions may be conceived as piercing through the hard shell formed by the international boundaries of the state. That is, other units than the state governments are drawn into international life:

The presence of such an authority, on the other hand, may set in motion the dynamics of pluralism in the member states. At first, some parties and interest groups of each member nation may support the new authority as against rival parties and interests in their own bailiwicks, thereby weakening the national unity and identity of interests. Then, the like-minded supporters of the union band together supranationally and thus induce their respective domestic opponents sooner or later to do likewise. Finally, these supranational alliances will face each other in the politics of the new central authority over their substantive differences of social, political, or economic interest rather than over the issue of union as such (*Haas*, 1960: 44).

It has been assumed that units will address their support and demands to those institutions whose decisions they expect to conform most to their wishes. Accordingly, when new decision-making institutions are established, this will induce those units from within the national political communities whose interests are affected by the decisions of the new institutions, to redirect their support and demands from the national governments to the new institutions. To a certain degree this will even occur when, as in the very first beginning of an integration process, the new institutions are of a predominantly intergovernmental kind, i.e., when they are not directly accessible to units other than governments. In this case those other units will still have to act through the national governments. But these actions will now be aimed at decision-making at the international level, and they will be inspired by interests as they are affected by decisions taken by the new institutions. Probably, realignments of interests and the formation of supranational groups will occur more slowly and to a lesser extent than in the case of the international institutions being directly accessible to and acting directly upon the non-governmental units.

At the same time the functioning of international institutions will induce cerain changes in the way bargaining over binding decisions takes place. Partly, these consist in a growing familiarity of the nego- tiators with each other. Besides, the creation of such institutions implies a measure of agreement as to their functions, and this, in turn, suggests that there existst room for decision-making by experts and on the basis of technical considerations (cf. *Haas*, 1958c: 291). In short, the estab- lishment of decision-making institutions creates conditions which are conducive to the identification of common interests and to compromise on the basis of considerations accepted as valid by all concerned.

Moreover, the subjects about which decision-making and bargaining take place are seldom or never completely isolated things. Generally they are closely linked with things that are, for the moment, outside the scope of decision-making. Social policies and taxation are closely connected with the costs of production of goods and services; coal, oil, natural gas, and nuclear energy all are important elements in the supply of energy, etc. Now decisions taken with regard to any one particular element in such a group will inevitably have certain conse- quences for the other elements to which it is related. But this implies that (international) decision-making in some particular field will also affect the interests of units operating in closely related fields. Accordingly, one may expect that such units will put forth demands aimed at adaptations to the changed situation, to redress what will be perceived as disequilibria and discrepancies. On the other hand such demands will also be made by units which were involved from the start, namely, when it is realized that the 'proper' decisions can only be taken by drawing in related subjects. In particular, this may be a method through which to resolve deadlock with respect to a particular subject. By drawing in other subjects more room is created for the exchange of concessions. The controversy may, in Haas's terminology, thus be 'redefined at a hagher level'; decision-making proceeds on the basis of 'upgrading the common interests'. It is of the essence of what Haas calls 'politicization' (cf. *Haas & Schmitter*, 1966: 262). In so far as units expect that such decisions in related fields can best be taken on the international level (i.e., in so far as they expect their demands to be met most adequately through the new institutions), they will demand an increase in the decision-making capacity of those international institutions. This is the 'expansive logic of sector integration' which Haas has made clearly visible with regard to European integration (cf. *Haas*, 1958c: ch. 8).

To sum up, the establishment of international institutions with a limited decision-making capacity, may initiate a self-sustained process of integration. Basically it rests upon the new institution's making decisions and proposals in such a fashion that, among a sufficient number of units, expectations arise that their demands will be met more adequately by working through the international institutions than through the national governments. If so, there will occur a redirection of support and demands on the part of the units, demands and support for the task expansion of the new institutions will be forthcoming, new units will be formed at the international level, while bargaining procedures will change. It is this complex of processes which Haas calls 'spill-over' (cf. *Haas*, 1958c: 313-317).

In this fashion an international institution will gradually acquire an increasing measure of legitimacy in a growing number of fields. At the same time and by the same token the pre-existing national governments will lose such legitimacy with regard to the subjects transferred to the international institution. On the other hand, continuing involvement in international institutions on the part of units will tend to make such units more dependent upon these institutions for the realization of their own interests. Generally, however, the realization of such interests requires compromise with other, often conflicting, interests, which may only be possible, if at all, through an extension of the international institution's task. All this may lead to a gradually growing and quite unintended enmeshment of the units in the international institution. In his *Tangle of hopes*, Haas finds many traces of this process with regard to the US's policies in the international organizations in which she participates (see, e.g., *Haas*, 1969: 22-23, 75, 78, 117, 130, 140, 157, 175, 217). This process does not rest only upon the rather instrumental considerations described thus far and explained on the basis of Haas's first postulate. For, according to his second postulate a growth in legitimacy may also be expected to result from the mere fact that the international institutions exist and function during a certain period. And presumably the longer this period, the higher the degree of legitimacy will be.

Thus far the new institutions themselves, that is, the people who man them in a more or less permanent fashion, their secretariats and executives, have been assumed to play a relatively passive role. In some cases, however, notably in that of the European Commission, the international institution itself can play the role of an independent political unit, rather than that of the passive executor of decisions taken by others. The institution may put forth demands itself; it may formulate proposals in such a fashion that it generates support on its own account. The mechanism with it utilizes thereto is the same as that via which decision-making in general proceeds – to seek a connection with the demands of a sufficiently strong, even though temporary and loose, coalition of units.

Political persuasion, moreover, rests less on golden words than on the sapient construction of coalitions with identical or converging interests. In short, purposes can be turned into functions, with the eventual cooperation of the parties concerned, if the tasks involved are part of the interests of a viable coalition of forces (*Haas*, 1964a: 102).

The organization need not even necessarily wait passively until such demands will be formulated explicitly by the units. It may also seek to link its proposals with values underlying such explicit demands so as to activate the making of such demands. In this way the organization increases its possibilities of manoeuvre, and it may consciously strengthen the forces leading to integration. These possibilities will be the greater in proportion as the organization is to a lesser extent of an intergovernmental character, and is more directly related to the various units within the states. For this increases the number and the variety of units and interests from among which coalitions may be built. But even when the organization is of the intergovernmental type, such manoeuvring and manipulation are not entirely excluded. Here, however, the organization can only act in a roundabout way – via the governments concerned. And its possibilities for independently mobilizing support and activating interests are greatly reduced.

In its actions the international organization may profit from the effects which autonomously follow from its existence. Through its policies it may to a certain extent consciously steer and channel the spill-over processes that will occur independently. Reorientation of demands and support in favor of the new institution on the part of the units concerned means an increase in the support of which it may dispose. But it also means an increase in the number and the variety of the units and interests from among which it may form coalitions. The changing bargaining procedures at the highest level make it easier to identify common interests and to reach compromises. But it also makes it easier to delegate decision-making to the organization itself. When forces working in the direction of task expansion occur, it means that more support becomes available. But when such a task expansion has taken place, the decision-making capacity of the institution is greatly increased since it enlarges the field of concessions that may be used in arriving at any one particular decision. By the same token the institution's room for manoeuvre, for stimulating support and for activating demands is greatly expanded. And, one may argue, the greater the scope of decision-making by the international institution, the greater the probability that it has effects outside of its proper field and, consequently, the more important spill-over processes will tend to be. Finally, the longer the institution exists, the more it will tend to acquire legitimacy, which in itself will induce demands to be addressed to it rather than to the national governments. This argument would thus seem to predict a more or less continuous process leading to the ultimate formation of a full political community. In Haas's words:

One important conclusion must certainly be that additional measures tending toward political community could be introduced as a result of the same fragmentation: a new treaty need merely be so constructed as to contain a large variety of otherwise unrelated provisions and thus appeal to a large enough constituency to establish another converging pattern of support (*Haas*, 1958c: 290).

4.3. *The international institution and its tasks*

Turning now to Haas's conception of the relation between integration and the character of the newly established international organization, it will already have become clear that if this organization is to stimulate an integration process, it should be one of a rather special kinds.

Governments will not readily transfer their competencies to a new institution when they cannot rather precisely estimate the costs and benefits involved. This will only be possible with regard to comparatively small matters or tasks of a limited scope. Consequently, the task of the new organization will be rather narrowly circumscribed initially. At the same time governments will allow such an organization to function more or less autonomously only in so far as they can agree among themselves on the kind of considerations on the basis of which it is to solve the problems associated with its task. That is, initially the organization's task will most probably be of a relatively 'technical' nature.

Nevertheless, if integration is to result the organization should not conceive its task in purely technical terms. For it has appeared from the foregoing discussion that this task is of an essentially political nature. It consists in making compromises and resolving conflicts between contending interests. And this cannot generally be done solely on the basis of exclusively technical considerations. Instead, it implies reckoning in terms of support, aiming at solutions which rest upon a sufficiently strong supporting coalition rather than upon the technical merits of the case. Indeed, an exclusive preoccupation with the technical aspects of its task will limit the organization to a marginal role in the process of integration (*Haas*, 1964a: 93 ff.). Accordingly, the organization should not primarily be an expert body, but rather a 'political' one (*Haas*, 1964a: 115).

In fact, the organization should function as a distinct political unit with its own interests, making its own demands, and actively seeking support for them. Of course, its interests will not automatically harmonize with those of the other units concerned. Generally there will be a certain tension between them (*Haas*, 1964a: 101), as between the organization's demand for task expansion and that of the governments to retain their own competencies. In general, the milieu in which the organization is to function is characterized by conflict. But far from shunning such conflict, the organization, i.e., its leadership, should seek to use it for its own purposes. By making proposals for its solution in particular cases so that it mobilizes converging patterns of support, it may both help to solve the problems themselves and set in motion forces leading to an expansion of its own tasks. This requires a dynamical and adaptative behavior on the part of the organization's leadership.

The leadership must learn *to use a crisis in the tension between organization and environment as an opportunity for self-assessment and self-redefini-*

tion, to profit from critical experience, to undergo growth in character and understanding. To be sure, a 'critical' decision cannot always be differentiated from a 'routine' one until the outcome is known. (. . .) The decision will nevertheless be 'critical' if it engenders a new affirmation of organizational objectives under a challenge from hostile or conflicting environmental pressures, if it thereby strengthens the sense of purpose of the organization's staff at the expense of environmental ties. But it is crucial to remember that unless the leadership is willing to examine useless old objectives and strike out in new directions with a revalued body of aims, it will merely reaffirm the stale old pattern, it will remain mired in routine (*Haas*, 1964a: 101).

Haas defines 'ideology' as 'the doctrines peculiar to a group' (*Haas*, 1958c: 6). For a certain group to act as a unit in the political process some such ideology will be necessary. That is, to be able to formulate demands there must exist among the members of the group a certain measure of consensus as to what its values are and how these are to be realized. Consequently, if the international organization is to act as a political unit, it also must have a certain ideology. And this ideology must enable it to formulate policy in particular cases and to mobilize sufficient support from among the other units participating in the integration process.

First, the ideology must be based on a minimum common denominator of shared goals among the member units; it must then be so construed as to point to the selection of a program that is inherently expansive, but acceptable to some viable coalition among the members.

Second, the ideology must be specific enough to act as a reliable guide for the organization's staff in making discrete programmatic proposals to the top policy-making organs, and remain true to the basic objectives.

Third, it must point to needs, expectations, and demands in the environment that can be transformed systematically as the program is implemented to meet explicit subgoals (*Haas*, 1964a: 119).

At the same time the organization must take care not to become too deeply involved in the conflicts and controversies of the day. If it is to play a role in the transformation of the political system in which it operates it must constantly be aware of its basic objectives and be oriented towards the future. Its daily policies must be attuned to its final objectives. This requires planning or programming. For,

What budgeting is to public administration, programming is to the international organization dedicated to systemic transformation: without a growth-oriented program there will be no impact on the sluggish and unfriendly environment (*Haas*, 1964a: 113).

It is aimed at the mobilization of support, the activation of interests which may serve the expansion of the organization's tasks. It is concerned with channelling future developments so as to serve the organization's final objectives.

Programming must proceed within the confines of the organizational ideology. Initial objectives must be divided into specific subgoals that appeal to specific groups of clients and supporters in order to assume the survival of the organization in the short run. Subgoals, however, should be defined so as to make operational and accepted the overall objectives. Subgoal dominance must be avoided by
   1. making programmatic innovation the responsibility of the top bureaucratic leadership in alliance with appropriate coalitions of clients;
   2. keeping in check the autonomy of specialists in the bureaucracy, and preventing the preparation of programs on the basis of simple 'problem-solving' by experts (*Haas*, 1964a: 128).

Accordingly, programming should feature consultation with the units concerned, rest upon compromises, and avoid rigidity and extravagant claims for uniqueness in order not to make later changes and adaptations too difficult (*Haas*, 1964a: 128). In order to avoid subgoal dominance and decision-making by experts, the organization should have an hierarchical structure with a 'political' top (*Haas*, 1964a: 114).
   Thus, an international organization which is to guide and stimulate a process of integration is one based upon an ideology sufficiently connected with the interests of the participating units, having an hierarchical structure and a dynamic leadership which is aware of the specifically political character of its task which it so programs as to strengthen its position in the course of time.
   The international organization to which Haas pays most attention is typically that of the more or less autonomous international Secretariat. It is the (international) bureaucratic or executive element in some process of integration. Usually, however, other elements are also involved in the process. The relations among the units in some integrating systems will also be governed by certain legal rules and practices, by particular bargaining procedures, while often a number of organs such

as a court, a parliament, and councils or committees of ministers or ambassadors, exist alongside the executive bureaucracy. And although among these the executive organization is of special importance, this does not mean that the other elements mentioned do not have an influence on the process of integration.

Thus, the creation of international judicial organs opens up new channels via which the units can solve some of their controversies and realize some of their demands. This, too, can cause a reorientation of loyalties (i.e., demands and support) on the part of the units (cf. *Haas*, 1958c: 474-475). The fact that in this case conflicts are resolved in a juridical way is hardly relevant in the context of the present theory; the politically relevant point is that here, too, certain interests conflict and that this conflict is resolved in a binding decision, albeit one made by a court and not a government.

An organ like a council of ministers is typically intergovernmental. But this does not warrant the conclusion that no positive integrative effects could flow from it. Thus, with regard to ECSC Haas concludes:

Hence, it cannot be accurately argued on the basis of ECSC experience that in a supranational system, intergovernmental techniques will invariably cut down the federal authority and reclaim all basic powers. Not only have the ministers encouraged the federal agency in several situations, but even the intergovernmental techniques of decision-making used and re-asserted carry the imprint of new procedures and attitudes which have 'spilled over' from the federal framework (*Haas*, 1958c: 512).

Deliberation and decision-making in the context of international parliamentary or quasi-parliamentary organs, too, may have positive consequences for integration. In this context Haas applies the term 'parliamentary diplomacy' about which he says:

Parliamentary diplomacy, as Dean Rusk defined it, implies the existence of a continuing organization with a broad frame of reference, public debate, and the statement of conclusions in a formal resolution arrived at by some kind of majority vote. (. . .) Since the institutional context in which parliamentary diplomacy can be practiced maximizes the representation of a variety of interests emanating from the same nation, it opens up areas of manoeuver which are foreclosed in negotiations exclusively conducted by carefully instructed single agents of foreign ministries. To that extent it facilitates a greater amount of integration even though it does not necessarily produce outcomes which upgrade common interests (*Haas*, 1961: 97).

But the political behavior of the units concerned is ruled by their expectations concerning what is most conducive to the realization of their values. And if a significant reorientation of their loyalties is to occur (an essential element in the process of integration) then there has to be created a more or less independent organ where substantial decision-making takes place and which can serve as a focus for the political attention of the non-governmental units. Viewed in that light it is not surprising that such reorientation does hardly occur with respect to mere parliamentary or ministerial international deliberating bodies, where *no* such substantial decision-making occurs.

Party lines may form internationally when programs can be criticized, when administrators can be questioned, when problems of political and economic wisdom can be shown up in a specific policy context. They cannot form easily when there are no administrators, ministers and civil servants committed to the execution of policies considered of vital and continuing importance by the parliamentarians (*Haas*, 1960b: 61).

And with regard to purely intergovernmental decision-making:

... integration is hampered if the ministerial decision-making cannot be fitted into an institutionalized mold of firm programmatic commitments enunciated and publicized by a supranational body of prominent experts (*Haas*, 1960a: 58).

Implicitly these considerations refer also to the character of the functions performed by international organs, or to the kinds of decisions that are made, and to their influence upon the integration process. It has already been mentioned that initially the tasks of international organizations tend to be narrowly circumscribed, since governments will not generally be willing to transfer competencies to such organizations when they are unable to make a rather precise estimate as to the costs and benefits involved. In this connection Haas uses the term 'specificity', as follows:

Organizational programs tied to the totality of all aspects of all national foreign policies never seem to enjoy implementation, whereas well-defined narrow programs conforming to parts of policies or certain states fare much better. In short, we can say that *functionally specific international programs, if organizationally separated from diffuse orientations, maximize both welfare and integration* (*Haas*, 1964a: 47).

Or

The more specific the task, the more likely important progress toward political community (*Haas*, 1961: 101).

For, not only that governments will not be inclined to transfer important competencies with regard to non-specific matters, but without such specificity a reorientation of the loyalties of the other units involved will be difficult to achieve. Thus, with regard to the Council of Europe Haas observes:

One can develop a specific ideology internationally when the issue is precise and when a pre-existing body of doctrine is considered applicable; but it is far more difficult to accomplish this feat when the sole issue is to be or not to be a 'good European'. In one setting party thinking thrives while in the other it is stultified (*Haas*, 1960b: 60).

Not surprisingly, this is especially relevant for the behavior of the leadership of an international organization:

It is the task of the organization – the leadership – to define aims *specifically* enough to act as a guide to policy, but *generally* enough to achieve rapport with an articulated body of values (*Haas*, 1964a: 101).

Thus, specificity alone is not enough. The organization's tasks should not be trivial, but must be concerned with interests that are important enough to induce the units to act upon them, i.e., to shift their loyalties to the new center (see *Haas*, 1964a: 83; 1960b: 63).

Although it has appeared that the organization must not shun conflict and controversial issues, on the other hand it should not announce its objectives too firmly and explicitly. This might mobilize negative support while it may also make later changes and adaptions more difficult (*Haas*, 1964a: 94).

It has also appeared that the process of integration rests to a large extent upon the fact that the functions which are performed by an international organization are generally not completely isolated and self-contained. Instead they will be connected with other things or fields in such a way that decisions taken with regard to one of them will have certain consequences in one or more of the others. Consequently, integration with respect to one such functional sector, or group of values, may set in motion integrative processes in related sectors – the 'expansive logic of sector integration'. Now presumably this will not occur to the same extent with regard to all possible functions. One may imagine that there are functions where such effects are almost entirely lacking (such as, perhaps, in the case of the international regulation of postal affairs), and others where such effects are very strong (e.g. in the case of a full economic union). Consequently, if integration is indeed to proceed continuously, the initial organizational functions should have what might be called a high 'spill-over potential':

The task, in short, must be both specific and economically important in the sense of containing the potential for spilling over from one vital area of welfare policy into others (*Haas*, 1961: 102).

And the program on the basis of which the organization frames its policy, should be 'inherently expansive' (*Haas*, 1964a: 119).

Now if it would indeed be true that all such functions, functional contexts, or sectors are linked with each other in the fashion indicated, a continuously expanding integration process ending in the formation of full political community becomes possible. However, on the basis of the actual course of European integration, Haas comes to a different conclusion which is at the same time a modification of his theory:

This survey of the functional lessons of European integration leads to the inevitable conclusion that functional contexts are autonomous. Integration forces which flow from one kind of activity do not necessarily infect other activities, even if carried out by the same organization (*Haas*, 1961: 102).

But it is necessary to distinguish here. For, as has appeared from the discussion in the last subsection (4.2), the 'expansive logic of sector integration' did not rest only on the assumption that functions are linked, but also on the kind of expectations of the units regarding the most effective way to have their demands met. In particular, units operating in fields beyond the purview of the international organization but whose interests are affected by the organization's decisions because of links between the sectors, will only demand organizational task expansion if they expect the chances of their demands to be met to increase as a result. But this is far from necessarily the case. For it might also be that their expectations were such as to demand an abrogation of integration in the original field (cf. *Haas*, 1964a: 51). Accordingly, Haas's modification of his earlier insights to the effect that functional contexts should now be assumed to be autonomous, seems to be made somewhat too rashly and cannot be accepted. The more so since the meaning of such terms as 'functional context', 'autonomy', and 'inherently expansive' is not spelled out very precisely by Haas. In fact, functional contexts, their interrelationships and the mechanism through which spill-over occurs are not yet analysed in a sufficiently precise and detailed fashion so as to render them capable of confronting empirical reality and to necessitate modification.

4.4. *The national communities and other units*

To a large extent the process of integration depends on the international organization's capacity to obtain support for its decisions and proposals by mobilizing coalitions of units. Other things remaining equal, this capacity is obviously strengthened by an increase in the number and variety of the units with which the organization can deal. For the greater the number of units, the greater the number of combinations that can be made. The larger the variety of units in terms of the interests they embody, the larger the variety of proposals which can be made by the organization and the more compromises can be reached by exchanging concessions from among different fields. Furthermore, the larger the variety and number of units concerned, the greater the probability that links exist with units not immediately involved in the integrative enterprise, thus increasing the probability that further integrative developments will occur. Consequently, international integration will proceed the more readily according as the national communities involved consist of a greater number and variety of units, i.e., politically articulate groups and individuals, with which the international organization can deal more or less directly.

Such variety in itself, however, is not sufficient. For the formation of coalitions from among the units on the level of the embryonic international community requires the construction of a basis of values or interests which are common to the participating units within the several national communities involved. In other words, the process of integration is stimulated by heterogeneity coupled with a certain measure of homogeneity, a combination which is called 'symmetrical heterogeneity' by Haas, that is,

... each country is fragmented along the lines of pluralism; but each group or class has it counterpart in the neighbouring country. In other words, no country is internally homogeneous, but the lines of cleavage and interest are regionally homogeneous (*Haas*, 1967: 320).

The above considerations also would seem to imply that integration will the more readily succeed if the populations of the communities involved are politically mobilized to a relatively high degree and are used to seek the realization of their values through political action and organization. Likewise a differentiated economic and social structure in the several communities will involve a large variety of different interests. Accordingly, one may expect integration to be more probable according as the communities involved have a higher level of political, social, and economic development.

Articulate voluntary groups, led by bureaucratized but accessible elites, compete with each other more or less rationally for political power and social status. The population is mobilized and participates in this process through affiliation with mass organization (. . .)
   Significantly correlated with industrialization we find the usual high degree of urbanization and evergrowing demands for government services and durable consumer goods. We also find increasing demands on limited natural resources and greater dependence on foreign (or regional) trade (*Haas*, 1961: 104; see also *Schmitter & Haas*, 1964: 34).

In this connection Haas also points to the significance of the similarity of the government bureaucracies of the participating units, as regards their structure and functioning, the backgrounds of their members, and the standards that are employed in the fulfilment of their tasks (*Haas*, 1967: 320). For such a similarity will greatly facilitate the introduction of common decision-making organs and bureaucracies, and the bargaining over and the execution of common policies.
   As has become clear already with regard to the concept of 'symmetrical heterogeneity', it is not only the characteristics of the individual political communities concerned which are relevant, but also (and perhaps even more so) the distribution of such characteristics within the integration system as a whole. Accordingly, Haas mentions three

macro-properties of such a system which could perhaps best be conceived as forms of homogeneity. The first is 'homogeneity of economic power', or, rather, of gross national products.

The more nearly homogeneous the countries are in economic power, the greater the chance of the union. Gross national product is used here as the measure of economic power (*Barrera & Haas*, 1969: 155; see also *Haas*, 1964a: 2).

The second property, which might be termed 'homogeneity of political power', is suggested by the following proposition:

Integration in any network of autonomous units is advanced if no single unit is the supreme repository of hopes, hates and tasks (*Haas*, 1964b: 86).

'Ideological homogeneity', finally, is defined as follows:

A given cluster of countries is ideologically 'homogeneous' if the divisions among the parties are, very roughly, the same among all the countries in the cluster, when the principles professed and the concrete socio-economic interests represented by the parties are roughly analogous on both sides of a frontier (*Haas*, 1964b: 105).

With respect to the latter, 'ideological homogeneity', an important element is the kind of nationalism which prevails in the communities involved in an integration process. While 'ideology' consists of the doctrines peculiar to a particular group within a political community, 'nationalism' refers to that community as a whole.

Nationalism is composed of values and claims acceptable to the great bulk of the population while also setting it apart from the values and claims of other political communities (*Haas*, 1958c: 6).

The character of a community's nationalism is an important determinant of that community's international behavior. And, consequently, it has an important bearing upon the course of an integration process in which the community participates. Haas distinguishes five forms of nationalism. The first of these, called 'liberal nationalism', is defined as follows:

This ideology regards the nation as a fraternal community whose purpose is the realization of the rights and liberties of *individuals*, thus contributing to the happiness of all. Liberal Nationalism has, of course, been closely related to ideologies of progress, both spiritual and material (*Haas*, 1964a: 465).

The second form, 'jacobin nationalism', differs from the first in that it attributes to the community the mission of disseminating liberal nationalism and bestowing it on other communities (*Haas*, 1964a: 465).

The third variety, 'traditional nationalism', seeks to protect the community against alien doctrines. It

. . . seeks to mobilize the people under the banner of an older pattern of life, harking back to feudal days and corporatist ways, tribal values, or the solidarity of a folk society. It emphasizes the rights of discrete groups, classes, guilds, or castes rather than of individuals. It always creates, or resurrects, a myth of golden ancient days of solidarity under which to organize the newly mobilized masses (*Haas*, 1964a: 465).

'Syncretic nationalism', the fourth form, is similar to traditional nationalism in that it attempts to protect the community against alien ideas. But it differs from it in that it is not entirely adverse to innovation and borrows such traits from those ideas as seem desirable (*Haas*, 1964a: 465-466).

Finally, in 'integral nationalism' all attention is focused upon the community itself rather than upon groups or individuals. It rigidly subordinates the good of the citizens to the survival of the community which is conceived as a monolithic organic whole (*Haas*, 1964a: 466).

Thus, integral nationalism, syncretic nationalism, and traditional nationalism, all seek to consolidate or strengthen the national community, which is not particularly conducive to integration at the international level. The missionary zeal of the jacobin variety would seem to be better suited for conquest or revolutionary wars of liberation than for participation in a process of peaceful international integration. Only the first form, liberal nationalism, seems to allow for an integrative development. It does not sanctify the national community; rather it conceives government in a more utilitarian fashion. It is not adverse to a variety of groups and individuals participating in a competitive political process.

Elites representing the various states are persuaded that some common or converging aim can be met more efficiently by political union. Normally,

economic considerations predominate. The institutions of the new federation
are always Liberal – Constitutional in inspiration. This is a matter of necessity rather than ideological conviction, since government by persuasion
and compromise can take place only in a system of defined powers and
rights. The pattern is thus Liberal Nationalist, even though the founding
fathers may not be Liberal Nationalists (*Haas*, 1964a: 474-475).

With regard to the kind of political system that may prevail in the communities participating in a process of integration, Haas distinguishes
three main categories: democracies, oligarchies, and totalitarian states
(*Haas*, 1962b: 324-325; 1964a: 129; see also section 5.4). As to economic development, the communities are classified as 'mature industrialized', 'rapidly industrializing', 'mature agricultural', and 'underdeveloped' (*Haas*, 1962b: 326; *Haas*, 1964a: 129-130; section 5.4).
The economic structure, finally, may be 'free enterprise', 'social welfare', 'communist', or 'corporatist' (*Haas*, 1962b: 326-327; 1964a: 130;
section 5.4).

Thus a system in which integration occurs can be characterized by
the distribution of the kinds of nationalism, political and economic
systems, political power, and the stages of economic development of
the communities concerned. This distribution is assumed 'to give us an
idea of the "general interest" or "shared aims" that the member governments profess at any one time, and that they seek to impose on the
international organization' (*Haas*, 1964a: 130). We have seen that
integration may be expected to proceed more readily according as the
communities involved have a higher level of political, social, and economic development. Probably, then, integration will be more sucess-
ful to the extent that those communities are 'industrial' and 'democratic'
(*Haas*, 1964a: 447-448), embracing a 'liberal nationalist' ideology
(*Haas*, 1964a: 474-475), while there are some indications that integration is positively correlated with the extent to which the communities espouse 'social welfare' aims (*Haas*, 1964a: 283, 312, 317, 323,
373; see also *Haas*, 1961: 105). It should be noted, though, that this
aspect of the theory has not been elaborated very much, as yet. The
relationships between integration and the categories mentioned have by
no means been established unequivocally.

All this also suggests a line of reasoning which might run as follows:
the greater the homogeneity (in the several respects mentioned) of a certain political system made up of autonomous communities, the greater

the probability that similar units and interests exist in those communities, and the greater the probability that demands for integration will be made and supported by coalitions based on converging interests. This aspect of the theory, too, has not been elaborated in detail by Haas.

Up to now an important question has been left out of consideration, namely, 'what makes units demand integration, and when?'. Of course, in a very general sense the answer is provided by Haas's first main postulate. That is, units will demand integration when they have come to the conclusion that their values cannot be realized any more in an adequate way through the national political institutions, and that international institutions offer more favorable possibilities. But, when will that happen and with respect to what units?

Haas does not deal very extensively and systematically with that problem. Actually, he largely limits himself to more or less incidental observations that do not carry us much further than the postulate just mentioned. Thus, he sometimes refers to the perception of military or economic threat that may result in demands for greater military or economic countervailing capabilities than those offered by the national community alone (cf., e.g., *Haas*, 1961: 107, 116; *Haas & Schmitter*, 1966: 188). Further, it is assumed that the desire for unity is reinforced to the extent that the actors involved perceive themselves to be dependent militarily, morally, and physically upon the external world (*Barrera & Haas*, 1969: 152). And similarly, the higher the pressure from the outside world, the more integration will be accelerated 'because of the postulated desire of the union's members to achieve a united common front against external forces' (*Barrera & Haas*, 1969: 152). He also attaches a certain weight to the amount of, and especially to the changes in, the transactions between the different communities involved (*Haas & Schmitter*, 1965: 2; 1966: 266 ff.; *Barrera & Haas*, 1969: 156). All this suggests a line of reasoning which links the occurrence of demands for integration to the amount, or changes in the amount, and character of certain transactions or, perhaps, to interpendencies existing among the communities involved. Unfortunately, however, it is not elaborated.

A corollary to the above problem is that of the relative significance of the units involved in an integration process with regard to the course that process takes. For, obviously, units differ in a number of respects, such as membership, ideology, financial power, etc. Such factors will presumably affect their behavior with regard to integration and the force with which they can put forward their demands. The weight which is attached to their support will equally differ. And for the success of an international organization, as for the entire course of a process of integration, it obviously makes a great difference what kinds of units compose the various coalitions supporting it. Also, some units will probably redirect their support and demands from the national to the international institutions more easily than others.

With regard to this last point, Haas mentions weakness, insecurity, and ideology, as factors which may stimulate a reorientation of loyalty. Thus he concludes, with regard to organizations of employees, employers, and businessmen in ECSC:

The insecure and frightened are the first to grope for a programme and a body of symbols implying supranational group integration, provided their previous value commitment was not solely to the national state (*Haas*, 1958c: 387).

In a different context, namely that of the International Labor Organization (ILO), it appears that weak governments more readily submit to the decisions of the international organization. What this weakness consists of is indicated as follows:

This combination of private and public pressures upon a government possessing few sources of revenue, highly dependent upon the support and good will of other nations, and having no developed public opinion standing behind its ruling clique brought some results (*Haas*, 1964a: 227; also 228, 262, 269).

Further, Haas mentions that the tasks of an international organization should be related to the interests of 'important national elites' (*Haas*, 1964a: 409), while the support of political parties is of special significance for an integration process.

Because of their appeal to an overlapping and diffuse group constituency political parties are far more crucial carriers of political integration or disintegration than even supranationally organised interest groups (*Haas*, 1958c: 437).

Apparently, the character of the interests of the units is also an important variable. Haas distinguishes four categories of expectations regarding the integration process. They form a 'scale' ranging from 'long-run positive expectations', to 'long-run negative expectations' (*Haas*, 1958c: 287-289).

'Long-run positive expectations' are concerned with demands whose fulfilment depends upon a continuing process of integration. The second category, 'short-run positive', is made up of demands whose fulfilment requires action by the international institutions, without being aimed at a continuing process of integration. This category is concerned with incidental demands, and with immediate benefits and costs, without implying a continuing support of and devotion to integration. 'Short-run negative expectations' involve opposition to specific decisions by the international institutions, without implying opposition to the process of integration as such and in the long run, which is of the essence of the fourth category, the 'long-run negative expectations'.

According to Haas, the two extremes of this scale will be characterized by relatively explicit and developed ideologies, while the two middle categories are concerned with more or less opportunistic considerations of expediency and of short-run benefits and costs. For the process of integration, however, these latter categories are of special importance. Their specificity and the absence of fixed ideological commitments render them particularly suitable for compromise; at the same time they are related to 'directly experienced needs and demands' (*Haas*, 1964a: 409) which stimulates the process of reorientation of loyalties.

Concerning this point, however, the actual course of European integration has led Haas to slightly modify his insights. That is, he has come to the conclusion that, as a result of de Gaulle's actions, European integration did not proceed as (Haas thought that) the theory would predict it.

The phenomenon of a de Gaulle is omitted; the superiority of step-by-step economic decisions over crucial political devices of the European social and economic structure is almost absolute (*Haas*, 1967: 327).

It should be noted, however, that the theory as developed thus far does *not* contain any postulate on the 'superiority' of 'step-by-step economic decisions' over 'crucial political devices', and neither can such a 'superiority' be deduced from it. In fact, as we have seen, the theory does hardly contain any definite proposition about the role of specific kinds of decisions or interests in the integrative process, while the categories used in the above quotation have not been defined properly. In othei words, the theory cannot be falsified at this point – not even by de Gaulle. At any rate, the above leads Haas to put a greater emphasis on the role of 'long-term expectations': in order to succeed, integration needs a firmer basis than one made up of short-term interests. Thus he writes:

... pragmatic interest politics is its own worst ennemy. The politician and the businessman who has abandoned an interest in high politics and devotes himself only to the maximization of his daily welfare is compelled, by virtue of that very concern, to make concessions to another actor who forces him to choose so as to sacrifice welfare. Pragmatic interests, simply because they are pragmatic and not reinforced with deep ideological or philosophical commitment, are ephemeral. Just because they are weakly held they can be readily scrapped. And a political process which is built and projected from pragmatic interests, therefore, is bound to be a frail process, susceptible to reversal. And so integration can once more develop into disintegration (*Haas*, 1967: 327-328).

In this connection he introduces a new distinction between the interests of units, this time one between 'dramatic-political' and 'incremental-economic' interests. In the first category one recognizes the 'long-term expectations' discussed earlier: 'dramatic-political' interests are concerned with issues of an ideological and emotional character relating to basic questions of political life, particularly those of foreign policy, defence, and the character of the political and economic order. 'Incremental-economic' interests are of a much more concrete character; costs and benefits can be recognized and calculated more easily which greatly facilitates compromise.

These two categories of interests are related by Haas to two categories of units – governmental and non-governmental. The resulting four possible combinations are assumed to have different consequences for the character of an integration process. This is represented by the following matrix (*Haas*, 1967: 329):

		aims of non-governmental elites	
		dramatic-political	incremental-economic
aims of statesmen	dramatic-political	integration either direct and smooth, or impossible	integration erratic and reversible
	incremental-economic	integration erratic and reversible	integration gradual but automatic

Of course, this is only a very rough scheme. As to the character of the interests involved, the categories used are of an extremely formal nature. And apart from the fact that they are not defined very precisely, adequate analysis would in all probability have to include other aspects concerning the substance of the interests as well. Similar considerations apply to the distinction between 'governmental' and 'non-governmental' units. Units differ in a number of respects among which their governmental or non-governmental position is merely one. In fact, from the foregoing discussion it appears that Haas himself does recognize some other relevant aspects. Consequently, the above scheme merely represents a possible starting point for a systematic analysis of the relationship between units and their interests and the process of integration.

It should be noted that Haas also distinguishes interest groups according to the *scope*, *intensity*, and *duration* of their interests (*Haas*, 1969: 43), such that 'only groups with specific, permanent, and intensively held views succeed in being heard regularly in Washington, and their influence is on specific issues of concern to them' (*Haas*, 1969: 57). This line of analysis, however, is not pursued very far, while it is not expressly linked to the problem of integration. As to the role of public opinion in the determination of foreign policy (of the U.S.), Haas conceives this as one of defining the area of consensus permitting the government to act and to justify its acts, rather than of prescribing or prohibiting specific governmental policies (*Haas*, 1969: 40). It remains to be mentioned finally that he also distinguished the aims of the units involved in integration according as these are 'identical' or merely 'converging' in the economic sphere, accompanied by 'strong' or 'weak' 'political commitments'. It is assumed that integration is stimulated to the extent that economic aims are 'identical' rather than 'converging', while they are connected with 'strong political commitments' rather than 'weak' ones (*Haas & Schmitter*, 1966: 269).

5. EMPIRICAL INTERPRETATION

5.1. *Outline of this section*

In this section I will discuss the way Haas empirically interprets the main elements of the abstract scheme of reasoning discussed above. I shall deal successively with integration (section 5.2); with units and their political behavior (5.3); and, finally, with some characteristics of the communities involved in a process of integration (5.4).

5.2. *Integration*

To begin with, it will be remembered that Haas conceives integration as the process whereby a political community is formed. A political community, in its turn, is characterized by the possession of central institutions to which the members, 'habitually and predictably over long periods', address their support and demands, and which are capable of making binding decisions. Accordingly, the concept 'integration' can be empirically interpreted through the various constituent elements of its definition: central institutions, the degree to which these attract the loyalties of the units, i.e., their demands and support, or the extent to which they acquire authority and legitimacy.

Haas does not give an explicit empirical interpretation of the concept 'central institution' or (international) 'organization'. Probably, though, this need not cause much difficulty. In general, the relevant institutions or organizations are relatively easily recognizable; one may think here of national governments and of international organizations such as the UN, the ILO and the EEC.

A different matter is that in his definition of political community Haas introduces the element of time. Also, his conception on integration as a *process* implicitly contains that same element. More generally, the outcomes of the processes through which integration is explained will be affected by the length of the period during which these processes occur. This is particularly important with regard to Haas's second (dissonance) postulate: probably, the longer people are made to behave inconsistently with their initial attitudes, the smaller the difference between attitudes and actual behavior will become. Accordingly, time will be an important variable in the explanation of, for example, the development of legitimacy on the part of political institutions. All this notwithstanding, Haas nowhere measures time in a precise fashion.

In the theory an important role is played by the concept of 'function' or 'task' performed by the (international) central institutions. Functions should be 'specific' and 'economically important', they must not be completely 'non-controversial'; and although 'functional contexts' are 'autonomous', they should also be 'inherently expansive'. Quite apart from the fact that the categories used seem to be inconsistent to some extent (an inconsistency which might disappear through more precise definition and elaborate analysis), Haas does not precisely determine the empirical contents of these concepts. For one thing, this makes it rather difficult to make empirical comparisons of international organizations with regard to their functions. Also, it will hardly be possible to determine empirically, with regard to an international organization, whether or not it shows functional growth or decay, or whether or not spill-over occurs. It renders the theory empirically indeterminate with regard to a crucial element.

No rules are given which would enable us to link the theoretical entity 'loyalty' (i.e., demands and support) in an unambiguous way to observable behavior. Also, Haas does not attempt to measure the *degree* to which the institutions of the emerging political community command the loyalty of the members. But since integration is conceived as a process, such loyalty must obviously allow for different degrees. As it is, it cannot be determined in any more or less precise fashion to what extent loyalties have shifted, increased, or decreased.

'Authority' and 'legitimacy' are concepts of a somewhat more limited scope. 'Authority', it will be recalled, denotes the extent to which the central institution's decisions are accepted as binding by the members, while 'legitimacy' concerns the extent to which the central institution as such is accepted by the membership. Both are particular forms of support commanded by the central institution. Clearly, both are aggregate measures, since they are concerned with the membership's support behavior in its totality. Consequently, a discussion of authority and legitimacy requires dealing with the support behavior of the individual units, although this more properly belongs to the subject matter of the next subsection.

It is in his *Beyond the nation-state* that Haas deals most extensively with the problem of empirically interpreting, and even measuring, authority and legitimacy. His treatment is characterized by two general traits. In the first place, he does not try to develop a fully general solution to the problem. That is, he offers a number of solutions which differ according as the context in which the problem arises differs. Secondly, he generally deals only with the support behavior of governments. In the context of the ILO this is justified in so far as it is the governments that have to carry out the organization's decisions. But however important governments may be, they are not the sole relevant actors. Accordingly, the significance of the solutions offered is limited.

Regarding the extent to which member states of the ILO conform to the recommendations of the Committee of Experts which is charged with the supervision of the national application of ratified Conventions in the field of labor conditions, Haas distinguishes four different forms of support behavior: a state may undertake 'full remedial action', 'partial remedial action', it may 'fail to remove infraction', or 'denounce Convention' (*Haas*, 1964a: 258). The number of cases in each category and during a certain period may be counted and calculated as a proportion of the total number of cases.

In order to determine the authority of the ILO with respect to labor standards, Haas uses a set of four 'indicators' (*Haas*, 1964a: 260).

In the first place he measures the 'fidelity with which annual reports on ratified Conventions are submitted'. This is concerned with an obligation of the member states under the ILO constitution, Haas distinguishes three forms of support here, namely, reporting 'regularly', 'intermittently', and 'sporadically' (*Haas*, 1964a: 261).

Secondly, he measures the 'regularity with which new ILO instruments are submitted to the competent national authorities'. Here Haas counts the number of states that, in a certain period, have submitted 'all', 'some', or 'none' of the Conventions or Recommendations of the ILO to the competent national authorities (*Haas*, 1964a: 263).

In the third place, it is determined which states comply 'regularly', 'intermittently', or 'poorly' with the ILO's demand to inform it of the reasons for non-ratification of its instruments and of the degree to which these instruments are applied even though not ratified (*Haas*, 1964a: 265).

Finally, 'the responsiveness shown by persistently delinquent states after they are placed on the back list' is measured. Here Haas distinguishes 'good', 'some', and 'no' improvement (*Haas*, 1964a: 267).

In order to determine the legitimacy of the ILO in the field of labor relations, Haas applies four indicators (*Haas*, 1964a: 269-270).

The first is 'the fidelity with which present and former colonial powers extend the provisions of the Code to their non-metropolitan territories – a step to which they are in no way legally obligated'.

A Convention is considered 'accepted' on behalf of 'almost all' colonial territories under the jurisdiction of a specific member state if that state submitted a declaration of acceptance *without* modification for the overwhelming majority of such territories.

A Convention is considered 'accepted selectively' (. . .) if that state submitted a declaration of acceptance *with* modification and/or has accepted the Convention only on behalf of a portion of its colonies.

A Convention is considered 'applied in almost all' territories if the member state is reported by the ILO as 'fully applying' the Convention, or if the state enacted legislation to give effect to the Convention in the overwhelming number of the colonies under its jurisdiction.

A Convention is considered 'applied selectively' if the member state is reported by the ILO as applying the 'substantive provisions' of the Convention, or where 'there appear to be beginnings of application' in all or some of the colonies under the member state's jurisdiction (*Haas*, 1964a: 271, table 7).

In the second place it is determined how many Conventions have been accepted by new states upon their acquiring independence and how many of these Conventions have been ratified by them since that time (*Haas*, 1964a: 275).

The third indicator of legitimacy is the extent to which states request the ILO's technical assistance in order to implement the Labor Code (*Haas*, 1964a: 277-279).

Fourthly, a certain number of monographic studies which have been prepared in order to ascertain the influence exercised by the ILO in specific states, are reviewed by Haas (*Haas*, 1964a: 279-283).

In a different context, namely, that of the several Industrial Committees of the ILO, Haas measures the support behavior of the member states through the way in which these states respond to the recommendations of these Committees. For this purpose he applies the following scheme of classification:

No reply – Government furnishes no response to a specific recommendation singled out for follow-up information by an Industrial Committee.

Evasive – Governmental response is vague and general.

Does not apply – Governmental response contends that local conditions render the recommendation inapplicable.

Complies fully – Government indicates that recommendation was used in introducing new national labor standards.

Complies in part – Government indicates that a portion of the recommendation was used in introducing new national labor standards.

No intent – Government makes clear that it has no interest in the recommendation and no intention of applying it.

Describes existing conditions as good – Government merely describes existing conditions in the industry that seem to conform essentially with the content of the recommendation.

Describes existing conditions as fair – Government merely describes existing conditions in the industry that seem to conform to some extent with the content of the recommendation.

Describes existing conditions as poor – Government merely describes existing conditions in the industry that seem not to conform with content of the recommendation (*Haas*, 1964a: 308).

On the basis of this scheme he measures mainly three things: first, the behavior of all reporting states; second, the behavior of those states *not* obliged to report (i.e. non-members of the Committees), what Haas calls 'special performance beyond the clear call of duty'; and, finally, the fidelity with which full members of the Committees discharge their obligations, by calculating the number of their responses in each category as a percentage of the total number of the committee's requests for information addressed to them (*Haas*, 1964a: 309-326). In this same context he also suggests that, as to the content of the resolutions of the Industrial Committees, their 'controversiality' could be used as an indicator. Apparently, the more 'controversial' the subject of the resolution complied with, the higher the authority of these Committees (*Haas*, 1964a: 328).

With regard to the extent to which ILO's jurisdiction as to disputes concerning the freedom of trade unions in member states is accepted, Haas uses the way the states fulfil the ILO's explicit recommendations regarding them as an indicator. There is 'great improvement' when 'the Committee's report acknowledges a change in policy or congratulates the government for having made improvements'; 'some improvement', when 'a part of the alleged violation was eventually rectified, although some other part might continue to give rise to correspondence'; finally, 'no improvement' occurs when 'the original allegations are made once more, whenever the Committee proclaims itself unable to dismiss the case because the government does not submit adequate replies, and whenever new cases are submitted alleging the same infraction already ruled on by earlier Committee decisions' (*Haas*, 1964a: 417).

A more complicated measure is developed with respect to human rights issues in the ILO. It is made up of:

(1) the response of the government to the Office's questionnaire inquiring about interest in preparing a Convention; (2) the vote of the government on the final text of the Convention; (3) ratification or non-ratification; (4) the degree of implementation, irrespective of ratification (*Haas*, 1964a: 371).

The different behavioral alternatives which are possible in each of the above categories are given numbers; some alternatives, in virtue of their greater importance, get a higher number – they are 'weighted'. (*Haas*, 1964a: 372).

Response to questionnaire		Ratification	
No response submitted	0	Ratified	2
Negative response	–1	Not ratified	0
Positive response	1		

Vote		Implementation	
Absent at time of vote	0	No report received	0
No delegation present	0	Report insufficient	0
Abstention	0	Convention is applied in part	1
No	–1	Convention is fully applied	3
Yes	1		

However, Haas does not explicitly specify the number system he applies, i.e., the relationships or the rules that are assumed to apply among these numerals; nor has he defined the concepts used so as to make them obey the stringent rules of a number system in which addition and multiplication are defined. Apparently, the different numbers only mean that the phenomena to which they correspond are different in the sense that the higher the number, the more important the corresponding phenomena are deemed to be. But these (ordinal) numbers do not automatically allow for the common arithmetical operations of addition and multiplication.

Consequently, Haas's 'human rights observation score' which is derived arithmetically from the above scheme cannot be accepted. This score is calculated as follows: First, for a certain state, and with respect to a specific Convention, the scores in each of the four categories mentioned are *added*; subsequently, for that same state, but now with respect to a group of selected Conventions, an *arithmetical mean* is computed from the totals for each individual Convention. The result is the 'human rights observations score' for that particular state. In view of the above considerations, however, no definite meaning can be attached to this score. It is interesting in so far as it represents an attempt to combine different forms of support behavior, instead of developing a set of indicators each of which may be interesting and significant in itself, but among which the relationships are far from clear.

Another concept by means of which the legitimacy of an international institution might be measured is that of 'coverage'. It is defined in the following terms:

The 'coverage' of a given kind of convention is computed by counting the *actual* ratifications and stating them as a percentage of *possible* ratifications for all member states in each category of political system, economic development, and economic institutions used in the discussion of the 'environment' (*Haas*, 1962b: 329).

This concept must be used with great care. For ratification of conventions by a state in and by itself does not yet tell us very much about the extent to which that state really supports the international institution. As Haas says:

Enough is known of the reasons for ratifying or refusing to ratify a Convention to cast doubt on the usefulness of this criterion as an indicator of authority. Many ratifications are deposited for trivial reasons, totally unconnected with a reasoned decision to submit local labor conditions to the upward dynamism of the International Labor Code (*Haas*, 1964a: 260).

Rather, 'coverage' can be used as an indicator 'for judging the existence of commonly experienced needs and interests' (*Haas*, 1961: 118-119).

To conclude, then: with respect to the concepts of 'integration', 'political community', and 'international organization' and its 'functions', 'authority', and 'legitimacy', Haas offers a relatively great number of indicators in order to give them an empirical interpretation. Their main weakness resides in the fact that generally they offer only partial solutions to the problem of operationalizing the concepts mentioned. Rather than the tools for a full and unambiguous empirical interpretation of the concepts mentioned, we are offered a number of more or less isolated suggestions.

5.3. *Units, their demands and support*

Haas does not give a separate and explicit interpretation to the concept 'unit'. In practice he is concerned with governments, political parties, interest groups, and international organizations acting as units. The identification of such units need not, perhaps, cause grave difficulties in itself. Here, however, some important problems of selection are bound to arise. In the first place, it will be recalled, a unit has been defined as an individual or group making political demands and, it should be added, being capable of support behavior. Especially in the case of the larger and more complex units, the problem is to determine what shall count as the political behavior of the unit; that is, whose demands and whose support behavior shall be identified as those of the unit as a whole. In the second place, in any political system there usually exist a multitude of different units. Not all of them, however, will be equally relevant with respect to some given political issue. Here the problem is that of determining which units are, and which units are not, relevant to the case under consideration.

Regarding these problems of selection Haas opts for an approach in terms of 'elites':

In our scheme of integration, 'elites' are the leaders of all relevant political groups who habitually participate in the making of public decisions, whether as policy-makers in government, as lobbyists or as spokesmen of political parties. They include the officials of trade associations, higher civil servants and active politicians (*Haas*, 1958c: 17).

This approach is justified as follows:

The emphasis on elites in the study of integration derives its justification from the bureaucratised nature of European organisations of long standing, in which basic decisions are made by the leadership, sometimes over the opposition and usually over the indifference of the general membership. This gives the relevant elites a manipulative role which is of course used to place the organisation on record for or against a proposed measure of integration.

A further important justification for the elite approach to the study of integration lies in the demonstrable difference in attitudes held at the leadership levels of significant groups, as contrasted with the mass membership. [In the latter there are found 'factual ignorance or general misunderstanding'; *Haas*, 1958c: 17-18; see also *Haas*, 1964a: 104, 110.]

Whatever may be the merits or demerits of this 'elite approach', it will have become clear that it does not completely dispose of the selection problems mentioned above. For how is it determined who participates 'habitually' in the making of public decisions? Besides, is everyone thus participating equally relevant? If not, how are such differences to be determined? In fact, it has appeared (cf. section 4.4) that units do differ as to their importance for a process of integration. In this connection Haas uses such expressions as 'insecure and frightened' (*Haas*, 1958c: 387), 'important elites' (*Haas*, 1964a: 409), 'viable coalition of forces' (*Haas*, 1964a: 102), etc. But no attempt is made to translate them into empirical terms.

No explicit empirical interpretation is given to the concept 'demand'. In practice Haas considers as such the oral, and especially the written expressions of claims and desires made by selected elites concerning the decisions to be taken by governments or international organizations. It has appeared from the discussion in section 4.4 that Haas distinguishes a number of factors which determine the relative significance of specific demands for an integration process. Thus there are 'strategic' demands (*Haas*, 1964a: 83); there are 'directly experienced needs and demands of important national elites' (*Haas*, 1964a: 409); a scale is constructed which ranges from 'long-term positive expectations' to 'long-term negative expectations' (*Haas*, 1958c: 287-289); and a distinction is made between 'dramatic-political' and 'incremental-economic' aims (*Haas*, 1967: 329). But no rules are given which would enable us to connect such categories unequivocally with observations.

In the context of the ILO and with respect to issues involving the freedom of trade unions, Haas distinguishes four categories of demands according to their 'controversiality': trade union rights, human rights, colonial issues, and cold war issues.

The least 'controversial' type of claim relating to the flourishing of pluralism involves specific charges of specific violations of the rights of a given union or a discrete set of persons. (. . .)

Next on the scale of 'controversiality', and more germane to the flowering of pluralism, is the category of issues we label 'human rights'. (. . .) here we are concerned with a challenge to the trade union movement as a whole, with efforts to destroy or weaken it. (. . .) Our third category – 'colonial issues' – takes cognizance of one of the major international currents in our period. Charges referring to any subject matter leveled in a context in which a national movement is seeking to weaken or descredit a colonial administration provide issues of this type. (. . .) Trade union violations put forth in the context of the Afro-Asian revolt against colonialism, then, provide our third type of issue. (. . .) Finally, the Cold War setting provides a rather typical context for charges of repressing trade unions. Again, the substantive charges may be the same as in the trade union and human rights categories. But the context is the discrediting of either West or East (*Haas*, 1964a: 386-387).

The significance of these categories is that they provide an indication of the degree to which the international organization in question has acquired authority and legitimacy. For the more controversial the demands fed into the organization, and decided upon by it, the greater its authority and legitimacy will be (see also *Haas*, 1964a: 328; see p. 149) above. At the same time the occurrence of the demands mentioned gives some indication as to the degree to which the international system concerned has been transformed, 'i.e., the extent to which autonomous social groups with articulate interests to defend make their appearance as actors' (*Haas*, 1964a: 386) at the international level.

To a large extent the empirical interpretation of the concept of 'support' has already been dealt with in the preceding subsection (5.2), that is, in the context of the central institution's or international organization's authority and legitimacy. This is also the context in which Haas deals most extensively with support behavior. It has appeared that his discussion of it is largely restricted to the actions of governments. As to the support behavior of other units, Haas does not attempt to formulate generally applicable interpretative rules. And apart from some occasional suggestions (see, for example, *Haas*, 1958c: 127, 212), no systematic effort is made to distinguish empirically different degrees or forms of support.

The empirical indeterminateness of the concepts 'units', 'demands', and 'support' makes it impossible to observe in any precise fashion whether and to what extent the theoretically extremely important process of reorientation of loyalties does in fact occur during a process of integration. To some extent only such reorientation of loyalties is measured by Haas with respect to units participating in elections in certain organs of an international organization.

Thus, with regard to roll-call votes in the International Labor Conferences (1919-1958), Haas constructs an 'index of dissent'. This index purports to measure the extent to which national ties are severed in favor of new international ties. As follows:

For each country the total number of votes was counted in which government delegates participated, excluding the few occasions on which the two government delegates opposed one another. Then the number of instances was counted in which labor and/or employer delegates from the same country voted differently from the government representatives. Abstentions by interest-group delegates were counted as dissenting votes whenever the government representatives did not abstain; conversely, affirmative or negative votes by the interest-group delegates were counted as dissenting whenever the governments abstained. Total disagreement with the government yields a figure of 100 per cent; total agreement results in a score of 0 per cent (*Haas*, 1962b: 338).

In order to determine to what extent new units have been formed, or to what extent cohesion has emerged of within certain selected groups of voting units, Haas constructs an index which he calls 'deviation of unanimity':

It is computed in the following manner: the total number of votes cast, or the number of votes on specific issues, is counted for a predetermined period; voters are indentified by nationality and affiliation with one of the three organized ILO groups (Governments, Employers, Workers). We then count the number of times each delegate votes with the majority (or minority) in his Group. The frequence of identification with the minority will then be specified as the percentage of the minority vote of the total vote. For this purpose it is immaterial whether the delegate whose votes are being counted voted 'yes', 'no', or abstained. The only concern is his identification with the minority or the majority, If the Group splits into three divisions on a vote, as happens frequently, the 'majority' is the division that includes the largest number of members voting, and the 'minority' is the sum of the two remaining divisions. This occasionally results in the 'minority' outnumbering the 'majority'. A deviation from the unanimity of 50 per cent indicates a complete splitting of the Group; a score of 0 per cent signifies complete unity (*Haas*, 1962b: 340; see also *Haas*, 1960b: 17 ff.).

Again, these indices can be computed only with regard to international organs where voting occurs, and with regard to units that participate in such voting concerning issues that are decided by voting. That is, they apply only to a limited class of phenomena; they do not fully determine the extent to which a reorientation of loyalties has in fact occurred in some integrating system as a whole.

5.4. *Background*

We have seen that Haas considers the number and variety of units within the political communities involved in a process of integration to be a major determinant of such a process, in the sense that the larger the number and variety of such units is, the higher the probability of successful integrative developments will be. In this connection Haas generally applies the term 'pluralism'. To determine the degree of pluralism prevailing in a political community, he uses the position of trade unions as an indicator. This is justified, since

In most countries, trade-union vigor and autonomy provide a yardstick for judging the existence of a strong pluralism in other contexts, such as service organizations, woman's groups, veteran's organizations, and other purely economic groupings (*Haas*, 1964a: 476).

The position of the trade unions is measured according to three criteria: 1. the legal context (i.e., whether the unions are or are not free to form, to strike, and to bargain collectively); 2. the character of their aims (i.e., purely economic and/or political); 3. their actual autonomy (i.e., the extent to which they are affiliated and/or subordinated to distinctly political formations) (*Haas*, 1964a: 476). On the basis of these criteria, Haas defines eight classes of pluralism:

Group 1. Full freedom; economic objectives and a bargaining mentality; no affiliation with political formations.

Group 2. Full freedom; economic objectives and a bargaining mentality; the maintenance of loose and informal political ties.

Group 3. Full freedom; mixed economic and political objectives, along with a tendency for a revolutionary mentality to take the place of bargaining; maintenance of full and open ties with political parties.

Group 4. Restricted freedom; mixed economic and political aims, the latter often taking precedence; maintenance of full and open ties with political parties.

Group 5. Restricted freedom; mixed economic and political aims; non-political trade unions based on weakness, timidity, and government restrictions.

Group 6. Extremely restricted freedom; it is difficult to speak of economic or political aims, since all union activity is subject either to the inclusion of the union elite in the governing oligarchy or to government toleration; non-political.

Group 7. Extremely restricted freedom; political aims predominate, since these unions are permitted to function only as a part of the official economic modernization plan; a tendency to be a part of the single ruling party.

Group 8. These trade unions are an arm of the state, permitted to function only as part of the total plan for society (*Haas*, 1964a: 476-477).

However, pluralism in itself is not enough. More specifically, among the communities participating in integration there should exist 'symmetrical heterogeneity' (section 4.4). To determine such symmetrical heterogeneity would require dealing with the ideologies of the different units existing in relation to the integrating international system as a whole, rather than as parts of the individual national communities. The above indicator, limited to one kind of units, restricted to the individual national community, and based on comparatively formal criteria, is not suited for a determination of such a macro-systematic property as symmetrical heterogeneity.

In order to determine the level of pluralism which obtains in an integrating system as a whole, it has first to be ascertained 'whether the prevalent mode of group within *each* of the participating states is functionally specific, universalistic, or achievement-oriented' (*Haas & Schmitter*, 1966: 267). Subsequently, 'the balance of pluralism for the union as *a whole*' (*Haas & Schmitter*, 1966: 267) should be established. (Note that this, in and by itself, does not yet inform us about the number and variety of units in the system).

The degree of pluralism is measured by means of two subindices: one of *articulation* and one of *modernization* (*Barrera & Haas*, 1969: 157-158). The first one is judgmental in character, based on ratings assigned to countries by Banks and Textor* regarding articulation 1. by associational groups, 2. by institutional groups, and 3. non-associational or particularistic groups.

A high degree of pluralism is indicated by high scores on the first two and a low score on the third. Since it was felt that potential for integration depended both on the level of pluralism and on the degree of heterogeneity within the union, a mean score was first computed for each bloc, based on the individual countries, and then this was multiplied by another measure representing one minus a measure of variability. This measure of variability consisted of the mean deviation divided by the mean score for the bloc (*Barrera & Haas*, 1969: 157).

Modernization was measured as follows. First, two *submeasures* were constructed: 1. *economic development*, based on per capita income and energy consumption, which measure was given a weight of 1; and 2. *social development*, based on education, urbanization, and communications – this measure was given the weight $1^1/_2$ (which is, it should be noted, a matter of judgment and more or less arbitrary). In order to combine (by simply adding the two weighted, standardized measures) these two measures both are, secondly, converted into standardized T-scores according to the formula

$$T = 50\frac{10\,(X_1 - \overline{X})}{s}$$

where X_1 represents the value of the variable (i.e., economic *or* social

* Arthur S. Banks and Robert B. Textor, *A cross-policy survey*. MIT Press, Cambridge (Mass.), 1963.

development), X the mean of that variable's distribution, and s its standard deviation (*Barrera & Haas*, 1969: 157). Like in the articulation index, the modernization scores are multiplied by one minus the mean deviation divided by the mean score of the bloc. Then the articulation measure is adjusted so as to bring it into the same range as the modernization scores.

This adjustment consisted of finding the means of the two distributions and then multiplying the ratio of larger mean to smaller mean by each of the scores in the smaller distribution. This transformed the small scores into roughly the same range as the larger ones, and they could then be added together (*Barrera & Haas*, 1969: 158).

Finally, the overall pluralism scores were computed by simply adding the final adjusted articulation and modernization measures.

An assessment of this pluralism measure is rendered difficult by the fact that Barrera and Haas only give a rather sketchy exposition of its construction. However, two of its more fundamental characteristics immediately strike the eye. In the first place, as has already been noted, it does not measure the number and variety of the units participating in the political life of the system. These are very important properties of the system, and they play a large role in the theory irrespective of the significance of the measures just discussed. Secondly, just as in the case of Haas's 'human rights observation scores', various arithmetical operations are performed on numbers, or, rather, 'numerals', that have not been defined so as to lend themselves to such operations (cf. p. 151 above). This applies in particular to the articulation scores which are basically judgmental in character, i.e., of an ordinal rather than a cardinal nature. This throws considerable doubt upon the entire pluralism index, of course.

Related to all this is the structure of the several communities involved in integration. Haas distinguishes in particular the character of the political system, economic development, and the character of economic institutions. As concerns the first element, here Haas distinguishes 'democratic', 'oligarchic', and 'totalitarian' political systems.

'*Democracy*' is considered to be the applicable political characterization of a state if there are agreed and regularly observed for peaceful change, if voluntary participation in politics on the basis of associational interest groups prevails, if free choice among two or more political parties is possible, and the rule of law is observed. A state is considered an *'oligarchy'* if there are no regularly observed rules of peaceful change, continuous participation in politics is limited to a small group of literate and/or wealthy citizens, the political scene is dominated by such institutional interest groups as the army, church, or bureaucracy, and if there is no consistent and reliable rule of law. (. . .) States are characterized as *'totalitarian'*, finally, if political leadership is monopolized by one group or party, peaceful change is possible within that group alone and not within any other actual or potential groups, mass participation in politics is compulsory and without choice of program or party, and the rule of law exists only within the limits of loyalty to the party and its programs (*Haas*, 1962b: 324-325) (my italics).

With respect to economic development states are distinguished as 'mature industrialized', 'rapidly industrializing', 'mature agricultural', and 'underdeveloped', as follows:

A *'mature industrialized state'* is characterized by a high or medium per capita GNP, a continuing high rate of investment, a preponderance of manufacturing in the total economy, and high technological inventiveness and adaptability. (. . .) A *'rapidly industrializing state'* possesses a medium or low per capita GNP, a very high rate of investment, a marked tendency to create new manufacturing facilities and to de-emphasize agriculture relative to industry, a managerial and administrative eagerness to adopt new techniques, and the likelihood of just having reached 'take-off'. (. . .) A *'mature agricultural state'* is characterized by a medium or high per capita GNP, a preponderance in the total economy of scientific and mechanized agriculture for export, high technological and managerial adaptability, and a rate of investment adequate to maintaining the position achieved. An economy is *'underdeveloped'* if per capita GNP is low or stagnant at a medium level, if there is very little or no capital investment, if there is little managerial or technological capacity or interest in acquiring it, and if the agricultural and/or mining sector is predominant and marked by low capital input (*Haas*, 1962b: 326) (my italics).

The economic structure of a community, thirdly, is classified as 'free enterprise', 'social welfare', 'communist', or 'corporatist':

A *'free enterprise economy'* prevails if the government, directly or indirectly, does not participate consistently in the growth of the economy, if there is no general interest in extensive social legislation, and if businessmen and farmers are expected to adjust to market forces. (...) A *'social welfare economy'*, however, prevails wherever the government seeks somehow to manipulate economic growth, where there is a general commitment to social legislation, where businessmen and farmers are deliberately cushioned against certain market forces. (...) A *'Communist' economic system* is characterized by the state's ownership and management of all major means of production, even if technically this is to be labeled 'state capitalism'. Finally, a *'corporatist economy'* prevails if business and labor groups, though permitted to exist, may influence economic life only through the medium of government-manipulated institutions, and if free market forces are not permitted unrestrained scope, in order to realize some doctrine of social harmony (*Haas*, 1962b: 326-327) (my italics).

While the above classifications and categories with respect to the character of the political communities involved in an integration process certainly seem to be interesting, it should be observed that their relevance for the theory as a whole has by no means been established in any unambiguous fashion. Actually, as may have appeared already from the discussion of section 4.4., this aspect of the theory has not been elaborated in great detail.

6. A BRIEF ASSESSMENT

One of the most striking characteristics of Haas's conception of the process of integration as it has emerged from the foregoing discussion is its generality. To be sure, Haas himself is concerned only with integration among states; that is, his empirical interpretation of the calculus developed in sections 3 and 4 was cast in terms of states, their structure, policies, constituent units, and the international organizations in which they participate. But, in fact, hardly anything in the abstract calculus would force us to choose just this particular interpretation. Thus, instead of in *inter*national terms, it could also be interpreted in *intra*national terms so as to make it fit processes of national integration. And, perhaps, it could even be applied to integrative processes at still lower levels – for example, those of provincial or municipal politics. Now, all this is not to deny that there may be important differences between integration processes at different levels or in different settings: the international political system will differ from intra-national systems; national governments are different from municipal governments; and the units participating at one level are generally different from those involved in politics at other levels, etc. The point is, however, that in its actual state of development Haas's conception of political integration seems to be wide and general enough to accommodate such differences. Actually it has appeared from the foregoing discussion that with regard to such questions as the definition of units and their behavior, that of the larger system or community in which they operate, and the classification of the differences that may exist between such units, systems, or communities, the theory has not been elaborated in great detail. This is a weakness in so far as it greatly limits its applicability in the study of any concrete process of integration. But on the other hand its generality and potentially wide applicability are brought out more clearly.

Haas's conception of the integration process, and in particular the way in which he conceives its inner dynamics, makes a strong impression of consistency and plausibility. Much less satisfactory, however, is the way he deals with the individual elements of that construction. As we have seen, questions regarding the character and significance of the central institution's functions, the various units involved in the integration process, their demands and support behavior, etc., are treated in a very incomplete fashion, if at all. This detracts considerably from the accuracy of the theory's explanation of integration. It only indicates the general lines along which an integration process might proceed. But it leaves open all questions regarding the degree to which the processes involved occur, the relative significance of the elements involved, the precise nature of the conditions under which the process does or does not occur, and so on.

The theory is clearly one about integration as a peaceful process. Virtually no attention is paid to physical violence and warfare. In itself this need not constitute a defect of the theory in so far as it does not purport to explain integration through military conquest. However, a certain amount of physical violence, or the threat of its use, presumably plays a certain role in other processes of integration as well. Between completely peaceful and voluntary integration and integration through outright conquest there is a variety of less clearcut cases – those of the formation of the European national states, for example. Consequently, a theory of political integration aiming at general applicability would certainly have to include an analysis of the role of physical violence, even when it is not intended for the explanation of military conquest as such.

In the theory relatively litlle attention is paid to the influence of events and processes outside of the integrating system upon developments within that system. That is, integration within a system constituted by a number of political communities is explained mainly in terms of what happens *within* that system, while more or less neglecting the role of what happens external to it (cf. *Kaiser*, 1968; see also *Haas*, 1968, author's preface). To a large extent, this relative neglect seems to be a consequence of the general incompleteness of Haas's treatment of the behavior of the various units involved in integration. For probably external events and processes will influence integration within a system primarily through the medium of the perceptions and reactions of the system's units. Accordingly, a more extensive analysis of the behavior of these units, and of the motives from which it springs, will in all probability lead to the inclusion of such external influences (see, e.g., *Haas*, 1961: 107-116; *Haas & Schmitter*, 1966: 288; *Barrera & Haas*, 1969: 152). In this connection it should also be recalled that Haas does not deal very detailedly with the problem of the origins of an integrative development. This is to say that the question why what units in what circumstances will demand integration goes largely unanswered.

The empirical interpretation of Haas's conception of the integration process is not very satisfactory either. In many cases rules to link the abstract concepts used to observations are lacking; and in so far such rules are given, they often lack precision. Thus the relation of the calculus developed to empirical reality remains to a large extent indeterminate. It is well-nigh impossible to test it, to confirm or falsify it. This puts Haas's 'revisions' of his theory (regarding the autonomy of functional contexts, and the limitation of 'pragmatic interest politics') in the proper light. Quite apart from the fact that these revisions or additions are far too little elaborated to be of much help, the above considerations throw doubt upon the justification for introducing them. For, in view of the relatively high degree of empirical indeterminateness of this theory, how could it possibly be observed that the theory were wrong and needed amendment? However, it should be added, the fact that the empirical interpretation is not definite and unequivocal enough for rigorous testing does not mean that the theory is altogether without empirical import. For, in fact, compared with the looseness of common discourse about these matters, the theory discussed often shows a definite advance in precision (cf. ch. 2 section 4.1).

BIBLIOGRAPHY

ANONYMOUS, 1966. *International political communities – an anthology.* Doubleday, Garden City (N.Y.).

BARRERA, Mario & Ernst B. HAAS, 1969. The operationalization of some variables related to regional integration – a research note. *Int. Orgn 23 (1)*: 150–160.

EASTON, David, 1965. *A systems analysis of political life.* Wiley, New York.

GRAUBARD, Stephen R. (Ed.), 1964. *A new Europe?* Houghton Mifflin/The Riverside Press, Boston/Cambridge.

HAAS, Ernst B., 1948. The United States of Europe – four approaches to the purpose and form of a European federation. *Polit. Sci. Q. 63 (4)*: 528–550.
HAAS, Ernst B., 1950. Imperialism and economic development in Asia. *J. int. Affairs 4 (2)*:
HAAS, Ernst B., 1953a. The attempt to terminate colonialism – acceptance of the United Nations trusteeship system. In: David A. Kay (Ed.), *The United Nations political system*, pp. 281–301. Wiley, New York, 1967.
HAAS, Ernst B., 1953b. The balance of power as a guide to policy-making. *J. Polit. 15 (3)*.
HAAS, Ernst B., 1953c. The balance of power – prescription, concept, or propaganda. In: James N. Rosenau (Ed.), *International politics and foreign policy – a reader in research and theory*, pp. 318–329. Free Press, New York, 1961.
HAAS, Ernst B., 1955. Types of collective security – an examination of operational concepts. *Am. polit. Sci. Rev. 49 (1)*.
HAAS, Ernst B., 1956. Regionalism, functionalism and universal international organization. *Wld Polit. 8 (2)*: 238–263.
HAAS, Ernst B., 1957. Regional integration and national policy. In: George A. Lanyi & Wilson C. McWilliams (Ed.), *Crisis and continuity in world politics – readings in international relations*, pp. 464–474. Random House, New York, 1966.
HAAS, Ernst B., 1958a. The challenge of regionalism. In: Stanley Hoffmann (Ed.), *Contemporary theory in international relations*, pp. 223–240. Prentice Hall, Englewood Cliffs (N.J.), 1960.

HAAS, Ernst B., 1958b. Persistent themes in Atlantic and European unity. *Wld Polit. 10 (4)*: 614–628.

HAAS, Ernst B., 1958c. *The uniting of Europe – political, social and economical forces, 1950–1957.* Stevens and Sons, London.

HAAS, Ernst B., 1960a. The comparative study of the United Nations. *Wld Polit. 12 (2)*: 298–322.

HAAS, Ernst B., 1960b. *Consensus formation in the Council of Europe.* Stevens and Sons, London.

HAAS, Ernst B., 1961. International integration – the European and the universal process. In: *International political communities – an anthology*, pp. 94–129. Doubleday, Garden City (N.Y.), 1966.

HAAS, Ernst B., 1962a. Dynamic environment and static system – revolutionary regimes in the United Nations. In: Morton A. Kaplan (Ed.), *The revolution in world politics*, pp. 267–309. Wiley, New York.

HAAS, Ernst B., 1962b. System and process in the Internation Labour Organization – a statistical afterthought. *Wld Polit. 14 (2)*: 322–352.

HAAS, Ernst B., 1964a. *Beyond the nation-state – functionalism and international organization.* Stanford University Press, Stanford (Cal.).

HAAS, Ernst B., 1964b. Technocracy, pluralism and the new Europe. In: Stephen R. Graubard (Ed.), *A new Europe?*, pp. 62–88. Houghton Mifflin/Riverside Press, Boston/Cambridge.

HAAS, Ernst B., 1964c. Toward controlling international change – a personal plea. *Wld Polit. 17 (1)*: 1-12.

HAAS, Ernst B., 1967. The uniting of Europe and the uniting of Latin America. *J. common Market Stud. 5 (4)*: 315–343.

HAAS, Ernst B., 1968. *The uniting of Europe – political, social and economic forces, 1950-1957*, 2nd impression, with a new preface by the author. Stanford University Press, Stanford (Cal.).

HAAS, Ernst B., 1969. *Tangle of hopes – American commitments and world order.* Prentice-Hall, Englewood Cliffs (N.J.).

HAAS, Ernst B. & Peter H. MERKL, 1960. Parliamentarians against ministers – the case of the WEU. *Int. Orgn 14 (1)*: 37–59.

HAAS, Ernst B. & Philippe C. SCHMTTER, 1965. *The politics of economics in Latin American regionalism – the Latin American Free Trade Association after four years of operation. Monogr. Ser. Wld Affairs 3.* University of Denver, Denver (Col.).

HAAS, Ernst B. & Philippe C. SCHMTTER, 1966. Economics and differential patterns of political integration – projections about unity in Latin America. In: *International political communities – an anthology*, pp. 259–299. Doubleday, Garden City (N.Y.).

HAAS, Ernst B. & Allen S. WHITING, 1956. *Dynamics of international relations.* McGraw-Hill, New York.

HANSEN, Roger D., 1969. Regional integration – reflections on a decade of theoretical efforts. *Wld Polit. 21 (2)*: 242–271.

HOFFMANN, Stanley (Ed.), 1960. *Contemporary theory in international relations.* Prentice-Hall, Englewood Cliffs (N.J.).

HOFFMANN, Stanley, 1963. Discord in community – the North Atlantic area as a partial international system. In: Francis O. Wilcox and H. Field Haviland (Ed.), *The Atlantic community – progress and prospects,* pp. 3–51. Praeger, New York/London.

HOFFMANN, Stanley, 1964a. Europe's identity crisis – between the past and America. *Daedalus 93 (4):* 1244–1297.

HOFFMANN, Stanley, 1964b. The European process at Atlantic cross purposes. *J. common Market Stud. 3 (2):* 85–101.

HOFFMANN, Stanley, 1964c. De Gaulle, Europe, and the Atlantic alliance. *Int. Orgn. 18 (1):* 1–28.

HOFFMANN, Stanley, 1966. Obstinate or obsolete? – the fate of the nation-state and the case of Western Europe. *Daedalus 95 (3):* 862–915.

KAISER, Karl, 1967. The U.S. and the E.E.C. in the Atlantic system – the problem of theory. *J. Common Market Stud. 5 (4):* 388–425.

KAISER, Karl, 1968. The interaction of regional subsystems – some preliminary notes on recurrent patterns and the role of superpowers. *Wld Polit. 21 (1):* 84–107.

KAPLAN, Morton A. (Ed.), 1962. *The revolution in world politics.* Wiley, New York.

KAY, David A. (Ed.), 1967. The United Nations Political system. Wiley, New York.

LANYI, George A. & Wilson C. MCWILLIAMS (Ed.), 1966. *Crisis and continuity in world politics – readings in internation relations.* Random House, New York.

ROSENAU, James N., 1966. Transforming the international system – small increments along a vast periphery. *Wld Polit. 18 (3):* 524–545.

ROSENAU, James N. (Ed.), 1961. *International politics and foreign policy – a reader in research and theory.* Free Press, New York.

SCHMITTER, Philippe C. & Ernst B. HAAS, 1964. *Mexico and Latin American economic integration.* Institute of International Studies, University of California, Berkeley.

TAYLOR, Paul, 1968. The concept of community and the European integration process. *J. common Market Stud. 7 (2):* 83–101.

1. INTRODUCTION

1.1. *A new language of politics*

Deutsch's work, perhaps even more so than that of Haas, is highly characteristic of the development of political science in general during recent decades. As noted several times before, this development is characterized chiefly by a transition from pre-scientific, speculative, and normative modes of thinking to more strictly empirical ways of inquiring into political life. Concomitant with this is an intensive search for a new vocabulary and for new ways to represent politics so as to make it more amenable to research. This search is not yet concerned primarily with the formation of theory in the proper sense of that word; rather it consists mainly of attempts to develop a vocabulary and a set of concepts in terms of which, it is hoped, theory construction will be possible eventually.

Deutsch's work can best be understood in the light of this relatively early stage of scientific development – as one great attempt to develop a new language of politics. In doing so he does not feel himself to be bound to political science as delimited traditionally or to any one of its more or less current conceptual schemes. On the contrary, he consciously explores other fields and disciplines in search of schemes and lines of reasoning which might be applied in political science. The result is quite fascinating and highly stimulating. On the other hand, the variety of approaches and terminologies which he applies and that of the levels of analysis at which he moves, render his work somewhat inaccessible, the more so since he is not an extremely rigorous thinker. Thus, intertwined with purely political considerations or detailed historical narration we meet with highly abstract cybernetic or communication-theoretical reasoning, and with general sociological analyses in which sometimes a Parsonian terminology is used. Often, however, such analyses are not elaborated in sufficient detail and with sufficient precision so as to enable us to judge their ultimate political applicability and relevance. At the same time the interrelationships between such distinct pieces of analysis are frequently left unspecified or they are only hinted at in loose and general terms.

Accordingly, before proceeding with the analysis of Deutsch's views on politics and on political integration, it will first be necessary to deal with some of his more general sociological and cybernetic insights (section 1.2). This may serve to put his political analyses into a proper perspective, and to avoid errors resulting from mixing up levels of analysis, problems, or conceptual schemes.

1.2.   *Cybernetics and 'sociology'*

Deutsch is keenly aware of the basic limitations of some of the main conceptions which have played a role in the historical development of the social sciences. He recognizes three such conceptions:

All three classical concepts were found to have major shortcomings. Mechanism cannot represent evolution; organisms are incapable of extensive rearrangement; models of historical processes have thus far lacked inner structure and quantitative predictability (*Deutsch*, 1952: 358; in the same sense *Deutsch*, 1963b: 38; see also *Deutsch*, 1948, 1951a, b).

As against this he thinks to have found in cybernetics a conceptual scheme lacking the weaknesses mentioned, one that is capable of accommodating such things as evolution, change, adaptation, and learning. Furthermore, he thinks it is possible to measure one of the most important cybernetic concepts, namely 'information', thus making for a quantitative theory. Accordingly, it seems attractive to try to conceive political problems in terms of communication and information, and political systems as cybernetic systems.

After the general discussion of systems analysis and cybernetics in chapter two (section 3.5) it is not necessary to deal with the general features of cybernetic analysis here. But it should be recalled that this mode of analysis is of an extremely general and abstract nature and that its application is any one particular setting, such as that of social life in general or of politics, requires its interpretation in terms of the domain to which it is applied. Thus, concepts such as 'system', 'steering', 'communication', 'information', 'environment', 'input', 'output', etc., should receive a meaning adequate to the domain for which their use is intended. The fact that such extremely important terms as 'communication' and 'information' do have a relatively well-established meaning in everyday discourse is of no avail in any sociological or political analysis in cybernetic terms. Failure to make the proper distinctions here will inevitably lead inquiry astray.

There is a certain connection between the concepts of 'communication' and 'information' as they occur in cybernetics and those of everyday life. To a certain extent this connection accounts for the importance Deutsch ascribes to these concepts, and probably it is one of the reasons why he finds cybernetics so attractive. For, it would seem, in ordinary life information and communication are concerned with knowledge of some sort and with its transmission. 'Knowledge' should here be taken in a very broad sense, including both scientific and non-scientific knowledge, and knowledge of a normative character, concerning values, preferences, etc. Perhaps its meaning could best be rendered as, roughly, 'intellectual or mental stimuli'. Now, one might say, in so far as man is not a machine which mechanically and purely automatically reacts to electrical and chemical impulses, it is especially these mental stimuli, 'knowledge', that are important in explaining man's individual and social behavior. This suggests that the cybernetic concepts of 'information' and 'communication' can indeed be given something of a psychological or social interpretation. Accordingly, Deutsch conceives human consciousness as an information-processing system (*Deutsch*, 1953c: 170; 1963b: 98ff.).

But it should be noted that in thus interpreting information and communication with the help of their ordinary meanings in human social life, we are moving at an extremely high level of abstraction and generality. Probably this interpretation of information and communication is much too wide and general to be of much use in actual research. Depending upon the problem investigated, or the character of the discipline within which it is to be investigated, the stimuli in question will have to be specified much more narrowly. Nevertheless, the above considerations may aid in understanding the rationale of Deutsch's most general, or 'sociological', analyses.

In most general terms Deutsch conceives of social life as consisting of people that interact. Interacting does not proceed wholly arbitrarily and randomly, but it shows certain more or less stable patterns, structures, and discontinuities. Accordingly, as a first step, human groups of any kind whatsoever might be characterized as particular local densities in the total web of interactions or transactions, in the sense that their members interact more with each other than with outsiders (*Deutsch*, 1953c: 36 ff.; 1968b: 75).

In this way, one may say, groups are defined in a purely statistical sense. Obviously, such a concept is insufficient to give an account of many of the most important features of actual human groups and societies. For example, the fact that such groups often display a remarkable stability and longevity, that they sometimes exhibit a high degree of cohesion, and that they may be very successful in performing common tasks both internally and externally. In order to explain such phenomena, a more specific concept is needed. And as Deutsch assumes that the stability, cohesion, organization, and the ability to perform common tasks of a human group requires a certain capacity to transmit information in the sense just described (cf. *Deutsch*, 1953c: 96; 1963b: 77; 1952: 367; 1953a: 273), it seems obvious that this new concept should be defined in terms of communication. Thus he introduces the general concept of 'community' as '. . . a group of persons who are able to communicate information to each other effectively over a wide range of topics' (*Deutsch*, 1953b: 169). Often, too, he uses the term 'people' which denotes essentially the same thing, namely '*A larger group of persons linked by such complementary habits and facilities of communication*' (*Deutsch*, 1953c: 96; see also *Deutsch*, 1953b: 169 and 1968b: 77-78). He also introduces the concept of 'culture', denoting an important regulatory mechanism in social life.

No terminology should try to be more accurate than life. 'Culture' and 'community' can be used interchangeably because they describe a single complex of processes. When we say 'culture', we stress the configuration of preferences or values; when we say 'community' we stress aspects of communication . . . (*Deutsch*, 1953c: 89).

This, however, seems to be rather unfortunate. For a configuration of values of preferences is something different from a communication structure. Conceived in terms of values and preferences, culture is a somewhat narrower concept than communication, and its theoretical function is different from that of the communication concept. While it may be understood as a particular form of information, and while it, too, is communicated, it also appears to be one of the major determinants of the flow of communication in any system.

In juxtaposition to the concept of 'community' Deutsch also introduces that of 'society'. But while the former is a relatively clear concept, the latter remains somewhat obscure. Thus he defines it in terms of the 'production, selection, and channelling of goods and services' (*Deutsch*, 1953c: 92); as 'a group of persons who have learned to work together' (*Deutsch*, 1953b: 169); or as 'a group of individuals united by the division of labor' (*Deutsch*, 1953c: 29). Moreover, a 'country' is described as 'a geographic area of greater economic interdependence' (*Deutsch*, 1953b: 169; 1968b: 76). Deutsch's ideas here show a markedly economic bias. Apparently, 'society' is that aspect of a human group (in the statistical sense described above) which consists of productive relations in the economic sense of that word. It is concerned with the sphere of the group's natural and human resources and their exploitation. Probably it is to be conceived as an economic interpretation of the generic concept of 'community'.

The concepts 'nation' and 'state', on the other hand, are of a more distinctly political character. A 'nation' is defined as 'a people which has gained control over some institutions of social coercion' (*Deutsch*, 1953b: 169), and a 'state' is 'an area within which certain laws can be enforced' (*Deutsch*, 1968b: 79). Disregarding the geographical dimension introduced here (as in the case of the concept 'country'), what is intended here is plainly a particular political interpretation of the 'community' concept. It should be noted, though, that this is only a first and approximative interpretation. Later we will meet with a political interpretation of the 'community' concept which is both more general and more precise, one in which the nature of the communication process involved is defined more sharply.

It should be recalled that in this subsection we are moving on an extremely high level of abstraction: social groups are first defined in purely statistical terms, while it is further indicated that on the basis of different interpretations of the concept of 'communication' ('sociological', economic, political) different conceptions of group life emerge. In this same context and at this same level of analysis, Deutsch also

shows an inclination to apply Parsonian language. To a large extent
this language exhibits the same pattern as what has been described thus
far (see *Deutsch*, 1963b: 116 ff.; 1968a: 14 ff.; 1964e).

Following Parsons, Deutsch conceives social life in terms of a social
system which is not defined *a priori* according to any one particular
criterion such as a political or economic one. For such a system to
exist and endure, four functions must be performed: 1. *pattern maintenance*, 2. *adaptation*, 3. *goal attainment*, and 4. *integration* (*Deutsch*,
1964e: 183). These functions, in turn, determine four different subsystems, each one of them fulfilling one function with regard to the
system as a whole, which together constitute the total social system.
Roughly, these subsystems can be identified with 'families', the 'economy', the 'political system', and 'culture', respectively (*Deutsch*, 1964e:
189). It should be noted that later Deutsch introduces two additional
functions, namely 'goal setting' and 'self-transformation' (*Deutsch*,
1968a: 15-17).

The different subsystems are interconnected. They are coupled in the
sense that the output of one of them serves as an input into one or
more of the others. Thus, families supply the economy with labor power
in exchange for income; they feed demands and support into the political system in exchange for certain political decisions, etc. In order to
facilitate such transactions, there may emerge certain standardized
means of exchange – *currencies*:

. . . transactions are made much more flexible and general by a social mechanism that is 'narrowly specialized in generality'. Such a mechanism we may
call a *currency* (*Deutsch*, 1963b: 117).

Thus money may be conceived as such a currency, while Deutsch also regards 'power' as such (*Deutsch*, 1963b: 120-122; 1968a: 41-42). Also,
with regard to the transactions between the subsystems, he applies
Parsons' well-known pattern variables (*Deutsch*, 1964e: 202 ff.).

All this has not been elaborated sufficiently to be of much help in
further investigation. Both with regard to the 'sociological' interpretation of cybernetics and the Parsonian approach with which we have
dealt in this subsection, the problem is rather the development of a
vocabulary than the formation of a theory in the strict sense. The high-
level considerations which have been sketched in this subsection can

perhaps best be seen as a matrix from which Deutsch's specifically political analyses emerge. Thus, the political system is merely one particular social communication system, the political process just one among many conceivable social communication processes, or merely one aspect of the social system conceived in Parsonian terms. It is only with politics that I shall be concerned for the rest of this chapter, while the other systems, processes, or aspects mentioned will only enter the analysis in so far as they are necessary to explain politics.

1.3. *Some notes on sources and Deutsch's theoretical development*

From the bibliography of this chapter (which contains most, but by no means all, of Deutsch's publications) it will be clear that Deutsch is an extremely prolific writer. Obviously, it is impossible to adequately summarize the whole of this voluminous production in a few sentences, or even in an introductory section such as the present one. Consequently, I shall limit myself to a few comments of a general nature and to drawing the reader's attention to a few of what I conceive to be his most important publications.

These publications, then, range over a period of some 25 years, and cover a comparatively large number and variety of topics. Since the early fifties, however, the dominant themes of this *oeuvre* have been politics and communications. Viewed as a whole, it displays a somewhat disappointing lack of progress and development. That is, to a large extent the substance of Deutsch's thinking can already be found in such comparatively early publications as *Nationalism and social communication* (Deutsch, 1953c), *Political community at the international level* (1954c), 'On communication models in the social sciences' (1952), 'Communication in self-governing organizations' (1953a), and 'The growth of nations' (1953b). Compared with these, his later publications do not in general really add much to the theory. They round off, or summarize, often reformulate, what has been developed earlier without, however, fundamentally changing or developing it. This applies especially to this *The nerves of government* (Deutsch, 1963b), *The analysis of international relations* (1968a), and to *Nationalism and its alternatives* (1969). But, it should be noted, these works, and in particular the first one, are indispensable precisely because they offer a comprehensive picture of what went before.

Actually, it is rather striking that Deutsch's later writings generally remain at the same level of abstraction, generality, and, it must be admitted, imprecision, as his earlier ones. The theory, though already substantially developed in his early writings, is not very much elaborated, refined, or rendered more exact and precise in his later publications.

The character of his empirical research, however, perhaps offers a clue to the explanation of the peculiarly static character of Deutsch's theoretical development just noted. For very often the link between his empirical research and the theoretical part of his inquiries is rather tenuous. Such research, it seems, has generally been undertaken in a very early stage of theoretical development, without his being sufficiently clear, that is, about its relevance or significance, about the place where and the way in which it fits into the theory as a whole. To do so would have required a much more detailed elaboration of the abstract reasoning involved. As noted, however, such elaboration is precisely what is largely lacking. Consequently, his investigations often seem to be guided by a somewhat crude empiricism – just measure and gather 'data', and important insights and relevations will spring forth automatically. Perhaps, however, it is fairer to say that his empirical research is typically explorative: meant less to apply and test some developed line of reasoning than to just see and discover what categories and schemes might be developed. Even so, one might well wonder whether a more intensive elaboration of the abstract reasoning contained in the early publications mentioned above would not have been both feasible and conducive to a greater theoretical yield of the empirical research done.

It remains to be noted that, like the investigations of Haas, those of Deutsch into political integration and into politics generally, concern a wide variety of historical and geographical settings. This suggests that the significance of what has been found and developed is not *a priori* restricted to any one particular political situation or configuration. And with special regard to the phenomenon of political integration, it also gives some indication as to the fundamental import of the problems involved.

2. POLITICS

2.1. *Outline of this section*

In this section on Deutsch's general conception of the political process, I will first deal with what he conceives to be the essence of politics (section 2.2); in section 2.3 I will discuss the political interpretation of his cybernetic vocabulary.

2.2. *Politics – demands, support, binding decisions; two postulates*

Deutsch defines the concept of 'politics' as follows:

Politics consists of the more or less incomplete control of human behavior through voluntary habits of *compliance* in combination with threats of probable *enforcement*. In its essence, politics is based on the interplay of these two things: habits and threats (*Deutsch*, 1967b: 232).

Interpreting the generic concept of 'community', discussed in section 1.2, in political terms gives us the concept 'political community', which is defined as

... a community of social transaction supplemented by both enforcement and compliance. In this sense, it is a community of persons in which common or coordinated facilities for the making of decisions and the enforcement of commands are supplemented by habits of compliance sufficiently widespread and predictable to make successful enforcement in the remaining cases of noncompliance probable at an economically and culturally feasible cost (*Deutsch*, 1954c: 40).

Both definitions together provide a sufficiently clear picture of what Deutsch understands by 'politics'.

In its essence, politics is apparently concerned with the control of human behavior; that is, decisions are taken which are accepted as binding by the participants in some political situation, either voluntarily or involuntarily through threats of enforcement. It is to be noted that Deutsch's definition allows for a very extensive interpretation of politics. Apart from the fact that we are obviously concerned with social life, the definition contains no further restrictions. Politics does not solely occur in just one particular social setting such as a state, but also in other human groups, or in the relations between them, for instance in international affairs.

Binding decisions do not occur in a void, of course. In order to explain them, Deutsch (much like Haas, incidentally) relates them to the same concepts as does Easton. His language, however, is somewhat less definite. Thus he uses the terms 'demands', 'interests', and 'needs' (cf. *Deutsch*, 1954c: 43-44; 1964b: 71; *Deutsch & Weilenmann*, 1964: 393; *Deutsch*, 1964e: 198). For the most part these notions can be treated as equivalent in his writings. For the sake of economy and clarity I will henceforth use only the term 'demand' in this context. Deutsch's own intentions, it seems, can be approximated most closely by conceiving such demands as the expressions of proposals for certain preferred binding decisions on the part of one or several of the participants in some political situation. The terms 'needs' and 'interests' (cf. *Deutsch*, 1968a: 51) could then be reserved for a 'deeper' level of analysis, namely in order to account for the voicing of certain demands by individual or groups. A demand, viewed as a proposal for some binding decision, in turn, derives from certain needs or interests.

However, to demand something does not result automatically in its being effectuated in the form of an actual binding decision. In order to explain this side of the matter Deutsch generally applies the concept of 'support', without, however, defining it explicitly. The way he uses it, however, suggests that 'support' concerns agreement with, or the willingness to behave in accordance with, decisions taken or to be taken, while disagreement with, or resistance to such decisions might be viewed as negative support. It goes without saying that support need not be given voluntarily; it may be induced through threats and coercion.

With these concepts politics can now be viewed as a kind of exchange process in which demands and support are converted into binding decisions, so that binding decisions in conformity with certain demands are taken in exchange for support. In this context Deutsch seems to apply two postulates of which at least the second one also appeared in Haas. *First*, a demand implies an offer of support; and, *second*, the extent to which support is given is determined by the extent to which demands are met in the decision taken or proposed. Thus a binding decision can be achieved by making it meet such demands as induce a sufficient measure of support (*Deutsch*, 1964e: 198). Or, as it is phrased in *The nerves of government*:

As regards the political system, households may be considered in the most simple case as making specific demands upon the political system. They offer specific support to rulers who in turn use this support to make and enforce binding decisions of the kind desired by their supporters. Thus, in effect, specific support appears exchanged for dependable specific decisions, responsive to specific demands, in a political analogy to economic barter (*Deutsch*, 1963b: 118).

Deutsch's conception of politics in general seems to be clear enough by now. Its further elaboration can proceed more appropriately in the context of the political interpretation of his cybernetic analysis.

2.3. *Political cybernetics; some postulates on learning*

After the foregoing the political interpretation of the key terms in the cybernetic vocabulary need not involve really fundamental difficulties. Apparently, political information consists of three different components: demands, support, and binding decisions.

A political system, then, should be conceived as a configuration of (political) information relationships in which demands and support (the information input) are converted into binding decisions (the information output). Its environment, made up of all those factors which together determine the nature of the information fed into the system, will in turn be modified by the system's binding decisions thus inducing modifications in the flow of demands and support that is put into the system. This is called feedback. It should be recalled (ch. two, section 3.5) that such a system should be conceived as a purely analytical category not to be identified in advance with any existing political entity, for example a 'state'.

A (political) system needs the organs or facilities to collect and to take in information (receptors), that is, demands and support. This function is performed by individuals, groups, or institutions, such as political parties, private interest groups, parliaments, etc.. The system also needs effectors, i.e., the facilities to implement and carry out its binding decisions. This function is typically performed by bureaucracies.

No communication system could be completely open in the sense that it could take in any information whatsoever from its environment. A system which would not proceed selectively and which would not limit its input would soon break down under the impact of information from the environment whose amount is, in principle, infinite. Consequently, the system needs certain rules which enable it to reject certain information as, for instance, 'wrong', 'absurd', or 'undesired', and thus to limit the incoming flow of information. Embodying certain priorities and preferences, such rules are also required to make the communication process reliable and dependable. In Deutsch's words:

The efficient functioning of any complex switchboard requires, therefore, some relatively stable operating rules, explicit or implied in the arrangements of the channels. These rules must decide the relative preferences and priorities in the reception, screening, and routing of all signals entering the network from outside or originating within it (*Deutsch*, 1963b: 94).

Through feedback processes such rules can be modified, of course (*Deutsch*, 1963b: 95).

The operation of this mechanism is clearly illustrated by the diagram which Deutsch has added to his *The nerves of government*. Here we find a selective screen in every major step in the communication process, symbolizing the operation of the rules described above (*Deutsch*, 1963b: 258). As is indicated in the above quotation, a distinction may be introduced between, on the one hand, the selective function or effect of the system's *structure* (the 'arrangements of the channels') and the system's more or less explicit *rules* on the other hand. And perhaps it is not too far-fetched to identify this latter component with the political system's *culture*, which is defined as

. . . a common set of stable, habitual preferences and priorities in men's attention, and behavior, as well as in their thoughts and feelings (*Deutsch*, 1953c: 88).

'Culture' would thus become one of the main mechanisms by means of which the system's communication processes are regulated. Consequently, it is difficult to see how a political system, let alone a stable and durable one, could exist without a certain common political culture.

The information fed into the political system, i.e., demands and support, after selection and combination with other information stored in the system's memory (of which culture is an important ingredient) has to be converted into binding decisions. This occurs in the system's *decision area*.

A decision area may be pictured as one where incoming messages are combined with recalled memories for determining the output of the system (*Deutsch*, 1964b: 62).

Such decision areas may be more or less institutionalized as in the case of the governments of states, but they need not be so. Thus, in international life both political systems and their decision areas often show a rather low degree of institutionalization. Actually there is a very wide variety of forms ranging from such things as the Concert of Europe in the nineteenth century, via present-day international organizations, to highly integrated national states. Deutsch's concept of 'political community', discussed in section 2.2, can be regarded as a comparatively highly institutionalized political system. The decision area functions as the political system's steering mechanism. It is here that the system's responses to its environment are determined; and it is here that the system's goals are selected, and that such behavior is chosen as is expected to realize those goals (cf. *Deutsch*, 1963b: 91).

The above leads to a question which is of major theoretical importance: given some political system, why are demands and support fed to some one particular decision area rather than to some other one, or that a decision area acquires the capacity to function effectively?

In the last subsection it appears that a demand implies an offer of support, and that such support depends upon the extent to which binding decisions meet such demands. Accordingly, it would seem obvious to assume that demands will be directed at those decision areas from which satisfactory decisions are expected.

This may be viewed also from the other side, that is, from the decision area itself. In this context Deutsch uses the concept 'authority'.

A *source* of messages that receives habitual preferential treatment as regards attention, transmission, and obedience in politics or social life may be said to possess *authority* (*Deutsch*, 1963b: 179).

Recalling that 'obedience' can be rendered in terms of support, this ('authority') can be interpreted as meaning the extent to which support is fed into the decision area in question. Deutsch also sometimes uses the concept 'legitimacy', without however very clearly defining it (e.g. in *Deutsch* et al., 1957: 8). As the concept of 'authority' is cast in terms of *habitual* preferential treatment, it may perhaps be conceived to also encompass the traditional notion of 'legitimacy' as a form of support *not* bound to the substance of *specific* demands and decisions. Or 'legitimacy' could be said to denote the extent to which some decision area's mere existence is thought to be right and proper, i.e., is supported.

How then does a particular decision area acquire authority and legitimacy? The two postulates mentioned before may explain how some specific decision is brought about and is supported. But it is of the essence of both authority and legitimacy as conceived by Deutsch that they involve support which is *not* thus bound to the nature of specific demands, and this cannot simply be explained by the postulates mentioned. In order to account for such more generalized support, Deutsch introduces another postulate. As follows:

When the decisions are acceptable to a certain number of individuals, general support for the government tends to increase. Making specific demands upon a government implies some offer of specific support. *If specific demands are met with reasonable frequency, given some threshold value, then generalized loyalty on the part of the population results.* The art of government consists in finding enough groups for whom specific demands can be met sufficiently so as to generalize loyalty to government and support for its role of responsibility for goal attainment in society (*Deutsch*, 1964e: 198) (my italics).

This may be conceived as a learning process. In this context Deutsch, seeking to apply some insights of psychological learning theory, formulates a few more specific assumptions:

... if people have experienced a high level of transactions, with substantial joint rewards at one time, they may be quite willing to accept joint deprivations at a later time, provided joint rewards come again still later.

... a group of people taught to identify with each other by means of initial joint rewards but then reinforced by a probabilistic mixture of joint rewards and joint deprivations will show greater cohesion and greater strength of habit than a group of people who have experienced nothing but joint rewards.

... rewards must become before the penalties, and rewards must be strong and frequent enough to initiate the habit (*Deutsch*, 1964b: 55).

This learning process, finally, requires a high degree of 'specificity'. Rewards and penalties must be clear and unambiguous.

Only by consolidating success and achievement along very specific lines will it be likely that enough habits and expectations are built up by the populations to then permit the establishment of a broad, diffuse government (*Deutsch*, 1964e: 207).

Unfortunately, however, Deutsch does not elaborate the above, and he does not employ the postulates in the construction of a more extensive argument. Accordingly the above should be regarded as a mere indication of a line of reasoning whose power has not yet been established.

We should further ask what determines the character of the system's input. In other words, how is the system's environment constituted, what factors, in what way, determine which demands or what support behavior is fed into the political system? In fact, we have already met with one such factor, namely culture. Presumably, however, many more things are relevant. Thus, certain social, economic, or technological developments might affect the interests or needs of individuals or groups. And this, in turn, will conceivably lead to changes in the character and/or amount of those actor's demands and support behavior. More generally, the problem is what causes demands and support behavior, and changes therein, and also what is the relative significance of various kinds of input in terms of such environmental factors. What, for example, is the significance of economic, industrial, or intellectual 'power' or of social status?

In general, Deutsch does not deal with these questions in a systematic and detailed fashion. To be sure, he often shows an awareness of the problems involved (e.g. *Deutsch*, 1954c: 39; 1961: 493 ff.; 1964b: 71; *Deutsch & Eckstein*, 1961: 270-271). But he does not develop elaborate analyses. Nor does he deal systematically with the relationships one may suspect to exist between, for example, the character of demands and that of support and the nature of the resulting decisions. It will be clear that in this situation we cannot acquire anything but the vaguest and most general insight into the feedback process, and the system's learning.

A system's existence and endurance implies the achievement of a certain relationship between it and its environment. More generally, a system will have goals (of which self-preservation may be one), i.e., it seeks to establish certain relationships with the environment (*Deutsch*, 1963b: 91 ff.). In order to do so, however, the system requires 'power' or 'capabilities' enabling it to influence the character of the environment, to prevail over it, or to overcome adverse developments in it. The terms 'power' and 'capabilities' or 'capacity' are, for all intents and purposes, equivalent in Deutsch's writings. Here, however, I shall generally prefer the term 'capacity'. Deutsch defines as follows:

Gross power can be thought of as the probability of a system acting out its internal program by imposing a given amount of changes upon the environment; and net power can be derived from this as the difference between the probability of these changes imposed on the outside world, and the probability of another critical or relevant amount of changes occurring in the inner structure of the system (*Deutsch*, 1963b: 111; see also *Deutsch*, 1968a: 22).

He also writes:

In an extended sense, we might define power (or 'strength', if another word is wanted) as the ability to act out a particular preference in behavior, or to reach a particular goal, *with the least loss of ability to choose a different behavior*, or to seek a different goal. Power in this extended sense is thus related not merely to the absence of imposed modification of behavior but also to the economy of commitment, and to the capacity for alternative commitments in the future (*Deutsch*, 1963b: 248; see also *Deutsch*, 1953c: 72-73).

In its essence, we are concerned here with the system's capacity to reach its goals despite a varying input from the environment, and this, in turn, implies learning. Accordingly, Deutsch writes:

More strictly speaking, what we are dealing with here might be called *learning capacity*: the ability of an individual or an organization to reallocate or recommit a large part of its resources to new uses, without destroying the organization as a whole (*Deutsch*, 1953c: 82).

It should further be noted that more recently he has developed a set of four categories purporting to make a more precise assessment of an actor's power possible; as follows:

The weight of the power or influence of an actor over some process is the extent to which he can change the probability of its outcome (*Deutsch*, 1968a: 24).

... the *domain* of power – the set of persons whose probable behavior is significantly changed by its application (*Deutsch*, 1968a: 28).

... the *range* of power (. . .) is the difference between the highest reward (or 'indulgence') and the worst punishment (or 'deprivation') which a power-holder can bestow (or inflict) upon some person in his domain (*Deutsch*, 1968a: 32).

By the scope of power we mean the set or collection of all the particular kinds or classes of behavior relations and affairs that are effectively subjected to it (*Deutsch*, 1968a: 34; cf. also *Lasswell & Kaplan*, 1950: 73 ff.).

What determines the capacity of a system? Deutsch recognizes three categories of factors:

In the long run, the strength or adaptability or 'learning capacity' of an organization may be expected to increase with three elements:
1. The total amount and variety of resources available to it;
2. The ease or speed with which these resources can be recommitted from one employment to another, without disrupting the essential minimum complementarity within the organization; and
3. The range of new patterns for recommitments available to the organization.

The first of these three factors is a matter of physical intake or receptivity, or of the ability to establish new channels of communications and control. The second is a matter of internal organization and reorganization. The third is a matter of 'invisible intake', of receptivity to new patterns of information, and of the ability not merely to store them, but to allocate on occasion physical resources to act on them (*Deutsch*, 1953c: 82-83).

Although he seems to conceive 'resources' chiefly as physical resources, in view of the political interpretation of the above it seems advisable to choose a somewhat wider conception. In particular it seems justified to consider the authority and legitimacy of the system's decision area, too, as resource. For these obviously help to determine the system's capacity vis-à-vis the environment. Such a wider interpretation also seems to link up better with Deutsch's conception of 'mobilization' and its relation to the system's capacity.

Social mobilization can be defined, therefore, as a process in which major clusters of old social, economic and psychological commitments are eroded or broken down and people become available for new patterns of socialization and behavior (*Deutsch*, 1961: 494).

And:

Generally, increases in capabilities require increasing social mobilization of the people (*Deutsch*, 1952: 453).

However, the effect of social mobilization cannot be predicted unambiguously, at least not on the basis of what has been said thus far alone. For such mobilization will also increase the amount and variety of demands fed into the political system: the information load will increase. And in order to cope with this increase, the system will need a higher capacity, or break down (cf. *Deutsch*, 1952: 453). In the absence of more information the result of mobilization is accordingly unpredictable. Deutsch offers a rather weak suggestion for a solution:

... the stage of rapid social mobilization may be expected, therefore, to promote the consolidation of states whose peoples already share the same language, culture, and major social institutions; while the same process may tend to strain or destroy the unity of states whose population is already divided into several groups with different languages or cultures or basic ways of life (*Deutsch*, 1961: 501).

It would seem justified to formulate this relationship in a somewhat wider sense and in terms of capacity: above a certain capacity mobilization will result in an increase of that capacity, while below that initial capacity it will tend to decrease that capacity.

Internal organization, in the second place, is concerned with the facilities to transmit (political) communication speedily and adequately. With regard to a political community Deutsch writes accordingly:

Its participants or participating groups must have continued and effective facilities for receiving signals concerning the most urgent needs of their partners, and for making responses sufficiently quick and appropriate to avoid serious conflicts or collisions (*Deutsch*, 1954c: 43).

And concerning governments:

To elicit full identification and loyalty, therefore, a government must be to a considerable extent accessible and predictable. It must be accessible to the questions, problems, needs, desires, and communications of its subjects; its office must be accessible to personnel recruited from their ranks; the minds of its decision-makers must remain open to the hopes, fears, and wishes of the population; and their commands and actions must be predictable in their impact on the lives and fortunes of its citizens (*Deutsch*, 1954b: 500).

The third element determining the capacity of a system ('receptivity to new patterns of information'), finally, may be interpreted as the system's capacity to take in, or to generate, new demands and support combinations. Perhaps the system, through its actions with regard to the environment, even could consciously steer or influence the emergence of such new inputs.

At any rate, a political system which could not take in and process new demands and support would presumably soon die from ossification.

It will be clear that the foregoing represents merely the barest outline of an answer to the question what determines the capacity of a political system. Many questions remain unanswered. For example, what resources give how much capacity, and in what way exactly? What is the exact meaning of the concept 'internal organization' of a system, and how precisely does it influence capacity? Also, how are we to determine the amount and composition of the system's input? This is not to say, of course, that Deutsch himself should, or even could, have provided solutions for all these questions. It merely serves to draw the attention to important gaps in the analysis, to indicate a few research problems, and to prevent unwarranted satisfaction with a few suggestive phrases.

Whether or not a system will actually reach its goals does not solely depend upon the system's capacity. For, apart from this capacity, this is determined by four other factors, that are defined as follows:

load: (. . .) the amount and rate of change in the international or domestic situation with which the government must cope.

lag: How much time do policymakers require to become aware of a new situation, and how much additional time do they need to arrive at a decision?

gain: (. . .) the speed and size of the reaction of a political system to new data it has accepted.

lead: (. . .) the capability of a government to predict and to anticipate new problems effectively (*Deutsch*, 1963b: 190).

Regarding these factors it is assumed that 'success', i.e., the extent to which the system indeed realizes its goals, is directly proportional to 'lead' and, to some extent, 'gain', while inversely proportional to 'load' and 'lag'.

A system may 'grow'. By this Deutsch – speaking about an 'organization', but this does not fundamentally affect the sense of the concept – understands the following:

First, an increase in openness – that is an increase in the range of the organization's channels of intake from the outside world; *second*, an increase in its inner complementarity or coherence – that is, in the efficiency with which information is transmitted and responded to from one part of the organization to another; *third*, an increase in the ability to change the environment of the organization in accordance with its projected inner patterns, policies, and needs; *fourth*, an increase in its learning capacity – that is, in the ability of the organization to learn rapidly and yet originally and creatively, and to change its own goals rather than remain the prisoner of some temporary goal or ideal and to fall victim to what A. J. Toynbee called the 'worship of ephemeral institutions' (*Deutsch*, 1952: 380).

Probably this growth can best be conceived as an increase in the system's capacity in the wide sense of that word discussed earlier. It may be already noted here that what is denoted here by the concept 'growth' seems to be closely related to the problem of political integration. For integration, too, seems to be concerned with the creation and development of the facilities as to increase some political system's capacity for joint action toward the environment, for the mobilization of its common resources, for adaptation and for survival.

Finally, it remains to mention that the conception which has been sketched thus far is – as in the case of Ernst Haas, incidentally – strikingly and obviously similar to that of David Easton. Here, too, politics is conceived as a process in which demands and support are converted into binding decisions – or 'authoritative allocations of values'. Political configurations are defined very abstractly as 'systems' into which demands and support are fed from the system's environment to which, in turn, the system's output (binding decisions) are addressed. There are a great many almost identical problems to be found in the different conceptions, such as that of the selection and limitation of the incoming flow of demands and support, that of the different forms of support (specific and general), and that of the legitimacy and authority, to mention only a few of them.

To some extent, of course, this reflects the fact that 'politics' somehow does pose common problems after all. At the same time it reflects the slow development of a kind of common scientific approach to politics, one that is increasingly abstract in the sense that it tries to transcend the traditional, and seemingly more concrete, political categories. Also, this approach seems to proceed along 'functional' lines, in the very wide sense of that word indicated earlier (chapter one, section 4). It has also appeared that traces of this more abstract and analytical approach to political problems can already be seen in the work of David Mitrany and the Functionalist school before World War II. As to the system-analytical and cybernetic vocabularies used, these cannot be said to contribute anything substantial to our knowledge of the political problems involved. One may even suspect that they introduce more obscurities than they dissolve. Their merit is, however, that they are healthily abstract, thus leading more easily to the development of new political conceptions by breaking through the traditional ones.

3. POLITICAL INTEGRATION – DEFINITION

3.1. *The concept's generality*

One of the outstanding characteristics of the political conception discussed in the last section is its generality. As noted several times before, it is concerned with politics at any level whatever – local, national, or international; institutionalized or non-institutionalized. The same applies also to Deutsch's analysis of the integration process. This, too, is concerned with integrative developments at the international and at the national level (e.g. *Deutsch*, 1954c; *Deutsch* et al., 1957), and even with integration in an urban political system (*Deutsch*, 1964b). Like that of Haas (whose empirical research, however, only concerns integration at the international level) Deutsch's integration theory thus acquires an extremely wide scope and generality.

3.2. *Integration – the formation of a political community*

In his inquiries into the integration process Deutsch applies a comparatively large number of somewhat different concepts. At times this is rather confusing since not all of them are defined with equal clarity, while some of them do not fit very well into the theory as a whole.

A difficulty of Deutsch's thinking here is that he seems to be interested in integration chiefly with regard to the problems of war and peace (cf. *Deutsch*, 1954c: 33; *Deutsch* et al., 1957: 3). Now, there are obvious links between these problems and those of politics generally. Even at first sight these links would seem to be particularly clear with regard to the problem of political integration. For it might be said that integration implies the establishment of peaceful relationships among the participating actors, or at least the limitation of warfare among them. Nevertheless it will be clear also that a definition of integration in terms of war and peace is after all different from one that is purely political. Thus, in so far as Deutsch conceives of integration in the context of war and peace, it will be necessary to reinterpret that context so as to make it square with his general political conception.

'Integration' is defined in relation to the concept of 'security community', as follows:

A *security community* is a group of people which has become 'integrated'.

By *integration* we mean the attainment within a territory of a 'sense of community' and of institutions and practices strong enough and widespread enough to assure, for a 'long time', dependable expectations of 'peaceful change' among its populations.

By *sense of community* we mean a belief on the part of individuals in a group that they have come to agreement on at least this one point: that common social problems must and can be resolved by processes of 'peaceful change'.

By *peaceful change* we mean the resolution of social problems, normally by institutionalized procedures, without resort to large-scale physical force (*Deutsch* et al., 1957: 5; *Deutsch*, 1954c: 33).

Deutsch regards such a security community as a special kind of political community. But in contradistinction to the latter, the former would be capable of excluding 'warfare' among its members (*Deutsch*, 1954c: 41; *Deutsch* et al., 1957: 5). Now, as defined earlier (see section 2.2) a political community is a group of people having the facilities, procedures and institutions, to convert the demands and support originating from the members of the group into binding decisions. It also appears from the definition that, in the great majority of cases, this process is enacted in a peaceful fashion, and that physical violence only plays a relatively marginal role. If not, the group cannot properly be said to form a political community at all. Herein we may easily recognize the 'peaceful change' from the above quotation.

Accordingly, it is difficult to see how Deutsch's view that political communities are not necessarily able to exclude 'warfare' or 'large-scale violence' among their members is to be reconciled with his own definition of political community. Of course, in cases of civil war and revolution, authority is being eroded or is altogether lacking, large amounts of negative support are fed into the political system, the community, in short, is breaking down. But then we may still speak of a 'political *system*', but certainly not of a 'political *community*'. And no existing political community can *a priori* be said to be immune from such developments. This, in turn, makes it somewhat unrealistic to define a concept ('security community') in terms of this immunity.

But if, on the other hand, we make that concept more relevant by allowing for some measure of physical violence, and for the possibility of ultimate breakdown through (civil) war and revolution, then it becomes difficult to see wherein the resulting concept would differ from that of 'political community'. The difficulty reappears in Deutsch's 'operationalization' of the concept 'security community':

The attainment of a security community thus can be tested operationally in terms of the absence or presence of significant organized preparations for war or large-scale violence among its members . . . (*Deutsch*, 1954c: 34).

However, what exactly are 'significant preparations'? And what has to be understood by 'war or large-scale violence' in this context? Moreover, it will often be exceedingly difficult to determine precisely against whom such preparations are made. The French strategic doctrine, *la stratégie des quatre azimuths* of de Gaulle, provides a revealing example: is Western Europe a 'security community' or is it not (on the assumption that that strategy would still be official French policy – which may be doubted)?

In view of the above considerations it seems advisable here to apply

'Occam's razor' and to banish the concept 'security community' from the theory. Political integration, then, will be conceived as the process of the formation of a political community in the sense described. I have applied the term 'process' here since this is how Deutsch views the problem. For him integration is not an all-or-nothing affair, but one allowing for different shades and nuances, one that can best be studied as a developmental process.

Accordingly he distinguishes three different kinds of political community. His criterion here is essentially that of the degree to which a political system becomes institutionalized, i.e., the extent to which it develops procedures and organizations via which its political processes are carried on.

The first form is that of a 'no-war community':

This is a limited political community within which, as in any security community, the only command expected and backed by relatively effective formal or informal sanctions is the command not to resort to war or large-scale violence in the settlement of disputes. In contrast to a security community, however, the possibility of war is still expected and to some extent preparations are made for it (*Deutsch*, 1954c: 41).

Apparently we are concerned here with a system of political units with a certain capacity to arrive at common decisions, but in which common institutions via which the process is carried on have hardly developed. The system's capacity for converting demands and support into binding decisions in a reliable and stable fashion is quite low. Accordingly, the use of physical violence and the occurrence of arms races remain possible (*Deutsch*, 1954c: 42).

The second form is that of a 'pluralistic community', that is:

A security community with few or no amalgamated institutions may be called a *pluralistic* security community (*Deutsch*, 1954: 41).

This definition does not establish a clear-cut distinction between a 'no-war community' and a 'pluralistic security community'. What is probably meant here is a political community displaying a somewhat higher degree of institutionalization than a no-war community, but considerably less than that of the third form, an 'amalgamated community'. This is a political community in which the political institutions of the participating units have merged into one common set for the community as a whole (*Deutsch*, 1954c: 34; 1964: 66; *Deutsch* et al., 1957: 6).

It cannot be said that these different forms of political community are defined very sharply. Nevertheless the general drift of the argument seems to be clear enough. Integration denotes the process of the progressive institutionalization of the political process in some political system, while the different forms indicated may be conceived as different stages in that process. In this context it may be observed that it would probably be better to conceive this process in a more analytical fashion along lines similar to those I have suggested earlier (introduction, section 3.3). If it is realized that integration is conceived here as the development of institutions capable of converting the demands and the support of the members into binding decisions, an alternative approach suggests itself rather naturally. That is, instead of trying to define a limited number of fixed stages or forms of integration, we might 'measure' its progress by estimating the amount, variety, or 'weight' of the demands and support the political institutions are capable of handling, as well as the extent to which they can, in fact, produce binding decisions.

Actually, it should be noticed that more recently Deutsch seems indeed to be working along such lines. For, analogously to the four dimensions of 'power' which he introduces (see section 2.3), he distinguishes four dimensions of integration. Thus he writes:

The *domain* of integration, like that of power, consists of the populations of the geographic areas integrated. Like power, integration also has *scope*, which is the collection of different aspects of behavior to which this integrated relationship applies (*Deutsch*, 1968a: 159).

Like power, too, integration has a 'range':

We may think of this range of integration as consisting of the range of rewards and deprivations of the component units, by which an integrated relationship is maintained among them (*Deutsch*, 1968a: 159).

The 'weight' of power, finally, is paralleled by 'cohesion' in the context of integration. As follows:

'An integrated system is *cohesive* to the extent that it can withstand stress and strain, support disequilibrium, and resist disruptions. Its cohesion, or cohesive power, could also be measured by the sustained shift which the system produces in the probabilities of the behavior of its components (as against the way in which they probably would behave if they were not integrated in the system) (*Deutsch*, 1968a: 160).

As already suggested (section 2.3) the above conception of integration might be linked to the notions 'growth' and 'capacity' of a political system. It does not seem too far-fetched to interpret integration as 'growth' of a political system, i.e., as an increase in its capacity. For through integration the system acquires a higher capacity to cope with demands and support fed into it.

4. POLITICAL INTEGRATION—EXPLANATION

4.1. *Outline of this section*

The problem of this section is the way Deutsch accounts for the occurrence or non-occurrence of political integration. I will begin with a discussion of his views on the mechanism of an integration process as a whole (section 4.2). In section 4.3 his ideas on the relationship between integration and the character of the behavior of the participating units will be dealt with. Finally, in section 4.4, I will go into various environmental or 'background' factors deemed relevant by Deutsch.

4.2. *The mechanism of integration*

Implicit in much Deutsch has written on the subject of integration is the assumption that it is not only the governments of the participating units that are the relevant actors. Such units, in particular the contemporary national states, are not to be conceived as completely monolithic and closed entities. Rather, they generally consist of a greater or lesser number of other political groups, such as political parties and various interest groups.

It has appeared that a political system can be viewed as a mechanism for converting demands and support into binding decisions. This can also be analysed in terms of the concepts 'load' and 'capabilities' as defined earlier (section 2.3). That is, a system is confronted with a certain (political) information load, i.e. a certain amount of demands and support, for whose processing the system may or may not have the requisite capabilities (cf. *Deutsch*, 1954c: 43-44). It has also appeared that integration may be conceived as the creation and development of new capabilities in a larger political system compromising the previously autonomous 'national' political systems. This way of looking at the problem already suggests that such new capabilities may be expected to occur in response to a perceived insufficiency of existing capabilities (i.e., of the 'national' system *and* of the existing 'international' one as actually organized) on the part of the units concerned. As Deutsch writes:

The issue of political integration thus arose primarily when people demanded greater capabilities, greater performance, greater responsiveness, and more adequate services of some kind from the governments of the political units by which they had been governed before. Integration or amalgamation were first considered as possible means to further these ends, rather than as ends in themselves (*Deutsch* et al., 1957: 87).

This can (and should, to my mind) be easily translated into the more direct language developed in sections 2.2 and 2.3. The above then reduces to the following. If, for some reason or other, certain existing political institutions fail to satisfy the demands (both new demands and existing ones) of their members, these institutions will lose support and thus some of their authority. Furthermore, if those demands concern matters pertaining to a larger political system, i.e. an international one, requiring binding decisions on the level of that larger system, *and* if it is thought that these can best be met through the creation of new institutions at that level, then demands for (international) integration will be made. So much follows from the postulates mentioned in section 2.2.

We may even go somewhat further. Assuming that new institutions do indeed emerge (requiring the mobilization of enough support for the demands concerned) they may gradually acquire authority. For if they succeed in making such decisions as meet the demands of a sufficiently large constituency with a reasonable degree of reliability, they will be supported and acquire authority and legitimacy. This can be explained by the postulates on learning mentioned in section 2.3. Thus, while the existing ('national') political institutions will lose some or all of their authority, the new ('international') ones will gain authority. In this way a new and progressively integrating political community might ultimately arise, superseding the pre-existing ones.

The proposition in terms of capabilities quoted above tends to hide from our view an important condition. It does not explicitly say that the demands for greater capabilities should concern capabilities of the *international* political system. For it may well be that the immediate reaction of groups and individuals to their perception of the failure of their *national* institutions is rather to strengthen *these* instead of demanding international integration. And if such strengthening does indeed occur, the result may be an increased seclusion from international life. This may well prejudge the chances for later integrative developments (see *Deutsch*, 1953c: 4; 1947: 625; 1960a: 155; 1961: 501; 1966c: 16-17; *Deutsch & Eckstein*, 1961: 299; *Deutsch* et al., 1957: 23-24).

In view of the assumption noted above, to the effect that the political communities concerned are not to be conceived as monolithic entities, it is hardly to be expected that demands for integration will be equally shared by all actors within the respective communities involved. And even among those actually demanding integration a variety of reasons, motives, and interests might be expected. Also, they will probably not all support the idea to the same extent. Consequently, concrete steps on the road toward integration will generally have to be taken on the basis of varying coalitions of supporting groups and individuals. Such coalitions need not rest upon complete identity of demands and motivations. Rather, they should display a certain measure of complementarity in that some integrative step must be seen by the actors concerned as conducing to the realization of whatever demands they may otherwise have. Thus:

The basis of such cooperation was not necessarily similarities of values or outlook, but rather complementarity – that is, an interlocking relationship of mutual resources and needs. A crucial condition for the success of the early leaders or promotors of integration movements was thus their skill in making compromises, or the lack of it (*Deutsch* et al., 1957: 90).

Since integration is concerned with a system consisting of several political communities, the conditions mentioned must not be restricted to individual communities. Rather, they should be made up of groups and interests from all of the communities concerned. At the level of the integrating system as a whole they can thus influence the policy of the international organs as more or less unitary, if temporary, groups. Their national components, on the other hand, can influence the national governments in more or less the same direction. For such coalitions to be at all possible, however, there must be interest configurations common to the entire system, and not restricted to the individual communities. Or, political cleavages should not all run along the boundaries of these communities. As Deutsch writes:

Often also the most salient political divisions within the emerging amalgamated security community become weaker, and – still more important – they shift away from the boundaries of the participating units. Political life then becomes dominated by divisions cutting across the original political units and regions. The more varied and salient these mutually *cross-cutting divisions* are, the better for the acceptability of the emerging union (*Deutsch*, 1968a: 197).

The above analysis in terms of pluralistic political communities, interest coalitions, and cross-cutting divisions, is obviously similar to, though less detailedly elaborated than, Haas's conception of the integration process. This also applies to another element – feedback. In Haas's analysis of the integration process a crucial role was played by his insight that common political institutions, once established, could, through their functioning, significantly modify the character of the system. This could well lead to a cumulative self-sustained process of integration. In Deutsch we find some traces of a similar line of reasoning. They are not elaborated in detail, however.

Thus Deutsch conceives of an integration process having a period of 'take-off':

In studying political movements directed toward integration, we may similarly speak of take-off as a period in which small, scattered, and powerless movements of this kind change into larger and more coordinated ones with some significant power behind them. Before take-off, political integration may be a matter for theorists, for writers, for a few statesmen, or a few small pressure groups. After take-off, integration is a matter of broad political movements, of governments, or of major interest groups ... (*Deutsch* et al., 1957: 83-84).

An integration process may pass a 'threshold', which may be a long historical period (*Deutsch*, 1955: 2; *Deutsch* et al., 1957: 32-35). This process may well be cumulative. It has already appeared how the new international institutions might gradually acquire authority and legitimacy. This depends upon the character of the tasks of these institutions, and in particular upon the way they carry them out. Feedback provides a basis for a process of self-sustained growth. For if the new institutions are perceived to function satisfactorily, and if they have an important range of such functions, one might expect both the willingness and the need (by virtue of the fact that such functions will be related to others outside of the institution's competence, while measures taken with regard to one of them will affect interests regarding others) to add new functions to the institution's competence to increase. Thus Deutsch observes:

But as the last of the conditions in each sequence are added to those whose attainment was assembled previously, the tempo of the process quickens. Background and process now become one. A multiplicity of ranges of social communication and transaction was a background condition for amalgamation, but the rapid adding of new ranges of such communications and transactions is a process (*Deutsch* et al., 1957: 70).

Whatever one may think about the phrase 'Background and process now become one', this clearly suggests a cumulative integrative development. And it does not seem too far-fetched to suppose that, if elaborated, the line of reasoning behind it would develop into something rather similar to Haas's spill-over idea.

The emergence of 'national' feelings, too, is explained by Deutsch as the result of feedback processes. Thus he writes:

Certainly, nationalistic or prenationalistic sentiments – feelings of loyalty to some territory, group, or state – played some role in all our cases. But in the case of any larger community these feelings were the results, not the causes, of political and historical processes that made for integration or disintegration. Produced by these processes, such feelings and memories then helped to modify the outcome of the developments which earlier had given them birth, but at all times the origin of these sentiments of patriotism (*Deutsch* et al., 1957: 83-84).

The development of such feelings could, perhaps, be deduced from the postulates on the learning process mentioned in section 2.3. At any rate, here, too, we find an indication of an important feedback process leading to the formation of a political community: new institutions may generate 'feelings of loyalty', i.e., a form of generalized support, which then could induce a strengthening of these institutions, etc.

In view of the rather obvious resemblance of the conceptions of Haas and of Deutsch, it is worthwhile to quote the latter's view on the significance of 'functionalism':

If a sudden jump to amalgamation is highly improbable, and if it is unwise to stress amalgamation as a goal but wise instead to emphasize national sovereignty, what room is left for progress toward amalgamation? It seems to us that functionalism offers perhaps the best intermediate ground for approaching either pluralism or amalgamation (*Deutsch* et al., 1957: 187).

4.3. *Political actors*

We must now deal with Deutsch's conception of the relationships between integration on the one hand, and the behavior of political actors on the other. More specifically, it is to be asked, what is the relative significance of the various groups, interests, their demands and support behavior, for the process of integration? Deutsch does not go very deeply and systematically into these problems; he treats them in a rather cursory fashion, and limits himself to a small number of more or less incidental observations.

It has appeared (section 2.2) that political actors will support decisions or policies and demands to the extent that these meet with their own demands. This does not make it very likely that demands for integration will find much support, unless they are clearly linked with rather more tangible and visible interests of various actors. For especially in the very first stages of an integrative development, integration may represent hardly more than a quite abstract ideal which will be unable to mobilize much support or even attract a significant degree of attention. As Deutsch observes:

So far as we could find, the motives of formerly passive groups or strata that came to support the movement [for integration] were primarily *local* in character. That is to say, these people were motivated by economic, political, or social concerns within their own political units, and they came to support the amalgamation or integration movement insofar as they expected from its success some gains in the local matters that concerned them. In addition to this, we found that formerly passive individuals or groups were frequently motivated to activity by seemingly accidental or adventitious pressures, such as famine, economic depression, and the like, with which their existing political institutions somehow failed to cope (*Deutsch* et al., 1957: 95-96).

From the last subsection (4.2) it appeared that the general mechanism which propels the process of integration is the formation of 'coalitions' of supporting groups resting upon configurations of complementary demands. What, then, determines the composition and effectiveness of such coalitions? Deutsch writes:

The choice of interests to be put forward in the pursuit of policy is in part also the result of potential allies and alliances that are available for their support. Once chosen and maintained for a longer time, however, each alliance and its outcomes in turn will strengthen or weaken the original interests for which it was invoked, and thus remake – reinforce or modify – the earlier interest configuration that gave it birth (*Deutsch & Weilenmann*, 1964: 407).

There is thus a certain reciprocity between the character of the demands made and that of the groups available for coalition formation. At the same time there is a feedback process. Such coalitions rest upon a certain interest configuration; their functioning, however, successful or unsuccessful, will in turn affect the underlying interest configuration. This seems to be plausible enough. Also, this insight seems to be extremely important. As it is not elaborated by Deutsch, however, it is impossible to determine its theoretical power.

One could argue that, in order to be successful, such coalitions should not be restricted to any one particular social group. Or, rather, that their effectiveness increases as they contain more, and more variegated groups. This might explain what Deutsch has to say about the composition of the leadership of a movement for integration in the early stages of the process:

Leadership in the early stages of an integration or amalgamation movement was furnished typically not by a single social class, but rather by a cross-class coalition (*Deutsch* et al., 1957: 88).

And with regard to the kinds of groups typically participating in the early supporting coalitions for integration, he writes:

Such a coalition characteristically united some of the 'most outside of the insiders' – that is, some of the less secure members of the established ruling class who were least closely connected with its other members – in a political alliance with the 'most inside of the outsiders'. These were some of the members of those social groups or classes outside the seats of power who had already become, or were in the process of becoming, the most serious contenders for a share of political power from among those strata hitherto excluded from it (*Deutsch* et al., 1957: 88).

This could perhaps be explained by arguing that the groups mentioned have relatively little to lose from breaking through the political status quo within their political community. On the other hand, they are close enough to the 'seats of power' so as to enable them to conduct effective political action.

Below the 'established ruling class' and its 'outside insiders' and 'inside outsiders' Deutsch distinguishes the population at large. In the early stages of an integration process this population plays a relatively minor role. This may change in the course of the process, however.

Popular attitudes, to be sure, set limits to what was politically practical from an early stage, both in regard to movements aiming at amalgamation or at secession; and the importance of these popular attitudes tended to increase with growing mass participation in politics. Active popular support, however, tended to come only at a later stage; but it is important to note that the enlisting of popular participation was one of the most successful methods used to promote successfully a movement for amalgamation (*Deutsch* et al., 1957: 93).

In Deutsch's view, an important role is further played in an integration process by so-called 'cores of strength', or 'core areas'. As follows:

Generally, we found that such integrative capabilities were closely related to the general capabilities of a given political unit for action in the fields of politics, administration, economic life, and social and cultural development. Larger, stronger, more politically, administrative , economically, and educationally advanced political units were found to form the cores of strength around which in most cases the integrative process developed (*Deutsch* et al., 1957: 38; in the same sense *Deutsch* et al., 1957: 72 ff.; *Deutsch*, 1955: 3 ff.).

Now, what does this mean exactly? It may be recalled (see section 4.2) that integration can be conceived as the creation of new capabilities in a (international) political system. Also, one might expect that these capabilities will be demanded if it is perceived that the existing capabilities are insufficient in relation to the load placed upon them. Prima facie there is no reason to suppose that communities already disposing of high capabilities will suffer from overload earlier than weaker ones. On the contrary, it might rather be supposed that overload would occur earlier in weak political systems. Accordingly, if interpreted in the sense that 'cores of strength' will support integration earlier and more readily than other political units, the proposition quoted sounds highly implausible – at least within the scheme of reasoning developed thus far. Moreover, it should be noted that 'capabilities' are significant only in relation to 'load'; and about this relationship the proposition is altogether silent.

Besides, what is meant by an integration process occurring 'around' cores of strength? Does it mean that such 'cores' use their capabilities to *force* the other units to integrate? Or that they force those other units to incorporate into the core areas – surely, a rather special form of integration? These are rather different things; they are also open questions, however. Probably the above proposition merely says that integration in some system will *not* occur without the active support of its strongest member, and that the character of the new system will conform most to its wishes. So much is implied by the concept of 'capabilities' at any rate (cf. section 2.3). Even so, it would be necessary to specify much more precisely than is done in the proposition quoted the *relative* capabilities of *all* the system's member units.

We have already seen that Deutsch makes some very general and relatively 'formal' observations on the character of the interests or demands involved in an integrative process. At a less formal level he attaches a special importance to 'expectations of greater social or political equality, or of greater social or political rights or liberties, among important groups of the politically relevant strata – and often among parts of the underlying populations – in the political units concerned' (*Deutsch* et al., 1957: 50 and 100). In the absence of any precise specification of the substance of 'social or political equality' (and the same goes for a second major class of demands, 'involving the development, strengthening, or defence of a distinctive way of life';

Deutsch et al., 1957: 100), this does not carry us very far. Probably, it does not go beyond saying that people will demand integration if, and in so far as, they expect it to result in an improvement of their political status, or the chances of realizing their highest values.

As a general rule Deutsch's treatment of the role of groups, interests or demands in integration suffers from vagueness. This applies to his analysis of interests and demands, as we have just seen, but it also applies to his treatment of the groups involved. Here he uses such concepts as 'ruling' or 'leading' 'class', and 'elite'; and he believes every political community to be governed by such a 'group' (*Deutsch*, 1953c: 32). One may suspect, however, that the picture which these expressions suggest is not entirely appropriate to the study of empirical politics which will probably show a more complicated situation.

A more satisfactory approach is used by Deutsch and Weilenmann in their study of Switzerland from the fourteenth to the sixteenth century. Here they more accurately distinguish several important groupings (urban elites, urban poor, peasants, rural nobles, churches, princes). These are related to a number of specific demands (main groups: trade, crafts, credit, employment, status, autonomy, integration; see *Deutsch & Weilenmann*, 1964: 394). Thus they can show how various coalitions were constituted or disintegrated. Although the categories used are to a large extent bound to a particular historical and geographical situation, the approach as such is not. Surely, it shows a marked advance over an analysis in terms of ruling 'classes' or 'elites'.

As concerns the methods to attain integration, finally, Deutsch formulates a list of 15 different possibilities (*Deutsch* et al., 1957: 101-105). The list displays little system. It includes such things as political strategies, e.g., propaganda, the use of symbols, military conquest; binding decisions, e.g., the setting up of common political organs, the creation of a monopoly of the legitimate use of force, legislation, demands, such as for the abolition of unpopular legislation or institutions, promises of autonomy or sovereignty. In Deutsch's view the most important methods are the mobilization of the population in a movement for integration, while a pluralistic community in which the independence and sovereignty of the participating units will be respected, should be emphasized as an ideal. The creation of a monopoly for the legitimate use of force, and military conquest would be the least effective strategies.

4.4. Background

In Deutsch's conception politics is concerned with the conversion of demands and support into binding decisions, i.e., decisions regulating the behavior of the participants in some political situation. Now one might argue that demands for such decisions will occur when, for those making the demands, the behavior of other units, that is, individuals or groups, has become sufficiently important. Thus it seems plausible to assume that the more interactions there are between a certain number of such units, or the more they are interrelated, the more important participating units will estimate the behavior of others to be, and, consequently, the more political demands there will occur among them. Also, it seems plausible to suppose that integration will only occur in a setting in which there is a sufficient amount of demands to be converted into binding decisions so as to warrant or to make possible the creation or growth of common institutions and stable procedures. Along these lines Deutsch's following proposition could conceivably be derived:

Only in the event that growth of transactions between the two countries would be clearly greater than its alternatives would there be *prima facie* evidence for a growth of conditions favoring integration or amalgamation – provided, furthermore, that this relative growth in transactions should be experienced by the participants as associated predominantly with rewards rather than frustrations (*Deutsch*, 1952: 458; also 1964b: 67).

In the second part of this proposition we find a trace of his postulates on learning (see section 2.3). This is no coincidence, of course. For the formation of new political institutions, or of a new political community, requires a reorientation of the participants' behavior – and this can be conceived as a learning process. It is to be noted, incidentally, that the above reasoning provides the context in which to make sense of Deutsch's measurement of 'communications' and transactions. These may be viewed as telling us something about developments in the environment of some political system. Without saying anything about that system itself, they may be used to explain (part of) the system's input. This is not yet sufficient, of course.

In his *Political community and the North Atlantic area* which reports the findings of investigations into a number of historical cases of integration, a distinction is made between 'essential' and 'helpful' conditions:

When we call certain conditions 'essential', we mean that success seems to us extremely improbable in their absence.
   . . . helpful but not essential: we found that integration occurred in their absence, and might well recur in this way in future cases (*Deutsch* et al., 1957: 12-13).

Thus are formulated twelve essential conditions:

   1. (. . .) compatibility of the main values held by the politically relevant strata of all participating units.
   2. (. . .) a distinctive way of life – that is, a set of socially accepted values and of institutional means for their pursuit and attainment, and a set of established or emerging habits of behavior corresponding to them. To be distinctive, such a way of life has to include at least some major social or political values and institutions which are different from those which existed in the area during the recent past, or from those prevailing among important neighbors. In either case, such a way of life usually involved a significant measure of social innovation as against the recent past.
   3. (. . .) widespread expectations of joint rewards for the participating units, through strong economic ties or gains envisaged for the future (. . .)
   Only a part of such expectations had to be fulfilled. A 'down payment' of tangible gains for a substantial part of the supporters of amalgamation soon after the event, if not earlier, seems almost necessary.
   (. . .) widespread expectations of greater social or political equality, or of greater social or political rights or liberties, among important groups of the politically relevant strata – and often among parts of the underlying population – in the political units concerned.
   4. (. . .) an increase in the political and administrative capabilities of the main political units to be amalgamated.
   5. (. . .) the presence of markedly superior economic growth either as measured against the recent past of the territories to be amalgamated, or against neighboring areas. Such superior economic growth did not have to be present in all participating units prior to amalgamation, but it had to be present at least in the main partner or partners vis-à-vis the rest of the units to be included in the amalgamated security community.
   6. (. . .) the presence of unbroken links of social communication between the units concerned, and between the politically relevant strata within them. By such unbroken links we mean social groups and institutions which provide effective channels of communication, both horizontally among the

main units of the amalgamated security community and vertically among the politically relevant strata within them.

7. (. . .) the broadening of the political, social, or economic elites, both in regard to its recruitment from broader social strata and to its continuing connections with them.

8. (. . .) the mobility of persons among the main units, at least in the politically relevant strata.

9. (. . .) a fairly wide range of different common functions and services, together with different institutions and organizations to carry them out. Further, they apparently require a multiplicity of ranges of common communications and transactions and their institutional counterparts.

10. (. . .) we found that it was apparently important for each of the participating territories to gain some valued services or opportunities. It also seemed important that each at least sometimes take the initiative in the process, or initiate some particular phase or contribution; and that some major symbol or representation of each territory or population should be accorded explicit respect by the others.

11. It was not essential that the flow of rewards, of initiatives, or of respect should balance at any one moment, but it seems essential that they should balance over some period of time.

12. (. . .) some minimum amount of mutual predictability of behavior (*Deutsch* et al., 1957: 46-57).

It has already appeared (sections 4.2 amd 4.3) that the process of integration rests upon the formation of common and converging interests (of which the formation of new institutions will be one, of course) at an international level. Assuming that the formation of such interests, in turn, requires certain common values or preferences on the part of the units concerned, the first condition becomes understandable by being deducible from the rest of the theory. Alternatively, from section 2.3 it appeared that the functioning of a (political) cybernetic system requires certain common preferences and values governing the communication processes within the system. Here, too, we meet with the necessity of a 'comptability of the main values' held by the various units concerned as mentioned in the first condition.

It should be noted, furthermore, that the expression, in the first as in other propositions, 'politically relevant strata' does not convey any additional information. For which group is relevant and which not cannot be determined once and for all in the abstract; it is precisely the thing to be determined by theorizing and empirical research. As it stands, the expression 'politically relevant strata' is merely vacuous. We are, and can only be, interested in 'politically relevant' strata, groups, or units, if only for the simple reason that in dealing with politically *ir*relevant groups we are not doing political research. Implicit in the expression is the assumption that not all groups are *equally* relevant – thus they may differ with respect to power, influence, economic strength, etc. The phrase 'politically relevant strata', however, does not go much beyond saying that it is the more 'important' strata which are crucial.

To a large extent the second condition ('a distinctive way of life') can be understood from the first one. That is, integration requires common values and preferences, or a certain measure of common culture. That it should be different both from the area's past way of life and from that of the area's environment can perhaps be understood by realizing that otherwise integration would have occurred earlier or would occur in a wider area. Furthermore, this 'way of life' should involve 'a significant measure of social innovation'. Apart from the fact of the development of that way of life itself (which may well be a major social innovation), it is difficult to see why this should be, or 'usually was', so. For integration might equally conceivably occur merely to defend an existing way of life (cf. *Haas*, 1960: 231).

In the conditions 3, 10, and 11, the postulates underlying Deutsch's conception of interest politics and of the political learning process (see sections 2.2 and 2.3) are easily recognizable. Besides, the third condition gives an indication concerning the nature of those interests that are crucial in the process of integration – 'social or political equality' and 'social or political rights or liberties'. This is not elaborated in detail, however; the nature of 'equality' or of the 'rights or liberties' in question is not specified more precisely. Perhaps the proposition can be understood as saying that integration will be supported most by those political units that expect to improve their relative position (e.g. their 'power', or access to decision-makers) in the political process by it.

It has already appeared (section 4.3) that the relationship between integration and the growth of the capabilities of the participating political communities is a far from unequivocal one. That is, such growth might well lead to a heightened degree of preoccupation with internal matters within the communities concerned, rather than to international integration. Accordingly, it is difficult to accept the fourth condition.

The more so since it only says something about a growth in capabilities, whereas the crucial thing is the development of the ratio between capabilities and loads, about which the proposition remains silent. In so far as economic growth, i.e. a growth of the resources of a system, constitutes an element in the growth of capabilities generally, the same considerations apply to the fifth condition.

That there must be 'unbroken links of social communication' both between and within the integrating communities (sixth condition) follows from the fact that we are dealing with communication systems. To a large extent the existence of such links (i.e., in so far as they are constituted by political institutions) is precisely the thing to be explained by the theory.

The seventh and eighth conditions can be understood in terms of the concept of 'social mobilization' as discussed earlier (section 2.3). In so far as such mobilization increases the load with which the existing political systems are confronted it may result in attempts to create new capabilities through integration. But in so far as it leads to an increase in the capabilities of the existing systems it may actually make integration more difficult to achieve, as we have seen already. Moreover, the occurrence of demands for greater social or political equality, rights or liberties, which is mentioned in the third condition, will probably constitute an important aspect of social mobilization. But this means that the relationship between integration and such demands also becomes ambiguous: they may or may not lead to integration.

Apparently, the existence of 'a fairly wide range of different common functions and services, together with different institutions and organizations to carry them out', is just the thing to be explained by the theory. Perhaps, however, this ninth condition can be read as suggesting that the development of fairly high capabilities in a political system in itself forms an important cause of the development of still more capabilities. In other words, the proposition could be read as suggesting a process of self-sustained growth beyond a certain level of integration.

The twelfth condition, finally, 'some minimum amount of mutual predictability of behavior', seems rather obvious. For without it communication will be hardly possible, and neither could stable (political) relationships develop – which is of the essence of political integration.

In the present context it may be worthwhile to see what factors Deutsch holds responsible for disintegration or the breakdown of an existing political community. He describes four factors, or groups of factors.

1. Common armies with light burdens and conspicuous gains in prestige or privileges, or short wars of similar character, were helpful, though not essential, to the deeper integration of a political community; but heavy military burdens with few conspicuous gains over the status quo tended to have the opposite effect.

2. (. . .) a substantial increase in political participation on the part of populations, regions, or social strata which previously had been politically passive. Such a substantial increase in political participation meant in each case that the needs, wishes, and pressures of additional social strata or regions had to be accommodated within an old system of political decision-making that might be – and often was – ill-suited to respond to them adequately **and in time.**

3. (. . .) the increase in ethnic or linguistic differentiation. Another aspect of the same condition is a rise in the political awareness of such differentiation as already may exist.

4. (. . .) any prolonged decline or stagnation, leading to economic conditions comparing unfavorably with those in neighboring areas.

– (. . .) the relative closure of the established political elite.

– (. . .) the excessive delay in social, economic, or political reforms which had come to be expected by the population – reforms which sometimes had already been accepted in neighboring areas.

– (. . .) any major failure on the part of a formerly strong or privileged state, group, or region to adjust psychologically and politically to its loss of dominance as a result of changed conditions.

On the other hand, instances of a successful adjustment to a loss of dominance tended to contribute to the preservation of a greater measure of political community than otherwise would have been likely (*Deutsch* et al., 1957: 59-64).

The points 1 and 2, and the first three propositions of point 4 may be derived from the general postulate that support is given by units to the extent that those units expect their demands to be met. Failure of the decision-makers to fulfil such expectations will erode their authority. Proposition 3 reflects the fact that the existence of a political community requires a certain basis of common values. In the fourth clause of point 4 one may suspect a vicious circle. For, could 'success' of the adaptation mentioned mean something different from, or could it be observed in any other fashion than as a strengthening of the community concerned?

Thus far we have only discussed Deutsch's 'essential' conditions. There are also certain 'helpful' conditions, however. About these he is rather vague; he writes:

Such helpful but non-essential conditions included previous administrative and/or dynastic union; ethnic or linguistic assimilation; strong economic ties; and foreign military threats (*Deutsch* et al., 1957: 44).

As a 'pluralistic security community' represents a weaker form of integration than an 'amalgamated' one, it seems obvious that the establishment of the former would require the fulfilment of less stringent conditions than that of the latter. According to Deutsch only three of the twelve conditions discussed previously are 'essential' for the establishment of a pluralistic community: compatibility of major values, mutual responsiveness, and mutual predictability of behavior (*Deutsch* et al., 1957: 66). The other conditions discussed are merely 'helpful' with regard to the weaker form of integration. However, the two forms of integration differ only gradually, while Deutsch himself does not provide the criteria to distinguish them in any precise fashion. On the other hand, the conditions themselves are not very precisely stated either. They hardly go beyond the level of generality of his general political conception (section 2), as we have seen.

It may have been noticed, incidentally, that to a significant extent the integrative 'conditions' discussed so far, and which are reported as the outcome of empirical research, may be deduced from the quite abstract scheme of reasoning discussed in the preceding sections. Actually, as concerns precision, specificity, and testability, these empirical propositions hardly go beyond what has been developed in the abstract. Neither do they add much of substance to the abstract reasoning. This illustrates what I have said earlier (section 1.3) about the explorative character of this empirical research; and it also suggests that with more elaboration of the abstract argument the theoretical yield of the empirical research done could have been considerably higher.

In some places (notably in 1954c and 1969) Deutsch distinguishes six different 'processes of integration': amalgamation, psychological role-taking, assimilation, division of labor, mutual responsiveness, and simple pacification (*Deutsch*, 1954c: 34-38). Now the first and the last processes can be understood as political processes properly so called. The others, however, should rather be conceived as developments in the political system's environment leading to the realization of some of the conditions upon which political integration proper is based. However, the precise relationships between integration and those processes are not spelled out in detail.

5. EMPIRICAL INTERPRETATION

5.1. *Outline of this section*

Inquiring into the way Deutsch empirically interprets the abstract scheme of reasoning discussed previously, I shall deal successively with the concepts of 'communication' and 'information' (5.2); with 'political community' and such matters as 'capabilities' and 'integration' (5.3); with 'demands', 'support', and 'binding decisions' (5.4); and, finally, with the political system's environment and with feedback (5.5).

5.2. *Communication and information*

I have already stressed several times the ambiguity of the term 'communication' in Deutsch's vocabulary. It has two meanings that are not always very clearly kept apart, thus leading to error and confusion. In the first place, in cybernetic terms politically interpreted, 'communication' consists of the transmission of political messages: demands, support, and binding decisions. Secondly, in its more or less everyday meaning, it is concerned with such things as mail flows and telephone calls. In this latter sense, too, the concept plays a role in the theory. It is concerned with developments in a political system's environment; it informs us about the extent to which people interact and this is, as has appeared from section 4.4, an important determinant of the amount and the nature of the political demands in some group of people.

In so far as he deals empirically with communication, Deutsch is mainly interested in this second kind of communication. Thus he measures the amount of the mail and telephone traffic between human groups, or the degree to which they interact in other ways (e.g. by means of trade; see *Deutsch*, 1956, 1957, 1960a; 1964c; *Deutsch & Russett*, 1963; *Savage & Deutsch*, 1960). But he hardly goes into the question to what extent *political* communication actually takes place.

A somewhat different point is that messages in themselves are not the most important things theoretically. What *is* important, is what really comes through, the *information* which is actually transmitted. To determine this would require rules enabling us to empirically separate information from 'noise'. It will be clear that this will be extremely difficult in social or political systems. The contents of the messages concerned would have to be analysed very carefully. In the political interpretation of his cybernetic vocabulary Deutsch ignores this problem. This means that it is not possible to determine precisely, or even measure, how a political information processing system actually functions. Deutsch limits himself to an enumeration of some of the factors thought to be relevant, without indicating how to observe, let alone measure them. Thus he mentions speed, accuracy, complexity, and volume (*Deutsch*, 1953c: 96).

5.3. *The political community and integration*

In using the concept of 'political community' Deutsch generally refers to 'states'. In so far as he deals with these more or less established and comparatively easily recognizable political forms, this does not cause much difficulty. This becomes different, however, as soon as he has to deal with political configurations of a less developed and a more fluid character. And it is precisely with these that a theory of integration is concerned. In such a theory it is imperative to be able to say whether and to what extent a political community actually exists, or to what extent a process of integration has actually progressed. Deutsch, however, does not develop clearcut rules linking the political community concept to empirical reality. This is not very surprising since, as has appeared from section 5.2, he does not give an adequate empirical interpretation to the concept of 'communication system' either. And in his conception a political community is first of all such a communication system.

The concept of 'integration' is operationalized by means of three groups of factors: 'compatibility of autonomous groups', 'distribution and balance of ranges of transactions', and 'volume and dimensions of transactions' (*Deutsch*, 1954c: 52-63). However, rather than integration as a political phenomenon or as a certain process within a particular political system, these factors concern certain factors in the environment of that political system, of the kind discussed in section 4.4. To be sure, such factors might be used in order to measure integration, but this would require the establishment of certain unambiguous relationships between them and integration, so that a particular value of any of these three factors (or of the three together) would correspond in a one-to-one fashion to particular stages in the integration process. As it is, these relationships are as yet unknown. Moreover, Deutsch does not develop the rules with which to observe or measure the factors concerned.

He also suggests that integration might be measured in two ways. 'In the first place by investigating the opinions of the people concerned with regard to integration. In the second place by the measurement of the tangible commitments and the allocation of resources with which people backed them' (*Deutsch* et al., 1957: 32). But he does not elaborate this.

Nor does he elaborate his remark that the erosion of 'party divisions which reinforced the boundaries between political units eligible for amalgamation, and the rise in their stead of party divisions cutting across them' (*Deutsch* et al., 1957: 76) could be used as a measure of integration. This suggestion rests upon the insight that the more integration proceeds, i.e., the more binding decisions are taken by the organs of the emerging international community, the more political formations aimed at influencing those decisions and cutting across the preexisting divisions will emerge.

Deutsch further develops a 'scale' of international integration in terms of the ratio between transactions within the (emerging) political community and those with the outside world (*Deutsch*, 1960a: 150; 1956: 160). In fact, however, this scale does not measure political integration, but the level of interactions within a certain system as compared with those with the outside world. It is concerned with an important factor in the political system's environment, but not with what goes on within that system. The same considerations apply to his 'index of relative acceptance' (*Deutsch* et al., 1967: 220; *Savage* & *Deutsch*, 1960: 32). Of more direct relevance are the concepts he develops in *The nerves of government*:

(. . .) the *political integration ratio*, that is, the proportion of persons extending generalized political support to the government or to political parties pledged to such support – including 'loyal opposition' parties. Similarly, a *political (alienation) ratio* could be estimated as the proportion of people denying generalized support to the country and its type of government, or supporting opposition parties repudiating any such generalized allegiance to the state and its regime. The *rates of political integration and alienation* are, then, the ones at which the respective ratios change over time; and a *rate and ratio of political neutralization* for the indifferent, the apathetic, and perhaps for those paralyzed by cross-pressures, might also be estimated in order to complete this part of the picture (*Deutsch*, 1963b: 126) (my italics).

However, as will appear from section 5.4, no satisfactory operational definition of 'support' or 'generalized support' is developed by Deutsch. Consequently, the above rates and ratios cannot be determined empirically.

The concept of 'capabilities' plays an important role in the theory. To a large extent integration can be conceived as the creation and development of new capabilities in a system made up of political communities. On the other hand capabilities figure (somewhat ambiguously, to be true) in Deutsch's explanation of the integration process. Such capabilities, it will be recalled, consist of three different elements: the amount and variety of resources available, the speed with which these can be recommitted from one employment to another, i.e., the internal organization of the system, and the system's receptivity to new patterns of information. From the discussion of the concept in section 2.3 it has already appeared that it is a far from simple one, and that even in the abstract it cannot be said to have been determined completely and precisely. It is not very surprising, then, that Deutsch does not develop the means for its empirical interpretation and measurement.

In his article *Towards an inventory of basic trends and patterns in comparative and international politics* (*Deutsch*, 1960b), he indicates a research strategy which might ultimately lead to a solution of the above problem. Roughly, the method is as follows. He constructs a number of (mainly ordinal) scales for a great number of measurable elements of capabilities. Thus he distinguishes five possible classes, denoted by the numerals '0' to '4', of the Gross National Product of a political community. On the basis of the membership of secessionist or revolutionary groups he similarly constructs a scale for the political homogeneity of a community (also denoted by numerals '0' to '4'). The results of the empirical measurements in these and a great number of other scales with regard to a particular political community are then brought together in what are called 'profiles'. Ideally, the capacity of some political community or, more generally, some political system would thus be expressed by a vector consisting of the values of a great number of different elements of capacity. Now it should be noted immediately that this ideal has not been realized by Deutsch. Thus we find very few data concerning the internal organization of a system, and virtually none on the system's receptivity to new information and its capacity to process it creatively. Finally, the vectors are made up mainly of ordinal numbers, which greatly limits the operations that can be performed upon them.

The actual functioning of a political system is not determined solely by its capacity, but also by 'load', 'lead', 'lag', and 'gain'. Regarding these factors we can be very short: Deutsch does not indicate how to give them an empirical meaning.

5.4. *Demands, support, binding decisions, and actors*

Deutsch does not give rules enabling us to observe and to distinguish demands empirically. It has appeared (section 4.3) that with respect to Switzerland from the 14th to the 16th centuries (*Deutsch & Weilenmann*, 1964) a number of specific demands or interests were distinguished. The method has not been elaborated and generalized to make it applicable to other geographic and historical settings, however. And even in the Swiss study no procedures are developed to unambiguously observe and measure the contents and the amount of demands. Neither do we find a systematic development of criteria or measurement procedures to establish the relative importance or 'weight' of demands for a political system. Consequently, it is impossible to estimate empirically the 'load' with which a particular system is confronted.

As the concept of 'culture' is not operationalized, and as culture was assumed to be one of the major elements governing the information processing by a system, it is difficult to acquire a clear picture of that process in some empirical (political) system. The same applies to the concept of 'memory' which also plays an important role in the explana-

tion of this process. No rules are developed to determine empirically
how such a (political system's) memory is constituted, how it functions, what information is stored in it, and how this information is
retrieved from it.

A systematic development of rules and procedures for the observation and measurement of support and for estimating the relative importance or significance of various forms of support behavior for a political
system is largely lacking. Consequently, we are not able to determine
empirically what precisely is fed into the system and what is the load
with which it is confronted.

In a somewhat different context, namely that of German foreign
policy (*Deutsch & Edinger*, 1959), a limited attempt to measure support is made. Following Almond, four different 'elites' (political, administrative, interest, and communication elites) are distinguished. The
attitudes of these elites on 16 specific 'foreign policy issues' are investigated and measured on ordinal scales running from '–3' ('strongly opposed'), via '0' ('indifferent') and '00' ('divided'), to '+3' ('very favorable') (*Deutsch & Edinger*, 1959: 208-212). It is remarkable that the
authors are led astray by the illusion caused by their use of numerical
signs to indicate certain differences in responses. That is, they treat
these numerals as cardinal numbers and through the arithmetical operations of addition and the computation of means with regard to the
ordinal 'satisfaction scores' they derive from these so-called 'aggregate
elite scores'.

Support is given by individuals and groups. Their character will be
an important determinant of the support's significance for the political
system. Deutsch does not deal systematically with this aspect of the
problem. In this context the following observation is interesting:

> Thus, the *potential* power of interest groups in the political 'market' may be
> thought of as roughly proportional to their share in the purchasing power in
> the national market. This purchasing power may be measured in terms of
> their share in the national product (*Deutsch & Eckstein*, 1961; 271).

In the first place, however, this is only concerned with one type of
political actor, the interest group. Secondly, when one thinks of intellectual or revolutionary groups, it becomes clear that the method described is not universally applicable, and that other elements would
have to be introduced. No rules are given to locate empirically such

groups as 'inside outsiders' and 'outside insiders' (section 4.3), or to observe and to estimate the significance of the coalitions formed by them.

With regard to the political system's output, i.e., the binding decisions achieved, Deutsch does not develop explicit operational definitions. Neither does he systematically distinguish various possible kinds of such decisions regarding their significance for the political system concerned or for the process of integration. He suggests that a government's capacity to keep its citizens alive, and to assure them a certain, unspecified, level of economic and cultural well-being, could provide a general measure for that government's functioning (*Deutsch*, 1964d: 144-145). He also writes:

The high level of government revenue to total income of the society usually correlates with a high level of integration (*Deutsch*, 1964d: 147).

This suggests a possible measure for a government's authority, and for the degree of integration of a community. It is not elaborated, however.

After the foregoing it will be clear that in view of the empirical indeterminancy both of a political system's input and its output, it is impossible to gain a clear empirical picture of, and test the assumptions concerning, the processes of feedback and of learning which play such an important role in the explanation of the integration process.

5.5. *Environment*

With regard to a political system's environment Deutsch is mainly interested in the quantitative analysis of human interactions. From section 4.4 it has appeared that the level of interactions in some human group may be one of the major factors governing the occurrence of political demands therein, which, in turn, is an important element in the explanation of political integration. To analyse such interactions, Deutsch develops what he calls I/O ratios (ratios of Internal to Outside transactions). That is, with respect to some human group or aggregate of groups he estimates the proportion of the transactions with the outside world among the total number of that group's transactions; and he compares the number of the group's internal transactions to those with the outside world. Thus he constructs a 'tentative scale of international integration and national autonomy', as follows:

I/O Ratio: internal to outside transactions	Percentage of outside transactions among total	Tentative interpretation. Degree of integration to outside world	autonomy or self-preoccupation of smaller unit
1 or less	50+	high	low
1-2	33-50	fair to high	low to fair
2-6	14-33	fair	fair
6-10	9-14	low to fair	fair to high
10-15	6-9	low	high
15 or higher	6 or less	extremely low	extremely high

(*Deutsch*, 1960a: 150; 1956: 160).

It is to be recalled, however, that the name 'scale of integration' is not correct. For what is measured is not political integration itself, but a factor in the political system's environment. In all probability several scales, differentiated according to the kinds of transactions involved, would have to be constructed, while the relationships between the measured ratios for each kind of transaction and integration would have to be established more precisely.

A refinement of this approach can be seen in Deutsch's development of transaction matrices. First a matrix consisting of the actual amounts of transactions, for example trade, among a certain group of units is constructed. Secondly, a matrix is constructed consisting of the computed amounts of these transactions that may be expected assuming that mutual transactions are determined exclusively by the share of each individual unit in the total amount of transactions of the group (see for the mathematical solution of this problem; *Savage & Deutsch*, 1960). Finally, a third matrix is constructed which consists of the percentual differences between the two other matrices. This method enables us to determine the extent to which units or groups of units interact more or less with each other than could be expected under the assumption of indifference. In this context, Deutsch speaks of an 'index' of relative acceptance' (RA Index):

(. . .) the Index of Relative Acceptance – the RA index – which measures the percentage by which the volume of actual transactions (such as, for instance, trade) between two countries exceeds or falls short of the hypothetical amount that would be proportional to the overall share of each of these countries in the total flow of transactions among all countries in the world. The index thus measures by how many more or fewer per cent these two countries deal with one another than they could be expected to do according to random probability and the mere size of their total foreign trade. The RA index separates, therefore, the actual results of preferential behavior and structural integration from the mere effects of the size and prosperity of countries (*Deutsch* et al., 1967: 220; see also *Deutsch*, 1960b: 458-459; *Savage & Deutsch*, 1960).

Again, however, it should be borne in mind that we are dealing here with one particular factor in a political system's environment, that the index would have to be determined for a variety of kinds of transactions (e.g., trade, military, economic, intellectual, technological, and cultural transactions), presumably of unequal, but unknown, importance, and that the relationship between the values thus measured and integration is by no means unambiguously clear.

Deutsch also develops a quantitative measure for the background conditions of the stability of a political system. He writes:

In principle, the background conditions for stability – though not stability itself – could be predicted from the ratio of two numbers: one indicating the rising burdens upon a government and upon popular habits of compliance or loyalty toward it; the other indicating the resources available to the government for coping with these burdens. An indicator of rising burdens could be found in the percentages of literacy, L, and of political participation, pol, together with data about the extent of inequality in the distribution of incomes, such as the percentages of total national income, Y, in the hands of the top 10 per cent of income receivers, written as y_{10}. A rough indication of the resources of the government could be found in the per capita national income, y, and perhaps – though this would have to be investigated – in the ratio, g, of the government sector – sometimes approximated by the national budget – to the total national income. Briefly put, the background conditions for stability would thus be indicated by some such ratio as

$$St = \frac{g}{L. \, pol} \cdot \frac{y}{y_{10}} \qquad\qquad (Deutsch, 1960b: 453)$$

Deutsch himself observes that the above merely gives a very rough characterization of some of the relevant factors involved (*Deutsch*, 1960b: 453).

Finally, he gives an indication of a possible method to determine quantitatively the 'saliency' of different units for each other.

Specifically, a nation is likely to treat messages from other countries, or concerning other countries, as more *salient*, the greater the proportion of foreign trade (T) – that is, the sum of imports and exports – is to its Gross National Product (GNP), and hence the greater the economic power base of foreign trade interest groups in that nation's political processes (*Deutsch &Russett*, 1963: 18).

It hardly needs emphasizing that this method is of limited applicability. Nevertheless, it would seem, it indicates a direction for further theorizing and research through the extension and generalization of the method to other kinds of relationship, such as cultural, military, and technological ones.

Incidentally, this last remark seems to apply to the whole of what has been discussed in the present section (5). That is, in the operationalization of Deutsch's reasoning with regard to politics and integration we meet with a relatively large amount of more or less incidental and unconnected suggestions and indications that are often hardly elaborated. Often, however, they do seem to provide promising starting-points for further theorizing and research.

6. DEUTSCH AND HAAS–TWO SIMILAR THEORIES

One of the most striking things about the theory discussed in the present chapter is its resemblance to that of Haas. This is all the more remarkable in view of the rather different vocabularies both authors use, or the different backgrounds from which they approach the problems involved. It forms a concrete illustration of the general point made earlier (chapter two, section 3.5) about the relatively inessential role of cybernetic and systems-analytic calculi in present-day political science.

Both authors develop a conception of politics in terms of demands, support, and binding decisions, which are, for all intents and purposes, identical. In both cases, too, this conception (and the same applies to their integration theories) is of an extremely wide character. Although both are concerned primarily with the national state and its problems, there is nothing, either in their conception of politics or in that of the integration process, which would preclude their applicability to other settings and configurations. Both authors conceive of integration in terms of interest politics which they appear to explain on the basis of largely similar postulates. Integration is seen as the result of compli- cated processes of feedback and learning, although here Haas uses somewhat different assumptions than Deutsch.

Both theories largely exhibit the same weaknesses which have been amply discussed in the foregoing and which I will not repeat here. To a large extent these weaknesses seem to be a matter of the lack of suffi- cient, and sufficiently rigorous, elaboration, rather than of fundamental flaws in the very basis of the argument. In this respect, incidentally, Haas's theory seems to show the higher measure of elaboration of the two. Finally, the complicated problem of a satisfactory empirical inter- pretation of their reasoning has not been solved by either of the two authors.

BIBLIOGRAPHY

Bryson, Lyman et al. (Ed.), 1945. *Approaches to national unity*. Harpers, New York.
Bryson, Lyman et al. (Ed.), 1947. *Conflicts of power in modern culture*. Harpers, New York.
Bryson, Lyman et al. (Ed.), 1953. *Freedom and authority in our time*. Harpers, New York.

Charlesworth, James C. (Ed.), 1966. *A design for political science – scope, ob- jectives, and methods*. American Academy of Political and Social Science, Philadelphia.
Charlesworth, James C. (Ed.), 1967. *Contemporary political analysis.* Free Press, New York.

Deutsch, Karl W., 1942a. The trend of European nationalism – the language aspect. *Am. polit. Sci. Rev. 36 (3)*: 533–541.
Deutsch, Karl W., 1942b. Some economic aspects of the rise of nationalistic and racial pressure groups. *Can. J. econ. polit. Sci. 8 (1)*: 109–115.
Deutsch, Karl W., 1944. Medieval unity and the economic conditions for an international civilization. *Can. J. econ. polit. Sci. 10 (1)*: 18–35.

DEUTSCH, Karl W., 1945. The economic factor in intolerance. In Lyman Bryson et al. (Ed.), *Approaches to national unity*, pp. 368–386. Harpers, New York.

DEUTSCH, Karl W., 1947. The crisis of peace and power in the atom age. In: Lyman Bryson et al. (Ed.), *Conflicts of power in modern culture*, pp. 608–657. Harpers, New York.

DEUTSCH, Karl W., 1948. Some notes on research on the role of models in the natural and social sciences. *Synthese 7 (6b)*: 506–533.

DEUTSCH, Karl W., 1951a. Mechanism, organism, and society – some models in natural and social science. *Phil. Sci. 18 (3)*: 230–252.

DEUTSCH, Karl W., 1951b. Mechanism, teleology, and mind – the theory of communications and some problems in philosophy and social science. *Phil. phenomenol. Res. 12 (2)*: 185–223.

DEUTSCH, Karl W., 1952. On communication models in the social sciences. *Public Opinion Q. 16 (3)*: 356–380.

DEUTSCH, Karl W., 1953a. Communication in self-governing organizations – notes on autonomy, freedom, and authority in the growth of social groups. In: Lyman Bryson et al. (Ed.), *Freedom and authority in our time*, pp. 271–288. Harpers, New York.

DEUTSCH, Karl W., 1953b. The growth of nations – some recurrent patterns of political and social integration. *Wld Polit. 5 (2)*: 168–197.

DEUTSCH, Karl W., 1953c. *Nationalism and social communication – an inquiry into the foundations of nationality*, 2nd ed. MIT Press, Cambridge (Mass.), 1966 (1st ed. 1953).

DEUTSCH, Karl W., 1954a. Game theory and politics – some problems of application. In: S. Sidney Ulmer (Ed.), *Introductory readings in political behavior*, pp. 289–296. Rand McNally, Chicago, 1961.

DEUTSCH, Karl W., 1954b. Cracks in the monolith – possibilities and patterns of disintegration in totalitarian systems. In: Harry Eckstein & David E. Apter (Ed.), *Comparative politics – a reader*, pp. 497–507. Free Press of Glencoe, New York, 1963.

DEUTSCH, Karl W., 1954c. *Political community at the international level – problems of measurement and definition*. Doubleday, Garden City (N.Y.).

DEUTSCH, Karl W., 1955. Large and small states in the integration of large political communities. *IPSA Congr.* (Stockholm 1955).

DEUTSCH, Karl W., 1956. Shifts in the balance of communication flows – a problem of measurement in international relations. *Public Opinion Q. 20 (1)*: 143–160.

DEUTSCH, Karl. W., 1958. The place of behavioral sciences in graduate training in tional decision-making – a possible research approach to international conflicts. *J. Conflict Resolution 1 (2)*: 200–211.

DEUTSCH, Karl W., 1958. The place of behavioral sciences in graduate training in international relations. *Behav. Sci. 3 (3)*: 278–284.

DEUTSCH, Karl W., 1959. The impact of science and technology on international politics. *Daedalus 88 (4)*: 669–685.

DEUTSCH, Karl W., 1960a. The propensity to international transactions. *Polit. Stud. 8*: 147–155.

DEUTSCH, Karl W., 1960b. Toward an inventory of basic trends and patterns in comparative and international politics. In: James N. Rosenau (Ed.), *International politics and foreign policy – a reader in research and theory*, pp. 450–468. Free Press, New York, 1961.

DEUTSCH, Karl W., 1961. Social mobilization and political development. *Am. polit. Sci. Rev. 55 (3)*: 493–514.

DEUTSCH, Karl W., 1962a. Supranational organizations in the 1960's. *J. common Market Stud. 1*: 212–218.

DEUTSCH, Karl W., 1962b. Communications, arms inspection and national security. In. J.K. Zawodny (Ed.), *Man and international relations*, Vol. 2, pp. 848–858. Chandler, San Francisco, 1966.

DEUTSCH, Karl W., 1962c. Towards Western European integration – an interim assessment. *J. int. Affairs 16 (1)*: 89–101.

DEUTSCH, Karl W., 1963a. Some problems in the study of nation-building. In: Karl W. Deutsch & William J. Foltz (Ed.), *Nation-building*, pp. 1–16. Atherton Press, New York.

DEUTSCH, Karl W., 1963b. *The nerves of government – models of communication and control*. Free Press of Glencoe, London.

DEUTSCH, Karl W., 1964a. External involvement in internal war. In: Harry Eckstein (Ed.), *Internal war – problems and approaches*, pp. 100–110. Free Press of Glencoe, New York.

DEUTSCH, Karl W., 1964b. Communication theory and political integration. In: Philip E. Jacob & James V. Toscano (Ed.), *The integration of political communities*, pp. 46–74. Lippincott, Philadelphia.

DEUTSCH, Karl W., 1964c. Transaction flows as indicators of political cohesion. In: Philip E. Jacob & James V. Toscano (Ed.), *The integration of political communities*, pp. 75–97. Lippincott, Philadelphia.

DEUTSCH, Karl W., 1964d. The price of integration. In: Philip E. Jacob & James V. Toscano (Ed.), *The integration of political communities*, pp. 143–178. Lippincott, Philadelphia.

DEUTSCH, Karl W., 1964e. Integration and the social system – implications of functional analysis. In: Philip E. Jacob & James V. Toscano (Ed.), *The integration of political communities*, pp. 179–208. Lippincott, Philadelphia.

DEUTSCH, Karl W., 1966a. On theories, taxonomies and models as communication codes for organizing information. *Behav. Sci 11*: 1–17.

DEUTSCH, Karl W., 1966b. The theoretical basis of data programs. In: Richard L. Merrit & Stein Rokkan (Ed.), *Comparing nations – the use of quantitative data in cross-national research*, pp. 27–55. Yale University Press, New Haven/London.

DEUTSCH, Karl W., 1966c. External influences on the internal behavior of states. In: R. Barry Farrell (Ed.), *Approaches to comparative and international politics*, pp. 5–26. Northwestern University Press, Evanston (Ill.).

DEUTSCH, Karl W., 1966d. Integration and arms control in the European political environment – a summary report. *Am. polit. Sci. Rev. 60 (2)*: 354–365.

DEUTSCH, Karl W., 1966e. Recent trends in research methods in political science. In: James C. Charlesworth (Ed.), *A design for political science – scope, objectives, and methods*, pp. 149–178. American Academy of Political and Social Science, Philadelphia.

DEUTSCH, Karl W., 1966f. Some quantitative restraints on value allocation in society and politics. *Behav. Sci. 11*: 245–252.

DEUTSCH, Karl W., 1966g. The future of world politics. *Polit. Q. 37 (1)*: 9–32.

DEUTSCH, Karl W., 1967a. Changing images of international conflict. *J. social Issues 23 (1)*: 91–107.

DEUTSCH, Karl W., 1967b. On the concepts of politics and power. *J. int. Affairs 21 (2)*: 232–241.

DEUTSCH, Karl W., 1967c. *Arms control and the Atlantic Alliance – Europe faces coming policy decisions*. Wiley, New York.

DEUTSCH, Karl W., 1967d. Communication models and decision systems. In: James C. Charlesworth (Ed.), *Contemporary political analysis*, pp. 273–299. Free Press, New York.

DEUTSCH, Karl W., 1968a. *The analysis of international relations*. Prentice Hall, Englewood Cliffs (N.J.).

DEUTSCH, Karl W., 1968b. The impact of communications on international relations theory. In: Abdul A. Said (Ed.), *Theory of international relations – the crisis of relevance*, pp. 74–92. Prentice Hall, Englewood Cliffs (N.J.).

DEUTSCH, Karl W., 1969. *Nationalism and its alternatives*. Knopf, New York.

DEUTSCH, Karl W. & Alexander ECKSTEIN, 1961. National industrialization and the declining share of the international economic sector, 1890–1959. *Wld Polit. 13 (2)*: 267–299.

DEUTSCH, Karl W. & Lewis J. EDINGER, 1959. *Germany rejoins the powers – mass opinion, interest groups, and elites in contemporary German foreign policy*. Stanford University Press, Stanford (Cal.).

DEUTSCH, Karl W. & Lewis J. EDINGER, 1962. The foreign policy of the German Federal Republic. In: Roy C. Macridis (Ed.), *Foreign policy in world politics*, pp. 91–132. Prentice Hall, Englewood Cliffs (N.J.).

DEUTSCH, Karl W., Lewis J. EDINGER, Roy C. MACRIDIS & Richard L. MERRIT, 1967. *France, Germany and the Western alliance – a study of elite attitudes on European integration and world politics*. Scribner, New York.

DEUTSCH, Karl W. & William J. FOLTZ (Ed.), 1963. *Nation-building*. Atherton Press, New York.

DEUTSCH, Karl W. & Walter ISARD, 1961. A note on a generalized concept of effective distance. *Behav. Sci. 6*: 308–311.

DEUTSCH, Karl W. & Morton A. KAPLAN, 1964. The limits of international coalitions. In: James N. Rosenau (Ed.), *International aspects of civil strife*, pp. 170–184. Princeton University Press. Princeton (N.J.).

DEUTSCH, Karl W. & William G. MADOW, 1961. A note on the appearance of wisdom in large bureaucratic organizations. *Behav. Sci. 6*: 72–78.

DEUTSCH, Karl W. & Richard L. MERRIT, 1965. Effects of events on national and international images. In: Herbert C. Kelman (Ed.), *International behavior – a social-psychological analysis*, pp. 132–187. Holt, Rinehart & Winston, New York.

DEUTSCH, Karl W. & Leroy N. RIESELBACH, 1965. Recent trends in political theory and political philosophy. *Ann. Am. Acad. polit. social Sci. 360*: 139–162.

DEUTSCH, Karl W. & Bruce M. RUSSETT, 1963. International trade and political independence. *Am. behav. Scient. 6 (7)*: 18–20.

DEUTSCH, Karl W. & J. David SINGER, 1964. Multipolar power systems and international stability. *Wld Polit. 16 (3)*: 390–406.

DEUTSCH, Karl W. & J. David SINGER & Keith SMITH, 1965. The organizing efficiency of theories – the n/v ratio as a crude rank order measure. *Am. behav. Scient. 9 (2)*: 30–33.

DEUTSCH, Karl W. & Hermann WEILENMANN, 1964. The Swiss city canton – a political invention. *Comp. Stud. Society Hist. 7*: 393–408.

DEUTSCH, Karl W. & Hermann WEILENMANN, 1967. The Valais – a case study in the development of a bilingual people. *Orbis 10 (4)*: 1269–1297.

DEUTSCH, Karl W. et al., 1957. *Political community and the North Atlantic area – international organization in the light of historical experience*. Princeton University Press, Princeton (N.J.).

DEUTSCH, Karl W. et al., 1966. The Yale political data program. In: Richard L. Merrit & Stein Rokkan (Ed.), *Comparing nations – the use of quantitative data in cross-national research*, pp. 81–94. Yale University Press, New Haven/ London.

ECKSTEIN, Harry (Ed.), 1964. *Internal war – problems and approaches*. Free Press of Glencoe, New York.

ECKSTEIN, Harry & David E. APTER (Ed.), 1963. *Comparative politics – a reader*. Free Press of Glencoe, New York.

FARRELL, R. Barry (Ed.), 1966. *Approaches to comparative and international politics*. Northwestern University Press, Evanston (Ill.).

FISHER, William E., 1969. An analysis of the Deutsch sociocausal paradigm of political integration. *Int. Orgn 23 (2)*: 254–290.

HAAS, Ernst B., 1960. The challenge of regionalism. In: Stanley Hoffmann (Ed.), *Contemporary theory in international relations*, pp. 223–240. Prentice Hall, Englewood Cliffs (N.J.).

HANSEN, Roger D., 1969. Regional integration – reflections on a decade of theoretical efforts. *Wld Polit. 21 (2)*: 242–271.

INGLEHART, Ronald, 1967. An end to European integration? *Am. polit. Sci. Rev. 61 (1)*: 91–105.

JACOB, Philip E. & James V. TOSCANO (Ed.), 1964. *The integration of political communities*. Lippincott, Philadelphia.

KELMAN, Herbert C. (Ed.), 1965. *International behavior – a social-psychological analysis.* Holt, Rinehart & Winston, New York.

LASSWELL, Harold D. & Abraham KAPLAN, 1960. *Power and society – a framework for political inquiry.* Yale University Press, New York/London, 1963.

MACRIDIS, Roy C. (Ed.), 1958. *Foreign policy in world politics.* Prentice Hall, Englewood Cliffs (N.J.), 1962.
MERRIT, Richard L. & Stein ROKKAN (Ed.), 1966. *Comparing nations – the use of quantitative data in cross-national research.* Yale University Press, New Haven/London.

ROSENAU, James N. (Ed.), 1961. *International politics and foreign policy – a reader in research and theory.* The Free Press, New York.
ROSENAU, James N. (Ed.), 1964. *International aspects of civil strife.* Princeton University Press, Princeton (N.J.).

SAID, Abdul A. (Ed.), 1968. *Theory of international relations – the crisis of relevance.* Prentice Hall, Englewood Cliffs (N.J.).
SAVAGE, I. Richard & Karl W. DEUTSCH, 1960. A statistical model of the gross analysis of transaction flows. *Econometrica 38 (3):* 551–572.

TAYLOR, Paul, 1968. The concept of community and the European integration process. *J. common Market Stud. 7 (2):* 83–101.

ULMER, S. Sidney (Ed.), 1961. *Introductory readings in political behavior.* Rand McNally, Chicago.

ZAWODNY, J.K. (Ed.), 1966. *Man and international relations,* 2 vols. Chandler, San Francisco.

5 AMITAI ETZIONI

1. INTRODUCTION

1.1. *A sociological approach?*

Etzioni's scientific background is somewhat different from that of the other authors discussed in this book. He is a sociologist, and he expressly presents his analysis of politics and of political integration as a sociological one. What exactly does this imply?

From the earlier discussion of what it means to define a particular science (chapter two, sections 2.6.1 and 2.6.2) it appeared that such a science is constituted by the way it defines some problem or complex of problems (its 'subject-matter') and that it further consists of everything which is deemed relevant to the explanation or understanding of its basic problem. Traditional disciplinary or, rather, academic distinctions are of a decidedly secondary interest. They are bound to more practical needs and interests and to the accidents of historical developments, rather than to the intrinsic merits of the substantive problems involved. Thus, assuming some common problem (e.g. political integration) different disciplinary approaches reduce to, at most, alternative theories within one scientific field. Whether that field be termed 'political' or 'sociological' is irrelevant. If not, the identity of the problems with which they deal must be merely apparent. Nevertheless, there is also a more practical point involved. That is, through his different educational background and the concomitant exposure to a somewhat different literature and range of problems, a sociologist might well introduce fresh research strategies or conceptual schemes and hit at solutions that may remain hidden from the professional political scientist. In other words, a sociologist might be free from some of the blinders with which the political scientist's training provides him. However, there is also a danger involved in such more or less extra-disciplinary ventures. Problems and lines of reasoning might get mixed up; and the result might merely be conceptual fuzziness and confusion from which neither sociology nor political science could derive any profit at all.

As will appear from the analysis of this chapter, Etzioni does indeed deal with typically political problems conceived in a way which does not differ radically from the way they are dealt with by the other authors discussed. What, then, characterizes his 'sociological' approach of these problems? To begin with, he thinks such an approach to have become possible only in the recent past. For:

So long as international relations are governed by highly calculative orientations, or by the exercise of force, there is relatively little that sociology can contribute to their study (*Etzioni*, 1963a: 407).

While this is thought to apply to the greater part of political history, more recently international relations would have become accessible to a sociological approach by virtue of the increasing importance of institutionalization and of ideologies therein (*Etzioni*, 1963a: 407). In his description of this particular approach he specifically argues against historical or legal ways of dealing with international affairs.

The sociological approach focuses on relations as we know them now rather than on those that existed among states in earlier periods; to the degree that the sociology of earlier periods is explored, it is with an eye to what we might learn from these periods to broaden our understanding of contemporary international relations. Moreover, this sociological approach is concerned with social, political, and economic forces; the formal structures of institutions are studied, but always in relation to the social forces that created the institutions and always with the question in mind: How well do these institutions fit international reality? Our approach combines a traditional power analysis with the Parsonian theory of action and with conceptions of cybernetics and communication theory introduced by Karl Deutsch (*Etzioni*, 1965: ix).

All this does not augur well for a theory concerning political phenomena. It will be clear that this is not a very precise and workable specification of his approach. That it is not historical or legal is merely trivial. And that it is presented as a 'new and rising approach to political science in general and international relations in particular' (*Etzioni*, 1965: ix), written as it is in 1965, sounds somewhat queer in view of the fact that for some decades so much of political science has emancipated from its early historical conceptions and concerns. The announcement that he will 'combine' 'traditional power analysis' with cybernetics and Parsonian conceptions should put the reader on guard. For this involves quite complicated problems, partly of a very abstract nature, with which Etzioni, however, does not deal.

A different point is that Etzioni is not expressly concerned with the formation of a theory in the strict sense. His ambitions in this respect are, or seem to be, more modest. Instead of a theory (of integration) he aims at a 'paradigm' which he describes as follows:

A paradigm is more than a perspective but less than a theory. It provides a set of interrelated questions, but no account of validated propositions. It provides a 'language', a net of variables, but it does not specify the relationships among those variables. It is less vague than a mere perspective, providing a systematic, specific, and often logically exhaustive set of foci for research and speculation. A paradigm is often a stage on the way from an old perspective to a new theory. The test of a paradigm is not only that of the validity of the theories constructed through its application, but also its fruitfulness in terms of the spectrum of significant problems whose study is facilitated by it (*Etzioni*, 1965: 2).

However, the distinction between a theory and a 'paradigm' should not be emphasized too much. For a theory, too, can be conceived as an interrelated set of questions. This merely depends on the degree to which the theory has actually been developed. Initially, many of the theory's statements will hardly be very specific and precise; that is, many of the relationships figuring in it will be extremely loose and vague, hardly amounting to anything more than questions to be answered by further theorizing and research. This is precisely the way insights and theory formation proceed. On the other hand, the formulation of questions, or the mere enumeration of variables, already presupposes quite an advanced stage of development. For it implies certain comparatively definite insights into the things that are relevant to the ultimate understanding of the problem at hand. The more so if it is asked that those questions really be significant and fruitful in guiding further research. In general, such questions can only be asked on the basis of the most advanced theory available (see on these matters especially sections 2.4.3 and 2.5.2 of chapter two). Also, it cannot be maintained that unlike a paradigm a theory would consist of 'validated' propositions'.

In view of all this there is no need here for a separate concept of 'paradigm'. Accordingly, I will analyse Etzioni's thinking in relatively straightforward terms and conceive it as a theory rather than as something else.

1.2. *Notes on the literature*

As can be seen from the bibliography attached to the present chapter, which contains most, though not all, of his publications, Etzioni, too, is an extremely prolific writer. He deals with a comparatively large number of quite different topics, not all of which are equally relevant in the context of this chapter. Thus he has written about the cold war and about American foreign policy in his *The hard way to peace* (*Etzioni*, 1962a) and *Winning without war* (*Etzioni*, 1964a). Rather than with purely scientific analysis, however, these books are concerned with the problem what policy to choose, by the U.S. in particular, in contemporary international life. Sociologically he has been concerned most with organizational theory in *Complex organizations* (*Etzioni*, 1961a), and *Modern organizations* (*Etzioni*, 1966a; also in 1959a and 1960), and with social change, in particular in *Studies in social change* (*Etzioni*, 1966b).

Political integration is dealt with most comprehensively in his *Political unification* (*Etzioni*, 1965) which also contains the essence of a number of isolated articles published earlier (*Etzioni*, 1962c, d, 1963a, b, c, 1964b). Indispensable to an understanding of his thinking, especially about the political process in general, is his *The active society* (*Etzioni*, 1968a). To a significant extent this book contains most of what is essential in his preceding publications. It is meant to be a comprehensive theory of society, aimed at forging the instruments enabling a society to consciously steer and control its life and development, i.e., a society that is 'active' in his terminology (*Etzioni*, 1968a: 3 ff.).

2. POLITICS

2.1. *The vocabulary*

In view of what has been said already about Etzioni's 'sociological' approach (section 1.1), it is not very surprising that he does not develop a very clear picture of what is to be understood by 'politics'. An added difficulty is constituted by his strong inclination to be over-generous in concept formation. That is, he forms a large multitude of different concepts which he often does not define very precisely, and that are often only very weakly interrelated, whose interrelationships are at any rate frequently left vague or unspecified. This makes it rather difficult to concoct a consistent general conception of the political process from his writings.

His description of the concepts of a 'community' and of 'political community' may serve as a starting point for this inquiry. He writes:

A societal unit is a *community* when it has autarkic integrative mechanisms – that is, when the maintenance of its boundaries, inner structure, and political organization are provided for by its own processes and are not dependent upon external units, supra-units, or sub-units. The communities we deal with here are political and not culturally, religiously, or otherwise circumscribed in scope. A *political community* is a community which has three kinds of autarkic integrative processes: It has sufficient coercive power to countervail the coercive power of any member unit or coalition of them; it has a decision-making center that is able to affect significantly the allocation of assets throughout the community; and it is the dominant focus of political loyalty for the large majority of politically active citizens. A political community is, thus, a state, an administrative-economic unit, and a focal point of loyalty (*Etzioni*, 1968a: 554; in the same sense *Etzioni*, 1965: 4).

Apparently, however, the first element ('coercive power') is the crucial criterion to distinguish political from non-political communities. For he writes:

The control of means of violence distinguishes a political community from other communities, such as religious and ethnic ones (*Etzioni*, 1965: 4; also *Etzioni*, 1968a: 554).

This is not wholly satisfactory. First a definition is given in terms of three different criteria, of which later merely one appears to be decisive. This raises questions regarding the interrelations of these different elements. One may also wonder whether the elements mentioned, combined or in isolation, do indeed constitute the essence of the political process. Do they really enable us to distinguish political processes from other processes, or do they rather distinguish one political configuration – a political community – from other, equally political, ones? They would, in other words, define the concept of 'political *community*', though implicitly presupposing some, unspecified, conception of the adjective. This seems to be confirmed by Etzioni's writing (*Etzioni*, 1968a: 554-555) that the loyalty mentioned is required only in 'political matters', but not in others, ' . . . unless, of course, these non-political identifications have or develop political corrollaries'. What, however, are these?

Etzioni writes that political processes fulfil two different functions, namely:

(. . .) to combine sub-units into a societal unit, to make out of parts a whole, and to guide societal action toward the realization of societal values as expressed via the political process (*Etzioni*, 1968a: 76).

The first function does not tell us very much about politics. Thus, sociologically, societies can be conceived of as combinations of smaller social units; anthropologically, cultures can be viewed as being made up of sub-cultures and, economically, most economies will consist of sub-economies. The point is that the statement quoted does not contain any information whatever about the nature of the 'combination', except that it be political . . . In other words, the nature of the first function mentioned is largely determined by the scientific point of view chosen. Or, while Etzioni is plainly concerned with a *political* process, his first function mentioned presupposes rather than defines the specific nature thereof. The second function promises to be more helpful; it points to 'guidance', to the coordination of the actions and behavior of the members of a community, and to the realization of their values in common actions of the community as a whole. In this connection he writes:

In short, we assume that for a societal entity to exist, political processes are required. We further assume that political processes are the main control mechanism of societal action (*Etzioni*, 1968a: 76).

Thus, the behavior of the community as a whole and that of its individual members is controlled via the political process. This suggests the exercise of power. And this phenomenon does indeed play an important role in Etzioni's thinking.

'Power', then, is described as follows:

Power is a capacity to overcome part or all of the resistance, to introduce changes in the face of opposition (this includes sustaining a course of action or preserving the status quo that would otherwise have been discontinued or altered) (*Etzioni*, 1968a: 314; also *Etzioni*, 1965: 8 footnote).

He distinguishes this from 'influence':

An application of *power* changes the actor's situation and/or his conceptions of his situation – but not his preferences.

(. . .) The exercise of *influence* entails an authentic change in the actor's preferences; given the same situation, he would not choose the same course of action he favored before influence was exercised (*Etzioni*, 1968a: 359-360).

And this, in turn, is distinguished from 'persuasion', as follows:

The difference between them rests in the depth of their effects; persuasion suppresses the actor's preferences without changing them; it, hence, resembles influence on the surface, but there is really an exercise of power beneath. The difference between persuasion and influence is analogous to the difference between propaganda and education (*Etzioni*, 1968a: 360).

So much will have become clear that the point in all these cases is that particular social actors (individuals as well as groups) are made to behave in accordance with the preferences of other actors. Since the distinctions described a moment ago, whatever may be their merits or demerits, do not play a role in the rest of the theory, I will henceforth only use the concept of 'power'. Power, then, will be conceived as some social actor's capacity to make other actors behave in accordance with his preferences, or, what comes to the same thing, as an actor's capacity to impose his decisions as binding upon other actors.

Consequently, Etzioni's conception of the political process as 'the main control mechanism of societal action' can be interpreted as meaning that in its essence politics is concerned with the exercise of power in social life. That is, it is concerned with the processes through which decisions binding upon the actors involved come about (see *Etzioni*, 1968b: 11). In view of the central place power and its exercise assume in Etzioni's thinking, this interpretation would seem to conform most closely to his intentions.

With regard to the means through which power is exercised, he introduces a distinction which does play an important role in his reasoning:

These sanctions, rewards, and instruments differ in their substance: They are either physical, material, or symbolic. This makes for a threefold classification of assets and powers: Power is either coercive (e.g., military forces), utilitarian (e.g., economic sanctions), or persuasive (e.g., propaganda). The classification is exhaustive (*Etzioni*, 1968a: 357; instead of 'persuasive', he often applies the term 'identitive'. See *Etzioni*, 1965: 38, and 1966a: 59).

In connection with the concept of 'power', that of 'assets' is defined as follows:

Assets are possessions that a unit or system has, regardless of those other units may have. Assets might be converted into power, as when a unit uses its economic assets to grant or withhold foreign aid in order to impose its wish on some other unit. On the other hand, a unit might consume these assets, accumulate them, or exchange them for others (*Etzioni*, 1965: 38).

As with power, three kinds of assets are distinguished:

Utilitarian assets include economic possessions, technical and administrative capabilities, manpower, etc. (. . .) *Coercive* assets are the weapons, installations, and manpower that the military, the police, or similar agencies command. (. . .) The term *identitive* assets refers to the characteristics of a unit or units that might be used to build up an identitive power. These identitive potentials are usually values or symbols, built up by religious institutions, national rituals, and other mechanisms (*Etzioni*, 1965: 38-39).

In these distinctions one easily recognizes a somewhat simplified version of Lasswell and Kaplan's reasoning regarding some actor's 'power base' (cf. *Lasswell & Kaplan*, 1950: 83 ff.). Power is differentiated according to the different kinds of resources on which it may be based. The above scheme, however, calls for some comment. In the first place, the categories in question are not defined very precisely. To indicate some examples is not generally an alternative for a clearcut definition. Of course, they could have been defined implicitly by postulating certain relationships between specific kinds of resources and power. This procedure has the important advantage of at once making clear why these distinctions rather than other ones are made. This, however, is hardly done by Etzioni. In the absence of such a more precise specification of the relationships between assets and power, one might, secondly, well wonder whether these two can, in fact, be always conceived as independent phenomena. For, often the very possession of certain resources already implies a measure of power; such resources will often be just as much the result of certain power relations as the cause thereof.

These considerations lead to a third, and more general point, namely the absence of any indication as to the nature of the relationship between resources and power on the one hand, and the specific character of the relations between the actors involved, on the other hand. Power is a relative notion. It is concerned with the relations of one social actor with one or more others. It is with regard to such relations that resources assume their significance. Accordingly, one would presume that it is not resources as such which give power to some actor, but rather the relationships existing between one actor's resources and those of others, within the context of the general nature of the relations between those actors. Thus, for example, 'utilitarian' assets will be relatively unimportant concerning the power relations of two equally autarkic and equally rich countries. The situation changes radically, however, in case these countries are equally rich, and/or (unequally) interdependent economically. Similarly, 'coercive' assets will be relatively unimportant between two countries whose going to war against each other is, for whatever reasons, extremely improbable. As a corollary to these considerations it should be noted – a fourth point – that Etzioni's scheme is silent on the precise ways assets are 'converted' into power which, however, would seem to be a quite complicated matter.

The significance of the distinctions made seems to reside chiefly in the reactions to the application of the different forms of power. This concerns especially the resistance, or 'alienation', which the application of power may provoke on the part of these to whom it is applied. Thus Etzioni writes:

The application of identitive power tends to be the least alienating (. . .); the application of force is the most alienating (. . .). The exercise of utilitarian powers, such as cutting the sugar quota and/or foreign aid, are less alienating than the use of force, but considerably more than the use of identitive power (*Etzioni*, 1965: 39-40).

At first sight this sounds plausible enough. Nevertheless upon somewhat closer scrutiny doubts immediately arise as to their fruitfulness and workability. Here specifically, it seems, the lack of a more detailed analysis of power and its application which was discussed above comes home to roost. In the first place, in view of the fact that identitive power is assumed to rest upon identitive assets, and that these, in turn, seem to involve common values and symbols (i.e., shared by both power-wielder and power-object), one may well doubt whether the first proposition ('the application of identitive power tends to be the least alienating') is not simply vacuously true. Apart from this, secondly, the propositions seem to be rather simplistic and superficial. For it seems quite conceivable for a moderate use of force to be much less alienating than an aggressive propaganda campaign. This would depend on the amount of, the way in which, and the period during which, force is applied; and, concerning propaganda, its contents, form, and tone, to name only a few of the seemingly relevant variables. All this would require much more specific and elaborated analysis.

Returning now to the concept of 'political community' as described earlier, the three kinds of power mentioned now become easily recognizable in its definition. It has appeared that in Etzioni's conception politics is concerned with the formation and application of power, or, to phrase it somewhat differently, with the process through which common binding decisions for the participant actors are achieved. In this perspective the political community can indeed be conceived as one particular political configuration among others. Apparently it is one where a center has emerged which disposes of a large amount of the three powers. Other configurations are possible. With some of them we will meet in the discussion of Etzioni's integration concept.

In connection with the concept 'power' that of 'elite' plays an important role in Etzioni's reasoning. It is defined as follows:

Elite refers to a unit that devotes a comparatively high proportion of its assets to guiding a process and leading other units to support it. It might be a person (for example, de Gaulle), a group of persons (for example, the British aristocracy), or a state (for example, the United States for the Western world) (. . .) When it is necessary to emphasize that we are concerned with a function, disregarding who or what is carrying it out, we use 'elite-unit' rather than simply 'elite'. Elite-unit is preferred over 'core area', used by Deutsch, because it might not be an area, but a social group. Unless otherwise specified, 'elite' throughout this volume is used to refer to units that exercise political leadership, not leadership in economic, cultural or other matters (*Etzioni*, 1965: 45; also *Etzioni*, 1968a: 113).

He also uses the concept of 'elitism':

'Elitism' refers to the concentration of power; it becomes higher the more the system is controlled by one or a few units; it becomes lower the more evenly power is distributed among the member-units (*Etzioni*, 1965: 45-46). (In this latter case he generally applies the term 'egalitarian'.)

These definitions offer some difficulties. Specifically: does an elite have, or does it not have power? Apparently it does. For an elite is 'guiding', and it exercises 'political leadership'. His definition of 'elitism' strongly suggests an elite with decisive power, while elsewhere an elite is thought of as a 'societal control center' (*Etzioni*, 1968a: 113). All this suggests an elite as a unit having power in relation to the rest of some political community. However, the above definitions could also be interpreted in a different way. According to this interpretation an elite is merely a unit devoting much of its resources to helping, or trying to shape the decisions binding upon the community as a whole, its policies and its destinies. In this second sense an elite may be just one among a large number of similar units. It would, perhaps, have power with regard to its supporters, but not necessarily with regard to the community in its entirety, at least not to the same extent.

These two alternative interpretations conform to two well-known similar tendencies in political thinking particularly with regard to the concept of 'democracy'. The first alternative is represented particularly clearly by Vilfredo Pareto, while the second one reappears in the more pluralistic conceptions of Schumpeter, Sartori, and Dahl. There is yet a third possible interpretation of the elite concept – in terms of the social characteristics of those who actually occupy certain positions of power in society. This last conception is essentially that of Mosca's and Bottomore's 'political class' (cf. *Bottomore*, 1964: 6 ff.; for a short discussion of the general problems involved, see also *Rustow*, 1966; *Friedrich*, 1963: 315 ff.).

Now Etzioni does not clearly indicate which of these rather different conceptions he has in mind. As regards this his vocabulary is rather loose. And he often writes about elites as if they were clearly and empirically identifiable political units, acting as such and exercising *the* decisive power in a political community – a conception which resembles that of Pareto. But one may strongly doubt whether such a conception would be at all adequate to an explanation of political processes in most of the contemporary societies. For here we meet with a rather large variety of political actors (such as parties and private interest groups) participating in the political process. Its outcomes, i.e., binding decisions, result from a complicated interaction process of all such actors, and it only seldom occurs that just one actor consistently and in all matters completely imposes his will over the opposition of all the rest. Of course, it may well be that the individuals involved most in this process share a number of social characteristics, such as income, prior profession, educational or cultural background, etc. Thus, one could empirically define some 'political class'. But to equate this political class with an elite in Etzioni's sense, that is, to conceive it as a political actor, would seem to be a gross oversimplification. In Rustow's words:

A meaningful elite theory must show that the rulers have some group identity derived from sources other than their political function – from prior group consciousness, from descent, from schooling, from appointment by previous rulers, from economic interest, or the like. But too often an author assumes what he ought to prove, and ends up with a tautology instead of a theory (*Rustow*, 1966: 711).

In view of these considerations the second ('pluralistic') interpretation of Etzioni's elite concept appears to be much more attractive. Such an interpretation, however, would have to involve a substantial amount of research into the interrelationships existing between the various elites participating in some political process, into their relative powers, and into their relation to the outcomes of the political process. But Etzioni's writings contain very little on this score. To be true, this interpretation involves all of the many problems of any group interpretation of politics. And one might even wonder why a special concept like that of 'elite' should be introduced here at all, the more so since it is not very precisely defined. This interpretation would, at any rate, have the considerable merit of pointing directly to a number of important research problems, instead of using a blanket term to hide both these problems and our ignorance concerning them.

I have paid rather considerable attention to Etzioni's concept of 'elite'. This is because it plays an important role in his integration theory, while the obscurities involved in it are at the root of some significant weaknesses of that theory. It is time, however, to turn to a different range of problems, namely those concerned with the explanation of the formation and application of power.

2.2. *Explanation*

An indication of the direction in which the explanation of the formation and application of power must be sought is furnished by what Etzioni writes about the state.

The state is more a mechanism of 'downward' political control than a mechanism of 'upward' societal consensus-formation. (. . .) We shall use the term *control networks* to refer to those networks in societies or collectivities which are used primarily for downward political flows, and *consensus-formation processes* or structures for those specializing in upward ones (*Etzioni*, 1968a: 107).

By 'consensus' he understands the following:

Consensus is a congruence in the perspectives of two or more actors. Since consensus-building is often only in part a conscious, deliberate process, the term 'consensus' is preferred to 'agreement' (*Etzioni*, 1968a: 469).

He further distinguishes between 'consensus-formation' and 'consensus-mobilization' according as the process originates among a unit's membership or in its power holders respectively (*Etzioni*, 1968a: 470). That is, consensus-formation is conceived as an autonomous process, while consensus-mobilization is one which is induced by the elite(s).

Thus Etzioni juxtaposes two political processes: one consists of 'the application of power and the specification of decisions' (*Etzioni*, 1968a: 480), and the other is that of consensus-building. The latter's purpose is 'to win the support of the member collectivities, their leadership and their membership' (*Etzioni*, 1968a: 480). This raises the question of the relationship between the two processes. An answer is indicated by the following proposition:

Consensus is needed because without it, no world state could have enough power to make the members comply. Legitimation is needed because a world state that relies on illegitimate power will be unstable and may experience civil wars as devastating as the worst international wars of the modern age (*Etzioni*, 1968: 565-566).

This proposition is restricted to a 'world state'. However, it does not seem too far-fetched to generalize it. The more so since, via the concepts of 'authority' and 'legitimacy', it is linked to that of power. As follows:

Authority is defined as legitimate power – that is, power that is used in accord with the subject's values and under conditions he views as proper (*Etzioni*, 1968a: 360; also *Etzioni*, 1965: 8 footnote).

Legitimacy could then be conceived as consensus regarding the application of power. But the latter, in turn, consists of the imposition of a particular behavior, the making and execution of binding decisions, as we have seen. And when power is legitimate, this apparently means that those decisions, or that behavior are in accord with the attitudes, opinions, or preferences of those to whom power is applied. Only in this case politics can be enacted relatively peacefully and in a stable milieu. Further,

Consensus and legitimation, in turn, cannot be created and maintained without community activities over and above the enforcement of law and order and disarmament, because enforcement generates alienation which undermines commitment; consequently, additional and different activities are needed to build up and sustain positive involvement. Also, inasmuch as any pattern of law and order protects a stratification structure, there must be a mechanism for the reallocation of assets so that the societal structure and the political organization will remain articulated. Without a promise of an arrangement for the peaceful inter-societal reallocation of assets, the 'have-not' nations are unlikely to support world-wide community-building; they cannot be expected to consent to the establishment of a world police force and to protect and, thus, rigidify the existing world wide allocative patterns (*Etzioni*, 1968a: 566).

This strongly suggests that consensus with regard to power is achieved through decision-making, or power application, which meets with the values, interests, or opinions of the participants in a political process.

It is tempting to interpret all this more widely and in more or less Eastonian language. That is, the units participating in some political process (individuals or groups) make demands regarding the behavior which should obtain among all of them and which is fixed in decisions binding upon them. The foregoing could be conceived as expressing the implicit postulate saying that such demands and binding decisions will be supported to the extent that they meet the preferences, values, or interests of the units involved. The binding quality of the common decisions could then be interpreted as their being supported to an adequate extent. Or, in other words, a decision is binding to the extent that it is supported, i.e., to the extent that units are prepared to abide by it, to behave in accordance with it. From the postulate mentioned it then would follow that such decisions will be made to the extent that the participants (or the power holders in some established political community) are capable of achieving such a consensus as sufficiently embodies the interests of all of them, or of a sufficiently strong coalition from their midst. Etzioni's three kinds of power (coercive, utilitarian, and identitive) could then be regarded as three different methods to acquire the support of the units involved in some political process. Such an interpretation of Etzioni's conception of politics would also come rather close to those of Haas and of Deutsch. Some provisos are in order, however.

In the first place this interpretation goes rather considerably beyond Etzioni's own formulation. Actually, he merely gives some rough and incidental indications. These indications are not very precisely stated; neither are they elaborated, nor are they explicitly interrelated. Secondly, the conception as sketched does hardly play an identifiable role in the rest of his theoretical scheme. Finally, he introduces a considerable complication, writing:

(. . .) *the state never merely reflects societal consensus* (or that of those who use it); it always has a power and perspective of its own. Like all organizational tools it not only serves a master but also affects what he is able and intends to do (*Etzioni*, 1968a: 110).

In the absence of further elaboration it seems rather difficult to square this with what went before, especially with the extensive interpretation of it which I suggested. The statement seems to introduce some entity, the 'state', willing and acting quite independently even from 'those who use it'. Probably nothing more inconspicuous is meant than saying that a particular organizational structure imposes its own constraints. Its channels and organs are selective and of limited capacity. But then this applies quite generally to any aspect of the physical or social environment of a particular political process. And there is hardly a need to specifically emphasize the state in this respect, unless, of course, it is meant to initiate an investigation into the precise character and function of such constraints. As it stands, however, the proposition quoted suggests a rather fundamental departure from the line of reasoning developed thus far.

With regard to the core problems of the formation and application of power, and the making and execution of binding decisions, Etzioni thus limits himself to a few relatively vague and unconnected hints. As will appear subsequently, this is not without some important consequences for his integration theory.

3. POLITICAL INTEGRATION–DEFINITION

Etzioni defines integration as:

(. . .) the ability of a unit or system to maintain itself in the face of internal and external challenges (*Etzioni*, 1965: 330).

Discussing his concept of 'political community' it has already appeared that this is defined in terms of three 'integrative processes' (*Etzioni*, 1968a: 554), or 'kinds of integration' (*Etzioni*, 1965: 4): coercive, utilitarian, and identitive power. Further he writes:

We shall refer below to the state of a system with respect to the three properties dicussed, as its 'level of integration'. It should be noted, though, that we are dealing with political integration, not with religious, economic, or general integration (*Etzioni*, 1965: 6 footnote).

The first definition quoted above seems to be a rather unfortunate one. Integration is *defined* in terms of the system's ability to withstand external and internal challenges. Now it may well be that there are certain links between a system's level of integration on the one hand, and the ability mentioned on the other. Thus one might presume that, given a challenge of a certain character and magnitude, the more highly integrated system may have a greater chance of meeting it successfully. Whether or not this is true, however, would be a matter for further investigations not to be solved by mere definitory stipulation. The two things are quite different and independent. The ability of a system to maintain itself does not only depend on its level of integration, but also on the kind of challenge with which it is confronted. To define the one in terms of the other would make sense only if one would be prepared to go to such lengths as to view only the strongest system imaginable as really integrated. Of such a queer conception not a trace is to be found in Etzioni's reasoning, of course.

The second definition quoted seems to be more relevant. Integration is conceived as the extent to which some political system has developed certain decision-making capabilities. That is, it disposes of some or all of the kinds of powers he distinguishes to a certain extent. Apparently, this implies certain common organizations or institutions for the system as a whole, since it is in the nature of the three forms of power, that they provide an identifiable focus for the loyalties of the units, are able to allocate the system's resources, and are able to command and apply force. All this is rather difficultly imaginable in the absence of more or less permanent institutions.

Etzioni also uses the concept of 'unification':

To the degree that the net effect of the process is to increase or strengthen the bonds among units, we refer to it as unification; to the degree that it reduces such bonds, de-unification is used, in absence of a better term (*Etzioni*, 1965: 3).

Obviously, this is rather vague. The following definition introduces somewhat more precision:

(. . .)unification – the bounding of units into supra-units. This bounding requires a shift in control from the unit to the supra-unit (*Etzioni*, 1968a: 421).

Apparently, unification is concerned with the formation of new units comprising a number of old ones. In view of the character of the political process, this may be rendered as the creation and development of new decisional capabilities, of new institutions commanding some measure of the various power forms, in a system made up of units thus far independent. It will be clear that Etzioni's concept of 'unification' does not differ essentially from that of 'integration' as applied by Haas and Deutsch. What, then, is the relationship between his concepts of 'integration' and of 'unification'?

He writes:

Unification is a more generic term which refers to the processes which lead to an increase in the level of integration, whether it reaches the community level or stops short of this (*Etzioni*, 1968a: 551).

However, terminological parsimony is served by abolishing the concept of 'unification' altogether, while it also has the advantage of bringing the vocabulary more in line with that of the other authors discussed. The term 'unification' does not serve any function which could not just as well be served by that of 'integration' conceived as processes leading to an increase in the 'level of integration' of some system. The same considerations apply to the separate term 'community-building' (*Etzion*i, 1968a: 551), denoting the process of the formation of a political community. For in view of the above and of the definition of 'political community' quoted earlier (section 2.1), it is apparent that integration, too, can be conceived in terms of the formation of a political community. Whether or not it actually reaches that level (anyhow, when is that precisely?) is immaterial. For, with regard to 'community-building', this, too, can be established only *after* the event. And *before* it, one could, in all probability, never apply the term 'community-building' at all.

As appears from the scheme reproduced below, a political community is conceived as an end-point on a continuum of various forms of, or stages in, a process of integration. In line with the definition developed, these forms are differentiated according as the political system involved has developed different amounts and mixtures of the three kinds of power as 'measured' in a five-point scale. As follows (*Etzioni*, 1965: 7 ff.):

Integrative continuum

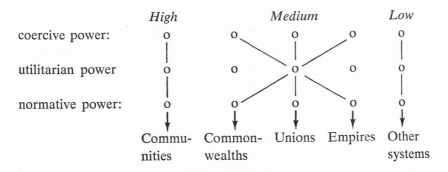

In this scheme the arrows indicate particular combinations of various amounts of the three powers, to which combinations Etzioni attaches such names as 'community' and 'union'. It represents an attempt to describe the various possible forms of integration of a political system. Etzioni pays most attention to the forms 'political community' and 'union'. The latter is further described as follows:

> If a system is less integrated [than a community] but its members are able to act in unison on a wide range of matters, we refer to it not as a community but as a union (of cities, of nations, etc.) (*Etzioni*, 1968a: 555; also *Etzioni*, 1965: 332).

Apparently, however, the above scheme is not complete. For Etzioni introduces also the concept of 'scope' as a different dimension of the integration process. This is concerned with the social sector with regard to which integration occurs:

> Social sector refers to all the activities of a social unit that serve a particular function for that unit (*Etzioni*, 1965: 11 footnote).

And thus:

> *Scope* is measured in terms of the number of social sectors of the member-units that the shared system penetrates (such as only military and economic) and in terms of the importance of these sectors to the survival of the units and the realization of their interests (for example, postal services versus defence alliance). It seems that, in general, *the higher the level of integration the broader the scope* (*Etzioni*, 1965: 11-12).

At first sight this seems plausible enough. The proposition quoted would seem to express an interesting relationship between integration, defined in terms of power, and scope, which concerns the substance of decision-making or the field in which power is applied. Upon closer scrutiny, however, it seems to reveal a certain vacuity. Thus the three power components have already been defined to what could equally be viewed as social sectors. For not only does coercive power, for example, *derive* from the possession of assets in a certain sector (the military or the police sector), but it also *implies* power *over* that sector. And similar considerations would apply to the other two components of power (utilitarian and identitive power). Accordingly, one could argue that a high level of integration, by definition implying a high degree of power, does by the same token imply a large scope. This suggests at least the need for a more detailed and precise elaboration both of the concept of 'power' and that of 'scope'.

Etzioni also uses the concept of 'harmonization':

The essence of the difference between high integration and high harmonization is that in the first case the units are partially fused together to form one system (for example, a nation out of tribes), while in the latter the units maintain their autonomy but work together. This is not the same difference as that between having and not having sovereignty, for sovereignty does not imply coordination or acting in unison. *The difference between harmonization and integration is that between two modes of coordination*: one that draws on a center of power above and beyond the member-units and one that seeks to do without it through interaction between the power centers of the member units (*Ezioni*, 1965: 300).

This definition would seem to strengthen the interpretation developed earlier according to which Etzioni's concept of 'integration' presupposes the formation of common institutions. For although in the above definition he does not explicitly mention institutions, it seems clear that it is precisely these that differentiate integration from harmonization.

It remains to be mentioned, finally, that the concept of 'integration' as developed in this section (like the whole theory intended to explain it) is not concerned solely with international affairs. In fact, it is meant to be of much wider application and validity. As Etzioni writes:

(. . .) the paradigm applies also to the formation of other political communities, such as national communities out of tribal, village, or feudal societies (*Etzioni*, 1962c: 44).

4. POLITICAL INTEGRATION–EXPLANATION

4.1. *'Epigenesis' or 'differentiation'?*

According to Etzioni there are two fundamentally different, even mutually exclusive, methods to study the development of social life: either by conceiving it as a process of 'differentiation', or as one of 'epigenesis'. In his view, 'until now sociology focused almost exclusively on differentiation models' (*Etzioni*, 1963a: 409). But there are several social units whose development cannot be understood in that fashion, he says. He describes both methods in the following terms:

(. . .) *the differentiation model*, which assumes that the 'primitive' social unit contains, in embryonic form, fused together, all the basic modes of social relations that later become structurally differentiated. While relations originally fused gain their own subunits, no new functions are served or new modes of interactions are molded (*Etzioni*, 1963a: 408).

Opposed to this is the 'accumulation approach':

(. . .) the accumulation (or epigenesis) approach, according to which 'adult' units emerge through a process in which parts that carry out new functions are added to existing ones, until the entire unit is assembled. Earlier parts do not include the 'representation' of later ones (*Etzioni*, 1963a: 409).

These descriptions are not excessively precise. They seem to come to this: in the differentiation (or 'preformist') scheme certain social units perform all the basic functions (i.e., 'adaptation', 'allocation', 'social and normative integration'; see *Etzioni*, 1963a: 416, and also *Etzioni*, 1959b: 10), for which later specialized structures are developed. Epigenesis, on the other hand, involves the formation of new units with new functions. Apparently, the latter occurs in political integration. For here new units do emerge which perform the function of achieving binding decisions for the original constituent units. However, one might say that this function is also performed in the absence of common institutions and of integration, for instance by means of warfare, diplomacy, or what Etzioni calls 'harmonization'. Accordingly, one can hardly say that the function in question really is a new one; and, viewed in this light, integration may be conceived both in terms of 'differentiation' and as 'epigenesis'.

Now the use of such terms as 'model' or 'approach' in the above quotations strongly suggests alternative methods to study the phenomena in question. That is, alternative sets of concepts and assumptions involving different ways of putting the problems and of solving them. Etzioni, however, does not describe these, and neither does he show what consequences follow from his choice of one of these so-called 'models' with respect to the problem of integration.

4.2. *Integration as a response to interdependence*

In attempting to account for the occurrence of integration Etzioni writes:

Thus, international exchanges and decisions concerning shared activities are like fluids in a pipe; up to a given level, increased flow can be carried by the old pipes and has little effect. If, however, the volume increases further, broader pipes must be introduced, i.e., more supra-unit controls and unification are required (*Etzioni*, 1968a: 564).

This suggests the following argument: an increase in the volume of international exchanges and activities requires an increase in the volume of internationally binding decisions. Beyond a certain level the latter cannot be carried by the existing international procedures. That is, harmonization does not suffice any more; and this creates the need for the creation of new international institutions, i.e., for integration.

In itself this is still a rather vacuous proposition: integration will or should occur if there are no other possibilities left. The point is, of course, to show how and why precisely this process will or will not occur. Nevertheless, the above contains a hint at one of the elements that could play an important role in such an explanation, namely the volume of the interactions or transactions occurring in a certain political system, or, rather, in its environment. Interpreting Etzioni's general political conception extensively (cf. section 2.2), the above could be reconstructed as follows: more interactions in certain fields (e.g. trade, cultural or military relations) lead to an increasing volume of demands regarding decisions binding upon all those involved in those interactions; by virtue of the volume and the character of those demands, such decision-making has to be organized on a more or less permanent and institutionalized basis; awareness of this on the part of the units involved will lead them to make demands for the formation of new (international) institutions. The relationship between such transactions and the occurrence of integration is a far from simple one, however. Some of the relevant variables involved are mentioned by Etzioni as he observes:

We would expect increased contact between actors to have a greater integration effect on their relations the more similar they were in interests, values, and cognitive perspectives and the more integrated their relations were at the outset. Increased communication can make the actors aware of a latent congruence which they can use to build up consensus, procedures for limiting conflicts, and integration. But when the values, perspectives, and interests of the parties are incompatible, increased communication, we expect, will make them more conscious of that which separates them and will increase tensions and conflicts and, quite likely, decrease the level of integration (*Etzioni*, 1968a: 559).

The same general line of reasoning is to be seen in Etzioni's description of the 'take-off' stage in an integration process – as follows:

The central variable for the 'take-off' of supranational authority is the amount of supranational decision-making required. This, in turn, is determined largely by the amounts and kinds of flows that cross the international borders (e.g., tourists, mail) and the amounts and kinds of shared international activities (e.g., maintaining an early-warning system). It should be stressed, however, that each flow or sharing activity has its own decision-making logarithm [*sic*]. Some flows can increase a great deal and still require only a little increase in international decision-making; others require much more (*Etzioni*, 1963a: 415; in the same sense *Etzioni*, 1965: 52-53).

But who, or what, 'requires' the amount of supranational decision-making? And how does this result in the formation of supranational institutions? Etzioni hardly deals with these problems. He merely observes that the establishment of new decision-making institutions will be more difficult than the extension of the 'power and scope' of existing institutions (*Etzioni*, 1963a: 415). He also writes:

We assume here that the *initiation* of unification requires interdependence among the participating units, that is, they constitute a system. The process by which an unrelated aggregate of units becomes interdependent is too rudimentary and common to be included in the concept of unification, and is excluded here by definition (*Etzioni*, 1965: 34).

Although it may be wise *not* to include the development of such inter-dependences in the *concept* of integration or unification, their analysis would have to assume an important place in a *theory* of integration. For it is difficult to see how an adequate integration theory could be developed without such an analysis of developments occurring in the environment of a political system. Moreover, the establishment and functioning of new political institutions will, in turn, influence those environmental processes. And without an adequate analysis of these environmental processes themselves, an understanding of such feedback relations will be difficult to acquire.

Etzioni, too, recognizes a certain dynamism inherent in a process of political integration. Thus, the core idea of the notion of 'take-off' mentioned above, is self-sustained growth (cf. *Etzioni*, 1965: 51). He further writes:

(. . .) *once a new center of control is established, on the supra-unit level, it tends to grow in power and in command of loyalties* earlier commanded by the member units (*Etzioni*, 1968a: 597).

And:

Once such a bureaucratic structure is established, a process often sets in whereby full-time, professional bureaucrats tend to usurp functions and authority from the part-time, political, 'amateur' superior bodies, thereby expanding the scope of the supranational authority. At the same time, the very existence of supranational control in one area tends to promote such control in others. The concept of spill-over, or secondary priming, which is used here to study the epigenesis of nations and unions, is applicable to the study of accumulation processes in general (*Etzioni*, 1963a: 415; see also *Etzioni*, 1965: 53-54).

Obviously, all this is not yet sufficient. For, what exactly is the role of an international bureaucracy in an integration process; how does it function, and through what mechanisms does it 'usurp' functions and authority? And how does 'spill-over' or 'secondary priming' occur?

Etzioni merely offers some suggestions instead of an elaborate analysis. Thus, in discussing the necessity of 'allocative power' in a political community, it is observed that:

Finally, it serves to focus the attention on the publics and of interest groups on the community rather than on the sub- or supra-units; this anchorages the formation of community-wide, horizontal cleavages that cut across the vertical, member-units, thus countervailing centrifugal forces (*Etzioni*, 1968a: 554).

He also writes:

After take-off, however, unification is expected to *proceed more and more in accord with the intrinsic needs of the emerging political union, less and less in accord with the internal needs of the merging units* (*Etzioni*, 1963a: 418).

In the absence of a specification of 'intrinsic' or 'internal needs', it is difficult to understand the meaning of the second statement. Nevertheless, the two propositions together and in connection with an extensive interpretation of Etzioni's general conception of politics, give some idea of the mechanism of the integration process. That is, decision-making by new international institutions would (on the basis of the postulate mentioned in the beginning of section 2.2) induce the units involved to direct their demands and support to those institutions instead of the national governments. Thus the international institutions may acquire authority. Due to the interrelatedness of sectors, decisions taken in one of them may lead to demands for international decision-making in others. This may lead to a broadening of the scope of the international institutions – the phenomenon of 'spill-over' or 'secondary priming'. However, Etzioni does not offer a detailed analysis of these processes. With regard to the general mechanism of an integration process he limits himself to a few rather general suggestions and hints.

4.3. *17 propositions on elites, power, and integration*

Etzioni's research into the process of integration is especially concerned with the role of elites and power in it. But it has also appeared (section 2.1) that he does not give a very precise and elaborate analysis of these concepts and that they offer many difficulties. Obviously, this entails grave consequences for a theory in which they are to play a central role. This becomes clear at once with regard to the concept of 'integrating power' which, in connection with that of 'elite', assumes a major role in his thinking. He writes:

> Which pattern they [that is, 'sociopolitical processes such as unification'] follow is in part determined by the *kind* of integrating power that various elites exercise and that the evolving union commands (*Etzioni*, 1965: 37).

This is a somewhat queer notion: Etzioni 'defines' it ('integrating powers') by merely referring to his definition of 'power' (*Etzioni*, 1965: 37 footnote). Apparently, it is concerned with the power of the elites involved in an integration process, while the above strongly suggests that this power is exercised on behalf of integration. That is, the concept is made up both of an elite's capacity to act or to impose its will, and the intention to achieve integration. It will be clear, however, that such a concept may quite easily lead to the assertion of vacuous truths. For, on the basis of Etzioni's definition of power, it is difficult to see what else than integration could be the result of the elite's involved disposing of integrating power. Similar dangers inhere in the application of the concept of 'elite', conceived as a unit having power, in the explanation of political processes.

Etzioni's insights into the role of elites and of integrating power in the process of political integration are embodied in a number of propositions which he attempts to test in his empirical investigations and which I will discuss in his own order (*Etzioni*, 1965: 94-96).

> 1. Unions that have fewer elite-units will tend to be more successful than unions that have more. In particular, unions having one elite will be more successful than those having two, and those with two more than those with three.
> 2. Egalitarian unions, whether they develop system-elites or not, tend to be similar in their degree of success to mono-elite unions.
> 3. Egalitarian unions tend to be less decisive than elitist unions, but more capable of generating commitments.

It is not immediately clear how to fit these propositions into the structure of Etzioni's reasoning as discussed so far. It would seem that their status is that of postulates rather than of theorems deduced from other propositions. Nevertheless, a certain link seems to be provided via another assumption, namely:

It would seem that when power is relatively concentrated in the hands of one or two units, coercion is more likely to be used; when it is fairly evenly distributed, identitive appeals are more common; and economic sanctions are frequently used in both elitist and comparatively egalitarian power distributions, but are more frequent in the elitist type (*Etzioni*, 1965a: 47).

Together with his assumption that coercive power provokes more resistance than utilitarian power, and utilitarian more than identitive power (section 2.1), the assumption just quoted could perhaps explain that egalitarian unions are more capable of generating commitments than elitist ones. This would seem to mean that in egalitarian unions positive support for the common institutions is forthcoming more readily, or, conversely, that these institutions more easily acquire authority. However, it has appeared already (section 2.1) that the connection between the kind of power applied and the resistance it provokes as postulated by Etzioni is of a very dubious nature.

Also, the ambiguity of Etzioni's elite concept is clearly manifest in the propositions mentioned above. If an elite were a unit that actually has decisive power, and if it is assumed that this elite actually wants integration (an assumption which is not made explicit by Etzioni, but which is necessary, nonetheless), then, of course, a mono-elite union will be more successful than one with more elites. For, in the latter case the various elites will perhaps not all want integration to the same extent or of the same form. In this case, however, an elite is apparently not a unit which has decisive power over the rest: it is one of a number of groups and individuals participating in the political process. And in this case integration will result from a complex process of struggle, bargaining, compromise, coalition building, etc., among those 'elites'. In this connection Etzioni concludes:

Finally, while three-member elite systems seem to us to be conflict-prone, the effect of a dual-elite structure on the success of a unification drive is determined largely by whether the elites are in conflict or coalition (*Etzioni*, 1965: 299-300).

This is particularly unconvincing. Why a distinction should be made at all between systems with two or three, or even more 'elites' is not made clear. In all these cases 'the success of a unification drive' will presumably be determined largely 'by whether the elites are in conflict or coalition' . . . And in connection with this it should be noted that in the propositions quoted no attention is paid to the interests, purposes, or demands of the elites concerned. But this element, too, will presumably have an effect upon the success of integration.

In the light of the above considerations one may also question the validity of Etzioni's ideas on 'egalitarian' unions. It will be recalled that in such unions power is not concentrated in one or a few elites, but is distributed more or less evenly over all the participants in the political process. In this case binding decisions (and among them the decision to establish or to strengthen new, international political institutions) will result from a complicated process of bargaining, coalition-building, intra- and inter-unit conflict and struggle, as indicated previously. How and why this should result in integration, and in particular why such egalitarian unions should be 'similar in their degree of success to mono-elite unions' is not made clear, however. On the basis of the previous discussion of mono-elite unions, this would actually be a rather astonishing result.

Now Etzioni distinguishes 'member-elites', 'external elites', and 'system-elites', according as the elites concerned are members of one of the communities that constitute a political system, are outside of that system, or are elites in the context of that system as a whole, respectively (*Etzioni*, 1965: 329). He then writes:

(. . .) *the most effective unions are expected to be ruled by system-elites rather than by member-elites.* A system-elite combines the decisiveness found in member-elites with the ability to generate commitment found in egalitarian unions; the decisiveness is gained from the existence of one superior center of decision-making, while commitments are generated because the system-elite is representing all the members of the union as a collectivity (*Etzioni*, 1965: 296-297).

That an integration process is more successful if there is a system-elite than if there is no such elite, is obvious. Not, however, because such an elite necessarily would be more decisive, nor because it would 'represent' all the members, but simply because its existence *implies* a successful integration process. For it means that, at the level of the system as a whole, a unit has emerged having decision-making capabilities. And that is precisely what the theory should explain. Similarly, it should explain whence derives the power of the one elite in a mono-elite union, and how it emerges, develops, and is exercised in a multi-elite union. Etzioni does not go very deeply into such matters, however.

He recognizes the role external elites may play in an integration process. Regarding this he formulates two propositions:

4. The external elite tends to enhance the success of unification the more the direction of its application of power coincides with the power structure of the emerging union, and to hinder it the more the application of its power is counter to the emerging structure.

5. As the level of integration and the scope of the union increase, the union tends to internalize the functions performed, as well as the authority held and the loyalties commanded by the external elite.

Now, apparently, Etzioni assumes that integration is actually taking place (for he is speaking about 'the emerging union'). This obviously means that the integrating system's 'power structure' (whatever that may actually mean) is directed towards integration. The application of some elite's power which 'coincides' with this structure merely means some extra impetus in the direction of integration. This is vacuously true. Of course, external units may exert some influence upon developments within some other system (and one may doubt whether an 'external elite' would still be an elite *without* some power over the system concerned). The generality quoted, however, does not provide any insight into this problem.

With regard to the second proposition (nr. 5), it is first of all necessary to inquire how Etzioni defines 'internalization'.

We refer to the process in which control of a system is taken over by member-elites from external elite-units as *internalization*, since control that was external to the system becomes internal (*Etzioni*, 1965: 483; of course, the member-elite may also be a system-elite).

However, integration consists of the creation of (institutionalized) decision-making capacities for a certain international political system. And the more power the new common institutions have, the more integrated the system is. Now as long as some external unit disposes of a considerable amount of power with respect to that system, that system as such cannot be said to be highly integrated. Or, rather, integration now concerns a different system – one *comprising* the 'external' unit. Integration here may assume the form of an empire or of a hegemonial system. But this is relatively insubstantial, because these, too, are forms of integration. In all those cases integration necessarily involves the 'internalization' of decision-making capabilities. If not, there is no sense in speaking of integration, except in the sense of integration *into* another system.

Viewed in this light Etzioni's 'internalization' merely means the process whereby some unit or group of units integrated within another system, e.g., a colonial or hegemonial system, becomes autonomous. This process need not necessarily result in a higher measure of integration within that unit or group of units itself. For,

If the external elite is more responsive than the internal elite, the result will be quite different. Note, for instance, the de-unifying effects of the internalization of control in the Federation of Rhodesia and Nyassaland, as power shifted from the British Colonial Office to the hands of the white settlers, a shift that accelerated African secessionist pressures (*Etzioni*, 1965: 293; It should be noted, incidentally, that here as elsewhere the term 'elite' seems to be used indiscriminately to denote states and non-state groupings, such as the white settlers of East Africa).

More generally Etzioni mentions three circumstances in which the process of internalization leads to tensions in some integration process:

a) The functions and powers internalized are taken over by member units from the external elite rather than by the union (. . .) b) The effect of such member- rather than union-internalization is even more de-unifying if some members' gains are not matched by those of others. Such uneven internalization increases heterogeneity, a factor that seems to make unification more difficult. c) If internalization is uneven among sectors, such as the economic and the military ones (. . .) (*Etzioni*, 1965: 293).

From these remarks it may be concluded that internalization involves an important number of rather fundamental problems concerning power and its application, the establishment and development of certain configurations of power-relationships, and the role of external units in some process of integration. The above analysis, however, is too rudimentary to be of much help in solving them.

Concerning the relationship between the character of power and the process of integration, Etzioni states three propositions:

6. The more identitive power the elites initiating and guiding unification command or the union-system builds up, the more successful unification tends to be.
7. The more utilitarian power the elites initiating and guiding unification command or the union-system builds up, the more successful unification tends to be.
8. The relation between the application of coercive power and the success of unification is curvilinear (That is, in contrast to the two other kinds of power, the higher application of force, above a given level is expected to produce less, not more, unification, all other things being equal).

These propositions would seem to follow directly from Etzioni's assumptions concerning the relationship between the kind of power applied and the resistance it tends to provoke. Upon closer analysis, however, these assumptions turned out to be of a rather dubious nature (cf. section 2.1). Naturally this also gravely affects the validity of the above propositions. Perhaps more important is that here, too, Etzioni largely ignores the problem how these kinds of power are acquired by the relevant elites, and why they are, and can be, applied in favor of integration. As it is, these propositions seem to verge on question-begging. For the thing to be explained by an integration theory would seem to be precisely how and why 'the elites initiating and guiding unification', or 'the union-system', do acquire and build up power.

9. A union is more successful the more effective its upward and downward *communication* channels are and the more *responsive* its power elites are to the communication received.
10. The stability of a union is undermined and its growth curtailed when the avenues of *political representation* are clogged or closed (Note: political representation is viewed as a central avenue of power-backed communication).
11. *Secession* of alienated units will be much more common than revolution in unions as compared to political communities.
12. The ratio will change in favor of revolutions as the process of unification increases the level of integration and scope of the unions.

All this can be deduced in a relatively straightforward manner from

Etzioni's general political conception, provided it is interpreted extensively and that what has been formulated as an assumption is indeed taken seriously as such. For, on the basis of what seems to be his most fundamental assumption concerning the relationship between support, demands, and binding decisions (see section 2.2), one may say that a stable power position for the institutions of an (international) political system requires the availability of a sufficient measure of support from the units involved. Such support will be forthcoming only if and in so far as the decisions taken by those institutions meet the substance of the demands made by the units. This, in turn, requires that sufficient facilities exist for such demands to be communicated to the institutions, and that the latter actually take them into account in their policy-making. In fact, this is what propositions 9 and 10 reduce to.

In order to attain a sufficient measure of consensus or support among a large number of more or less heterogeneous political units, a 'multi-level consensus formation structure' may be required, in Etzioni's view:

Consensus among a large number of units can, however, be reached by breaking the participants into groups, each group working out an agreement among its members, with the group's representatives working out a general consensus (Etzioni, 1962a: 194; see also *Etzioni*, 1962d: 928; 1964c: 186-187).

That the occurrence of secession and of revolution depend upon the measure of integration attained in a political system is rather obvious; actually, this is largely a matter of definition. Revolution is directed against the institutions of a political system, and aims at overthrowing or changing them. This will happen only if such institutions do in fact exist and have developed to such an extent, and the units involved have developed such a measure of political interdependence, as to make it worthwhile to continue to operate within the same political system. As a general rule these conditions are met only in a highly integrated system, i.e., in a political community. Secession, on the other hand, implies the separation of a unit with its own decision-making institutions from an existing political system and its institutional framework. The mere existence of such units already means that the original system was not a very highly integrated one.

In connection with the above, Etzioni's concept of 'exchange' may be discussed. He writes:

The relationships among members of a union can be fruitfully examined as exchanges in which assets that are an output of one unit are an input for one or more other units; that is, the outputs of one unit are exchanged for those of the others. Two key variables here are the rate of exchange and its substance. In completely egalitarian relationships the *rate of exchange* is one, that is, each unit is giving the same amount it is receiving. In follower-elite relationships the rate of exchange is a ratio expressing the amount of power the elite has over the follower; the smaller the ratio and the less favorable the exchange is to the follower, the greater is the power of the elite (*Etzioni*, 1965: 77).

A more elaborate analysis of this concept of 'exchange' could have led easily to a more satisfactory conception of the problem of the *formation* of power. For it clearly reveals the two-sided character of power as a relationship between the elite or the political institution and the members of the political system, and it suggests a certain interaction between these two. This interaction, in its turn, could perhaps profitably be analysed in terms of demands, support, and the substance of the binding decisions made, and on the basis of what seems to be Etzioni's fundamental assumption regarding their interrelationship quoted earlier (section 2.2). Etzioni, however, does not develop a detailed analysis of the concept. Instead, he applies it to denote power-relationships. But it is rather difficult to see what this adds to the understanding of those relationships. The more so since he conceives the 'substance of exchange' as consisting of 'assets', that is, possession that can be 'converted' into 'power'. It has already been shown (section 2.1) that both 'assets' and 'power', and their interrelationships offer many difficulties, and that their nature can hardly be said to have been determined precisely and unequivocally. In these circumstances the whole concept of 'exchange', together with the remark just quoted, remain in mid-air. Accordingly, it is not very surprising that Etzioni concludes that he hardly needed the concept in his investigations (*Etzioni*, 1965: 315).

Etzioni does hardly deal systematically and in detail with the kinds of demands or interests of the units involved in an integration process, and with their role in such a process. With regard to the elites guiding an integration process he concludes that

(. . .) contrary to a widely held belief, *their main interest in unification does not seem to be improving their utilitarian rates of exchange.* The data suggest the contrary; that leading a union, to the degree it is in the hands of a member-elite or an external elite (as distinguished from a system-elite), seems to require, on balance, investment of some utilitarian assets by the elite in exchange for some symbolic (identitive) gratification, such as that gained from the status of leadership (*Etzioni*, 1965: 315).

As noted on various occasions, the concepts involved in this proposition are not very clearly defined; and neither has the above been analysed elaboratedly, nor does it fit in with such a systematic analysis.

Etzioni's last five propositions, finally, run as follows:

13. The amount of power needed to *increase* the level of integration and to extend the scope of a union tends to be higher than that needed to *maintain* a given level of integration and scope.

14. Integrating power needed tends to be greater to maintain a *premature* unification effort than a *mature* one; and even smaller, at least in the initial stage, to maintain an *overdue* one.

15. *Acceleration* strategy tends to be more successful in the mature and overdue unions and *deceleration* strategy in the premature unions.

16. For the initial stages of unification, building up the union, *rather than reallocation* among units or subunits, tends to be more effective.

17. The *coercive showdown* of a union tends to come at a particular point in its life history: a) as the power of external elites declines, b) before the union's utilitarian and identitive systems and power are built up, or c) after they have weakened.

It may be recalled that 'the level of integration and scope' denotes the degree to which the institutions of an (international) political system dispose of decision-making capabilities, that this is the crux of Etzioni's concept of 'power', and that, in fact, 'level of integration' is defined by him in terms of power. Consequently, proposition 13 amounts to little more than a vacuous truth. The use of the term 'power' in it suggests an explanation in terms of an independent variable. It appears, though, that this variable is anything but independent; accordingly, it can difficultly be used in an explanation. But its use does definitely obscure the real problem: how is a certain level of integration maintained or increased? The proposition quoted does not answer that question.

For the understanding of the next proposition (14) it is first of all necessary to see what is meant by the terms 'premature', 'mature', and 'overdue'. Etzioni defines as follows:

Premature unification occurs when the population of the member-units have strong vested interests in the regulation of utilitarian processes on the unit rather than the system level, desire unit-control of coercive power, and strongly identify with the unit as compared with the system.

Mature unifications are those in which the level of vested interests in the unit is medium to low, in which there is no unit-control of coercion or only a limited one, and in which the population's identification with the units is weak and progressively weakening.

An *overdue* unification is one in which there are widely felt needs for more interunit, union-wide regulation of utilitarian processes and control of the means of violence than is available and in which the population's identification with the system is higher than is needed for the existing level of integration (*Etzioni*, 1965: 81).

At best this could be viewed as the beginning of an analysis of the interests of the units involved in a process of integration. For in the above statement integration is related to the interests and needs of the participants with regard to the three components of power. It is not elaborated, however. But, still more important, Etzioni's definitions threaten to render his fourteenth proposition, too, simply vacuous. For, 'premature', 'mature', and 'overdue' unifications are defined in terms of the strength of the units ('populations', &vested interests') in favor of integration or, conversely, opposing integration. And his definition of power seems to imply that the more resistance or opposition there is, the more power is needed to overcome it (cf. section 2.1). This exactly is what proposition 14 amounts to.

On 'acceleration' and 'deceleration' in relation to the elites in control Etzioni writes:

On the one hand, they might *decelerate* unification to allow more time for adjustment and to reduce the de-unifying pressures by curtailing the changes introduced. That is, they hope to reduce unification to the level the integrating power can carry. Or, the elites might marshal a grand offensive to *accelerate* unification and bring it to a level at which, hopefully, new supportive power will arise (because new vested interests have been centered around the evolving structure, its values have become more visible, or less integrating power is necessary now that resistance has been broken) (*Etzioni*, 1965: 321-322).

Besides, he suggests that acceleration will be most successful at a moment of 'success' and least successful at a moment of 'crisis'. But since he does not describe precisely what these strategies consist of, and how they influence the integration process, it is rather difficult to see what precisely is meant here.

The alternative mentioned in proposition 16 makes a somewhat dubious impression. For 'building up the union' implies the creation of certain decision-making capacities that, in turn, are presupposed in 'reallocation'. That is, 'reallocation' requires a fairly large amount of such decision-making capacities; and it is thus doubtful whether, in the initial stages of integration there really is an alternative. Whereas 'reallocation' seems to be concerned with the communities' resources or with economic assets, 'building up the union' seems to refer to such things as 'community sentiments, institutions, and integrative forces' (*Etzioni*, 1963c: 189). This could be interpreted as suggesting that the alternative mentioned is concerned with the differential effect of two kinds of interests upon integration. Thus, in the initial stages of an integration process, attempts at strongly affecting economic interests would tend to make integration more difficult and interests of a more general nature, not deeply affecting the units involved should be stressed instead. This idea rests upon two assumptions, namely:

1. The marginal alienation of the groups from which benefits are taken is going to be greater than the marginal gratification of the groups to which benefits are given. For instance, the alienation of those farmers who will lose subsidies is greater than the gratification of the taxpayer who will pay less taxes or buy cheaper food. 2. The alienation of the deprived groups will be more concentrated and politically better articulated than that of the gratified ones (*Etzioni*, 1963c: 192).

Several things should be noted, though. In the first place, whereas the above suggests a generalized analysis of the differential effect of kinds of interests and binding decisions upon integration in terms of the positive or negative support for integration which is forthcoming, it is not elaborated sufficiently. More specifically, the kinds of interests involved in the above proposition are hardly defined with sufficient precision by Etzioni. And in the absence of further analysis the two assumptions just quoted are not too convincing. In the second place, it would not seem too far-fetched to suppose that the growth of 'community sentiments' could be induced via decisions or policies concerning more tangible, economic interests. In other words, 'building up the union' might well proceed precisely through 'reallocation'. To decide this point, however, would require much deeper analysis and detailed empirical research.

Proposition 17, finally, is concerned with a 'coercive showdown' which may occur in an integration process.

In almost every unification there are one or more units or subunits for which the prospect of further unification is comparatively highly alienating; as unification progresses, the active resistance of such units increases. Even if there are constant efforts to make the union profitable to such units, or to appeal to their value commitments not to obstruct unification, or to threaten them with the use of force, often a point is reached at which – if unification is to be continued – the power of such an alienated unit 'needs' to be reduced or at least its weakness vis-à-vis the union has to be demonstrated in order to make it cooperate and in order to retain the cooperation of the other units (. . .) Since the test tends to require the use of coercive power and to occur in a limited period of time, we shall refer to it as the 'coercive showdown' (*Etzioni*, 1965: 87).

And:

Earlier (i.e., before the 'showdown', DV), disunity is minimized and showdowns are avoided because they might strengthen the control of the external elite and discredit the party that forces the showdown. On the other hand, delaying a showdown until the union's system and integrating powers are built up will tend to prevent an alienated unit from affecting the structure of the emerging union (*Etzioni*, 1965: 88).

Etzioni's 'coercive showdown' apparently refers to a particularly critical and decisive application of physical force. As an example, he points to the American civil war. After such a showdown the union is established – it is a final confrontation between integrative and disintegrative forces. It can hardly be maintained, however, that this is a sufficiently precise determination of the concept. What exactly is the difference between such a showdown and other applications of physical force, or other forms of armed conflict? And in particular, why a *showdown* instead of a long period of adaptation and armed confrontations? The circumstances in which a showdown tends to occur, and that are indicated in the 17th proposition, all seem to refer to a situation in which the powers of the union's institutions still are quite low. But this does not yet explain why what kinds of violence play what role in an integration process.

4.4. *Sectors, spill-over, and stability*

It has already been shown (section 4.2) that Etzioni recognizes the possibility of an integration process acquiring a certain momentum of its own. It has already appeared that his writings contain some suggestions as to how to explain such processes as 'spill-over' or 'secondary priming' and the self-sustained growth of integration. It may now be asked to what extent these processes are dependent upon the character of the sectors with regard to which integration or the building up of decisional capabilities occurs. Etzioni writes:

The data cast some light on the 'functional' approach. They suggest that in gradually building up the scope of a union, the critical questions are what sectors are tackled first and how extensive the functional effort in each of these sectors is. If they are low spill-over sectors, or if integration in high spill-over sectors is below the take-off point, a broad-scoped unification process will not be primed (. . .) In short, it seems that the 'functional' approach in itself is neither valid nor false; it is not specific enough. The scope-broadening effect of functional integration depends on which sectors are selected and how each is integrated (*Etzioni*, 1965: 309).

Etzioni himself assumes the following order among sectors with regard to what might be called their 'spill-over potential':

(. . .) I would order international organizations in various sectors with respect to their spill-over tendencies – from low to high – as follows:
a. organizations that deal with services such as postal services, allocation of radio frequencies, police cooperation, etc.;
b. organizations dealing with labor, health, and cultural exchange, i.e., services to which 'human values' are attached;
c. tariff agreements and military organizations;
d. economic unions or common markets.
The spill-over phenomenon points to the fact that societal sectors differ in the degree to which they are inter-related. Integrating some of them triggers unification tendencies in many other sectors; while integrating some other sectors has comparatively small repercussions. The military sector,

for instance, is highly segregated and autonomous, unless industrial mobilization is involved. (. . .) Economic integration, on the other hand, affects all societal groups – consumers, producers, management, labor, farmers, small business – and therefore tends to have extensive political repercussions. In contrast, tariff agreements, especially to the degree that they cover only some goods and concern only reduction but not abolition of tariffs, affect only some exporters and importers and a limited number of related industries (*Etzioni*, 1962d: 931).

Thus the crucial point is apparently the number and character of groups that are affected by integration in some sector – either directly, or indirectly. The more groups that are affected, the higher the 'spill-over potential' of the sector concerned.

In this context Etzioni also uses the concept of the 'dominant function'. This concerns the major or most important function that is served by some integrating system in some stage of its development. In Etzioni's view this is an important variable.

For instance, we can already suggest that some functions – especially the political, social, and ideological ones – require higher integration and broader scope than others (for example, individual-oriented consumption). Hence, the level and scope at which the unification process is terminated and the nature of the function serviced collectively are crucial variables that both affect and are affected by the dominant function of the new unions and communities (*Etzioni*, 1965: 63).

Here, too, it would seem that the point is the number and kinds of the groups concerned with or affected by integration.

The above is related to the problem of the stability of unions and of communities. As follows:

The highest degree of stability is reached, we suggest, only when a full-fledged political community is established; that is, when integration on all three dimensions (monopoly of violence, center of decision-making, and focus for identification) is high, and unification has penetrated all major societal sectors. Unification might stop short of high integration and full scope, and the resulting union might exist for a considerable period of time; moreover, high integration and full scope might be more difficult to attain and, hence, more risky to aim at than some less integrated and less encompassing form of unification. All that we hypothetically suggest is that, once attained and in the long run, unions that have become highly integrated and have a broad scope are more stable than those that are not so well integrated or inclusive (*Etzioni*, 1965: 56; in the same sense *Etzioni*, 1968a: 958).

However, the relationship between stability and level of integration and scope is anything but a simple one. For,

It is quite possible that a less maximally integrated structure will prove stable, since it allows for more expression of unit loyalties and vested interests (*Etzioni*, 1965: 62).

But, on the other hand,

(. . .) the more integrated a community is (by other standards), the more unit autonomy it can tolerate (*Etzioni*, 1965: 62).

Although,

The broader the functional scope of an international organization, the more consensus-formation required; hence, the fewer the number of nations at each level (or more precisely, the lower the degree of heterogeneity) it can tolerate without loss of effectiveness (*Etzioni*, 1964c: 188).

It seems to be difficult to square the four propositions just quoted. Anyhow they suggest that the relationship between the level of integration and stability has not been determined unequivocally, and that much more analysis and research are needed.

5. EMPIRICAL INTERPRETATION

On the operationalization of the foregoing scheme we can be brief. Etzioni does not deal specifically and systematically with the problem how to link his concepts unambiguously with observations. As already observed (ch. two, section 4.1), this does not mean, of course, that the reasoning analysed above is entirely devoid of empirical content. Rather, it means that its empirical content does not exceed that which a more or less refined common understanding of the concepts employed gives it. In a scientific theory, however, it should be possible to unambiguously determine whether or not something is the case in empirical reality and to what extent. And to accomplish this with respect to the concepts Etzioni applies, common understanding will not generally suffice. Thus, questions such as 'how far has integration proceeded?', 'is A an elite, and if so to what extent?', 'how much power, and of what kind, does A command with respect to B?', to mention only some of the more obvious ones, remain largely unanswered. Etzioni's insights into empirical integration processes thus are a matter of more or less impressionistic judgment rather than of empirically testable conclusions.

6. ASSESSMENT

As I have already said in the 'introduction' the main purpose of the present inquiry is to see whether and to what extent contemporary theorizing in the field of political integration provides a starting-point for further elaboration, research, and theory formation.

From this point of view the scheme analysed in the present chapter is rather disappointing. Its defects are quite obvious. It employs a superabundance of concepts and technical terms. These, however, are not very clearly and precisely defined. Neither does their meaning become much clearer through their application in the propositions that are formulated. These, in turn, are generally stated in a rather loose fashion. Whatever may be their *prima facie* plausibility, closer analysis often reveals important uncertainties that leave their meaning in mid-air, or they turn out to be more or less vacuous truths. Accordingly, the entire theoretical structure suffers from vagueness and ambiguity. It also exhibits a strong tendency to remain at the surface of things. Time and again it turned out that important problems were ignored, or that propositions stated appeared to involve questions an answer to which was imperative in order to make the proposition concerned at all meaningful. Thus, a lack of elaboration and deeper analysis entailed particularly grave consequences for the application of two of the more fundamental concepts introduced, namely 'power' and 'elite'. Compared with these crucial defects, the lack of a sufficient operationalization of the scheme is of a decidedly minor importance. And in view of the above one may even doubt the use of any attempt to provide such operationalization. It has also appeared that inasmuch theorizing did reach deeper levels, it displayed elements suggesting a line of reasoning and analysis not unlike that found in the thinking of Haas and of Deutsch. However, they have been elaborated too little to be of much help in understanding the problems involved.

BIBLIOGRAPHY

ANONYMOUS, 1968. *World peace through world economy (6th int. Study Conf., Youth & Student Div. Wld Ass. Wld Federalists).* Van Gorcum/Prakke & Prakke, Assen (Netherlands).
ANONYMOUS, 1966. *International political communities – an anthology.* Doubleday, Garden City (N.Y.).

BOTTOMORE, T. B., 1964. *Elites and society.* Watts, London.

ETZIONI, Amitai, 1959a. Authority structures and organizational effectiveness. *Admve Sci. Q. 4 (1)*: 43–67.
ETZIONI, Amitai, 1959b. The functional differentiation of elites in the kibbutz. In: *Studies in social change,* pp. 9–29. Holt, Rinehart & Winston, New York, 1966.
ETZIONI, Amitai, 1959c. Alternative ways to democracy – the example of Israel. In: *Studies in social change,* pp. 157–179. Holt, Rinehart & Winston, New York, 1966.
ETZIONI, Amitai, 1960. Two approaches to organizational analysis – a critique and a suggestion. *Admve Sci. Q. 5*: 257–278.
ETZIONI, Amitai (Ed.), 1961a. *Complex organizations – a sociological reader.* Holt, Rinehart & Winston, New York.
ETZIONI, Amitai, 1961b. Industrial sociology – the study of economic organizations. In: Amitai Etzioni (Ed.), *Complex organizations – a sociological reader,* pp. 130–141. Holt, Rinehart & Winston, New York.
ETZIONI, Amitai, 1962a. *The hard way to peace – a new strategy.* Collier Books, New York.
ETZIONI, Amitai, 1962b. The decline of neo-feudalism – the case of Israel. In: *Studies in social change,* pp. 180–197. Holt, Rinehart & Winston, New York, 1966.
ETZIONI, Amitai, 1962c. A paradigm for the study of political unification. *Wld Polit. 15 (1)*: 44–74.
ETZIONI, Amitai, 1962d. The dialectics of supranational unification. *Am. polit. Sci. Rev. 56 (4)*: 927–935.
ETZIONI, Amitai, 1963a. The epigenesis of political communities at the international level. *Am. J. Sociol. 68 (4)*: 407–421.
ETZIONI, Amitai, 1963b. European unification and perspectives on sovereignty. *Daedalus 92 (3)*: 498–520.

ETZIONI, Amitai, 1963c. European unification – a strategy of change. In: *International political communities – an anthology*, pp. 175–197. Doubleday, Garden City (N.Y.), 1966.

ETZIONI, Amitai, 1964a. *Winning without war*. Doubleday, Garden City (N.Y.).

ETZIONI, Amitai, 1964b. On self-encapsulating conflicts. In: *Studies in social change*, pp. 115–135. Holt, Rinehart & Winston, New York, 1966.

ETZIONI, Amitai, 1964c. Atlantic union, the Southern continents, and the United Nations. In: Robert Fisher (Ed.), *International conflict and behavioral science – the Craigville papers*, pp. 179–207. Basic Books, New York.

ETZIONI, Amitai, 1964d. The West Indian Federation – a constitution against reality. *6th Congr. IPSA*, (Geneva, 1964).

ETZIONI, Amitai, 1965. *Political unification – a comparative study of leaders and forces*. Holt, Rinehart & Winston, New York.

ETZIONI, Amitai, 1966a. *Modern organizations*. Prentice Hall, Englewood Cliffs (N.J.).

ETZIONI, Amitai, 1966b. *Studies in social change*. Holt, Rinehart & Winston, New York.

ETZIONI, Amitai, 1966c. A psychological approach to change. In: *Studies in social change*, pp. 79–109. Holt, Rinehart & Winston, New York.

ETZIONI, Amitai, 1968a. *The active society – a theory of societal and political processes*. Collier–MacMillan, London/Free Press, New York.

ETZIONI, Amitai, 1968b. Introduction. In: J. P. Nettl & Ronald Robertson, *International systems and the modernization of societies – the formation of national goals and attitudes*. Faber & Faber, London.

ETZIONI, Amitai, 1968c. Next steps for the third world – an internationalist view. In: *World peace through world economy (6th int. Study Conf. Youth & Student Div. Wld Ass. Wld Federalists)*: 35–46. Van Gorkum/Prakke & Prakke, Assen (Netherlands).

ETZIONI, Amitai, 1969. Toward a Keynesian theory of social processes. *Wld Polit. 22 (1)*: 139–147.

ETZIONI, Amitai & Frederic L. DUBOW, 1967. Some workpoints for a macrosociology. In: Samuel Z. Klausner (Ed.), *The study of total societies*. Doubleday, Garden City (N.Y.).

FISHER, Robert (Ed.), 1964. *International conflict and behavioral science – the Craigville papers*. Basic Books, New York.

FRIEDRICH, Carl Joachim, 1963. *Man and his government – an empirical theory of politics*. McGraw-Hill, New York.

KLAUSNER, Samuel Z. (Ed.), 1967. *The study of total societies*. Doubleday, Garden City (N.Y.).

LASSWELL, Harold D. & Abraham KAPLAN, 1950. *Power and society – a framework for political inquiry*. Yale University Press, New York/London, 1963.

NETTL, J. P. & Roland ROBERTSON, 1968. *International systems and the modernization of societies – the formation of national goals and attitudes.* Faber and Faber, London.

RUSTOW, Dankwart A., 1966. The study of elites – who's who, when, and how. *Wld Polit. 18 (4):* 690–717.

1. INTRODUCTION – A SECOND–GENERATION THEORY

In Lindberg's research into the process of international integration one may distinguish two different stages. The first one comprises *The political dynamics of European economic integration* (*Lindberg*, 1963), *Decision making and integration in the European Community* (*Lindberg*, 1965), and *Integration as a source of stress on the European Community system* (*Lindberg*, 1966a). The second, more recent stage is represented by *The European Community as a political system . . .* (*Lindberg*, 1966b), his and Scheingold's *Europe's would-be polity . . .* (*Lindberg & Scheingold*, 1970), and his *Political integration as a multi-dimensional phenomenon . . .* (*Lindberg*, 1970).

In the first three publications mentioned (*Lindberg*, 1963, 1965, 1966a) he largely remains within the theoretical framework as developed by Ernst Haas, his former teacher. In them he basically seeks to apply and to elaborate Haas's theoretical scheme, rather than attempting the independent construction of a fundamentally new theory of integration. While Haas, in his *The uniting of Europe*, was concerned with the establishment and development of the European Coal and Steel Community, Lindberg, in *The political dynamics of European economic integration*, deals with the European Economic Community. Thus, one of the beneficial results of this research strategy is that we now dispose of two fairly sophisticated analyses, applying a common theoretical perspective, of two important successive stages in the process of contemporary European integration.

The second stage in Lindberg's research differs from the preceding one by the fact that here an attempt is made to apply Easton's systems-analytic vocabulary to the field of international integration. However, one should not attach too much importance to this difference. For it has already appeared how very close Haas's thinking, and thus, by implication, that of Lindberg, is to that of Easton – whether a specifically systems-analytic terminology is used or not (see in particular chapter three, section 2.4). Accordingly, the application of this vocabulary in itself can hardly be expected to result in any fundamental departure from the original theoretical scheme.

Lindberg's investigations differ from those of the other authors discussed so far in that they are concerned exclusively with just one instance of an integration process, namely that occurring among the six states of the European Common Market. At first sight this would seem to seriously limit the significance of Lindberg's theoretical efforts. Theorizing could be biased because of the rather special characteristics of this contemporary European integration process. Nevertheless, this restriction of research to only one empirical case does not in itself preclude the formation of an integration theory of much wider validity and applicability. For what empirical setting constitutes the immediate stimulus for theorizing is, after all, of relatively minor importance. And no amount of empirical cases investigated in the process of theory formation can make the theory proof against falsification in particular future cases. The restriction of research to just one case may even be positively advantageous in that it provides an opportunity for much more intensive and detailed research than would otherwise be feasible. This advantage may well compensate for the possible drawbacks of such a restriction.

The above already suggests an important difference between Lindberg on the one hand, and Haas, Deutsch, and Etzioni, on the other. Whereas the latter three were concerned with attempting to develop *new* theories, in a field where there had been virtually no such activities before, the former (Lindberg) can, and does, build upon the foundations laid by the others, especially Haas and Deutsch. Thus, Lindberg may be considered as a theorist of the second generation. Accordingly, his writings display less originality and less preoccupation with the fundamentals of the trade than do those of Haas and Deutsch in particular. Much of what constituted problems for the latter, it would seem, is more or less taken for granted by Lindberg. And, as has appeared from the preceding chapters, while even Haas and Deutsch were none too explicit as concerns their basic presuppositions and the character of their argument, Lindberg generally proceeds in an even less explicit fashion. This, however, makes it all the more difficult to avoid the errors of the predecessors. Besides, it renders it difficult to really build upon, refine, elaborate, and advance over what has already been done.

It remains to be mentioned, finally, that Lindberg's *Political integration as a multi-dimensional phenomenon* represents what may be counted as the most intensive attempt made thus far to operationalize integration. From the preceding chapters it has already appeared that this constitutes one of the most important unsolved problems in the theory of integration. And although it cannot be said that Lindberg does offer a solution, he at least clearly shows the many and varied problems involved in such operationalization, and a possible strategy for their eventual solution.

2. POLITICS

2.1. *Politics and the political system – the vocabulary*

In *The political dynamics of European economic integration* Lindberg writes:

The essence of a political community, it seems to me, is the existence of a legitimate system for the resolution of conflict, for the making of authoritative decisions for the group as a whole (*Lindberg*, 1963: 7).

This indicates that politics is concerned with the process through which, in some human group, decisions binding upon all of its members come about. This does not differ too much from Easton's conception which Lindberg later adopts (*Lindberg & Scheingold*, 1970: 32; *Lindberg*, 1966b: 346; 1970), in terms of 'authoritative allocations of values'. These decisions or allocations are explained in terms of the well-known concepts 'demands' and 'support' (*Lindberg*, 1966b: 352 ff.). Furthermore, he introduces the concept of 'actor', as follows:

By 'political actor' we mean any person or group of persons acting in concert who engage in activities that are relevant to the political system. They make, support, or resist demands for particular policies or decisions, or they may actually occupy official positions in the decision-making process itself (*Lindberg & Scheingold*, 1970: 122-123).

A group of such actors among which a political process occurs may be conceived as constituting a political system. Such a system consists of a set of processes through which the actors' demands and supports (the system's input) are converted into authoritative decisions (the system's output; cf. *Lindberg & Scheingold*, 1970: 111). It should be noted that this system is of a purely abstract, or 'analytical' nature, not necessarily to be identified with anything existing as, for example, a geographical unit:

The political system is separated from other systems by *system boundaries* which, though in many cases lacking in geographical or empirical referents, can be identified through the observation of distinctive behaviour patterns. These sorts of boundaries separate the political system from other intra-societal systems such as ecological, personality, and social systems. An example of a boundary dividing a social from a political system would be the different behaviour patterns anticipated from one man when he is acting as a father writing to a son and as a citizen writing to a legislator (*Lindberg*, 1966b: 346).

Likewise, the system's environment should be conceived abstractly as consisting of everything which determines the character of the system's input.

At this point it may be useful to briefly discuss a number of subsidiary notions and distinctions which Lindberg introduces in relation to the concepts mentioned above. To begin with, support is distinguished on the basis of two dimensions: basis of response and level of interaction. These, in turn, allow for a distinction into 1. identitive and systemic support, and, 2. utilitarian and affective support respectively:

The first pair, composed of identitive and systemic support, is offered to enable us to make distinctions between the development of links among the peoples of the Community (identitive) and the development of links with the system itself (systemic). Identitive support, thus, gauges what might be termed 'horizontal' interaction among the broader publics of the system, while systemic support probes 'vertical' relations between the system and these publics. In accordance with the empirical political theory of David Easton, we further subdivide the category of systemic support among the possible 'objects' of that support; community and regime. The second pair, utilitarian and affective, permits distinctions between support bases on some perceived and relatively concrete interest (utilitarian) and support which seems to indicate a diffuse and perhaps emotional response to some of the vague ideals embodied in the notion of European unity (affective) (*Lindberg & Scheingold*, 1970: 40).

(For lack of data, as he writes, Lindberg omits the third Eastonian object of support – the authorities (*Lindberg & Scheingold*, 1970: 40 footnote). It should be noted that the concept of 'community' which is used here is that of Easton, and refers to the division of political labor among a group of people; it is altogether different from the concept of 'community' as defined in relation to that of 'integration'. As is well known 'regime' refers to the structure of institutions and procedures existing in some political system.)

The distinctions introduced here are put in matrix form (*Lindberg & Scheingold*, 1970: 40):

	Basis of response	
	utilitarian	affective
Levels of interaction — identitive		
systemic community regime		

Although this scheme, in striking contradistinction to what is done with regard to 'demands', the other main input variable, does not provide for a distinction of support according to the nature of the supporting actor, some such distinction is implicit in much of what Lindberg writes (e.g. *Lindberg & Scheingold*, 1970: 283-284). Presumably, the same actor categories could be used for this purpose as are introduced below with regard to demands.

For demands, secondly, are distinguished according to the nature of the actors concerned and their perceptions of their own interests. The former is further specified on the basis of 1. the character of their aims, and 2. the scope of their 'power and sphere of responsibility'. As to the aims, Lindberg largely adopts Haas's distinction into 'dramatic-political' and 'incremental-economic' aims.

Elites (or actors) with dramatic-political aims are those who are concerned with 'high politics', with 'deep ideological or philosophical commitment', with national self-assertion, prestige and grandeur, power in the world. Elites with incremental-economic aims devote themselves to the maximization of their daily welfare concerns and have 'abandoned an interest in high politics' (*Lindberg & Scheingold*, 1970: 123).

That Lindberg here adopts Haas's distinction should not be read as implying that he also agrees with Haas's insights as to the relative roles of these aims in politics or in an integration process (cf. *Lindberg & Scheingold*, 1970: 123-124). With regard to the power and responsibility of national political actors, he further writes:

We must also distinguish between political actors whose power and sphere of responsibility is as broad as the national system and those concerned with the interests or welfare of a subgroup, that is, a region, an industry, a trade union. The former would include nationally elected officals (premiers, presidents, cabinet members, members of parliament), high civil servants, and national political party leaders. The latter include primarily interest groups or their leaders, lower level officials and civil servants, local or regional politicians (*Lindberg & Scheingold*, 1970: 124).

This distinction has here been defined in terms of one kind of political system namely a national one. The definition, however, can easily be generalized; in this more general case the terms 'system-' and 'sub-system-actors', rather than 'national' and 'subnational-actors', would seem to be appropriate. The second major classificatory criterion for the demands made by actors is provided by the way actors perceive their own interests in relation to some given policy or issue, in this case integration. Lindberg introduces a threefold subdivision:

Broadly speaking, we can classify actor perception of interest in integration as follows: actors see their interests served by *further integrative moves*; actors see their interests served by *conserving* the level of integration already achieved; and actors see their interests served by vetoing integrative moves or *undoing* or *rolling back* the integration already achieved (*Lindberg & Scheingold*, 1970: 126).

However, all this is merely concerned with the classification of individual demands. But one should also be able to classify larger aggregates of such demands, since a political system will normally be confronted with a multitude of more or less different demands, rather than with individual and isolated ones. In this context Lindberg introduces the terms 'identical' and 'convergent' in order to denote different *patterns* of groups of demands:

We will classify such patterns as either identical or convergent. For our purposes, a pattern of identical interests will be one where all or most actors perceive their interests served in the same way by the same policy or decision. A convergent pattern will find supporters (or opponents) anticipating different gains (or losses) from different aspects of the policy or decision *Lindberg & Scheingold*, 1970: 127).

In order to be generally applicable for any group of demands, and not just to those involving some measure of consensus, this scheme should obviously be supplemented by some such category as 'divergent interests or demands'.

In his most recent paper (*Lindberg*, 1970) he tries to develop a scheme for the eventual estimation of the total flow of demands fed into the political system. Following Easton, he conceives this flow as a function of the *volume* and the *variety* of demands. At the same time he attempts to link these concepts to those used in the classification of individual demands as discussed above.

The *volume of demands* made for collective action will some function of the number of actors who develop demands relative to the collective arena, the power of influence or resources (usually in the constituent systems) of the authors of these demands, the intensity of their concern, and the extent to which they mobilize to press their case. The *variety of demands* will be determined both by the substantive policies desired and by the type of action being requested (*Lindberg*, 1970: 39).

It is indicated that the distinctions between system and subsystem actors, and between dramatic-political and incremental-economic aims, refer to the actors' power, influence, and resources; while those concerned with the actors' perception of their own interests regarding some policy have to do with the variety of demands (*Lindberg*, 1970: 39-40).

The analysis of the two basic input components, demands and support, by Lindberg, seems to exhibit a marked asymmetry. While demands are analysed in some detail in terms of the characteristics of the actors who make them, support is discussed mainly in terms of its motivation and its objects. But obviously demands, too, can be analysed in terms of their objects and the underlying motivations; while, conversely, support could well be analysed in largely the same terms as have been applied with regard to demands. Thus, for example, one could meaningfully speak of a 'volume of support', defined in terms of 'the power or influence or resources' of the actors, its 'intensity', and the extent to which they [the actors] mobilize'. And similarly the 'variety of support' could be defined in terms of 'substance' (e.g. the 'weight' of support), and of the 'type' of support behavior (e.g. voting, lobbying, or demonstrating). After all, the two concepts seem to be closely related. It is rather difficult to imagine demands being made without involving some measure of support – if only the support of those making the demand. It seems to me that the analysis would have gained much from a more comprehensive and uniform approach.

With regard to a political system as a whole Lindberg distinguishes between its *scope* and its *institutional capacity* (*Lindberg & Scheingold*, 1970: 65 ff.). 'Scope' is further subdivided into *extent* and *intensity*. The former refers to the range of decision-making performed by the political system, that is, the range of the decision-making areas, subjects, or functions with regard to which authoritative decisions are made. Lindberg lists 22 such areas or functions in four main groups – *external relations, political-constitutional, social-cultural,* and *economic functions* (*Lindberg & Scheingold*, 1970: 67; for a somewhat different listing, see *Lindberg*, 1966b: 359). 'Intensity' refers to 'the relative importance of Community decision-making processes as compared with national processes in any given area' (*Lindberg & Scheingold*, 1970: 68). Here Lindberg is obviously speaking about the European Economic Community; in more general terms 'intensity' can be said to refer to where decisions are taken – by the system as a whole or by some constituent subsystem. In between these two extremes three stages are distinguished, namely (in somewhat more general terms than Lindberg actually uses) 'only the beginnings of a system-wide decision process', 'policy decisions in both but subsystem activity predominates' and 'policy decisions in both but system activity predominates' (*Lindberg & Scheingold*, 1970: 69). The second main element, 'institutional capacity', is not defined very precisely. It is concerned both with a political system's decision-making structures, or institutional set-up, and with the rules and norms that come to regulate the behavior of subsystems toward each other (*Lindberg & Scheingold*, 1970: 82 ff.).

Together these two elements, a system's scope and institutional capacity, constitute a system's *internal resources* (*Lindberg & Scheingold*, 1970: 111). *External resources,* on the other hand,

(. . .) include *systemic supports*, that is, willingness among elites and mass publics to use the system or to consider its existence and operation as legitimate and proper, and the *actual efforts at leadership*, which are made available by national and supranational elites (*Lindberg & Scheingold*, 1970: 112).

'Leadership' is described in terms of its functions:

In terms of our model, leadership is a crucial activator of coalitions that conduce to system growth. It is the function of leadership to aid in the identification of problems; to evaluate, store, and retrieve information; to see to it that differences are handled in acceptable ways; to articulate goals for the collectivity and to symbolize them effectively: to build up support in the legitimacy of the system; and to engineer consent by organizing bargaining and the exchange of concession (*Lindberg & Scheingold*, 1970: 128).

A political system uses these resources in order to produce certain outcomes, that is, authoritative decisions and their effects. To a large extent this occurs through a process of bargaining. Here Lindberg applies Haas's familiar categories to denote three different bargaining patterns: 'accommodation on the basis of the minimum common denominator', 'accommodation by splitting the difference' and accommodation by 'deliberately or inadvertently upgrading the common interests of the parties' (*Lindberg*, 1963: 12).

A system's outcomes are classified in various ways. Thus, in a rather formal way, 'scope' does already involve some sort of classification of outcomes. Another classificatory criterion is that of the 'saliency of issue areas' (*Lindberg*, 1966b: 360-361). This refers to the importance actors attach to the decisions produced by a political system. On this basis (following Theodore J. Lowi) three kinds of policies, assumed to be increasingly salient, are distinguished:

distributive policies (. . .) that allocate some value (money, prestige, rights) to a relatively small segment of society (farmers, shareholders in corporation, residents of a coastal city) with the rest of the society not perceiving any loss,

regulatory policies (. . .) those that allocate values so that some win and some lose, but the losers do not perceive their deprivation as a major or fundamental one,

redistributive policies allocate values to a very broad segment of society,

with other broad segments perceiving their loss as a major relative deprivation (*Lindberg*, 1966b: 361-362).

Outcomes are also classified according to the nature of the resulting
obligations or commitments. Lindberg distinguishes two kinds of obligations:

(. . .) on the one hand, to carry out specific, agreed functions or to obey
specific rules, and on the other hand, to institute an ongoing Community
[he refers to the EEC] decision-making process which was to translate general goals into specific rules and policies. The former represents a commitment to execute agreements already arrived at (. . .). The latter implies a
commitment to seek such agreements by means of joint processes and institutions (. . .) (*Lindberg & Scheingold*, 1970: 135).

Moreover, obligations may be *fulfilled*, *retracted*, or *extended* (*Lindberg & Scheingold*, 1970: 102-103). These two classifications are combined in the form of a matrix in which they are linked to certain developmental sequences of the system as a whole. As follows (*Lindberg &
Scheingold*, 1970: 136):

Obligations	Outcomes		
	Fulfilment	*Retraction*	*Extension*
To participate in a joint dec.-making proc. (i.e., to make new policy)	forward-linkage model	output-failure model	
			systems
To implement agreements, and the routine enforcement of specific rules (i.e., to administer a previously agreed area of joint activity)	equilibrium model	spill-back model	transformation model(s)

The various concepts used here are defined as follows:
Forward linkage describes a sequence whereby commitment to participate
in joint decision-making has initiated a process that has led to a marked
increase in the scope of the system or in its institutional capacities. (. . .)

Output failure refers to a situation in which such a commitment was accepted but where the system was unable to produce an acceptable set of policies and rules and where the capacity and scope of the system hence were not enhanced. (. . .)

Equilibrium occurs when an area of activity is routinized or institutionalized. Rules are established and recognized, and there is little need for new intergovernmental bargaining. Nor is there any increase in scope or in institutional capacity (. . .)

Spill-back refers to a situation in which there is a withdrawal from a set of specific obligations. Rules are no longer regularly enforced or obeyed. The scope of Community action and its institutional capacity decrease. (. . .)

Systems transformation means an extension to specific or general obligations that are beyond the bounds of the original treaty commitments, either geographically or functionally. It typically entails a major change in the scope of the Community or in its institutions, that often requires *an entirely new constitutive bargaining process* among the member states, entailing substantial goal redefinition among national political actors (*Lindberg & Scheingold*, 1970: 137).

In his *Political integration as a multi-dimensional phenomenon* (*Lindberg*, 1970), Lindberg offers a much more elaborate and comprehensive analysis of the crucial properties of political systems than has been discussed above. To a large extent the present analysis is put in a larger and more comprehensive perspective. It is broadened rather than superseded. Here I will discuss briefly the framework's outline. Before proceeding with the discussion, however, it should be noted that in Lindberg's most recent writings, in particular in the last two (*Lindberg & Scheingold*, 1970; *Lindberg*, 1970), he is concerned with political systems that already show some institutional and procedural provisions for collective decision-making (cf. *Lindberg & Scheingold*, 1970: v; and *Lindberg*, 1970: 1-21); accordingly, the analytical framework which he develops is not automatically suited to the analysis of other kinds of political systems, for example those characterized by warfare or the threat of it. To increase its applicability in that sense would probably require a more or less extensive reformulation of such concepts as 'support', 'demand', and the system's 'scope' and 'capacity', to mention only a few of the more obvious ones.

A 'collective decision-making system', then, can be described, according to Lindberg, in terms of three basic categories: its *level*, its *animators* or *activators*, and its *consequences* (*Lindberg*, 1970: 7). 'Level' refers to 'the extent to which the constituent countries actually make decisions as a group' (*Lindberg*, 1970: 7; see also p. 9). The term 'animators' (or 'activators' – both are used) denotes a set of properties which are meant to describe 'the energy available to the system at the time of analysis' (*Lindberg*, 1970: 7). The term 'consequences', finally concerns the effects the system's outputs have on its environment (*Lindberg*, 1970: 8). These three elements are further subdivided, thus yielding a group of 10 properties. It should be noted, incidentally, that the reasoning behind the introduction of these properties remains largely implicit. Although the relevance of the properties would seem to be plausible enough, this relevance is not spelled out with sufficient clarity. In particular, it is *not* shown why these three (or ten) properties must characterize a political (or, rather a 'collective decision-making') system, rather than some different set – why not more or fewer properties? (see also ch. 2, section 2.4.4).

A system's level (*1*) is composed of (*1.1*) the *scope* of collective decision-making, (*1.2*) the *range* of participation in joint decision-making, and (*1.3*) its *decisiveness* in 'determining public allocations at different stages of the process and in different issue areas' (*Lindberg*, 1970: 11).

Scope (*1.1*) is then defined to increase with increases in (*1.1.1*) the number of issue areas concerned, and (*1.1.2*) their salience (*Lindberg*, 1970: 27). With regard to the former Lindberg uses a somewhat revised list of decision areas as was introduced earlier in order to estimate a system's *extent* (see above, p. 276). Here, too, he applies the basic categories *external relations, political-constitutional, social-cultural*, and *economic functions* (*Lindberg*, 1970: 22). Salience, on the other hand, is assumed to vary with, and in the same direction as, the *intensity* of preferences and feelings in a particular area, the *power* of the actors whose preferences are involved, and the nature of the *deprivations* they anticipate ('whether conflicts are perceived as zero sum, or subject to resolution with nobody losing very much of importance'; *Lindberg*, 1970: 26).

Following Lasswell and Kaplan, the range (*1.2*) of participation in categories *external relations, political-constitutional, social-cultural*, and stages in a process of decision-making. Lindberg distinguishes six stages: *collective problem-recognition, specific action alternatives defined collectively, collective decisions on policy guidelines, detailed collective goal-setting, implementation by national rules, decisions on policies and rules directly binding on individuals,* and, finally, *collective implementation and enforcement* (*Lindberg*, 1970: 30).

In order to estimate the decisiveness (*1.3*) of collective decision-making, Lindberg uses basically the same categories as introduced earlier (see above, p. 276) to determine a system's 'intensity' (*Lindberg*, 1970: 33 ff.).

The second major property of a decision-making system, its animators or activators (*2*), dissolves into *demand flow* (*2.1*), *resources* (*2.2*), *leadership* (*2.3*), and *bargaining modalities* (*2.4*) (see *Lindberg*, 1970: 11 ff.).

Concerning the first element, *demand flow* (*2.1*), it has already appeared that Lindberg here follows Easton in distinguishing between the *volume* and the *variety* of the demand flow (see above p. 278; cf. *Lindberg*, 1970: 37 ff.).

The concept of 'resources' (*2.2*) is defined in a very broad fashion. It is assumed to vary with, and in the same direction as, the following five groups of sub-elements (*Lindberg*, 1970: 43 ff.).

1. Prior agreement on what can be decided colllectively (existing level).
2. Decision-making norms.
3. Supranational structures.
a) supranational structural growth
b) resources of supranational structures
c) national-supranational transactions
4. Financial resources.
5. Support resources.
a) expectations of future gain
b) belief in legitimacy
c) belief in common interest
d) sense of mutual political identification

As concerns leadership (*2.3*) a distinction is made between supranational leadership, on the one hand, and national leadership on the other (*Lindberg*, 1970: 64 ff.). The activities of the former are analysed in terms of five 'types of activity', it being assumed that 'supranational leaders will be likely to maximize their potential to the extent that they engage' in them (*Lindberg*, 1970: 69). The categories are *goal articulation and advocacy*; *consultation, co-optation, and coalition building*; *recruitment and organization*; *redefine goals and expand scope*; and *brokerage and package deals* (*Lindberg*, 1970: 69-70). The activities of the national leaders, on the other hand, are classified according to the following categories (the classification is concerned with activities relating to an ongoing process of integration): *asserts a 'natural' leadership role*; *expansive proposals*; *commitment to system*; *support and responsiveness*; and *bargaining activity* (*Lindberg*, 1970: 72).

The term 'bargaining modalities' (*2.4*) refers to the nature of the bargaining in which actors engage, to their expectations and their strategies (*Lindberg*, 1970: 13-14, 72 ff.). Haas's familiar three accommodation patterns (minimum common denominator, splitting the difference, and upgrading common interests; see above p. 277) can be viewed as a first attempt to classify such modalities in a more precise fashion. By making use of certain game theoretic concepts, Lindberg seeks to improve upon this early attempt. He constructs a list of six such modalities; and since he is interested in integration the modalities are ordered according as they involve an increasing measure of cooperation. As follows:

1. Competitive zero-sum unit veto model: No possibility of increasing utilities through cooperation or collusion (. . .).

2. Competitive zero-sum-minimum coalition model: Limited cooperation or collusion to maximize gain of a winning coalition (. . .).

3. Cooperative constant sum game – simple log-rolling model: All may reorder preferences and make limited sacrifices and trades in own interest. (. . .) Side payments and exchanges of votes only on limited range of closely related issues.

4. Cooperative variable sum game – complex log-rolling model: Unrestricted side payments make possible extensive log-rolling and trades over wide range of issues. (. . .)

5. Cooperative variable sum game – complex log-rolling model: As 4 except that players combine to create new resources and institutions. (. . .)

6. Cooperative variable sum game – general benefit. Progressive taxation model: Cooperation to optimize the interests of society itself. Acceptance of notion of an overriding collectivity interest distinct from maximization of individual utilities (. . .) (*Lindberg*, 1970: 75) [I have somewhat altered the presentation].

The third major property of a decision-making system is termed 'consequences' (*3*). This, in turn, is subdivided into (*3.1*) the *penetrativeness*,

(*3.2*) the *compliance with*, and (*3.3*) the *distributive consequences* of the decisions produced by the system (*Lindberg*, 1970: 8).

The first element, 'penetrativeness' (*3.1*) is concerned with the general question: 'whose behavior is changed, and how much, as a consequence of the existence and activities of a given collective decision-making system? (*Lindberg*, 1970:80). The question is an extremely difficult one, and Lindberg does not offer an elaborate answer to it. He points out that, on the one hand, individuals and collectivities may change their behavior as a direct consequence of collective decisions (*Lindberg*, 1970: 80-81); and, on the other hand, they may change their orientations and attitudes toward the system as a result of the experience of participating in its activities (*Lindberg*, 1970: 81-82). Regarding this latter effect, the concept of 'actor socialization', introduced in *Europe's would-be policy*, is relevant:

We can well imagine how participants engaged in an intensive ongoing decision-making process, which may extend over several years and bring them into frequent and close personal contact, and which engages them in a joint problem-solving and policy-generating exercise, might develop a special orientation to that process and to those interactions, especially if they are rewarding. They may come to value the system and their roles within it, either for itself or for the concrete rewards and benefits it has produced or that it promises (*Lindberg & Scheingold*, 1970: 119).

Secondly, 'compliance' (*3.2*) is described as 'the likelihood that the formal decision outcomes of a collective decision-making system will be complied with by those to whom they are addressed' (*Lindberg*, 1970: 84). Here Lindberg largely limits himself to mentioning some of the ways in which this likelihood could be determined empirically (*Lindberg*, 1970: 85-86), but with which we need not concern ourselves at this stage of the inquiry.

As concerns the 'distributive consequences' (*3.3*) of collective decision-making, Lindberg writes:

It seems to me that there are at least three major questions involved. First, are *new* advantages, or benefits or resources or disadvantages created as a consequence of the system and its works? Second, if there are such new benefits (or costs), how are they distributed? Third, what is the impact of collective decisions on the overall distribution of benefits and costs in the member societies? (*Lindberg*, 1970: 87).

Besides, a distinction should be made between 'public goods' and 'private goods'. Public goods are goods, services or functions, from which nobody can be excluded and which are available to all (*Lindberg*, 1970: 88). In the case of private goods, on the other hand, it is, at least in principle, possible to indicate the individual actors to whom the benefits (or costs) accrue. To estimate the distributive consequences of collective decison-making is, however, an extraordinarily complex problem, for which no clearcut solution is developed here.

By now, it seems, Lindberg's vocabulary concerning politics and the political system in general has been discussed in sufficient detail. The terminological apparatus introduced is of a quite complex nature. But it is still merely a *vocabulary*, a more or less interrelated set of terms. In order to make it work, that is, to apply it in the explanation of politics or of some specific political phenomenon such as integration, we need assumptions or postulates linking the concepts introduced and enabling us to derive other propositions. These will be discussed in the next subsection (2.2).

2.2.   *Some basic assumptions*

As concerns his basic assumptions about the political process, Lindberg is none too explicit. It will be recalled that the political process is conceived as one in which actors demand and support certain policies or decisions that are to be imposed authoritatively upon all the participants in the process. Although it is nowhere explicitly so stated, Lindberg's most fundamental assumption concerning the relationship between demands, support, and authoritative decisions would seem to be that actors will support demands and comply with decisions to the extent that their substance meets with their own preference or interests as they perceive them (cf. *Lindberg*, 1963: 9; 1970: 12 and 86; *Lindberg & Scheingold*, 1970: 126 ff.).

However, the actors participating in some political process will not generally have precisely identical interests. And accordingly the support of all of them cannot be taken for granted in any specific decision. Apparently, what is required in order that some demand be converted into a binding decision is merely that support *for* it exceeds support *against* it. That is, some specific demand or policy will usually rest upon a more or less restricted supporting coalition from among the actors participating in some political process. To be effective, i.e., to have its demands translated into binding decisions, this coalition needs to be stronger than coalitions supporting alternative policies.

Such coalitions, as his already appeared above (see p. 275), may be based either on *identical* demands or interests, or on merely *converging* ones. The former are thought to be more stable than the latter, since:

They are less likely to be affected asymmetrically by most kinds of stress. A convergent pattern will be more vulnerable, since political actors receive different benefits from different sources (*Lindberg & Scheingold*, 1970: 217).

Coalitions may occur in several ways, or, as Lindberg writes, via several mechanisms. He distinguishes four of them: *functional spill-over, side-payments and log-rolling, actor socialization*, and *feedback* (*Lindberg & Scheingold*, 1970: 117). They are defined as follows:

In functional spill-over, actors are brought in because they find that tasks (or policy-making areas) are functionally related to one another. That is, because of the nature of the task or area involved, actors discover that they cannot do *A* (or cannot do it satisfactorily) without also doing *B* and perhaps *C*; or, having done *A*, they so change the circumstances of *B* and *C* that joint action there may become necessary in order to prevent inconvenience or disruption (*Lindberg & Scheingold*, 1970: 117).

(*Log-rolling and side-payments*) These represent ways in which actors are brought into a growth-inducing coalition because of the disparity of their interests and priorities in integration. [The reference to integration and the growth-inducing character of the coalition is of course inessential in the present context.] (. . .)

Log-rolling refers to bargaining exchanges within a given decision area, while side-payments involve their extension to other (often functionally unrelated) areas (*Lindberg & Scheingold*, 1970: 118-119).

Actor socialization has already been described above (p. 283).

In the case of the feedback mechanism, it is the outputs of the Community that have an impact on attitudes and behavior. And it is primarily the perceptions and behaviors of non-participants that are involved. (. . .)

In sum, the feedback mechanism is stimulated primarily by the perceptions people have of the Community decision-making system and its outputs (*Lindberg & Scheingold*, 1970: 120; here, too, the reference to a particular system, that of the EEC, is plainly irrelevant in the present context).

As can be clearly seen in the above definitions, the formation of coalitions is initiated or stimulated through changes (either occurring autonomously, or through conscious manipulation) in the actors' perceptions of their interests, in the substance of the demands or decisions made, or in the overall balance of costs and benefits of the actors, i.e. also involving elements not directly at issue. It may also have appeared from the foregoing that coalitions need not be conceived as tightly organized, more or less permanent groupings. They may also be organized very loosely or not at all, their composition may fluctuate continuously, and they may be restricted to some isolated issue, never to emerge again once that issue has disappeared from the political stage.

From the fundamental assumption mentioned above, i.e., that actors will support demands and comply with decisions to the extent that their substance meets with their own preferences, it seems to follow that the more nearly identical actors' preferences or interests are, the more they cherish the same set of values, the greater the likelihood that they will feed a large measure of support for some decisions (or institutions) into the political system. This would seem to be the essence of another of Lindberg's assumptions, one that is stated explicitly this time:

Our assumption will be that substantial mutual identification will be more supportive of joint problem solving by Community institutions, simply because projects will be presumably less vulnerable to nationalist challenges (*Lindberg & Scheingold*, 1970: 39; in the same sense *Lindberg & Scheingold*, 1970: 26). (Mark, however, that what is stated here as an assumption or postulate actually has the status of a theorem by virtue of its being deducible from the postulate mentioned.)

According to Easton's analysis support may assume two forms: specific support and diffuse support. Specific support is directly related to particular demands or decisions, while diffuse support is not (see Easton: 1965; 267 ff.). The former may roughly be defined as agreement or compliance with, or behavior (both overt and covert) aimed at the realization or effectuation of certain demands or decisions. The latter, on the other hand, is concerned with agreement with or acceptance of the political system (or particular aspects thereof) as such. It may be described as a kind of second-order support. And it is this kind of support Lindberg seems to have in mind in introducing his notion of 'systemic support' (cf. p. 272 above). Also, it does not seem too far-fetched to suppose that Lindberg assumes that no political system could endure without this form of support. However, how does this kind of support emerge? For whereas it has appeared that specific support is conditional upon the degree to which the supporting actor's demands are (expected to be) fulfilled, no such direct link exists in the case of diffuse, or systemic support.

Especially in his most recent writings Lindberg formulates several assumptions that could possibly be used in accounting for the emergence of this form of support. Thus he writes:

The more intense and sustained are transactions the more likely is it that norms of conflict resolution will develop, thus facilitating bargaining and joint problem solving (*Lindberg*, 1970: 54; see also *Lindberg & Scheingold*, 1970: 95).

This could be read as saying the more intense and sustained transactions among the political actors of some system are, the greater the likelihood will be that diffuse support for some kind of regime (see p. 272 above) for that system will emerge. Somewath more generally it is suggested that:

(. . .) when people have experienced a high level of transactions, and when these tend to bring rewards rather than deprivations, they will come to like them (*Lindberg*, 1970: 86).

This could be interpreted as meaning that the higher the level of transactions among actors, and the more frequently their demands are met, the greater the likelihood that diffuse support both for the regime and for the 'community' (see p. 272 above) of that political system will build up (in the same sense, *Lindberg*, 1970: 54). On the basis of some such postulates as have been mentioned here, one could well explain how the mechanisms of 'actor socialization' (p. 283 above) and 'feedback' (p. 285 above) could result in the emergence of systematic support in some political system. They are essentially learning mechanisms whose results, according to the above assumptions, depend upon the frequency and intensity of the interactions among political actors, and the degree to which these interactions are rewarding, i.e., the extent to which the supporting actors' demands have been, are, or are expected to be, met.

Thus far, and without offering any kind of explicit definition, I have treated the concept of 'support' in the more or less familiar sense of, roughly, any kind of overt or covert behavior on the part of some demand or decision (cf. also *Easton*, 1965: 155, 162 ff.). But I have deliberately glossed over the fact that Lindberg attaches a somewhat different meaning to the term. For he views 'identitive support' also as a form of support (see p. 272 above). Now identitive support has to do with the development of links among the people included in some political system, perhaps in the sense indicated on p. 286 above. It is not, however, concerned with any behavior more or less directly aimed at the realization of demands or decisions. Rather, as indicated by the argument just mentioned (pp. 286-287), it is to be conceived as one of the factors explaining the flow of support into the system, that is, as an environmental variable. Lindberg's not sharply distinguishing between these different notions seems to be rather misleading. Accordingly, I will continue to use the term 'support' in the sense just delineated, and will not consider 'identitive support' as a form of support properly so called.

In conclusion of this section it remains to be mentioned that the actual binding decisions that are produced by some political system cannot be explained solely on the basis of the concepts of 'demands' and 'support'. Or, rather, if one views these two as the basic variables in terms of which decisions are to be explained, the way in which demands and support are actually converted into binding decisions will also be determined by a number of parametric factors characterizing the system at some particular moment. Thus, some specific decision results from a particular configuration of demands and support *at the time when, and the place where such a decision is to be actually made*. But what demands and support are available there and then is, in turn, determined by a number of other factors, or parameters, such as that system's institutional structure, the procedures governing bargaining, and the resources available for effectuation or implementation of decisions, to name only a few of the more obvious things involved. Accordingly, Lindberg writes:

The decisions of a collective decision-making system will be determined by demands, resources, and bargaining modalities as they operate within a collective area of a given scope, stages, and decisiveness (*Lindberg*, 1970: 14).

However, apart from his attempt to operationalize the variables involved (to which purpose *Political integration as a multi-dimensional phenomenon* is mainly devoted), he does not try to fix the character of that function.

3. POLITICAL INTEGRATION – DEFINITION

After the preceding analysis of Lindberg's general conception of the political process and of the political system, his concept of 'integration' does not offer great difficulties.

For the purposes of this study, political integration will be defined as a *process*, but without reference to an end point. In specific terms, political integration is 1. the process whereby nations forego the desire and the ability to conduct foreign and key domestic policies independently of each other, seeking instead to make *joint decisions* or to *delegate* the decision-making process to new central organs; and 2. the process whereby political actors in several distinct settings are persuaded to shift their expectations and political activities to a new center *(Lindberg,* 1963: 6).

Lindberg, too, conceives integration as the process of the formation of a political community, that is, the development of a

(. . .) legitimate system for the resolution of conflict, for the making of authoritative decisions for the group as a whole *(Lindberg,* 1963: vii).

He stresses the fact that integration is concerned with a *process*, and that it need not necessarily result in the establishment of a full political community or a state-like organization. While such a community might be conceived as an end point of an integration process, integration may well occur without that end point ever being reached *(Lindberg,* 1963: 5).

The translation of this into Lindberg's systems-analytic vocabulary is fairly obvious. Integration can be said to occur when a political system, or a collective decision-making system, increases its capacity to process demands and support into authoritative decisions (cf. *Lindberg,* 1966b: 352 ff., 372). And in terms of the 10 fundamental properties of collective decision-making systems, summarized under *level, animators,* and *consequences* (cf. pp. 279 ff. above):

In general, we can say that the higher the score or ranking on any of the above properties, the more integration there is (*Lindberg*, 1970: 18; similarly, although less elaborately, in *Lindberg & Scheingold*, 1970: 99).

It should be noted, though, that there is an alternative conception. That is to say, rather than defining integration to occur when the values of *all* the variables mentioned increase, one could also relate it to merely one particular group of variables, namely *level*. For *level* directly refers to the extent to which a collective decision-making system is indeed capable of collective decision-making; it measures, one could say, such a system's 'capacity'. As against this, the two other variables, called *animators* and *consequences* respectively, seem to play a rather different role. Although Lindberg does not, unfortunately, precisely spell out the relationships involved, it does not seem too far-fetched to argue that *animators* (with some reformulations, of course) refers to what gives a system its capacity (what explains it), while *consequences* refers to the effects of such capacity upon the actors concerned and upon the environment. Now it would seem entirely legitimate to *define* 'integration' more simply as an increase in a system's level, whereas the other two (groups of) variables could well be limited to the role of *explaining* a process of integration. This would have several advantages. In the first place it would make the *concept* of 'integration' somewhat simpler. Secondly, as the properties do seem to have rather different relationships to integration, it would separate things that should be separated and thus contribute to conceptual clarity. Finally, it would more directly pose the problem of the interrelationships between the various variables, thus contributing to theoretical development and elaboration.

In Lindberg's conception of integration, common institutions figure somewhat less prominently than in that of the other authors discussed thus far. The way he defines it, integration might conceivably occur in the absence of common institutions. After all, they are merely one factor among others. In practice, however, their role in Lindberg's research, too, is extremely important. And in actual fact he is only concerned with integration involving institutions and their development. Theoretically, as has already been noted (p. 279 above), he tends to presuppose some degree of institutionalization. Accordingly, the very wide applicability or scope of this conception of integration remains largely potential.

In principle integration could be achieved through the application of violence. That is, through military conquest and coercion some political actor might forcibly increase the capacity of some political system. As is implicit in the way Lindberg deals with integration generally, and as, more recently, he states explicitly (*Lindberg*, 1970: 1), he conceives integration to be a peaceful process.

4. POLITICAL INTEGRATION – EXPLANATION

4.1. *Outline of this section*

In this section I will discuss the way Lindberg seeks to explain the occurrence (or non-occurrence) of a process of (international) political integration. I will focus successively on the general mechanism of the process (section 4.2); the role of the newly established political institutions in that process (4.3); the role of the various other actors concerned (4.4); and, finally, on the role of environmental, or 'background' factors (4.5).

4.2. *Integration – the mechanism*

International integration is concerned with the transformation of a political system constituted by states. These states, in turn, are political systems in which collective decision-making institutions and procedures have already developed to a relatively high degree. International integration means that the actors constituting these national systems (their governments included) are led to redirect their demands and support from the pre-existing national political institutions to those of the new (international) system, that they comply with the decisions made there, and that they conform to the decison-making rules and procedures evolving in that new system. And while, in the absence of integration, internationally binding decisions may be, and actually are, made on an *ad hoc* basis, (specific) support being provided according as actors perceive their demands to be met sufficiently, integration requires the development of what Lindberg calls 'systematic support'.

From the postulate mentioned in section 2.2 (p. 284 above) it follows that actors will direct their demands and support to those institutions where they expect their demands to be met most satisfactorily. Accordingly, one would expect integration to occur, or, rather, demands for it to be raised, when actors think that the existing political institutions do not any more provide sufficient guarantees for the making of satisfactory decisions, *and* when they expect new international institutions to do just that. One might also say that integration will occur when, for some reasons or other, the existing national institutions fail to cope with certain demands. These institutions may be said to suffer from 'demand-input overload':

Thus, initially, demand-input overload at the national level was a condition of the emergence of the European Community system. What we know about the dynamics of this system suggests that a continued inflow of demands that cannot be processed at the national level is a condition of its further evolution and perhaps of its persistence (*Lindberg*, 1966b: 374; see also *Lindberg & Scheingold*, 1970: 94-95).

And conversely:

Increased capabilities to process demands autonomously, or a diminished flow of demands or a change in their content, whatever the reason, would thus constitute a source of stress on the Community system. This might result from high prosperity (for economic demands) of from a diminished perceived military threat (for security demands). In both cases the system may be wholly or in part responsible for the changed conditions that resulted in stress (this is evident in the case of NATO). Much of the literature on the European Communities has argued, however, that the kinds of demands upon which that system is based cannot *by their nature* be satisfied by any of these units acting autonomously (*Lindberg*, 1966b: 374).

While all this sounds plausible enough, it is also fairly general. It raises a host of more specific questions such as 'why did overload, and concerning what matters and actors, occur?, or 'how much overload is required?', or 'why did it result in integration rather than, for example, revolution?'. As concerns such problems, however, Lindberg does not indulge in an elaborate theoretical analysis. Unfortunately (though quite legitimately, of course), in his latest book he explicitly assumes new (international) political institutions to have been established already (*Lindberg & Scheingold*, 1970: 5), i.e., he is concerned with a relatively advanced stage in the process.

That, as a result of demand-input overload at the national level, demands and support for integration will be forthcoming, does not imply that all actors concerned will be identically motivated, that they will seek to realize identical values through it. On the contrary, such a situation will only rarely occur; it is clearly a marginal case. It has already been discussed (p. 284 ff.) how Lindberg conceives decision-making to proceed generally through the construction of various supporting coalitions. Integration, too, can be seen to proceed via a number of different steps supported by varying coalitions of actors who did agree in some specific demand or decision, but for a variety of different, sometimes even conflicting motives (cf. *Lindberg*, 1963: 10, 298; 1965: 79; 1966b: 379).

At the outset of an integration process, when institutions and procedures through which binding decisions for the international system concerned can be made do not yet exist, it is only the participating national governments that can make such decisions – including that of establishing new international institutions. Accordingly, the coalition initially supporting integration need at least comprise those national governments. And as long as governments have the power to withdraw from the collective enterprise, i.e., in particular in the first stages of the process, their support for the building up of the collective decision-making structures remains a precondition for further integration (cf. *Lindberg*, 1963: 11, 285; 1965: 65).

According to the postulate mentioned earlier (p. 284 above) governments will support integration to the extent that they expect it to improve the chances that their demands will be satisfied. And this has to be 'measured' against a certain loss of autonomy which is implied in integration. To make this judgment, however, will be rather difficult when the powers or competencies of the new institutions are described in a wide and vague fashion. This renders it plausible that the tasks of new institutions will initially be circumscribed in a rather precise and restrictive fashion. For the immediate formation of a full-fledged 'federation' with all-inclusive powers will probably be perceived as a jump in the dark by the governments concerned, who cannot, in any precise way, estimate the 'costs' and 'benefits' of such a step.

However, once this first step has actually been taken, and some kind of an international decision-making structure has been established, a process may be set in motion over which the participating governments only have a limited measure of control. That is, a process of political integration once being started might develop a dynamics of its own.

To begin with, when the newly established international decision-making structures actually produce authoritative decisions, this may lead those actors who expect their interests to be affected to reorient their demands and support. While these had to be directed to the existing national institutions, since the relevant decisions were made there, demands and support may now be shifted from these to the new institutions. According to the postulate mentioned before (p. 284 above) this will happen to the extent that such actors expect those institutions to provide better opportunities for the realization of their demands than the pre-existing national ones. If so, actors will adjust their tactics and activities to the institutional structures and procedures of the new collective decision-making system (cf. *Lindberg*, 1963: 7). By the same token, as the political arena is enlarged one may expect new actors to form at the new international level (e.g. the formation of supranational interest groups) in order to more effectively advance their interests in the larger sphere (cf. *Lindberg*, 1963: 288).

Now if political interactions in the new system are frequent and rewarding enough, this will, as has already appeared (see p. 287), lead to the development of systematic support on the part of the actors concerned. Actors do not merely support the international institutions in so far as they produce decisions in conformity with the specific demands made, but support is now being extended to those institutions *per se*. But since the politics of the participating states are also determined, partly at least, by the demands and support of the non-governmental actors involved in the integrative process, their supporting the international institutions and procedures (or, rather, the new system's *authorities, regime,* and *community*) will render it more difficult for the governments concerned to withdraw from the collective enterprise.

Furthermore, the integrative process may itself create situations and pressures such as to conduce to more integration. We have already discussed the four basic mechanisms through which this may occur (p. 285 above). They all concern the bases for the formation of coalitions supporting the increase of the system's integration level: functional spill-over, log-rolling and side-payments, actor socialization, and feedback (see also *Lindberg*, 1963: 10-11).

All this suggests a process of self-sustained, and even self-accelerating growth. For the higher the level of integration (its *scope, range of stages*, and *decisiveness*; see pp. 280-281 above), the more actors will reorient their demands and support. This may well increase and intensify political transactions in the system. And provided that those are rewarding for the actors concerned, systemic support may consequently grow. The growth of systemic support increases the system's *resources*, and it does not seem too far-fetched to suppose that this, in turn, will increase that system's decision-making *decisiveness*, and, consequently, its *consequences* for the national systems concerned. But this together with a high level will again tend to make for more functional spill-over and feedback. And a high level of integration presumably increases both the necessity of and the occasions for log-rolling and side-payments, while it might also lead to more and more intensive actor socialization. Thus one might imagine a seemingly irresistible system of accelerated growth of a collective decision-making system. In the process the participating national governments lose more and more of their decision-making functions, and (national) systemic support will accordingly dwindle. The end result would be the formation of a full-fledged state in the formerly international system in which the role of the erstwhile national governments would be relegated to the performance of minor administrative tasks.

However, that integration would actually be such a smooth and continuous process does indeed seem to be somewhat implausible, to judge from the actual course of, for example, contemporary European integration. Nevertheless, this rough sketch of an argument (of which Lindberg only gives the barest hints) serves to show some of the potentialities of the theoretical scheme which has been developed thus far. It should be borne in mind, though, that one of the main assumptions upon which the above argument rests is that (an increasing number of) actors expect and perceive integration to be rewarding, its benefits clearly outweighing its costs. But it does not seem very probable that this could be realized always and continuously in actual fact. Thus, certain actors (for example those with a highly protected and privileged position in their national political system) may feel acutely threatened by integration, while those actors whose interests are affected through functional spill-over may be led to demand the restriction or even abrogation of the integrative process, rather than its extension and further growth. Accordingly, as has already appeared (see

p. 279 above), Lindberg distinguishes several possible outcome patterns of which 'output failure', 'equilibrium', and 'spill-back' refer to precisely such situations of standstill or retrogression. It will be clear that to predict which of these cases will actually occur a much more detailed and elaborate analysis than has been developed thus far is necessary. This is the moment to turn to a somewhat more detailed investigation of a few of the major aspects of the scheme which has been outlined thus far.

4.3. *Leadership*

We have already seen (section 3) that in Lindberg's conception the concepts 'level', 'animators', and 'consequences' can be said to 'measure' a collective decision-making system's degree of integration. On the other hand, as has just appeared, this degree of integration itself will probably influence the further course of a process of integration. In this subsection I will focus on one particular aspect of a developing decision-making system, namely the role of the international institutions. This is because such institutions, or rather their leadership, in certain circumstances may play an active role in consciously guiding and controlling an ongoing process of integration. It will be recalled that Lindberg considers such institutions as resources (p. 281 above); that their role may be that of providing leadership to the process of integration (p. 281 above); and that their functions are related to a system's level, i.e. its *scope, range of stages* and *decisiveness* (p. 280 above).

According to Lindberg, the availability of leadership is a crucial variable in the explanation of an integration process:

If demands are to be processed, if often conflicting purposes are to be reconciled and a consensus evolved for a particular joint policy, if political actors are to be mobilized, a political system requires leadership. Indeed, leadership is the very essence of a capacity for collective action. In terms of our model, leadership is a crucial activator of coalitions that conduce to system growth. It is the function of leadership to aid in the identification of problems; to evaluate, store, and retrieve information; to see to it that differences are handled in acceptable ways; to articulate goals for the collectivity and to symbolize them effectively; to build up support in the legitimacy of the system; and to engineer consent by organizing bargaining and the exchange of concessions (*Lindberg & Scheingold*, 1970: 128).

In general, international institutions may perform this leadership through their making decisions and framing demands, e.g. in the form of proposals for action, so as to be sufficiently rewarding for sufficiently large coalitions of actors to mobilize an adequate degree of support. Decisions and demands may be devised in such a fashion as to maximize the possibilities for the formation of the various growth-inducing coalitions (p. 285 above). In principle, and to some extent at least, international institutions may thus consciously guide a process of integration and stimulate its growth.

Although Lindberg does not elaborate this in detail, it would seem plausible to assume the institutions' capacity for this kind of leadership will increase with increases in a collective decision-making system's degree of integration. For the higher a system's level, i.e. the larger its scope, the greater the range of decision-making stages involved, and the greater its decisiveness; the greater the demand flow, the more resources, and the more cooperative its bargaining modalities ('animators'); and the greater its consequences (penetrativeness, compliance, and distributive consequences) – the more occasions for, procedures through which, the greater the freedom with which, and the greater the number and variety of demands, supports, and actors from which to build up coalitions will be provided. This sounds reasonable enough. But although Lindberg occasionally seems to hint at such a line of reasoning (e.g. *Lindberg*, 1963: 7-8; 1970: 28, 56), he offers no systematic and elaborate analysis.

This argument and Lindberg's concept of 'functional spill-over' suggest the significance of the nature of the international institutions' task for the process of integration. That is, that task may be linked to other fields or decision-making areas outside the initial scope of the institution in such a way that decisions and policies concerning it will have consequences for those other fields. This may lead to demands for further integration, i.e. for increasing its scope on the part of those affected by it. However Lindberg agrees with Haas in that he recognizes that 'functional contexts are autonomous'.

The 'autonomy of functional contexts' means that the fact that a coalition of political actors favors integration in one particular area does not imply that the impulse to integrate will necessarily spread to another area in which different groups are involved and hold power (*Lindberg & Scheingold*, 1970: 109).

This will limit the possibilities for integration to occur as a more or less continuously spreading and progressing process (see also *Lindberg,* 1963: 288). On the other hand, it is to be recalled that in Lindberg's conception 'functional spill-over' is merely one of the mechanisms through which integration may proceed.

It remains to be mentioned, finally, that an international institution, if it is to play the role assigned to it in the above scheme, must be one of a somewhat special character. Although technical expertise may be an important asset (*Lindberg & Scheingold*, 1970: 129) the institution should not conceive its task in a restrictively technical fashion and be dominated by exclusively technical concerns. As has appeared above, its task is essentially a political one; it involves a clear awareness of the institution's purposes, sensitivity to the opportunities provided by the political milieu in which it is to functon, and the capacity for quick, coordinated, and autonomous action. According to Lindberg:

The organization has to learn how to reconcile internal aspirations with external environment, and the real work of organizational leadership lies in managing this process of dynamic adaptation. Several specific tasks are implied here: 1. the definition of the institutional mission and role – these must be specified and recast in terms of external and internal capabilities; 2. an institutional embodiment of purpose – purpose must be built into the social structure of the organization (by staffing and recruitment); and 3. a defense of institutional integrity vis-à-vis external forces – this involves the major adaptative mechanisms of ideology and co-optation (*Lindberg*, 1963: 66; similarly in *Lindberg*, 1970: 66 ff.; see also *Lindberg & Scheingold*, 1970: 93-94).

4.4. *Political actors*

Lindberg does not deal very extensively and systematically with the problem of the relative significance of different political actors for a process of integration. It has already been argued (p. 293 above) that at the outset of an integration process the support of the governments concerned is minimally required. And as long as these national governments still play an essential role in the process (for example because it is *they* who have to bargain over, and to conclude the formal treaties required for increases in the level of integration), and to the extent that they do so, most other actors would seem to be only *indirectly* relevant. That is, such actors as private interest groups and political parties would be important mainly in so far as their activities may influence governmental policy. Accordingly, the significance of the demands and support of non-governmental actors for the process of integration would then be a function of their significance, their 'weight' or 'power', vis-à-vis the *national* governments. Conversely, in order to promote the process of integration the international institutions should mobilize such supporting coalitions as may influence governmental policies. Some such reasoning seems to be behind Lindberg's speaking in terms of 'actors with political power in the national communities' (*Lindberg*, 1963: 94), and of 'significant elites' (*Lindberg*, 1963: 94); as well as the attention he pays to the attitudes and support of 'elites' as distinguished from 'mass publics' (*Lindberg & Scheingold*, 1970, esp. ch. 2 and 3); and his notion that the 'saliency' of an issue area increases with the 'political power' of the actors concerned (p. 280 above). It is not systematically elaborated, though.

In this context it should be mentioned that Lindberg considers the European Community the work of a relatively restricted group of 'elites':

The Community is primarily a creature of elites and even within this category the Community's immediate clientele tends to be restricted to those officials and interest group leaders who are directly affected by its work (*Lindberg & Scheingold*, 1970: 41).

This poses the question of the significance of the support of those non-elites who are not directly involved in the enterprise – the support or attitudes of mass publics as revealed for example in opinion surveys. In Lindberg's opinion such support should be understood in terms of a 'permissive consensus'. By this term he seems to mean, roughly, a form of support which is not actively promoting anything special, but rather *allows* certain things to happen (*Lindberg & Scheingold*, 1970: 41, 62, 252 ff.). It can be thought of as providing room for elite activities.

Actors have been distinguished (p. 273 above) as 'dramatic-political' and 'incremental-economic' as regards their aims; as 'system' and 'subsystem' as regards their 'power and sphere of responsibility'; and according as they perceive their interests to be served by 'further integrative moves', by 'conserving the level of integration', or by 'undoing or rolling back' integration already achieved. However, except for the rather obvious significance of the last-mentioned distinction, the theoretical relevance of the other two distinctions is by no means clear. The more so since Lindberg does not accept Haas's initial assumptions in making the distinction between 'dramatic-political' and 'incremental-economic' actors or interests, namely that the former will generally be dominant (*Lindberg & Scheingold*, 1970: 123-124). Nevertheless, from his discussion it would seem to follow that Lindberg is inclined to consider 'dramatic-political' and 'system' actors to be somewhat more important than 'incremental-economic' and 'subsystem' ones (see in particular *Lindberg & Scheingold*, 1970: 283-284).

Finally, 'leadership' may not only be exercised by international institutions, but also by 'national leaders' by which Lindberg seems to understand governmental actors (*Lindberg*, 1970: 70 ff.). This role essentially derives from the fact to which I have referred in the opening paragraph of this subsection, that such actors, especially in the initial stages of the integration process, occupy a rather special position in the political systems concerned (*Lindberg*, 1970: 70). Lindberg considers their leadership role to be dependent upon the support of their populations (*Lindberg*, 1970: 71). For the rest he limits himself to enumerating some possible kinds of leadership behavior (pp. 281-282 above).

4.5. *Environment*

As to Lindberg's treatment of the environment of integrating political system we can be short. He does hardly deal with it. That is, no explicit and systematic discussion of what determines the character of the system's inputs, support and demands, except in so far as these are influenced by the political process as described thus far, is provided. To be true, it has appeared that Lindberg assumed that, roughly, the more mutual identification there is between actors, the greater the likelihood that they will support common policies and institutions (see p. 286 above). This can clearly be seen as (the beginning of) an attempt to explain support in terms of an environmental variable: in this case (perhaps) identity or complementarity of values patterns. Also, I have argued that what Lindberg calls 'identitive support' is not concerned with an input into the system, but with something determining the character of such an input, namely support (see p. 298 above). In that context he is concerned with such things as the feelings people have about other countries, travel, mail flows, trade, and transnational economic and social organizations (cf. *Lindberg & Scheingold*, 1970: 45 ff.). Generally, however, he limits himself to indicating that things like that are relevant, without providing a detailed analysis of their connection with the system's input. Perhaps it is not too far-fetched to suppose that he assumes that the more links and relations of the kinds mentioned there are, the greater the probability that support for common policies and institutions will become available. The specific result will, however, also be determined by the kinds of demands to which these relations, and the way they are structured, will give rise. On these problems, though, Lindberg is altogether silent. Moreover, in the context of his discussion of the possible future developments of the European Community (*Lindberg & Scheingold*, 1970: 249 ff.) an awareness is shown of such things as value patterns, cultural assimilation, and social or economic class, as possible relevant environmental variables. But in all these cases Lindberg's analysis is of an extremely limited nature – relevance is indicated or assumed, but no detailed and elaborated analysis is offered. It remains to be mentioned, finally, that as concerns the influence of 'external' systems or processes upon what happens within the integrating system, Lindberg explicitly states that these will work through the system's (or subsystem's) actors. Consequently, there is no need, at least not at the level of analysis at which he is moving, to provide for a special concept of 'external influences' (*Lindberg & Scheingold*, 1970: 226).

5. EMPIRICAL INTERPRETATION

5.1. *Introductory*

In general one may say that in his earlier publications (*Lindberg*, 1963, 1965 and 1966a) Lindberg does not expressly go into the problem of the operationalization of his conceptual apparatus. He tends to treat the concepts he uses as of sufficient empirical determinateness. But although it cannot be said that those concepts are altogether empirically empty, their meaning is not generally so (empirically) clear and unambiguous as to suffice for the development of a testable theory (cf. ch. 2, section 4.1). In his later writings (*Lindberg*, 1966, 1970; *Lindberg & Scheingold*, 1970) Lindberg concentrates upon the operationalization of the concept of integration, so much so indeed that he tends to neglect the other parts of his theoretical scheme as described above.

In this section I will first deal with Lindberg's attempts to give an empirical interpretation to the concept 'integration' (section 5.2). In section 5.3 a few of the more important other concepts used will be dealt with.

5.2. *Political integration*

The way Lindberg deals with the problem of operationalizing the concept 'integration' differs somewhat in his various publications (in particular in *Lindberg & Scheingold*, 1970; *Lindberg*, 1966b, 1970). These differences are not of a really fundamental nature, however. Rather, they represent stages in the progressive development of what is really one conception, as may already have become clear from the previous discussion of the political system and of integration (sections 2.1 and 3). Accordingly, in this subsection I will largely limit myself to Lindberg's analysis in *Political integration as a multi-dimensional phenomenon* (*Lindberg*, 1970), which clearly represents the most advanced stage in his thinking on the subject.

As is indicated by the title of that paper, and as has appeared from the discussion of sections 2.1 and 3, Lindberg defines 'integration' in relation to a set of several (10) properties (arranged in three groups, designated by the names 'level', 'animators', and 'consequences') of a collective decision-making system. That is, 'integration' is defined to occur if, in some collective decision-making system, the values assigned to the ten variables increase (cf. also *Lindberg*, 1970: 96 ff.).

Thus, to interpret this geometrically, which may aid the understanding of the problems involved, integration might be conceived as some spatial configuration defined within a 10-dimensional space in the same way as, for instance, a curve can be defined in a 2-dimensional space, i.e., a plane. Lindberg himself repeatedly suggests an algebraic interpretation (e.g. *Lindberg*, 1970: 24, 27, 101); that is, integration, or indeed any of its three compound properties ('level', 'animators', 'consequences'), could be conceived as a vector made up of the numerical values of the ten simple properties mentioned (of course, in the case of the three compound properties individually the vectors involve a smaller number of properties).

But although such interpretations may be useful heuristically, they also call for some qualifying observations. In the first place, it is not certain that the various properties have been defined in a really independent way so that each one of them individually may vary without necessarily implying variations of one or more of the others (cf. *Lindberg*, 1970: 93). Thus, for example, one may doubt whether the properties 'scope' and 'decisiveness' on the one hand, and 'penetrativeness' and 'distributive consequences' on the other, have indeed been defined in such an independent fashion (see pp. 280-281 and 283 above).

In the second place, the character of the function linking integration to the properties mentioned has been defined in an extremely weak fashion. Integration is said to occur when their values rise. But it is not specified how much, and, still more importantly, it is not determined how they, together and mutually interrelated, relate to integration. What, for example, if some of them rise and others fall, or some rise more strongly than others? Of course, Lindberg himself is not blind to these problems (see e.g. *Lindberg*, 1970: 18-19, 100-101). To some extent they inhere in the analysis of any complex (or 'multi-dimensional') phenomenon, and no patent solution for them is available. Such difficulties are compounded, however, by the rather common tendency to introduce all kinds of concepts merely because they somehow seem to have something to do with the subject under consideration, or because they have traditionally been thought so. Too often, however, the most important second step is not made, that is, to carefully think through and explicitly argue why precisely there concepts and their meanings, rather than any others, must be used (see on the rationale behind this point ch. 2, section 2.4.3). As concerns this point, however, it cannot be maintained that Lindberg is altogether blameless.

In the third place, finally, the problem of measuring the values of the various variables in a sufficiently strong way so as to render mathematical solutions for the above-mentioned problems possible, has not been solved by Lindberg. Nevertheless, the mathematical notions referred to may be useful heuristically in that they may point to lines of reasoning via which, ultimately, the problem of measuring integration might be solved.

I shall now briefly discuss Lindberg's operationalization of the ten properties one by one. Since this operationalization is generally presented as tentative only, I will limit myself to indicating the general lines along which Lindberg suggests the problems might eventually be solved. It will be recalled (see pp. 280 ff. above) that the ten properties concerned were: *scope, range, decisiveness* ('level'); *demand flow, resources, leadership, bargaining modalities* ('animators'); and *penetrativeness, compliance,* and *distributive consequences* ('consequences').

Scope is measured in terms of 1. the number of issue areas subject to collective decision-making, and 2. their salience (*Lindberg,* 1970: 23 ff.; p. 280 above). The former is to be estimated on the basis of government documents, those of collective institutions, news reports, etc., applying Lindberg's list of issue areas. The second element, salience, could be measured by using expert coders. With regard to each individual issue area, these are to assign a rating of the 'intensity', 'power of actors' and 'anticipated deprivations' concerned on a five-point scale – from 'low', 'little', and 'all gaining & nobody losing' to 'intense', 'most potent', and 'only one wins, rest lose', respectively.

As to the *range* of participation in collective decision-making, we have seen (p. 280 above, *Lindberg,* 1970: 30) that Lindberg distinguishes six such stages. Together they constitute a kind of six-point scale, ranging from 'collective problem-recognition' ('1') to 'collective implementation and enforcement' ('6'). Each collective act within some specific issue area is to be assigned a position on this scale; and for each issue area a distribution of the acts as to *range* could then be established.

Decisiveness (*Lindberg,* 1970: 33 ff.; pp. 281 and 276 above) is to be measured in a five-point scale, ranging from 'all decisions made by individual governments', through 'only the beginnings of European-level decision authority', 'both, national predominates', and 'both, Community predominates', to 'all choices are subject to joint decision in the European system'. Ratings will have to be made by expert judges.

With regard to *demand flow* it has appeared that Lindberg here distinguishes its 'volume' and its 'variety', and that he suggests these to be estimated in terms of the position of the actors concerned ('system' or 'subsystem'), their interests ('dramatic-political' or 'incremental-economic'), the extent to which they mobilize, the character of their expectations regarding integration, and of their demands concerning it (*Lindberg,* 1970: 39-40; pp. 273 ff. above). As to the operationalization of all this, however, Lindberg limits himself to indicating the possible relevance and usefulness of such things as surveys, the analysis of interactions, the measurement of the rate at which new interest groups form, the growth of their staffs and budgets, and the content analysis of various communications (*Lindberg*, 1970: 41-42).

Many things are included in the concept '*resources*' (pp. 281-282 above; *Lindberg*, 1970: 45 ff.). 'Prior agreement on what can be decided collectively' is to be estimated through an analysis of existing treaty obligations and of past decisions. This is concerned with the extent to which the participating governments have agreed to the making and implementing of decisions by the international institutions. It refers to the existing level of integration (*Lindberg*, 1970: 45). This seems to be an instance of the non-independent character of the variables (cf. p. 303 above). The extent to which 'decision-making norms' have actually developed should be measured by analysing interactions within the collective decision-making system in order to estimate whether or not they involve invocations or rejections of, or conflicts over collective norms (*Lindberg*, 1970: 47).

'Supranational structural growth', it is suggested, could be estimated on the basis of such things as the size of the administrative staff and budgets of the collective institutions, the number of organizational sub-units, the number of meetings held by the institutions, and the number of proposals made by them (*Lindberg*, 1970: 49-50). The 'resources of supranational institutions' are concerned with 'attributed prestige and legitimacy', 'treaty-granted "power" of initiative', and mastery of technical expertise' (*Lindberg*, 1970: 51). The first of these could be estimated by analysing the behavior of governments and other actors vis-à-vis the collective institutions (requests for assistance, expressions of confidence, attitudes, etc.) by interaction analysis and content analysis, as well as by opinion surveys. The second element, 'power of initiative', could be determined on the basis of treaties instituting the system, or by expert coders. 'Technical expertise' could be estimated from the growth of administrative staff, in particular in high-level and professional categories (*Lindberg*, 1970: 52-53). The volume of 'national – supranational transactions' is to be estimated in terms of the frequency with which national civil servants participate in the activities of the collective institutions, the flow of communications (phone calls, mail, or telex) between such participating civil servants and their home ministries, the number of administrative units in national bureaucracies which are directly concerned with the collective activities, and the number and duration of meetings of intergovernmental bodies and expert groups (*Lindberg*, 1970: 55).

The 'financial resources' of the collective decision-making institutions can be estimated from their budgets, for example as a percentage of the aggregate GNP of the states involved (*Lindberg*, 1970: 56).

No detailed indications are provided for the estimation of a decision-making system's 'support resources'. These include (p. 281 above; *Lindberg*, 1970: 60 ff.) 'expectations of future gain', 'belief in legitimacy', 'belief in common interest', and 'sense of mutual political identification'. To some extent, it is suggested, these could be determined through surveys and attitude research, and by analysing the behavior and communications of such actors as political parties and interest groups.

Leadership (the third 'animator') may be of a supranational and of a national kind. It has already been shown that Lindberg distinguishes several categories of leadership activities (p. 281 above). Instructions are provided so as to allow coders to assign the actual activities of supranational and national leaders to the appropriate categories (*Lindberg*, 1970: 70-72). In this context it should also be mentioned that Lindberg suggests that 'the extent to which an organizational ideology has developed' in the international institution (see p. 298 above) could be estimated through content analysis of the statements and proposals of supranational leaders (*Lindberg*, 1970: 67). He further writes that it is especially the 'time-in-service of the occupants of top policy-making positions' of an international institution which could serve as an indication of the extent a cohesive staff has developed (*Lindberg*, 1970: 67-68).

The several *bargaining modalities* which may characterize some collective decision-making system (the fourth 'animator', see p. 282 above) are again to be coded by an analysis of actual bargaining and on the basis of instructions that are described in some detail (*Lindberg*, 1970: 75).

The third main group of variables, finally, termed 'consequences', consists of *penetrativeness*, *compliance*, and *distributive consequences*. Lindberg suggests that *penetrativeness* could be determined by using survey data in order to see whether and to what extent attitudes and opinions have changed in regard to integration, and by analysing national policies as to whether these have grown more similar or dissimilar

(*Lindberg*, 1970: 83). Furthermore, he indicates that collective decisions should be analysed as to the degree to which these are binding for the various actors concerned, or the constraints they impose upon those actors (*Lindberg*, 1970: 83-84). It would seem, however, that *penetrativeness* here overlaps *decisiveness* and *scope*; it seems to be another example in which the concepts used have been defined non-independently.

Compliance could be measured in terms of such things as the number of national court rulings challenging collective rules; the number of complaints made or suits for rule violation; boycots; the frequency of invocation of escape clauses and demands for exceptions from collective rules; the number of requests for interlocutory rulings by collective legal institutions on the part of national legal authorities; and the number of judgments by national courts interpreting and/or confirming the rules of the collectivity (*Lindberg*, 1970: 85-86). These, it is to be noted, are offered merely as suggestions by Lindberg. Finally, no definite measures are offered to precisely and empirically determine the character and magnitude of the collective decision-making system's *distributive consequences*. Here Lindberg limits himself to pointing out the possible relevance, but also the empirical *and* theoretical indeterminateness, of such things as economic growth rates, flows of investment capital and trade, imponderables like military security and a higher status in the world's power-hierarchy, and changes in access to or influence over decision-makers (*Lindberg*, 1970: 86 ff.).

It has already been discussed that this approach to the phenomenon of political integration poses the problem of the combining and interrelating of all the various observations and measurements regarding the ten properties. This problem has not been solved. Quite apart from this, however, it will have become clear from the above brief account of the lines along which Lindberg seeks to link the ten properties described with observable reality that this, too, can hardly be said to be a complete success. That is, in most cases only suggestions and hints as to the direction further research might take in order to solve the problem of the empirical interpretation of the concept of integration were given. Now, given the extreme complexity of the problem one could expect hardly more. And it certainly is not the least one of the merits of this attempt to have brought out this complexity in a very clear and sharp way.

5.3. *Actors, demands, and support*

I have already said (section 5.1) that Lindberg tends to concentrate on the operationalization of the concept of integration, to the virtual exclusion of the other elements in the scheme. It should be recognized, though, that to some extent at least such other elements (e.g., 'actors', 'demands', and 'support') *are* dealt with in relation to the concept 'integration'. This perspective, however, also introduces a certain bias. That is to say, in particular with regard to demands and support Lindberg concentrates upon finding aggregate measures at the level of the system in its entirety. He is concerned most with the character of the total demand flow fed into the system, and with the total amount of systemic support available to it, while much less attention is paid to specific demands and support of individual actors. Of course, an analysis of aggregate support and demand flows will ultimately reach down to individual and specific demands and support as the constituent elements of the total flows. In general, however, Lindberg's analysis has not been elaborated to such detail.

As to support, Lindberg concentrates upon its systemic and identitive forms. I have already argued why I think 'identitive support' should be considered as a 'background' or 'environmental' variable rather than as a form of support properly so called (cf. section 2.2). Very little attention is paid to the analysis and empirical interpretation of specific support, i.e. support aimed at specific objects, interests or purposes, nor does he pay much attention to an analysis of the forms such support behavior may assume and their relative significance in a process of integration. In this connection it may be mentioned that, in *The European Community as a political system*, he does make an attempt to construct a kind of 'support scale', as follows:

4 equals intense and uncritical support (super-patriotism) and action.
3 equals strong supportive feelings and political activity.
2 equals strong supportive feelings but no action.
1 equals moderate feelings of support, not intense, no action.
0 equals indifference, passive acceptance.
−1 equals moderate opposition.
−2 equals strong opposition.
−3 equals strong opposition, political action.
−4 equals very deep hostility, and violent disagreement (*Lindberg*, 1966b: 376).

It will be recalled that interests have been classified as 'dramatic-political' and 'incremental-economic', as well as on the basis of the actors' expectations with regard to the consequences of integration. Also, the 'power and responsibility' of the actors is an important classificatory criterion (p. 274 above). All this, however, has not been elaborated very much.

In order to determine the relative significance of various forms of demand and support behavior it would presumably be necessary to relate these to certain properties of the actors concerned. Obviously, not all actors have the same political status or weight, or play the same roles in the political process. Lindberg does not deal systematically and in detail with these matters, however. He distinguishes actors in terms of the scope of their power and responsibility (system-wide or limited to some subsystem), as we have seen above; and he also repeatedly speaks in terms of 'elites'. But apart from the fact that these categories are not defined very precisely, if at all, no rules are given through which they can be empirically interpreted. Occasionally, some more exact measures are given. Thus, in order to determine the significance of certain trade agreements for particular participating states in EEC, Lindberg uses data on the composition of imports and exports, their significance for the national economies concerned, the economic sectors involved, the composition of the labor force, and the height of tariffs (*Lindberg*, 1963: 111 ff.). He also uses the composition of the labor force as a measure for the 'political weight' of one of its elements, in particular with respect to the agrarian population (*Lindberg*, 1963: 226).

All this is not elaborated, however. Nevertheless, it would seem, it suggests a kind of analysis through which such things as the 'weight' or 'importance' of certain actors, the 'significance' or 'importance' of certain interests for them, could be related to empirically measurable and observable phenomena. It has already been noted that this is also highly relevant for any more elaborate analysis of demands and support behavior, in particular in view of determining the relative significance of its various manifestations.

However, in all the cases discussed in this subsection, the basic weaknesses involved seem not to reside primarily in defective operationalization, or even its complete absence. Rather, it seems to be a matter of the low degree to which such elements as have been mentioned here have been elaborated in the abstract scheme analysed in the preceding sections. Before the question of empirical interpretation can be posed in a meaningful way with regard to such elements, much more purely abstract analysis would seem to be required.

6. ASSESSMENT

It will have become clear by now that Lindberg's integration theory does not differ fundamentally from that of Haas, the much larger role the systems-analytic vocabulary plays in it notwithstanding. This is not to deny, of course, that there are no differences between the two theories. Thus, Lindberg pays much more attention to the analysis and empirical interpretation of the concept of integration than does Haas. While Haas expressly defines 'integration' in terms of common institutions, Lindberg's conception of integration is, at least potentially, wider: in his most recent publications integration is conceived as the growth of a collective decision-making system. One of the elements of such systems *may* be common institutions, or organizations, but, in principle, integration might be conceived to occur even in their absence – namely, if the values of the other variables characterizing the system increase. On the other hand, however, common institutions and their resources are extremely important; one might even presume that from a certain level on integration will not further proceed in their absence. Also, it has been noted that Lindberg tends to presuppose the existence of such institutions in his theorizing. Accordingly, in practice common institutions assume much the same importance in his treatment of the subject as in that of Haas. Furthermore, the concept of spill-over is defined in a somewhat narrower sense by Lindberg than by Haas, while he also shows more awareness of its limitations than Haas did in his early publications. On the other hand, however, in his mechanisms of coalition formation we meet with largely the same mechanisms which underlied Haas's conception of the process.

But such differences would merely seem to concern matters of detail. They do not detract from the very fundamental similarity between Lindberg's and Haas' theorizing (and by implication that of Deutsch, too) as to the structure of the argument in general, and the conception of politics, of integration, and of the mechanism of the process in particular.

On the other hand, however, it can hardly be maintained that Lindberg's theorizing goes beyond that of Haas or of Deutsch, that is, further develops their theories in any fundamental sense. No really new insights are offered and neither does his theorizing elaborate, refine, or add precision to, what could already be distilled from the writings of Haas and Deutsch. One of the main reasons for this is, of course, that neither Haas nor Deutsch really do present in their publications theories of such a clear and explicit form as to lend themselves easily to further development and elaboration. And in so far this provides a clear example of the way the lack of clear and explicit argument on the basis of explicitly stated assumptions and through clearly stated inferences, may impede scientific progress. In Francis Bacon's words: 'Truth emerges more readily from error than from confusion'. Another reason is, however, that Lindberg himself does not proceed in a very clear and explicit fashion either. If anything, it seems that with regard to such crucial matters as the character of the political process and that of integration he leaves even more things implicit than did Haas or Deutsch (cf. sections 2.2 and 4.2 in particular).

The above does not wholly apply to Lindberg's analysis of the concept of integration and its empirical interpretation, of course. Here he does indeed refine and elaborate to a fairly high degree. Nevertheless, here, too, his treatment seems to suffer from a certain lack of explicit argument and reasoning, as has already been observed (cf. section 3 and 5.2). Given the complexity of the problems involved, one may not expect a conclusive, or at any rate a satisfactory, answer to the question of the empirical interpretation, let alone measurement, of the concept of integration to be developed on short notice. The basic flow of Lindberg's attempt at operationalizing the concept 'integration' resides in the isolated character thereof. That is to say, 'integration' is treated largely as an individual concept to be empirically interpreted in isolation from the rest of the theoretical scheme constructed. As I have already observed earlier (cf. ch. 2, section 3.3.3), however, one cannot generally isolate individual concepts from the calculus in which they occupy a position and which determines their meaning. The empirical interpretation of such concepts, too, involves the entire calculus from the very beginning. This applies the more strongly to the concept 'integration', as it is a highly abstract theoretical construct embedded in a calculus of a very general and abstract nature.

BIBLIOGRAPHY

EASTON, David, 1965. *A systems analysis of political life*. Wiley, New York.

LASSWELL, Harold D. & Abraham KAPLAN, 1950. *Power and society – a framework for political inquiry*. Yale University Press, New York/London, 1963.

LINDBERG, Leon N., 1963. *The political dynamics of European economic integration*. Stanford University Press, Stanford (Cal.)

LINDBERG, Leon N., 1965. Decision making and integration in the European Community. *Int. Orgn 19*: 56–80.

LINDBERG, Leon N., 1966a. Integration as a source of stress on the European Community system. *Int. Orgn 20*: 233–265.

LINDBERG, Leon N., 1966b. The European Community as a political system – notes toward the construction of a model. *J. common Market Stud. 5 (4)*: 344–387.

LINDBERG, Leon N., 1970. Political integration as a multi-dimensional phenomenon requiring multi-variate measurement. Mimeo; to appear in *Int. Orgn.*

LINDBERG, Leon N. & Stuart A. SCHEINGOLD, 1970. *Europe's would-be policy – patterns of change in the European Community*. Prentice-Hall, Englewood Cliffs (N.J.).

7 TOWARD A THEORY OF POLITICS AND OF INTEGRATION

1. OUTLINE OF THIS CHAPTER

In this chapter I will be concerned with an attempt to draw a few general conclusions from the analyses of the preceding chapters, and to see whether some kind of synthesis can be concocted from them. Section 2 will be devoted to a discussion of a few of the more important formal or methodological characteristics of the investigations analysed so far. In section 3 I will try to sketch what seems to emerge, as a theory of politics and of integration, from the analyses of the preceding chapters. In section 4, finally, I will make some brief observations on the general significance of the problem of political integration.

2. THE THEORIES – INSTANCES OF EARLY SCIENCE

2.1. *Observations on scientific development*

As indicated earlier (cf. introduction, section 2) the main purpose of the preceding inquiries has been to see whether and to what extent there have emerged theories of political integration in the strict sense of the term 'theory' discussed in chapter two, i.e., that of an empirically testable system of concepts and postulates through which politics and integration can be explained. To this end it has been attempted, on the basis of a fairly explicit and elaborated notion of what a scientific theory is or should be, to distill from what has been written by the several authors theories in the sense indicated. In other words, a particular metascientific conception of theorizing has been used as a kind of filter through which to study the authors' writings – retaining what could be made to fit into the structure of a scientific theory and rejecting everything else.

In itself this perspective is fundamentally a-historical. That is, for the reconstruction of the theories or for an evaluation of their scientific adequacy, their strengths and weaknesses, it does not really matter whence derive the conceptions and notions involved, how their authors are influenced, or what went before and what comes after. On the other hand, however, it has been seen (cf. section 2.5.2 of chapter two) that the acquisition of knowledge, theorizing, and the construction of reality, actually are historical processes. What is being done and what is developed in a particular period is indeed connected with and based upon what went before, while it in turn provides the starting point for further developments. Accordingly, in order to gain a proper understanding of the significance of the theories under discussion a purely formal or metascientific evaluation of its products (i.e., whether they meet the criteria of scientific theorizing) is not enough. It might well be that a theory, though grossly inadequate from a strictly scientific viewpoint, is nevertheless to be judged as of the highest importance and significance because it represents, or leads to, a major breakthrough in the historical development of science, and provides a basis for fundamentally new tance of the purely scientific standards. On the contrary, for it is precisely the theory's inadequacies and weak points that ultimately appear to be its historically most important and fruitful elements. This is not to say, of course, that in evaluating a theory one should play down the importance of the purely scientific standards. On the contrary, for its is precisely through a strict application of such standards that the theory's weak and strong points emerge, and that its historical significance can be estimated.

In seeking to communicate some sense for the development of science in general, and for that of theorizing in the field of integration in particular, I have placed the preceding analyses against the background of earlier developments in the field (chapter one). And although theories should in general be formulated in a logically strict and rigorous fashion, in my reconstruction of the several integration theories I have generally sacrificed logical rigor to faithfulness of presentation. For, since the writings of the authors discussed do not, for the most part, exhibit a clear and explicit logical structure, a logically strict reconstruction of the authors' arguments would have required adding too much to and going too far beyond what they actually wrote. By keeping more closely to the texts the developmental character of theorizing may emerge more sharply since continuities and discontinuities with respect to the central problems, the vocabularies applied, and the kinds of arguments used, between the literature analysed and the preceding tradition may thus become somewhat more easily visible.

In speaking about the historical development of science and of theorizing this should not be understood as implying a smoothly continuous progress of knowledge. To conceive this development as a 'cumulative process of gaining knowledge', when meant to denote a continuous and progressive enrichment of some pre-existing fund of knowledge, is slightly misleading. Surely, in general knowledge does progress and insight does deepen; loosely speaking, we do know and understand more now than in the past – even with regard to political integration. Several important qualifications should be borne in mind, however.

In the first place, the process may be an extremely slow one. And its most important stages may well be characterized by significant problems being raised rather than by the addition of important pieces of substantive knowledge to the existing store. Thus, with regard to the subject under discussion it appeared that it took some centuries before even the more significant questions were merely asked. Besides, science may proceed through discarding existing problems as irrelevant, rather than solving them, while putting new problems in their stead.

In the second place, the process need not occur in a chronologically neat fashion. New ways of thinking may emerge slowly, and even with present-day communication facilities the old and the new may coexist for a considerable period. Thus, in the field of international integration, it appeared that an important part of the pre-scientific tradition, notably a considerable portion of federalist thinking, is strictly contemporaneous with the theorizing discussed in this book. More generally, thirdly, in an important respect scientific development is of necessity a *dis*continuous affair. As has appeared from chapter two (see in particular its section 2.5.2) theory formation does not merely *add* something to knowledge and understanding of a pre-existing reality but consists of the construction of a (partly) new reality for whose understanding the pre-existing stock of knowledge is not automatically relevant.

It will have become clear from the preceding chapters that no satisfactory theory of integration has been developed as yet. In fact, theorizing as it has been discussed here bears all the characteristics of an early stage in the development of science. Reasoning proceeds in an extremely loose and informal fashion; concepts are formed in a rather undisciplined way; empirical propositions often rest upon impressionistic judgement rather than upon careful and precise observation; while suggestions and brief hints very often take the place of strict argument. In all this the theories are still very close to the notions and linguistic habits of everyday discourse.

All this is important enough, of course, but it is insufficient for evaluating the significance of the theories discussed. For against it should be set the fact that, for all its technical defects, a new way of thinking about politics and integration, a more or less consistent vocabulary and some sketches of argument could indeed be seen to emerge. Actually, as I will argue below, some of the theories' weaknesses (and some very important ones at that) were altogether avoidable; accordingly, more *could* have been achieved; but if one is aware of what it takes to form new and original theories, that is, to break through established conceptions and ways of thinking, one can hardly fail to feel impressed, especially since theory formation is, to a fairly large extent, a matter of imagination and originality, and not one of the application of some simple rules.

2.2. *The lack of argument*

2.2.1. *Introductory*
The purpose of the preceding analyses has been to construct rather than to criticize. The character of this work implies that I have always sought for what I conceived to be the best possible interpretation of the authors' writings. I will not repeat or summarize all the various points of critique made with regard to the individual authors discussed. There is, however, one more general point pertaining to all the authors concerned to a fairly high degree which deserves to be discussed in somewhat greater detail. It may be summarized through the phrase 'the lack of argument', and it concerns three major aspects of theory formation: reasoning, i.e., the way conclusions are derived from certain assumptions, concept formation, and operationalization.

2.2.2. *On assumptions and conclusions*

It is really striking how little reasoning with a semblance of strictness one encounters in the literature investigated. As may have become clear from the preceding analyses basic assumptions are only seldom stated clearly and openly. Often they have to be culled from the way they appear to be used in different contexts. When one does meet with explicit formulations these are frequently offered in a casual and loose fashion. Although the subjects dealt with (both the political process in general and political integration) are of a very general and extremely complicated character, these are attacked with only a minimal apparatus of presuppositions openly so stated. Moreover, there is a strong tendency to forget about such presuppositions once they have been stated. That is to say, once formulated one seldom finds them used and mentioned in arguments based upon them. Of course, it generally seems plausible enough that it is *these* postulates rather than others from which the propositions made by the authors derive. It should be recognized, however, that in the absence of a clearly formulated argument involving them we can never be entirely sure about that. It might well be that the author concerned did have something different in mind after all.

It should be obvious that this method, or, rather, lack of method, entails some important weaknesses and dangers in theorizing. I have already indicated that in the absence of explicit argument reasoning is essentially uncontrolled – one may never be entirely sure as to what assumptions were actually applied, while, conversely, auxiliary assumptions can be introduced *ad libitum* whenever some statement is under attack. Another point is that in this fashion theorizing tends to be restricted to a level of fairly uncomplicated and rather primitive reasoning. That is, when one does not argue in a strict fashion on the basis of openly formulated assumptions, only such conclusions will be drawn as appear to be immediately obvious, and chains of argument will not extend beyond what can be seen immediately and in a glance – which probably is not very far. Moreover, by not arguing explicitly one can hardly exhaust all the potentialities of the assumptions that are introduced. Thus, although the basis of postulates applied in the foregoing analyses was an extremely narrow one, on several occasions I have indicated that it allowed for the derivation of much more than the authors themselves were apparently aware of (see, for instance, ch. four, section 4.4

on Deutsch's discussion of the 'background' conditions for integration; and ch. six, section 4.2 on Lindberg's treatment of the mechanism of an integration process). On the other hand ignoring crucial assumptions sometimes led inquiry astray (see, for example, chapter three, section 4.3, concerning Haas's modification of his ideas on spill-over and the autonomy of functional contexts).

2.2.3. *On concept formation*

However, the phrase 'lack of argument' does not only refer to the character of the reasoning involved in the theories discussed, but also to the way concepts were formed and applied. Surely, reasonably clear definitions were provided for the most obviously important concepts used, while (still more important, perhaps) the relevance of such concepts in the theory was generally made sufficiently clear. Thus, neither the description of the nature of the political process in general, nor that of political integration, did raise too much difficulties on this account. Matters often become somewhat different, however, as one reaches down to 'lower' levels of analysis, that is, levels of analysis where it is attempted to explain, for example, a political system's input in terms of environment variables, or where the system's output has to be related to such environmental variables. One is tempted to say that the greater the 'distance' between the theories' central concepts 'politics' and 'integration' and other concepts applied, the more obscure and uncertain the latter's theoretical position and role tend to be.

What is at issue here is not merely a matter of explicit definition. The concepts involved might well be defined in an unimpeachable fashion. Nonetheless their theoretical significance may remain wholly unclear and dubious. And rather than upon considerations derived from the theory being developed, their introduction may well rest upon nothing more than the fact that they are traditionally thought to be important, or only the vaguest idea that they have something to do with the matter at issue. A particularly clear example is provided by the rather common treatment of so-called 'economic' factors in relation to political integration.

Thus, almost all authors discussed pay a more or less considerable amount of attention to such 'economic' environmental variables as trade flows. It is thought, and probably rightly so, that these are important things in explaining processes of political integration. Nevertheless, it is only rarely spelled out with sufficient clarity why exactly they are important and wherein this importance resides. The introduction of 'trade flows' at this level of analysis would, in general, seem to rest upon some such assumption like 'the greater the trade flows between actors, the higher the probability of political integration occurring there'. Now even if openly so stated (and, to a large extent, one is free to introduce any kind of assumption whatsoever) such an assumption leaves much to be desired. In the first place, and disregarding the fact that the above proposition is rather imprecise and stated in a highly simplified fashion, its introduction is highly dubious from a formal point of view. If we, as do all the authors discussed here, either explicitly or implicitly explain politics first of all (i.e., at a first or 'highest' level of analysis) in terms of demands, support, and binding decisions, political integration being conceived as a political phenomenon in the first place, then, by the same token, it is inadmissible and inconsistent to relate such a political phenomenon *directly* to something like trade flows. One thus would bypass the variables (demands, etc.) in terms of which one had declared earlier to explain politics. In systems analytic terminology: demands and support are input variables while trade flows (and the same applies with equal force to such things as communication flows, GNP's, military and administrative capabilities, language, culture and culture patterns) are 'environmental' ones.

Thus, from a purely formal point of view, the introduction of the concept 'trade flows' along the lines indicated, fails completely to determine its role and position in the theory. But, secondly, this has important substantive consequences. Briefly, to link trade flows directly to political integration is a rather crude and unsophisticated strategy, since trade flows (so much seems to follow from research done in the field) are in all probability merely one factor among many others that are responsible for the occurrence of integration; it seems highly unlikely that one could establish such an unambiguous relationship between integration and trade flows. In disregarding the concept 'demands' and 'support' and the various postulates governing their use, one bypasses an opportunity to develop a more refined and realistic construction. That is to say, such things as trade flows might then relate to integration *via* the behavioral and motivational characteristics of the various actors making demands and lending support, *together* with a number of other environmental influences. And, conversely, even if such a direct link between integration and trade flows would have been established empirically, it would merely constitute something to be explained – for which explanation one would presumably have to turn again to such concepts as 'demands' and 'supports'.

As may be seen from this example, the important thing is, here as elsewhere, that in order to make theoretical sense, introducing a concept merely by means of a definition does not suffice. In addition, certain assumptions have to be formulated so as to link the concept concerned to the rest of the theoretical structure. And, conversely, nothing should be introduced which makes no sense in terms of such assumptions. What is to be introduced should be based upon what are thought to be the needs of the theory, and *not* on what has been developed in some other sphere, for example, that of everyday discourse or of practical politics (see for a deeper justification ch. 2, section 2.4.4).

As it is, however, the theoretical reasons for introducing some concept very often remain implicit, thus leaving the concept's function in the theory undetermined. And this, too, offers an example of what I have phrased the 'lack of argument' characterizing present-day theorizing in the field of political integration. Incidentally, the lack of explicit reasoning also prevents the use of the powerful tool of the implicit definition, which does require postulates openly so stated (cf. ch. 2, section 3.3.2).

2.2.4. *On operationalization*

In the third place, lack of argument is exemplified by the way it is generally attempted to give an empirical interpretation to theoretical constructs. Inasmuch as such interpretation can be conceived as the introduction of observables into the theoretical structure, largely the same considerations as described above with respect to concept formation in general apply here too. With regard to this problem of operationalization three specific points deserve some additional, if brief, comment: the common practice of seeking to operationalize the calculus' central concepts in a direct and isolated fashion; the misuse of 'indicators'; and the problem of measurement as it is dealt with in the theories under discussion.

It may have been noted that in so far as the authors discussed do expressly attempt to operationalize their theoretical schemes, this usually involves an attempt to directly confront or 'compare' such schemes' central constructs (in particular that of 'political integration') with empirical reality in an isolated fashion. That is, such attempts usually involve but little argument, or only very short chains of reasoning, anɑ/or they are made in virtual isolation from the rest of the calculus hardly applying its postulates and other concepts. Now it has already been pointed out that it is somewhat misleading to conceive of a calculus's operationalization in terms of its constituent concepts as more or less isolated entities to be directly 'measured' against or 'compared' with observable 'things', especially when these concepts are highly abstract and complex constructs (cf. chapter two, section 3.3.3). Such a direct empirical interpretation will normally be possible only with regard to very elementary and simple concepts. And it is through these that the other elements of the calculus will receive an indirect empirical interpretation. But it will be clear that this again involves argument and reasoning. For it is through the calculus' apparatus of postulates, *plus* the additional assumptions linking its more elementary concepts with observables, that its more abstract and complex constructs can be said to receive an interpretation. This may lead to quite complex and lengthy arguments involving much more than a simple observing whether or not political integration, for instance, is the case. Thus, instead of seeking a direct empirical referent for the concept 'political community', a directly observable 'thing' to be called a political community, its empirical interpretation will have to proceed via certain assumptions that link observables to what the calculus deduces from the occurrence of a certain measure of political integration (understood as the formation of a political community). For example (and to mention merely one among many possible arguments), on the basis of certain postulates about 'demand behavior', the way political actors spend 'resources', and the definition of 'political integration' or 'community', the calculus might predict that if integration occurs then there will be an increase in the 'amount of resources' spent in certain 'forms of demand behavior' at a supranational level. Via the introduction of some *additional* assumptions linking 'amount of resources' and particular 'forms of demand behavior' to *observables* (e.g. to 'the amount of money invested in the hiring of international staff by private interest groups'), one might thus operationalize the concept 'political community'. In actual fact, of course, the empirical interpretation of the political community concept will be a matter of much longer and much more involved constructions than the one indicated here. The above merely serves to show how such interpretation will in itself be a matter of theoretical construction, involving both the calculus and a number of additional concepts and assumptions.

In practice one often seeks to solve this problem by means of what are called 'indicators'. Sets of a greater or lesser number of such empirical indicators are constructed, involving more or less direct observations, and purporting to 'measure', or to be correlated with, the concept in question. Surely, this can be viewed as a first step toward a more sophisticated approach to the problem of operationalization. In the first place the use of a number of different indicators, meant to relate to different 'aspects' of the phenomenon at issue, means already that more relevant elements are drawn into consideration, which would, when elaborated, presumably mean a progressive involvement of the calculus itself in the enterprise. Still more important, secondly, is that the use of indicators does imply some kind of argument and reasoning. For, briefly, the application of indicators involves some such assumption as 'if there is smoke, then there will be fire'. It can be easily seen that upon giving this proposition a suitable interpretation in terms of the domain under discussion, some kind of argument becomes possible.

Several things should be noted. First, the crucial assumptions are rarely stated explicitly. Second, the chains of argument are generally extremely short, for the most part not exceeding one link, which is hardly adequate for the complexity of the issues involved. Finally, and largely as a consequence of all this, the interrelationships among the various individual indicators are generally left unspecified (see, e.g., ch. 3, section 5.2 on Haas's operationalization of the concept 'integration', and ch. 6, section 5.2 on that of Lindberg).

Similar problems are posed by the way it is attempted to measure political phenomena. In the preceding analyses several examples of such measurement were met with. Usually these were of an extremely weak form (nominal or ordinal). The reason why I mention these problems here, however, is that the way such measurements are made frequently suffers from the same lack of argument as can be observed with regard to other aspects of theorizing discussed. That is, only rarely one finds the nature of the number system chosen spelled out clearly. Neither is it sought to determine whether or not the relationships obtaining in the empirical domain satisfy the requirements of that number system (see, e.g., Haas's and Deutsch's attempts at scale construction in ch. 3, section 5.2, and ch. 4, section 5.4, respectively). Again, all this is largely a matter of the construction of arguments upon the basis of postulates and assumptions explicitly and clearly stated. Its absence may well be responsible for the rather common error of performing all sorts of arithmetical operations on numbers for which these are not even defined. This also suggests the inadequacy of the logical and mathematical insights that are brought to bear upon the problems concerned.

2.2.5. *Lack of argument – significance, origin and a qualification*

I have paid considerable attention to, and rather strongly emphasized, what I have termed the 'lack of argument' characterizing so much of the theories analysed. This is basically for two interconnected reasons. In the first place, argument is of the essence of theorizing, and something lacking it can hardly be called a theory. In the second place, in the absence of explicit argument, scientific progress becomes difficult indeed. When crucial assumptions are left unstated, or are stated only in an obscure and ambiguous way, when lines of reasoning are merely suggested or hinted at rather than described fully and precisely so that the interconnections between the different parts of the theory cannot be made visible – then it becomes very difficult to evaluate such a theory, to avoid the errors made in it, to use it as a basis for further theorizing and research, and to build upon it. As I have indicated, in the absence of open argumentation theorizing tends to remain at a level of superficial and rather primitive knowledge.

It is rather difficult to account for this peculiar lack of argument in the theories discussed. For, at first sight at least, it can hardly be explained through the fact that we are concerned here with a very early stage in the development of (political) science, since it would seem that openly stated argument is *always* possible, in any stage of development whatsoever. Perhaps the authors concerned share in the rather general feeling of uncertainty as to the feasibility of social science theory formation making any attempt at more rigorous and formalized theorizing seem futile. However this may be, it is hoped that the preceding analyses have demonstrated that, for all its defects, enough has been achieved as to warrant some cautious optimism – something has been achieved indeed.

The above picture of the theories' general lack of argument may have been painted in somewhat too violent colors. Several qualifications are in order. In the first place, the picture is somewhat distorted because it lumps together a multitude and variety of observations on different authors. Of course, they do not all display the traits noted to the same extent. Also, those traits may characterize their treatment of some elements of their theories but not others. For the sake of the exposition's clarity and economy, such differences have been ignored. Furthermore, in the second place, in many cases arguments could be fairly easily reconstructed. And finally the criticisms made do not imply that the problems involved allow for some easy solution or that such solutions are within easy reach and would merely require a greater measure of explicit argumentation. The problems of operationalization and measurement in particular turn out to be extremely thorny and difficult. Their solution surely is not something to be expected in the very near future.

2.3. *A note on continuity*

Throughout this book I have stressed both the discontinuities and the continuities between scientific theorizing and common sense and everyday discourse. As noted, the basic reason for not carrying my (re-) construction of the theories discussed further than I actually did was precisely to bring out more sharply the links between them and the preceding tradition and everyday discourse (see section 2.1). In important respects the theories turned out to be rather close to the preceding tradition and to common sense. Nevertheless, and for all their important weaknesses, they were also scientific theories – at least, significant steps on the road toward such theories. This raises a point of a more general nature, namely, that scientific theorizing is not totally alien to more traditional and common discourse, and that it should not be separated from the latter by an impassable chasm. I have already indicated the nature of the *dis*continuities involved. It is equally important, though, to be aware of the continuity between the two. In particular it may have become clear that the way of reasoning applied in scientific theorizing, though applying longer chains of argument and proceeding in a much more explicit and precise fashion than in ordinary life, is not fundamentally different from that used in more common or traditional knowledge; or, conversely, that a more strict analysis of the latter may well bring out a structure of reasoning that is not unlike that employed and developed in a scientific theory. This, incidentally, is also the reason why, in the present section, I have generally spoken in terms of 'argument' and 'reasoning', terms which, however, denote essentially the same things as, in more formal or rigorous theory formation, 'deduction' or 'derivation'. Also, the development of more formal and rigorous theories would seem to be a rather 'logical' or 'natural' step in our search for more precise and reliable knowledge. Theories, even mathematical theories, are *not* the mysterious and esoteric entities they are often taken to be; they are not to be put into boxes that are wholly separate from 'life', 'man', or 'practice'. Rather, they represent perfectly natural, though none too common products of our quest for better, i.e., more reliable and precise knowledge.

3. AN ATTEMPT AT SYNTHESIS

3.1. *Introduction*

3.1.1. *One theory or many?*
When I originally conceived the idea of these investigations I hoped (and expected) to find a number of fundamentally different, alternative theories of political integration contained in the writings of the various authors. The more so since a first and superficial glance over some of the relevant literature seemed to reveal considerable differences as to vocabulary, conceptions, and lines of reasoning employed. To reconstruct several alternative theories seemed attractive as it would allow for choice. Their weak and strong points could be compared; what would have remained unsolved in one theory would perhaps have been solved in another; and although there would certainly have remained a number of problems unsolved by any of the theories, the confrontation of different approaches to them would perhaps suggest solutions or lead to a new look at them – *du choc des opinions jaillit la vérité*.

Appearances proved to be somewhat deceiving, however. For, as I have repeatedly indicated during the course of the preceding analyses, far from resulting in a number of really different theories, the investigations revealed what should rather be called 'variations on a common theme'. Obviously, this is not to deny that the several authors discussed *do* display certain differences as to the way they attack the problems involved. Thus, they differ with regard to the vocabulary applied; they do not all focus upon the same problems or aspects with equal intensity; their theories show different degrees of elaboration; the backgrounds from which they take their basic ideas differ; and, finally, one might perhaps say that the nearer one gets to the periphery of the theories (i.e. where one has to deal with such problems as explaining the behavior of political units, the role and nature of a political system's 'environment', 'background variables', and the operatioalization of the theoretical scheme) the greater the differences become.

But it also appeared that differences in vocabulary, and the extra-political background from which the theories emerged, proved to be hardly essential. In fact, the theories' most central parts, i.e., their conceptions of politics and of integration, the kinds of concepts employed in their explanation, and the avenues along which such explanation was undertaken, proved to be remarkably similar. And the one theory that departed most from this common train of thought (Etzioni's) was also the least satisfactory one – so much so indeed that it, too, cannot be said to provide a real alternative to the others.

It is this common theoretical core which I shall seek to describe in the next section. As may appear from the literature mentioned at the end of this chapter, however, the authors discussed so far have not been the only ones to have occupied themselves with the theory of political integration. Generally speaking, however, and as far as I could see, such other contributions are either of a too limited nature, dealing only with certain aspects of the problem of integration, or they do not sufficiently advance beyond, or differ from what has been presented thus far, as to justify detailed discussions in separate chapters. The relevant elements from these writings will be mentioned or discussed in the appropriate places in the discussion of the present section.

Another point is that such an attempt at synthesis trying to uncover what seems to be contained in the theorizing under discussion, already implies a certain advance over what was originally given; the more so since I cannot, for the most part, refer to any explicit formulation by some individual author. As a general rule I have kept as closely as possible to what has already been discussed or suggested, or what is explicitly so formulated in other literature; only in case its omission would be very obvious and glaring have I added something more, while I have also kept the discussion at a rather informal level.

3.1.2. *Outline of this section*
This section will consist of three main sub-sections: on politics in general (3.2), on political integration (3.3), while 3.4 will be devoted to a critique of what emerged in the preceding subsections. The discussion of sections 3.2 and 3.3 will proceed in three steps, that may roughly be said to represent different levels of analysis. The first ('the problem') is concerned with the definition of the phenomenon under discussion (politics and integration, respectively). The second ('the mechanism') is concerned with the postulates and variables in terms of which this phenomenon is initially explained. Although I will not use any systems-analytic language (which is not to say that I shall not, occasionally, use the general term 'system'), the familiar term 'environment' seems entirely appropriate for designating the third level of analysis. This concerns the explanation of the actual values of those variables assumed to be given in the second stage (i.e. the 'mechanism').

3.2. *The political process*

3.2.1. *The problem*
On the way politics is conceived in the literature considered here, i.e. on what is thought to be the nature of the phenomena to be explained or on what renders them interesting to the political scientist, we can be relatively brief. After all, this is to a large extent a matter of definition – be it one of fundamental importance to any subsequent theorizing. But although there is, consequently, a certain measure of freedom here, there also appeared to obtain a remarkable measure of consensus with regard to this point. To a very large extent, be it with different degrees of explicitness, one common notion as to the nature of politics turned out to underly the theorizing under discussion. And even when no, or seemingly different, definitions were provided this did not entail really fundamentally different conceptions. It appeared that in practical research the problems actually selected for study, and the phenomena deemed relevant to their solution were not radically different from those with which others were concerned. That is to say, that notwith-

standing differences in wording and terminology, here, too, an apparently similar conception of the nature of politics appeared to guide actual research and theorizing.

According to this common conception, politics is essentially the process through which decisions binding upon the members of some collectivity are made. In some way or another the members of the collectivity or their representatives arrive at decisions (in such varying forms as laws, decrees, agreements, conventions, or resolutions) by whose provisions the collectivity's behavior is henceforth to be ruled. Such decisions may be the unilateral acts of some 'elite' or 'power-holder' imposing his wishes upon the collectivity; or they may be agreements, freely consented to by, and embodying the more or less common interests of, the members of the collectivity. Their binding quality may range all the way from unenforced obligations to pay lip-service to their substance, to those sanctioned and enforced by law and physical violence. Also, it should be noted, in certain circumstances the outcome of the process need not be a 'decision' in an explicit and formal sense. As Bachrach and Baratz have pointed out, the process may also consist in 'non-decision-making', i.e. the avoidance of such explicit and formal 'decisions' in some political system and regarding certain issues (cf. *Bachrach & Baratz*, 1963).

As indicated, even in case the process is initially defined or described in somewhat different terms, the above conception appears to remain valid. Thus, it may be recalled that Etzioni in particular approached politics in terms of 'power' and its application. Nevertheless, it turned out that what was at stake here is essentially the same thing. For roughly, power was conceived as the capacity to impose one's wishes on others. That is to say, it is concerned with the ability to take binding decisions for some collectivity (and notice that a collectivity may be anything up from two individuals or groups). And the application of such power is really nothing more than the making and execution of binding decisions. This is mainly and somewhat restrictively defined for two kinds of collectivity: national states and groups of such states. Moreover, this conception of politics would seem to be strongly molded by political experiences in the national state. That is, this notion would be derived from the form the political process seems to assume in national states, or at least in institutionalized settings. It is conceived in terms of *acts*, *decisions*, by somebody or some body (such as a government or a conference), i.e. in a fashion which is rather similar to the way one generally learns to identify the laws, decrees, and regulations made by kings, dictators, or governments in states. This is not very surprising in view of the history of political science. As may have appeared already from the preceding analyses, however, and as I will seek to make clear in section 3.4 this political conception as outlined here is not without some rather grave limitations.

As I have already repeatedly indicated in the preceding chapters the conception sketched here is very close to that of Easton. He conceives (and Lindberg explicitly follows him here) politics in terms of 'authoritative allocations of value' (*Easton*, 1953: 134; 1965: 21). What he has done in defining politics is, in fact, to construct an *explication* in the sense defined earlier (ch. 2, section 2.6.1) of what commonly goes under the name 'politics' (this is particularly clearly exhibited in *Easton*, 1953: 126-134). It will appear subsequently (section 3.4) that his definition allows for a more general interpretation at least more easily so, than one in terms of 'decision-making'. As far as the literature under consideration here is concerned, however, 'binding decisions' and 'authoritative allocations of values' can practically be considered as equivalent things.

3.2.2. *The mechanism*

At the level of analysis at which we are at present, the occurrence of binding decisions in some collectivity is quite generally explained in terms of two basic concepts that may be called 'demand' and 'support'. Their meanings are relatively clear. A 'demand' may be conceived as a proposal on the part of some individual or group for some decision binding upon some collectivity, i.e., it is a desired decision. 'Support', on the other hand, can be viewed, rather widely, as behavior aimed at, or on behalf of, the achievement, effectuation, or implementation of some state of affairs (cf. also *Easton*, 1965: 159). It may both consist of overt actions, and of mere favorable attitudes or of the passive acquiescence in some situation as in the case of the passive obedience to, or acceptance of, the policies of the government. Note that according to this definition support may be given to *demands*, to *binding decisions*, and to the *political system* as such. That is, it is not exclusively concerned with the political system and its several aspects (authorities, regime, and political community) as Easton's treatment of the subject might suggest (see *Easton*, 1965: 171 ff.), a treatment which is narrower than is necessitated by his own definition of support, which reads as follows:

We can say that A supports B either when A acts on behalf of B or when he orients himself favorably toward B. B may be a person or group; it may be a goal, idea, or institution (*Easton*, 1965: 159).

Thus, at this most general level politics can be conceived as a process involving three basic variables: demands, support, and binding decisions. This can be interpreted in more colloquial terms, as follows. Politics is concerned with a particular kind of interactions between groups and individuals, say 'actors'. Such actors have all kinds of wishes, preferences, or interests, which they seek to have imposed on, effectuated by or recognized by the other actors with whom they trade in some collectivity. Thus they are led to make 'demands' for 'binding decisions'. In order to realize such demands, to have them carried out and to carry them out, they engage in all sorts of activities, such as seeking to convert the others to their ideas, to fight for them, to combine with like-minded actors in order to acquire such strength that they may impose their wishes, to vote for those with whom they agree, to force others to agree with them, or to just passively and docilely obey the decisions actually made. That is, they lend 'support' to certain 'demands' or 'binding decisions'. It should be noted that such support may also be of a 'negative character', consisting in disagreeing with, or resisting certain demands or binding decisions.

With regard to the concept of 'support', it is to be observed that in the literature (see, e.g., sections 2.2 of chapters three and four, and *Easton*, 1965: 171 ff.) there is a tendency to define it in relation to such things as 'institutions', 'organizations', 'governments', or 'political systems', as more or less fixed and established political configurations of actors and rules governing their behavior (cf. Easton's preoccupation with support for the political system and its several aspects noted above).

These configurations, actors or rules, rather than demands and decisions themselves, are supported. In actual fact, however, many decisions (e.g. those resulting from incidental bargaining or warfare between actors) occur outside of such more or less established systems, and in the absence of institutions, organizations, or rules governing the behavior of the actors. In order to be able to explain such decisions on the basis of actors' demands (and note that in a general theory of politics the existence of rules and institutions cannot be taken for granted – the political system is precisely the thing to be explained by a theory of integration) a somewhat wider conception of 'support' seems required: one in which support is primarily *aimed at binding decisions*, or mobilized *behind demands*. Thus, the concept is not directly and exclusively connected with institutions or political systems, but with demands and decisions (see also sections 4.2 of chapters three and four, and *Easton*, 1965: 157-159). The point is that support for some decision within a political system cannot be automatically taken to imply support for that system itself.

One cannot *explain* the occurrence of binding decisions merely on the basis of the *definitions* of a few concepts. We need some assumptions or postulates relating such concepts in order to accomplish such explanation. Two main postulates would seem to underly the theorizing as discussed in the preceding chapters – be it too rarely in a fully explicit form. They could probably best be phrased as:

I   *A demand is supported by an actor to the extent that it agrees with the substance of his own demands or interests.*

II *A decision is supported by an actor to the extent that it agrees with the substance of his own demands or interests.*

In such a rather loose formulation these two postulates seem intuitively reasonable enough – perhaps this is precisely the reason why one seldom bothers to state them explicitly. In these assumptions one seems to meet with somewhat specialized versions of what is quite frequently introduced under the label of an 'assumption of rationality' (cf. for example, *Buchanan & Tullock*, 1962: 18; *Harsanyi*, 1969a: 370; *Harsanyi*, 1969b: 515; *North*, 1968: 319; *Riker*, 1962: 22; *Schelling*, 1960: 4; *Valkenburg*, 1969: 23-24). Roughly, this assumption says that if an actor can choose among several behavioral alternatives, and if he can rank these as to the degree to which he likes or prefers them, he will choose the one he likes or prefers most.

It is not to be assumed that actual collectivities are made up of actors all having identical wishes, preferences, or interests, and making identical demands. Normally, they will contain a greater or lesser number of actors who differ and who make different even conflicting demands. While it will occur only relatively rarely that one actor is able to consistently and in all matters impose *his* decisions upon the rest, to achieve such decisions will most often require the collaboration of other actors. That is, decision-making will normally be a matter of the construction of such supporting alliances or coalitions behind particular demands as are strong enough to have these demands realized over the opposition of the other actors in the collectivity. This notion of decision-making played an especially prominent role in the theories of Haas and Deutsch (see also *Riker*, 1962: 11-12). As noted several times one should not conceive such coalitions as being necessarily tightly organized and permanent groupings. Also, it is not necessary that they rest upon a basis of fully identical interests on the part of the members. It is merely required that these interests, whatever be their nature, converge into a common demand strongly enough so as to induce the actors concerned to cooperate.

Underlying all this seems to be the assumption that:

III   *The decisions that will actually be taken at some moment are those that are supported by a stronger coalition than any of the relevant alternative decisions.*

This poses the question of what is a 'stronger' coalition. Suffice it here to say that this is essentially a matter of measuring the 'weight' or 'magnitude' of the various possible forms of support behavior and that of the supporting actors. The support of a large group is different from that of a small group, the use of arms in support of a demand has a different value than casting a vote, etc. Such questions, however, can better be dealt with at the next level of analysis ('environment').

With regard to the above picture of the political process, several things should be noted:

1. First of all, it is *not* a conception inherently 'democratic', or based upon a typically 'democratic' or 'pluralistic' ideology. It is meant to be universally applicable, both with regard to democratic and to non-democratic political systems. It would be a very unrealistic idea that a monarch, a dictator, or a despot, could do without support, or that 'his' decisions could consistently ignore the interests of the coalition on whose support he depends. Other groups will be involved, such as the army, a single party, a bodyguard; to some extent the collectivity may be organized in such a fashion as to exclude or limit the possibilities for the formation of other coalitions; other means, such as large-

scale terror and the use of concentration camps, may be employed – but the above conception remains fully valid in such cases, too. Part of the error indicated seems to flow from overlooking the fact that in particular the concept of 'support' may assume many forms, and may be induced by a variety of means. Voting as an expression of support is merely one form among others.

2. In the second place it should be noted that the category of 'actors' applied here should not be conceived too restrictively. In particular, it should not be assumed that it is only those who explicitly voice demands or who occupy some recognized position in the political structure of a collectivity who are to be viewed as 'actors'. For actual decisions do not come about solely on the basis of the support, expressly offered by such actors, but those who remain passive and silent, who may perhaps docilely accept almost any binding decision are equally important. Their silence is just as important in the total political situation from which decisions emerge as the explicitness of the others.

The notion of the 'silent majority' points to this. This might be overlooked by using such expressions as the 'politically relevant members of the system' (see ch. 4, section 4.4: see also *Easton*, 1965: 154), and conceiving this in terms of 'influential members'.

3. It may be well once again to stress the fact that the above scheme of the political process is meant to apply to *all* political settings and situations, not merely to, e.g. a national state's domestic processes, but equally to the relations between such states, i.e., to international politics. Of course, there are differences between international politics and national politics. They would seem to differ mainly in the degree to which the political process has become institutionalized, a phenomenon to be dealt with in 3.3. Note that physical violence and coercion occur in both settings, and cannot, therefore, be used as a criterion to distinguish the two (cf. *Burton*, 1968: 102). In view of the above, several writers have stressed the basic similarity between international politics and that in 'primitive' political systems (cf. *Barkun*, 1968: 33-34; *Masters*, 1969) or even in small groups (*Galtung*, 1968a). Others reject any rigid distinction between national and international politics (*Easton*, 1953: 137-138; *Easton*, 1965: 484; *Rosenau*, 1966: 53 ff; *Russett*, 1969a), while no such distinction was made by the authors discussed in the preceding chapters.

In this context it remains to be mentioned that in the literature discussed in the present book, no consistent interpretation of warfare or political violence as a political mechanism has been developed.

4. Finally, what has been described here in loose and informal terms would seem to be a rather common conception of the political process. In one form or another these ideas seem to underly most of current political science. It is, however, none too often made explicit. And although, from a scientific point of view, my presentation of it was very imprecise and informal, still, measured against common discourse and most of history and political science, it represents a comparatively high degree of formalization. Also the conception sketched here is not particularly new. Simplifying somewhat, one may suspect that some such reasoning as developed here underlies the so-called contract-theories of politics. Even more clearly this conception comes to light in the writings of Hobbes and especially in those of Spinoza (see *Hobbes*, 1651; *Spinoza*, 1670-1677). At least this gives some indications regarding the pace of scientific progress.

3.2.3. *The environment*

As indicated this subsection is devoted to a discussion of how to explain the actual values of the variables discussed in 3.2.2: demands, support, and binding decisions. The problem of the present subsection should be distinguished from that of the preceding one. Thus it appeared that support may be induced through making certain kinds of decisions or demands. Here, however, I will be concerned with how to explain the character and significance of support in terms of what might be called 'extra-political', 'environmental', factors, from the 'outside' as it were. Similar considerations apply to the other two variables (demands and binding decisions) and their interrelationships, of course. It has to be observed that, as a general rule, most authors are none too explicit as concerns the formulation of specific assumptions regarding the relationships between 'environment' and the variables discussed above. Here, too, one must often guess and conjecture. Some general tendencies seem to emerge, though.

One of the first questions which more or less naturally arises in this context is: why precisely do actors actually make demands? On several occasions during the preceding discussion I have hinted at a line of reasoning along which the question might be answered, and that seemed to underly to some extent what the authors had to say about the 'environment' (see in particular ch. 4, section 4.4; and ch. 5, section 4.2). It seems plausible to assume that:

IV *Actors will make demands if and to the extent that the behavior of the other actors in the collectivity concerned is important to them for the realization of their own goals.*

It does not seem too far-fetched either to assume that:

V-1 *The more frequently an actor interacts with other actors the more important will be the behavior of these latter for the realization of that actor's goals.*

However, not all things will be equally important to an actor, and it seems reasonable to assume that, for some actor, the behavior of others will be important to the extent that an actor's goals involved in his interactions are important. As follows:

V-2 *For any actor, the behavior of other actors with whom he interacts is the more (less) important for the realization of his goals, the more (less) highly preferred the goals involved in those interactions are by the actor.*

These three postulates together would seem to underly the high importance which appears to be ascribed to the analysis and measurement, of the amount and character of 'interactions' or 'transactions' among political actors (see also *Jacob & Teune*, 1964: 11-12; *Nye*, 1968a; *Brams*, 1966; *Barkun*, 1968: 52, 57; *Merritt*, 1963: 72; *Nye*, 1967a: 62; *Reinton*, 1967). They also seem to cover the essence of such concepts as 'interdependence' of actors, and their 'saliency' or 'importance' toward each other – in so far as these things are politically relevant, that is (see also *Galtung*, 1968b: 378; *Nye*, 1968a: 868; *Brams*, 1966: 882 ff.).

It has appeared from the previous subsection that decision-making generally involves the construction of supporting coalitions behind common demands. Regarding this, it seems reasonable to assume that:

VI *The more similar actors are with respect to their goals, values, and preferences, the greater the likelihood that they will make similar demands.*

Some notion like this would seem to be behind the often-mentioned condition of cultural similarity, or similarity as to values, on the part of the actors in, for example, an integrative process (see also *Ake*, 1967a: 2; *Ake*, 1967b: 486; *Jacob & Teune*, 1964; *Nye*, 1965b: 209, 250; *Galtung*, 1968: 378-9).

Several things should be noted in regard to these four postulates (IV, V-1, V-2, VI). First, at least intuitively they seem highly plausible and obvious – so much so, perhaps, that they are only very rarely stated openly. Besides being applied in the theories discussed in the preceding chapters, and in the literature indicated above, here, too, it seems that their (implicit) use is much more widespread than is indicated by the few examples given. In the second place, the relationships, goals, values, or preferences involved have not been specified. In other words, they can, and in all probability should, be interpreted in many different ways, depending upon the problem at hand. Thus one may think of such things as cultural, emotional, economic, military, or technological 'interdependence'; or of values and goals as diverse as military security, economic growth, cultural preëminence, or the recognition of religious truths. This poses the problems of the nature of values, or 'issues', and of the relationships between this and the kinds of demands made. This problem will be dealt with mainly in relation to the concept 'support'. Finally, especially with regard to postulates nr. IV and V, it has to be noted that these do *not* say that the more actors interact the more friendly their relations will be, or the higher the probability for integration to occur between them. Actually, an increase in the volume of demands might just as well lead to enmity and to warfare. Similarly, nr. VI does *not* say that similar demands can always be easily accommodated. While it would seem that some such similarity is indeed a prerequisite for coalition-formation and decision-making, it is conceivable that in some circumstances it is precisely such similarity (e.g. that of two states for one strip of territory) which precludes coalition-formation, and which may lead to decision-making through warfare. Apparently, intensive elaboration is needed here.

With regard to the notion of 'support' the question why support is given or not given has already been answered by the postulates I and II. However, in view of the third postulate it has to be determined how 'much' support will be attached to some demand in relation to that attached to alternative demands, in order to be able to explain actual decision-making. Three different things seem to be involved here: (1) the nature of the supporting actors or coalitions of actors, (2) that of the kind of support behavior they engage in, and (3) the character of the demand concerned.

The first element comes to light in such notions as the 'strength', 'power', or 'influence' of actors. The second concerns such things as the relative political significance of forms of political behavior such as voting, passive obedience, the application of physical force, propaganda, and street demonstrations. The third one is intimately related to the problem of finding a classification of 'values', 'interests', 'issue-areas', or 'social or functional sectors'. The literature reviewed here is none too outspoken on either of these aspects.

1. (the nature of the supporting actors) With regard to the first element then, it would seem that at least the following ideas underly much of theorizing in the field under discussion:

VII   *The significance of support, its magnitude, or the strength of a supporting coalition increases as the number of individuals involved increases.*

VIII *The more physical, economic, intellectual, moral, organizational, or propagandistic resources an actor or coalition of actors commands, the greater the significance of its support.*

IX   *The greater an actor's or coalition's access, i.e., the closer it is to actual decision-makers, the greater the significance of its support.*

So much seems at least to be implied by the frequent use of such phrases as 'powerful' or 'influential actors', 'elites', 'politically relevant' actors, in order to denote especially significant actors, or rather, the significance of their support in relation to that of other actors.

2. (the kind of support behavior). On the second aspect of support the literature under discussion here is virtually completely silent. Nevertheless, it seems, the various possible forms of support behavior that come to mind rather easily and some of which have been mentioned above, do differ with regard to their impact on, or significance for, decision-making. Apparently, it makes a good deal of difference whether people use arms to advance their cause or merely cast votes for their most preferred party or candidate once every four years. Part of the difficulty in determining wherein precisely such differences reside, and what is their significance, is the problem of finding a common denominator for such forms. A first step is suggested by VIII, arguing that

these forms differ with regard to the amount of resources invested in them, tentatively assuming that:

X   *Support is the more significant, the more resources are invested in it.*

It should be noted, though, that inasmuch the authors dealt with in previous chapters restrict themselves largely to peaceful political processes, for them at least the scope of the problem is also of a more restricted nature.

3. (the character of the demand). The third-mentioned support aspect, finally, is intimately related to the other two main variables introduced in the preceding subsection (demands and binding decisions). For it is concerned with the substance of what is demanded, decided, and supported.

Demands or decisions, then, would seem to differ with regard to their substance's political 'importance' or 'significance'. Thus, to bring about a fundamental re-orientation of a collectivity's external policy, or a redistribution of its income, would seem to be much more 'important' and usually involves more intense political struggle than to grant diplomatic recognition to a newly independent state or to reach a compromise on the voting age. That is, the nature of the issue involved in decision-making would seem to have a bearing upon the character of the political process: not all actors will be equally interested in all issues; for some they will be prepared to battle much more fiercely than for others; with regard to some issues actors will disagree more than with regard to others, etc.

We have met with this general problem (i.e. that of the influence of the nature of demands or decisions, or of groups of these, upon the character of the political process in general and of the integration process in particular) at various occasions in the preceding chapters, especially in that on Haas where it was posed under the heading of 'functional sectors'. Often, too, it emerges as that of political 'issues-areas', i.e. groups of substantially different demands or decisions. The leading idea is that such sectors or areas are of supreme political significance in that the nature of the issues concerned determines to a large extent what political actors will be drawn into the political arena, what the process through which decisions are achieved will be like, and what will be the consequences of such decisions for the members of the collectivity. In fact, one might say, such issues, demands or decisions, define more or less distinct subsystems in the total political life of the collectivity (cf. *Barth & Johnson*, 1959; *Lowi*, 1964; *Kaplan*, 1967: 99; *Rosenau*, 1967b: 11-13; *Rosenau*, 1966: 74 ff.).

Both the literature mentioned, the preceding chapters, and the reasoning developed thus far suggest several things about decisions and demands that are relevant. These seem to follow in a straightforward way from the postulates already introduced and do not seem to require the formulation of additional ones. Thus, given some level of interactions among a set of actors, the nature of the values or goals involved, and the height of the preferences concerned, will help to determine which actors will be mobilized in the process of making some specific decision. Or, more accurately, they will determine the nature and significance of the support that will be fed into the political system (according to postulates I, II, and V-2). Also, the nature of the values and goals, and the height of the preferences concerned, and in particular their distribution among a set of actors, tell us something about the probability of a particular decision being made. That is, the higher the preferences involved and the more *dis*similar the goals or values at stake, the lower the probability that some decision will be achieved tends to be (postulates I, II, III and VI). And from postulates I and II it seems to follow that the higher preferences are involved, the greater an actor's propensity to invest resources in his support behavior will be. Accordingly, one might expect that in the situation just described (i.e. dissimilar but highly preferred goals) there will be a tendency to increasingly strong or significant support, but coupled to dissimilar demands, being fed into the system. That is, in such situations the decision-making process will be characterized by intensive political struggles.

The above suggests that one of the crucial things at issue here is the relationship which obtains between, on the one hand, the values and preferences involved in the demands or decisions, and, on the other hand, the distribution of such values and preferences among the collectivity's actors determined in terms of their support characteristics (VII, VIII and IX). For, in the context of the present theory, it is through the relationship mentioned that the nature of actor's goals and preferences become, in its turn, relevant for the explanation of the decision-making process. And this, in turn, suggests that the crucial dimensions involved in determining the nature of such demands or decisions are the height of the preferences at stake (see above)*, the number of people affected (postulate VII), the resources at stake (see above; postulate VIII), and the political position of the actors concerned (postulate IX).

To a large extent the above is already concerned with, or is at least relevant to, 'feedback', i.e. the effects of binding decisions taken and/ or implemented upon those factors in terms of which the present section seeks to explain the occurrence of demands and the character and significance of support. Thus, binding decisions will affect the resources and the political position of a more or less extended number of actors or people, and to the extent that they do so, and dependent upon the height of the preferences involved, such decisions will determine the nature of the demands made and the magnitude or significance of the support which will be forthcoming. Furthermore, and at a 'deeper' level, such decisions, by altering the situation in which people or actors find themselves, may lead them to change their values, goals, and preferences. For example, a collectivity's decision to go to war, and the implementation of that decision, may rather profoundly affect the kind of goals actors have or think most important – even on the part of those actors not directly concerned with the original decision.

Such feedback, it may be recalled, played an important role in the theories discussed previously, in particular in that of Haas. There it is concerned most with the re-orientation of the flow of demand and support toward new decision-making centers, on the one hand, and the emergence of new interests and actors, or perhaps, forms of support, on the other. Now the former can be explained relatively easily on the basis of the postulates I and II in particular. The latter, however, poses some problems of a general and rather involved character. At first sight it seems rather reasonable to regard the information of a new actor, a party or an interest group, as a more or less direct and almost automatic reaction on the emergence of a sufficiently important common interest, goal, or value for the members. In view of the postulates VII

* With regard to this aspect of the matter, i.e. the height of preferences, no particular postulates could be found in the literature reviewed here (apart, perhaps, from V-2). Nevertheless, it will be clear that this element plays a particularly large role in any assumption of 'rationality' whose basic importance I have already indicated in the context of my discussion of the first two postulates (see p. 331).

and VIII, it would seem rather natural for people to band together and form a group or an organization as soon as an important common interest arises, so as to increase the likelihood of their demands concerning it to be heeded in the relevant decisions (postulate III).

However, as has been shown with particular force by *Olson (Olson,* 1965: *Olson & Zeckhauser,* 1968; see also *Stevers,* 1968), the information of such groups and the concomitant emergence of new support flows, actually constitutes a major problem and cannot be expected to proceed automatically or mechanically. Roughly, the problem is as follows. The formation of such groups normally involves certain 'costs' for the participants; it requires them to sacrifice certain resources (if only some of their time, or some minimum financial contribution) or some of their freedom of action. However, if the (potential) group is relatively large, and if the resulting benefits (some particular binding decision, or the expectation of it) are of a 'collective' nature, i.e., if they accrue indiscriminately to all of the participants, then neither the postulates discussed here, nor a more extended assumption of rationality will straightforwardly predict the formation of a group or organization. For, in the situation sketched, individual participants or, rather, potential participants will not have the incentive to make any sacrifice for such a group. The formation of such actors would require what Olson calls 'separate and selective incentives' (*Olson,* 1965: 51), that is, additional benefits that accrue only to those participating in the group but not to those outside it. It will be clear that here lies an important area for further research, that is of the utmost importance for any theory (such as an integration theory) dealing with important transformations of political systems involving the emergence of new actors.

It should be recognized, though, that in all probability the above will not necessitate important changes in the set of postulates developed thus far. That is, they could still serve the explanation of the formation of new actors as indicated, provided it is realized that in order to perform that task the definition of one common interest may well be insufficient, and that actual behavior of the participants will be ruled both by this common interest *and* by other interests (if only the gratification expected from participation in, and belonging to, the new actor) providing the necessary 'separate and selective incentives' indicated above. This would mean that such behavior will have to be explained by syndromes of interests, rather than by single ones. But, given such

342 *Toward a theory of politics and integration*

syndromes, the postulates mentioned already will remain fully relevant.

In this section on 'environment' I have not expressly dealt with such things as 'culture' or 'economy' often held to be important categories in the explanation of political life. To some extent this seeming neglect results from the necessarily sketchy and brief character of this section which does not allow for extensive attempts at reinterpreting the discussion in more common and current terms, or the discussion of empirical examples in any elaborate fashion. On the other hand, it should be recognized that the main part of what is usually sought to be conveyed through such concepts is already contained in the above scheme. Thus, things like 'goals', 'values' and 'preferences' concern what seems to be most relevant in the 'culture' or 'political culture' concept. Largely the same applies to the 'economy': this enters the picture via such concepts as 'resources' (and the distribution of them), 'goals', 'values' and 'preferences', in so far as they originate within it, and 'the degree to which people interact', or 'interdependence'. These necessarily brief remarks may indicate how such problems are to be solved in the present scheme. Of course, in this context many more problems may be posed than those I have discussed. For example, at still another level of analysis one may seek to account for the formation of preferences, motivations, and goals, under the impact of various 'psychological', 'economical', or 'sociological' phenomena and developments.

3.3. *Political integration*

3.3.1. *The problem*
Generally political integration is conceived to be concerned with the way a political process comes to be ordered, regulated, or structured by means of decision-making institutions. But, clearly, there are other ways of conducting politics, in the absence of common decision-making institutions, such as warfare or traditional diplomacy. Accordingly, to define political integration immediately raises the problem of distinguishing integration from such other forms of conducting politics. However, what forms are there? As indicated already three of them seem to be distinguished in the literature: politics by means of warfare, through bargaining or diplomacy, and via institutions. In other

words, actors may fight, bargain, or submit to common institutions in order to arrive at binding decisions (in a similar sense, *Boulding*, 1964: 78; *Boulding*, 1966: 27).

The defects of such a classification are rather obvious, though. For, in the first place, the criterion or criteria on which it is based are anything but clear. Related to this, then, the distinctions between them are rather vague, and the categories seem to show considerable overlap accordingly. Thus, insofar as bargaining is governed by commonly accepted rules and procedures such as, for instance, in international diplomacy, it seems to acquire some important characteristics of an institutional process. This becomes even more visible in the case of the establishment of more or less permanent, or periodically gathering, bilateral or multilateral diplomatic bodies. But even warfare, inasmuch as it is commonly accepted and does proceed according to certain rules, limited though they may be, cannot be entirely denied an institutional character. Also in diplomacy or bargaining military moves or threats of physical violence, coming close to actual warfare, often play an important role, while physical violence and (civil) war often occur in institutionalized settings.

What, then, underlies this rather common distinction? In terms of the theory developed thus far, two things seem to be relevant: the kind of support behavior on the one hand, and some sort of political division of labor on the other. Thus, as has been indicated in 3.2.3 in connection with postulate X, at least one of the crucial characteristics distinguishing warfare (or the application of physical violence generally) from the other forms mentioned would be the kind of support behavior it represents. Also, restricting ourselves for the moment to the *international* political system, both warfare and diplomacy have a rather incidental nature. They come into play only when some specific need for them arises. They are conducted by the same actors, the states, that make the demands concerned. As against this, integration or an institutionalized political process seems to be characterized by the fact that individuals or organizations, functioning more or less independently from the states, process demands on a more or less regular basis. That is, it can be conceived as a kind of division of labor occurring in the (international) political system (similarly in *Eisenstadt*, 1963: 95-96). Furthermore, it seems that institutionalization is characterized by a restriction of the kinds of support behavior to be fed into the political system, in that it would tend to limit or even exclude warfare or the application of physical violence on a large scale.

The above fits in rather nicely with the conception of political integration which emerges from the literature. For integration turned out to be conceived quite generally as the process of institutionalization of a political system. This conception involves some important problems, however.

These problems arise as soon as one attempts to make sense of the very general notion of integration as a *process*. For this would seem to imply that it allows for different stages, or that it can be ordered according as there is 'more' or 'less' integration. In some cases, as we have seen, attempts were made, notably by Deutsch and Etzioni, to identify separate forms of integration such as, for instance, amalgamated and pluralistic security communities, or commonwealths, unions, and empires (for similar attempts, see *Plischke*, 1964b: 3-5; *Nye*, 1967a; *Nye*, 1968a: 866). It turned out, however, that generally such attempts were not very satisfactory in that they often were rather unsystematic; also, they quite needlessly sought to restrict the range of possible forms to a very small number.

As exemplified especially clearly by Lindberg, there is an alternative approach to this problem which is more systematic and theoretically relevant. Since integration is concerned with the creation and development of decision-making institutions in some political system, one could well 'measure' integration in terms of those institutions' capacity for making such decisions. And this, in turn, suggests several important dimensions along which such measurement should proceed.

To begin with, integration can then be defined as *any increase of the decision-making capacity of the common institutions of some political system*. In its turn, such capacity may be viewed as a function of both political input (notably the kind of support fed into the political system, as discussed above), and of political output (i.e. the binding decisions produced through the institutions). And this again suggests that decision-making capacity might be defined to be 'greater':

1.   the greater the binding force of the decisions made is; and/or

2.   the greater the amount and/or variety of the decisions is (variety i.e., the greater the number of 'sectors,' or 'issue-areas' included, see 3.2.3); and/or

3.   the more 'important' or 'salient' such decisions are; and/or

4. the more effectively certain kinds of support behavior, in particular those involving the actors' use of physical violence, have been
restricted.

This raises the question whether it is at all necessary or useful to
define integration in terms of institutions or organizations. That is,
integration could perhaps be defined as any increase of a political
system's decision-making capacity, instead of as an increase of the
decision-making capacity of such a system's *institutions*. For it is at
least conceivable that the decision-making capacity in the sense defined
above increases (which could then be defined as integration), without
separate political institutions being formed. Thus, in primitive political
systems, institutionalization may be extremely low or even non-existent
without therefore ceasing to be relatively effective decision-making
systems (see *Barkun*, 1968 and the various contributions to *Cohen* and
Middleton, 1967). Even at that low level of organization the concept
'integration' in the sense indicated might well be usefully applied.

It has appeared that it is especially Lindberg who came rather close
to such a wider conception of integration. But it has also appeared that
in practice he limits himself to integration which does involve common
political institutions. In the wider perspective just indicated such *institutional* integration may be conceived as a particular stage in the
integration process. And it may well be an extremely important stage
at that, since it may be presumed that in the absence of common organizations and a certain division of political labor, the growth possibilities of the capacity of a political system will be severely restricted.
That is, it may be that from a certain level of capacity onwards additional demands and support (both in terms of amount, variety, salience,
and kind) cannot be processed by the system unless common organizations are available. To determine this level would be one of the crucial
problems for a theory of integration; it is to be noted, incidentally, that
the problem is at least implicitly raised by such questions as 'when will
integration occur?'

It should be noted that in such a wide conception the possibility must
be faced that the emergence of an effective 'threat-system', based upon
mutual threats of violence and annihilation, but which might nevertheless (and perhaps even by virtue of those threats) show an increase
in decision-making capacity, would also have to be counted as 'integra-

tion'. This may well be justified; in the literature dealt with here, however, not a trace of such a conception is to be found.

The problems discussed above concerning 'forms' of integration should not be confounded with those that are often discussed under the same heading but that nevertheless concern wholly different matters. Sometimes attempts are made to distinguish various kinds of integration, such as 'economic', 'cultural', 'social', 'attitudinal', or 'communicative' (see, for example, *Galtung*, 1968b: 375-376; *Landecker*, 1952: 394; *Nye*, 1968a: 858 ff.; *Weiner*, 1965: 53-54). Such non-political 'forms' of integration, though, should be taken for what they are: either politically irrelevant; or relevant in that they are linked, preferably through explicit assumptions, to political integration properly so called in which case they may be viewed as certain phenomena or developments in the political system's environment.

3.3.2. *The mechanism*

The political theory developed thus far (section 3.2) was completely general in treating the concepts of 'demands', 'support', and 'binding decisions'. Now a distinction has to be introduced. One range of problems is to explain the production of binding decisions *within* some political system, taking for granted its structure, institutions, rules and procedures. These may be called problems of 'first-order politics'. As against this, integration (and the same goes for the problems of the nature of the 'political order') is to be conceived as a problem of 'second-order politics', since it is concerned precisely with the political system, its institutions, structure, rules and procedures, itself (for a similar distinction, see *Daudt*, 1962: 11). The theory is concerned here primarily with demands, support and binding decisions having as their objects the political system and its various aspects *as such*. This requires some new concepts and postulates as will be seen presently.

Thus, a crucial aspect of an integration theory will be the explanation of the development of support for an emerging political system itself. It is here that the commonly used concept of 'legitimacy' is relevant. As generally applied, it can be said to refer to a crucial aspect of support behavior, namely, one having as its object not any particular demand or decision, but rather the actors, institutions, or procedures by whom or through which binding decisions are produced. That is, legitimacy (of an institution, etc.) may be defined as a willingness on the part of the actors concerned (i.e., individuals, interest groups and political parties, but also in international life, states or their governments, etc.) to accept or support that institution as such independently of the particular decisions produced or to be produced by it. It may be thought of as the extent to which actors link it right and proper to direct their demands and support to that institution rather than to some other one. It is a kind of reservoir of goodwill of which such an institution disposes (cf. *Easton*, 1965: 278 ff.). To a large extent the problem of integration is concerned with the development of such legitimacy for new institutions.

This, however, cannot automatically be explained by the postulates formulated in section 3.2.2, in particular Nos. I and II. For these have been cast in terms of demands and decisions and *not* in those of systems or institutions. Legitimacy is (at least to a large extent) independent of any specific demand or decision; rather it is concerned with a general willingness to support the institutions and the decisions reached through them, often even when these turn out to be disadvantageous to the actor concerned (cf. Easton's discussion of 'diffuse support' in *Easton*, 1965: 267 ff.).

As becomes particularly clear in the context of the process of integration, it is not to be assumed that legitimacy is something a political institution receives in full at the very moment of its inception. Rather, its development will be a matter of time, a more or less gradual process – if it occurs at all, that is. Apparently, it involves the formation of habits in the behavior of actors, the building up of more or less stable attitudes, or, more generally, the learning of (new) behavioral and attitudinal patterns on the part of the actors concerned.

As can be observed often enough in political history, some government or regime, though originally established by brute force and the most illegitimate methods, may, after a certain period of time, be accepted and recognized as fully legitimate. Things like these may be the source of what is perhaps the most deeply ingrained, and most often applied (be it usually implicitly rather than explicitly) postulate on politicals learning – the popular adage 'might becomes right'.

It may be recalled that Haas (ch. 3, section 2.2) went somewhat further in formulating a 'dissonance postulate', while Deutsch (ch. 4, section 2.3) offered several postulates linking the formation of habits or attitudes to the course of time and to the experience or expectation of benefits on the part of the actors concerned (see also *Boulding*, 1966: 37-38; *Hovland* et al., 1953: 229; *Merelman*, 1966; *Raser*, 1969). They may perhaps be summarized as follows:

XI   *The longer an actor is made to behave in a particular fashion, the greater the likelihood that he will actually prefer this behavior.*
XII *The more often some behavior or relationship has led to, or contributed to, the realization of an actor's interests, the greater the likelihood that the actor will think it right and proper.*

These two postulates link behavior to the development of preferences or attitudes concerning that behavior, and the context in which it occurs (note that they are phrased in terms of *likelihoods* only). They thus allow for the explanation of the emergence of a political system's legitimacy on the basis of support (both voluntary and coercive) for specific decisions or policies. It does not seem necessary to go any further and equally adopt Deutsch's proposition to the effect that habits or attitudes are reinforced by a probabilistic mixture of rewards and penalties (cf. also *Kuhn*, 1963: 81-82): it hardly plays a role in the literature under discussion here, while it is not needed to explain the development of support for a political system at the present level of analysis.

How then to account for the occurrence of political integration in some system? To begin with, it should be noted that the establishment of common institutions for a group of hitherto autonomous political systems is a matter of a common decision of these systems that, in turn, results from the concurrent decisions produced by each of these systems individually. And these again are reached by or through the governments of the participating states, resulting from political processes within them. That is, those governments should at least be included among the actors supporting the step. This point is important since it clearly shows both the essential role of governmental actors at the outset of the process, and its limitations since these actors, too, require the support from other, non-governmental actors.

In the context of the problem at hand postulates I and II may probably be interpreted as saying that actors, including governments, will support demand for integration or decisions to integrate only in so far as they expect their other demands to be met more 'adequately', with a higher probability, than through the existing decision-making facilities, notably those of diplomacy and of warfare. Now this will have to be conceived in a rather wide fashion. For such expectations will not merely concern more or less direct 'positive' benefits, but also 'costs' involved in the different decision-making facilities and procedures. It will rather be a matter of an overall balance of such benefits and costs. The latter could here be interpreted as, for instance, the likelihood (in particular for governmental actors) of losing support through the impossibility of attaining the right kinds of decisions in a reliable fashion through existing facilities. Or they may refer to the moral and material costs of warfare whose likelihood may be judged to be too high in the existing structure.

The above may also be rendered in somewhat different terms. That is, integration will be supported if and to the extent that actors have come to perceive existing institutions and procedures (both of the states and of the interstate milieu) as inadequate for meeting the actual flow of demands fed into them. Accordingly, integration may be said to be one possible response to what may be called 'demand input overload'. Such conceptions were developed by Deutsch and Etzioni, as we have seen (similarly, *Easton*, 1965: 57 ff.). It is implicit in much earlier discussion about the obsolescence of the nation-state in contemporary international life, notably in Mitrany's thinking; and in a remarkably sophisticated version, anticipating Deutsch's vocabulary, it is to be found in Clarence Streit's ideas (cf. *Streit*, 1939: 65 ff., 70). Of course, to speak in terms of increases in the flow of demands in a certain political system does not mean that it is only a matter of the quantity of demands; as indicated above, it is just as much a matter of their quality, in that existing facilities may be unsuited to process certain kinds of demands, for instance because they involve many more actors than are comprised by any individual state.

According to postulate III, the decision to integrate, i.e. to set up common political institutions in some system, will be taken if there is more support available for it than for any alternative to it, most notably that of continuing the status quo with respect to decision-making facilities. Like every political decision, this is a matter of the construction of a sufficiently strong supporting coalition, that is, one whose total support is more important or significant than that of alternative coalitions as determined by the postulates VII, VIII and IX. This does *not* say that integration necessarily results from identical demands, interests, or motivations. Such a situation will seldom occur. Rather, as has been made clear especially by Haas, such coalitions will generally rest upon a basis of different though converging interests or motivations. The coalition's common demand (for integration in this case) will normally be a kind of compromise in which the participants expect to realize their own different demands to a sufficiently high extent so as to induce them to support it. Also, the above does *not* mean that for integration to occur there must be overwhelming, positive, explicit, and enthusiastic support for it on the part of all actors concerned – governments, parties, interest groups, as well as the population at large. For while, as has been noted previously, the positive support of the governments concerned is indispensable, it may well be that their support is significant mainly to the extent that other actors are not concerned at all, or merely passively support the idea, or simply abstain from feeding negative support concerning it into the system. And as will appear from the next subsection (3.3.3) this situation is not so extremely improbable as it may perhaps seem to be.

Now assuming that new decison-making institutions are indeed established, this may set in motion various processes through which integration may acquire its own dynamism. If such institutions succeed in making decisions that are experienced by actors as rewarding, or if they succeed in inducing expectations that future decisions will be rewarding, or if, in certain matters, they provide the only channels via which certain demands can be realized, the postulates XI and XII predict that those institutions will gradually acquire legitimacy. In so far as it is justified to assume that the converse of these postulates (XI and XII) also hold, the same mechanism would explain a gradual loss of legitimacy for the existing institutions of the states.

However, much more is involved. Specifically, if the new institutions, or their personnel or leadership rather, have some, perhaps limited, capacity for behaving as independent actors, i.e. when they themselves can make demands and significantly affect the outcomes produced though them, they can to some extent consciously steer and control the process of integration. Thus, utilizing the mechanism formed by the first two postulates, they may seek to make such demands, in the form of proposals, or to make such decisions as to attract the support of an increasing and increasingly significant coalition of actors. On the one hand this may (through postulate XII in particular) strengthen their legitimacy; on the other hand, it may strengthen their position vis-à-vis the government of the states. For if they succeed in acquiring the support of important non-governmental actors in the different states (in the sense of the postulates VII, VIII and IX) the likelihood increases (through III) that those governments will equally follow policies favoring the institutions (see also *Cox*, 1969). That is, the institutions can to some extent consciously utilize and manipulate the mechanism of coalition formation from among the system's actors, both governmental and non-governmental. But quite apart from this, their functioning and their producing decisions that affect the interests of certain actors in a way perceived as rewarding by them will induce them to support the institutions (postulate II). This is sometimes expressed by saying that institutions will induce the growth of 'vested interests' around them (e.g. *Galtung*, 1968c: 25-26).

Furthermore, the emergence of a new decision-making center, comprising a larger number of actors than the pre-existing states individually may be expected to have two effects that together may lead to the formation of new actors on the international level. In the first place, if actors perceive that such decision-making will affect their interests they will tend to address their demands to the new center. In the second place, however, due to the increase in the number of actors in the system, the relative significance of their support will diminish, according to the postulates VII, VIII and IX. And this again will provide a stimulus for the formation of new actors, i.e. 'supranational' groups, as alliances, coalitions, or combinations of similar groups, previously operating individually in the various states, in order to recover what has been lost. That is, the formation of new decision-making institutions may be expected to result in the growth of new groups, private interest groups and political parties, at the new level (see also *Chambers*, 1963: 39 ff.; *Watts*, 1966: 342).

Another thing is that decisions (and the same applies to demands or interests, and to actors) are not totally unconnected things. Thus, some one particular decision requires for its implementation additional decisions in other fields; certain decisions may rule out the possibility of other decisions. Decisions made to satisfy a particular kind of interests may well, through its consequences, affect other interests. Actors will be linked, in that the behavior of one of them influences what the others can do; and what happens to one of them may well affect the interests of the others. Consequently, one may expect that in so far as decision-making by the newly established international institutions does have such consequences outside their initial field of activities, i.e. when it does affect actors and interests not initially concerned with them, new demands will be made in order to compensate for possible losses incurred in that way, to redress what will be felt to be imbalances, or in general to adapt to the changed situation. Now, in so far as this is seen to require additional decision-making at the new level, and in so far as actors expect beneficial decisions from the new institutions, or are not prepared to demand their demise and the abrogation of the integration that has actually been achieved so far, one may expect the occurrence of demands for further integration and the extension of the institutions' field of activities.

This is behind what is variously termed 'spill-over' (by Haas and Lindberg in particular) or 'secondary priming' (by Etzioni). Here again the leadership of those institutions may seek to consciously utilize this mechanism in that it seeks to formulate such demands and decisions as can be predicted to have consequences outside their original scope of activities. In that way it may seek to stimulate, or manipulate, the formation of growth-inducing supporting coalitions demanding decisions that can only be made through the expansion of the task of the institutions.

All of the above suggests that integration may acquire its own dynamism. For, as will appear from the next subsection, there is reason to expect that the various tendencies and forces described will occur the more strongly the further the process has developed. In other words, it may be that political institutionalization has the character of a process of selfsustained growth, a tendency which, more or less explicitly, has been observed in various settings (see, for instance, *Wheare*, 1963: 237 ff.; *Eisenstadt*, 1963: 95 ff.; *Russett*, 1969a: 124-125; *Galtung*, 1967a: 314-316; in particular *Elias*, 1936, Vol. 2: 222 ff.).

One should not, however, too easily assume this process to be an 'automatic' one; or, one should recognize the limited nature of the 'automaticity' involved. In particular, all stages of the argument involved postulates I and II, and it had to be assumed that actors indeed saw the new institutions as beneficial and expected them to produce decisions sufficiently meeting their demands. To a large extent, namely in so far as it involved postulate XII, the same applies to the process through which the institutions acquire legitimacy. However, it does not seem very likely that this condition will always be met in practice: certain participants will be disappointed, they will lose rather than win, and be punished rather than rewarded. And this may induce them to feed negative support into the system and to reject integration altogether rather than to ask for more of it. The actual results will depend upon what actors will be thus affected and mobilized, i.e. what the significance of their (negative) support is. Also, an important role is played by the leadership of the international institutions. It cannot be taken for granted that it has the motivation and the skills to actively seek the expansion of the institutions' tasks and to promote integration. The most that can perhaps be said is that the process' automaticity resides in the fact that the creation of new decision-making institutions forces the participants to reorient their political demands and support; it creates a new political structure to which they will somehow adapt. One *cannot* simply assume the occurrence of a smooth and continuous process leading to the formation of a full-fledged state of political community.

3.3.3. *The environment*
In seeking to account for the occurrence of demands in section 3.2.3 it was assumed that the propensity to make demands was the greater the more actors interact and the more important the values involved (postulate V). From the foregoing section 3.3.2 it appeared that demands for integration will occur only if actors think existing decision-making facilities incapable of meeting with the actual flow of demands fed into the system. And this, in turn, is most likely to occur when that flow of demands has increased more or less considerably both in terms of its quantity and of its quality. Consequently, demands for integration are most likely to occur when the level of interactions between actors has increased as well as its importance to them. However, one should proceed carefully here. For such a situation may also have radically different outcomes. Instead of leading to demands for integration, it may equally result in attempts to unilaterally impose certain binding decisions through warfare or the threat of it. Rather, one should say that an increase in the amount and importance of transactions and the consequent increase in the flow of demands will lead to demands for *changing* the existing decision-making facilities and structures. Whether

or not this change will be integration will again be dependent upon a number of other considerations. For instance, what is the character of the increasing demand flow, how high are the costs and the chances of success of warfare estimated by the actors concerned, compared to their estimation of the costs and probability of attaining beneficial decisions through a more integrated structure? Questions such as these have hardly been posed by the existing literature on integration, let alone investigated in depth. In fact, it will be recalled that (in such writers as Deutsch and Etzioni) even the above line of reasoning was merely hinted at, but not precisely and explicitly stated and elaborated.

At any rate, if integration is to result from such an increase in transactions, then it should lead to demands made and supported by sufficiently important (in the sense of postulates VII, VIII and IX) actors from within the various states concerned as follows from the third postulate. And from VII, VIII and IX it would then follow that such interactions would have to involve substantial parts, or perhaps even the greater parts, of the states' populations, and/or the various kinds of resources of which they dispose, and/or groups or individuals with a high position in the political structures involved.

Here, too, one should proceed very carefully, however. For it should be recalled that what is at issue here, and what may make actors demand integration, is their awareness that existing facilities are insufficient for processing their demands in a satisfactory fashion. Now the reaction of non-governmental actors to such a situation may well be limited to demanding all kinds of adaptions and compensations, and the safeguarding of their interests in international negotiations. All this may well proceed within the bounds of existing structures and institutions, and without such private actors even considering any deeper-going structural adaptation such as integration. Their attitude towards this could even be negative, due on the one hand to the state's government's legitimacy vis-à-vis them, and on the other hand, to their fear of losing their acquired position with respect to the state's government in the larger setting of an integrated system. Thus, one would expect that in general it will be the governments concerned, rather than private actors, who, most early and most sharply, come to feel the burden of the inadequacy of existing channels for the processing of an increased amount of demands. For it is they who have to do the actual work of decision-making; and it is they whose position is most directly dependent upon their capacity to generate satisfactory decisions. All this means that one cannot take it for granted that demands for integration will originate from private actors, not even from those that are most intensively involved in the increased interactions. One would rather expect such demands to be made initially by governments or politicians, or by those actors most intensively concerned with the functioning of the political structure as such, for instance groups of intellectuals and sometimes political parties. And this is, in fact, the overwhelming impression which emerges from the literature on the subject (see, in somewhat different contexts, also *Eisenstadt*, 1963: 13; *Nye*, 1965b: 18ff.).

However, governments, too, need support for their demands. This may consist in a mere passive acquiescence on the part of non-governmental actors or in overt support behavior. The former will presumably occur in case non-governmental actors do not perceive their interests, tangible or intangible, to be at stake while the latter will occur when they do perceive their interests to be at stake. This situation involves some difficulties. For one may presume that the former case will occur when the issue under consideration is of a very general nature remote from most of the daily concerns of actors. With regard to such matters, however, it is not very likely that governments will be prepared to make integrative steps. For, whereas integration involves the relatively clear cost of a transfer of decision-making capabilities to a new center, its magnitude, as well as that of the benefits to be expected from it, will be difficult to estimate in the case of integration concerning such general and remote issues. And in this case it is improbable that postulates I and II will lead such governments to support the step.

Thus governments may be expected to initiate and support integration only to the extent that it will concern relatively specific and down-to-earth issues, with regard to which they can form a relatively precise estimate of the costs and benefits involved. By the same token, however, such matters will also involve non-governmental actors to a much larger extent.

Accordingly, as has been described most elaborately by Haas, such integrative steps will involve a quite complicated process of the formation of sufficiently strong supporting coalitions, a process which has to be enacted in all the states participating in integration. As we have seen the construction of such coalitions requires the formulation of such demands or decisions, compromises in fact, as to induce the support, for whatever further reasons or motivations, of a number of different actors. Again, it should be emphasized that this conception is not 'Western' or 'democratically' biased, but that it applies to all kinds of political systems or organizations. Such differences as actually exist between various kinds of political systems concern the kind of actors participating in the process, the means employed by them in their political actions, the rules governing their behavior, etc., but *not* the conception just sketched as such.

Complete identity in interests will only very rarely exist between actors. More commonly they will have both similar and dissimilar interests. Accordingly, the formation of coalitions will involve compromises and the exchange of concessions. And the common decision or demand around which the coalition is built up will normally consist of a more or less complex set of elements so made up as to persuade the individual actors that *their* interests are sufficiently realized to induce them to participate in the coalition (postulates I and II). One may assume that actors will more easily make the necessary concessions, the lower the preferences involved are, i.e. the less important the issues are to them since one will be more prepared to compromise with respect to such matters than with respect to highly preferred ones. On the other hand, similarity with regard to their more important interests will render such actors all the more willing to compromise over less important ones. Such similarity with respect to highly important interests, some basic common purposes, or a common outlook, provides the basis for making compromises over less important interests, the stimulus for an actor to pay a 'price' in terms of less important concessions in order to realize the more important interests. Thus one would expect that 1. *the formation of coalitions will be the more easy, the more similar participants are with respect to their more important interests, while, for each one of them individually, the differences with the others concern relatively less important interests.*

In the second place one may presume that 2. *the more specific and tangible the interests concerned are the greater the likelihood that a coalition will be formed tends to be.* For with regard to such issues gains and losses will be more easy to determine and to compute. The magnitude of concessions can accordingly be determined and weighted more easily than with regard to more general and intangible interests.

Furthermore, 3. *the possibilities for the formation of various coali-*

tions increase the greater the number and variety of political actors in the system, and the greater the number and variety of interests for which they are organized. This renders it possible to choose different groups of actors from which to form coalitions according as is required for each step in the integrative process; it tends to lessen the common institutions' or the governments' dependence on any one particular actor or group of them, while it also increases the range of interests from which concessions may be exchanged which will increase the institutions' freedom of maneuver with respect to the kinds of things they wish to undertake (see for a similar reasoning regarding rank incongruences in the size and power of actors, *Schmitter*, 1969b: 328). This is the element of 'pluralism', strongly emphasized by Haas in particular.

The preceding considerations suggest that the possibilities for coalition formation are the greater, the greater the number and the variety of interests and actors to be found in the social structure, *and* the greater their similarity with respect to the more highly preferred values or interests.

Especially during the course of the integration process, it will be necessary to construct coalitions combining actors from the different states involved, cutting across their boundaries. This is particularly important in case the common institutions, rather than the individual governments concerned, are to play a leading role. Again, the chances for such developments to occur are the greater the more pluralistic the political systems concerned are *and* the greater the similarity as regards the more 'important' interests. But now all this regards the system as a whole. It is here that Haas's notion of 'symmetric heterogeneity' is relevant. For in order to construct coalitions cutting across the states' boundaries, configurations of interests that equally cross these boundaries are required. In other words, while there should be a variety of different interests, the differences should not run along the boundaries, and be confined to the various states.

In the above one easily observes the relevance of, in most general terms, a common culture among the participants for integration. This may be said to provide the similarity regarding the more important, or 'deeper' and more 'fundamental' interests necessary for coalition formation. The above, however, involves more things; it also indicates the relevance of the states' economic and political structure for a process of integration. For it is these, through the kinds of activities undertaken, and through the rules, procedures, and institutions through which they are undertaken, that significantly affect the kinds of actors and interests occurring in the states. Also, through the postulates VII, VIII and IX, they affect the significance of the support behavior of which such actors as may be found are capable, and thus what kinds of interests and actors will have to be included in the coalitions to be formed. And in so far as this is the case, it suggests that coalition formation (and through it integration) is the more easy, the greater the similarity between the individual states' political and economic structures, and the higher the extent to which there exists a common culture.

As a corollary to this, it would seem that the political systems of the participating states should be 'open' in the sense that the formation of coalitions cutting across the states' frontiers requires that actors may establish contacts with, and be accessible to, actors from among the other states. Also, to play an effective leading role the new international institutions should have access to actors within the individual states in order to be able to persuade them to give their support, and to bargain over compromises on which coalitions are to be formed.

It should be noted, finally, that the common interests that may induce or facilitate coalition formation and integration may also originate from external developments. Thus, the perception of a common military threat confronting a system of states, or the emergence of a powerful diplomatic or economic competitor, may give rise to common interests within the states concerned for meeting it. By the same token, such threats or competitors may make actors realize that existing decision-making facilities are insufficient to process their demands for military security or for greater diplomatic or economic stature. While such interests have presumably played an important role in the political history of mankind it should be recognized that they merely represent one kind of interest among many others, and that the relative significance of all such interests in integration or state-building processes is anything but clear. At any rate, such interests, too, must be supported from *within* the states if they are to lead to integration.

From the previous discussion it appeared that integration is most likely to begin in a rather narrow fashion. That is, it will most probably be concerned initially with interests or values of a rather specific kind, while the competencies of the common institutions established with respect to them will be equally narrowly circumscribed. Once started, however, several important things may happen that tend to broaden the process. To begin with, in the course of time the institutions may acquire legitimacy or strengthen whatever legitimacy they might have at the outset. This, in turn, will make it somewhat easier for them to reach binding decisions, while actors may be somewhat more prepared to broaden their scope of activities.

Furthermore, the decisions that are made through them, and the actors that are directly concerned with them, are not completely isolated entities. Thus, decisions made with respect to one kind of actor and one kind of interest will have consequences with respect to other interests and actors – a phenomenon which has been analysed most thoroughly by Haas. As we have seen, this may lead to demands for further integration with respect to additional actors and interests. Thus far the picture is relatively clear. What is not so clear, and what has hardly been analysed in the literature, however, is wherein this 'spill-over potential' of decision-making actually resides.

The preceding analyses suggest the following. Two things seem to be at issue: 1. actors that are already directly concerned with integration may demand additional decision-making in related fields in order to satisfactorily implement and realize what has already been decided (e.g. tax harmonization in order to make a common market work more satisfactorily); and 2. actors not immediately involved in the process may find that their behavioral alternatives are affected by decision-making by the new institutions (such as ministers of finance and presidents of central banks with respect to exchange rates in a common market with regulated prices). In both cases decision-making affects actors' interests; it suggests that 'spill-over potential' is the greater the more interests are affected, and/or the more highly preferred interests are affected, and/or the more significant the actors whose interests are affected. And, on the basis of postulates VII, VIII, and IX, one would expect that this potential is the higher, the more people and resources are involved, and the more it affects actors' access.

And these considerations, in turn, suggest that the more important and far-reaching the decisions of the common institutions, the more important spill-over will become, i.e., the stronger the pressure for further integration and an enlargement of the institutions' scope will grow. By the same token, it will become more difficult to undo the process or to reverse it; the more actors and interests are involved in it, the greater the possibilities for coalition building and for exchanging concessions from different fields. Also, the more non-governmental actors from within the several states concerned come to direct their demands and support to the new institutions, the less likely it will become that the governments of these states will find sufficient support for decisions and policies aiming at restricting, undoing, or abrogating the enterprise. And as the common institutions increasingly gain legitimacy, while the states' governments lose more and more of their functions, one may expect them to gradually lose legitimacy as well. At the same time, as noted in section 3.3.2, new actors organized at the level of the system in its entirety and focused upon the new institutions rather than upon the individual governments may be expected to form at a progressive rate the more integration proceeds.

As integration proceeds, and as the number of issues subject to decision-making by the new common institutions increases, the possibilities for coalition formation, for reaching compromises through exchanging concessions from different fields, or for accommodating differences of interests among actors also increase, as has just been noted. Compromises may be assumed to reduce stress. Accordingly, the system becomes more stable in the sense that the possibilities of coping with stress caused through demands fed into it are greater (cf. *Galtung*, 1968c: 32; *Russett*, 1969a: 124).

Not much attention is paid in the literature to the political structure of the evolving system, i.e., to the problem of describing and analysing the ways there emerges a network of interconnected actors whose relationships are regulated through institutions, rules and procedures that equally emerge in the process. Apart from introductory descriptions of the institutional make-up of the integrating systems, to be found in most investigations, or from purely legal analysis by lawyers, political scientists tend to concentrate upon the typically 'political' and most central parts of the system's structure, such as the Commission in the case of the EEC. However, such a system's structure normally involves much more. Even within the jurisdiction of the common institutions, one may suspect that there will be a variety of facilities, rules, procedures, and institutions through which demands and support are processed, binding decisions produced, and conflicts resolved. Some matters may be decided by relatively unofficial bargaining between actors, perhaps under the auspices of some common organ or organization; some may be decided through national governmental institutions that here may act as organs of the evolving institutional framework rather than in a purely national quality; in part decision-making may be of the legal kind and proceed through courts, both national and international ones.

These are merely a few conceivable ways of decision-making in the international system. They may be viewed as various possible avenues along which demands and support may be processed by the system. They, too, involve the same political processes, although, as in the case of courts, decision-making may be more tightly regulated. And they need not reach the system's highest level or most central institutions. And it is at least conceivable that these kinds of decision-making, too, will have more or less important integrative consequences (see, with respect to the role of courts, *Wheare*, 1963: 74).

With regard to this structure and its differentiation, i.e., the creation of ever more additional, subsidiary, and supplementary decision-making institutions and facilities, it does not seem too far-fetched to assume that this obeys the same mechanism as has been sketched in the beginning of this subsection with regard to integration generally. That is to say, it may be conceived as a response to the perception of the inadequacy of existing facilities. And from this, in turn, it would follow that such differentiation will increase the greater the amount of demands and support fed into the system, or the greater the amount and variety of decision-making required of it. In other words, structural differentiation would increase with increases in the degree of integration. Also, one would expect that the more legitimacy is acquired by the evolving structure, the greater the scope for more tightly regulated or routinized ways of decision-making and conflict resolution. For legitimacy implies support for the 'rules of the game'. Accordingly, it might be expected that the higher the degree of integration attained, the greater the incidence and importance of typically legal decision-making by courts. Conversely, the greater the number and variety of opportunities for decision-making offered to actors, the greater the stability of the system would tend to become, since the system becomes capable of accommodating more and more varied demands (cf. *Galtung*, 1968c: 26). And this, in turn, may make actors more prepared to feed their demands and support into the new structures rather than into those of the states.

All this strongly suggests a conception of integration as a process of self-sustained growth. Several provisos are in order, though. To begin with, all the qualifications described with regard to the process's 'automaticity' at the end of 3.3.2 apply here too. In addition, it is to be noted that nothing is said about the length of the period required for integration to progress toward a new 'state' or political community. In fact, it may well be that an entirely different kind of political structure will emerge. More generally, the conception sketched here is rather imprecise. In order to be able to reach more definite conclusions about the process we would have to dispose of much more information – questions such as: 'how great is the existing decision-making capacity of a system?', 'to what extent is it perceived as insufficient by whom?', 'what is the relative significance of various (positively and negatively) supporting actors?', 'what are the effects of decision-making in one field upon actors and interests in other fields?' come readily to mind but have not been answered.

It remains to be mentioned, finally, that not much is known, as yet, about further feedback effects of integration processes. Nevertheless it seems reasonable to expect that integration, especially as it progresses to high levels, during long periods of time, will change people's preferences and values; entirely new interests and actors might emerge; and the challenges with which the system is confronted in international life may equally change. These few examples at least suggest an important area for further research.

3.4. *Comment*

The preceding subsections (3.2 and 3.3) were meant to indicate what seemed to underly the theorizing discussed in the present book both as concerns the political process as such, and the process of political integration. This involved a significant measure of conjecture, since, unfortunately enough, basic concepts and principles are only rarely to be found in explicit form, in particular as they concern the political process in general. Accordingly, I have stressed intentions rather than precise and fully consistent formulations in my presentation; in fact, the preceding scheme has been rather loosely and informally worded. Moreover, the scheme is certainly and obviously incomplete. In the present subsection I will be concerned with some less obvious and more substantial weaknesses of the conception sketched so far.

I will be concerned mainly with the conception of politics in terms of decision-making (section 3.2.1). This conception defines politics in relation to binding *decisions*. That is, the conception is cast in terms of human *acts, choices* from among sets of alternatives, more or less identifiable endpoints in a process. As will appear below, such a conception is not without some important difficulties and dangers. Of course, to a large extent this is merely a matter of definition. One could surely so define decisions as to avoid all of the possible pitfalls to a decision-making conception of politics. The point is, however, that the actual choice of a decision-making language is no mere accident. It seems to derive from a historically understandable institutional bias in our conception of politics. It seems to be strongly modelled upon what happens in (what one has learnt to identify as) established 'states' where 'governments', 'leaders', or 'rulers' actually seem to *make* decisions binding upon the population. The decision-making language also seems to contain an 'anthropomorphic' bias as it were, in that it seems to be modelled on decision-making, acting, or choosing by individual man. And although, by means of the choice of suitable definitions, the defects of a decision-making language might well be remedied, it will first be necessary to identify those defects, while one may fear that many of those who actually employ this language are not always completely free from the ideas, images, and associations that are at its roots.

1. To begin with, such a conception can easily be interpreted too narrowly, so as to exclude a phenomenon such as war from the domain of political science. But it cannot be denied that an important part of political life is conducted via precisely this mechanism. Its outcome cannot straightforwardly be qualified as 'decisions', nor the process itself as one of 'decision-making', especially not since wars often do not end in any formal treaty or 'decision', without, therefore, ceasing to end in a definite result of sometimes great binding force.

2. Perhaps, too, it is precisely the kind of general political conception indicated which may explain a large part of the neglect of warfare and violence in the theories discussed. This leads to a second point, namely that it is also rather difficult to conceive the results of purely unilateral political actions, such as the occupation of the Rhineland by Hitler, or the installation of missiles on Cuba by the Soviet Union, as 'decisions', even when they come to be sanctioned and accepted by the others. The important thing in both the first and the second point is

that while the thing to be explained (e.g. the result of some war or the actual occupation of the Rhineland) may be viewed as *resulting from* a number of 'decisions' made by the actors concerned, it cannot *itself* be simply conceived as a *decision*.

3.   This leads to a third point which is that this conception tends to hide from view that the political process sometimes may go on for very extended periods (even indefinitely so, at least in principle) without resulting in anything which could properly be called a 'decision'. Thus the relations between national states may be characterized by a continuous process of bargaining, strategic moves and countermoves, minor armed clashes, and unilateral acts of a limited nature, without ever leading to some identifiable 'decision'. However, in any stage of the process their behavior is limited to relatively well-defined alternatives. They cannot transgress the boundaries 'prescribed' to them as this will invite retaliation by the other(s), i.e. war – which again seems to be of the essence of what politics is about.

4.   Furthermore, one may fear, this conception tends to limit the attention to just one point in the political process: namely, that point where some more or less easily recognizable act of the making and promulgation of what can count as a 'decision' occurs. The whole subsequent process of implementing or executing such a 'decision' is easily lost sight of, however. There does not seem to be any cogent reason, though, why political science should not be interested in that phase, too. The more so, since (as emerges again most clearly in international politics) this stage, too, may be typically 'political' in that it involves various actors contending for benefits and seeking to have the most advantageous way of implementing the decision.

It should not, however, be understood that the above only concerns the inadequacy of the decision-making conception for *international* politics. To be true, it is in that setting that the weaknesses mentioned stand out most clearly; precisely because, lacking institutions of the kind found in national states, an institutional bias is more readily exposed. But such things as warfare (in particular civil war and revolution), unilateral acts and *faits accomplis*, inconclusive processes of bargaining going on indefinitely, and struggles about the execution and implementation of decisions, are not restricted to the international scene.

5.   The 'anthropomorphic bias built into the conception discussed may equally easily obscure our view of politics. It tends to focus attention

on the acts of individuals or bodies or groups (confusingly modelled, incidentally, upon individuals and individual behavior), and it tends to view the outcomes of the process in terms of such more or less individual acts (this is particularly clearly visible in Etzioni's treatment of 'elites'). This conception, too, breaks down in the face of such phenomena as warfare or the 'game' of strategy made up of threats and counterthreats. Whatever may result from such phenomena, it can hardly be conceived as a decision made by some individual or group of individuals. But even in the case of such regularly constituted groups as governments, conferences, parties or party committees, and so on, one may strongly doubt whether what is counted as the 'decisions' of such groups can really be adequately viewed in these terms. That is to say, it would seem more appropriate and more generally applicable to take such outcomes for what they are: outcomes of processes about which, incidentally, not too much is known as yet. Attention should consequently be focused upon the *process* of which 'decisions' may be an outcome; and while such a process will be made up of numerous individual decisions, of course, its outcome results from the *interaction* of such individual decisions – not to be automatically identified as, or modelled on, such a decision itself. This anthropomorphic bias might well be responsible for the rather common tendency of indiscriminately applying postulates on behavior both to individuals and to compound actors, as will be discussed below.

Now it should be recognized that all this is not merely a question of words and terminology. The points made above concern very substantial aspects of political science. The important thing is that the conception described easily conduces to ignoring or neglecting important aspects of political life, or to applying the wrong concepts or assumptions (as in the indiscriminate application of the postulates described both to individuals and to compound actors, as will be discussed below) to the process. To some extent this may indeed be conceived as a matter of definition. One might so define the term 'decision' as to remedy many or even all of the defects of a decision-making conception of politics. This would seem to be precisely the strength of Easton's conception of politics in terms of 'allocation of values' (see *De Vree*, 1968b: 73 ff.).

Another important problem is that of the basic variables in terms of which the political process is explained. Quite generally the process is explained in terms of two ('input') variables – demands and support. Upon closer scrutiny, however, these offer some curious problems. To begin with, one may well doubt the wisdom of indiscriminately applying the term 'support' both to *actions* or *behavior* concerning demands, decisions, or the political system as such, and to the *attitudes* or, rather, *preferences* in terms of which, according to the theory sketched here, such actions or behavior are to be explained (cf. section 3.2.2). To account for the actual behavior of actors (in terms of given preferences or attitudes) is a problem which lies at a rather different level from that of explaining the formation of those attitudes or preferences themselves. This became already clear from the foregoing analysis in which different sets of postulates were needed for each of the two problems (i.e. I, II, IV and V, as against XI and XII). To use the concept 'support' at both levels of analysis might easily lead to a neglect of the rather essential differences between the problems involved there.

But if one does make this distinction, i.e., if one only applies the term 'support' to refer to *actions*, there arises another problem concerning the relationship between support and demands or decisions. For, it would seem, one does not merely support, but one supports *something*. And in the scheme discussed so far this 'something' cannot be anything else than a demand or a decision (either *within*, or *with respect to* a given political system; see also the discussion concerning support in section 3.2.2). And even in case some actor would lend support in a completely arbitrary and undirected fashion, not expressing any wish or desire of his own, still, in the scheme discussed here, this can only be considered as support for some demand, be it one made by others. This is perfectly in order, of course. For whatever may be the ideas, motivations, or lack thereof on the part of some actor lending support, the political significance of such behavior can only be that of support for the demand or decision concerned. And since in the present theory a decision presupposes demands for it, the above can be summarized by saying that supporting behavior implies demand behavior. Conversely, if some actor puts forward a demand this also means that some support for that demand (be it merely by the actor himself) is fed into the political system. So much is already indicated by postulate I.

What does all this mean? Perhaps nothing more inconspicuous than that support and demand are *aspects* of behavior, rather than different forms of behavior, and that it is always the two of them together which are fed into the political system, rather than two separate inputs, as is suggested by the present vocabulary. Nevertheless this does point to an alternative conception of the political process: instead of two inputs into the political system, demands and support, the system's input might well be conceived to consist of only one, 'demand behavior' (i.e. behavior aimed at the realization or implementation of some binding decision). 'Support' (or another term such as 'weight') could then be used to refer to those characteristics of demand behavior which render it more or less effective – which, by the way, is also its function in the present theory, as embodied in postulate III.

The difficulty of operating with the two separate concepts is clarified by considering unilateral political acts or behavior. For example, Hitler's entry of the Rhineland might be viewed as his making of a demand. Disregarding for the present moment the behavior of others in that context, the support behind the demand is nothing more than certain characteristics of that demand behavior itself, such as the number of troops employed, the means applied (i.e. military forces rather than diplomacy), or, more generally, the resources invested in it. But one can just as easily, and more economically, consider other political behavior in the same light. Thus, casting a vote or staging a street demonstration, too, may well be considered as forms of demand behavior that may be characterized in the same way, i.e. in terms of the means employed or the resources invested in it. Consequently, Occam's razor can be applied here, and one of the two concepts can be eliminated from the vocabulary. As indicated, though, this applies merely to the rather wide conception of 'demands' and 'support' chosen here as well as in the theories discussed. Such a wide conception seemed necessary in order to be able to economically accommodate the fact that both 'demands' and 'support' occur in many different forms – explicit and implicit, overt and covert, verbally or by means of actual behavior to be interpreted on demands or support behavior. Perhaps, however, 'support' ought to be interpreted much more restrictively, merely concerning actors' behavior, or propensity to behave, in accordance with certain demands, such as manifested in obedience to, acquiescence in, or a favorable disposition with regard to certain demands (or decisions). 'Demands' could then be interpreted more widely still as behavior aimed at bringing about such obedience, etc., while everything else usually denoted by 'support' could then be viewed as an aspect of such demands or demand behavior.

The postulates formulated in the preceding subsection, too, present important problems. Their most obvious defects have already been indicated. Even so, as may have appeared from the preceding chapters, they are not entirely lacking in some explanatory strength. And they are explicit enough to serve as a starting point for more disciplined and purposeful further inquiry. They do exhibit, however, one grave defect which is somewhat less obvious and should be spelled out here. As I have already hinted, it can perhaps be explained as a consequence of an 'anthropomorphically' biased conception of politics. It consists in indiscriminately applying such postulates both to individuals and to compound actors, i.e., those made up of a number of individuals. In particular this concerns postulates I and II (or, indeed, any wider assumption of rationality) saying that an actor supports a demand or decision to the extent that it agrees with his own demands or interests.

However, this does not automatically apply to groups of individuals. More or less intuitively one may already have reservations about such groups making estimations or calculations concerning 'their' interests. But, more importantly, it should be recognized that the making of a demand by any aggregate of people, or the determination of the common interests of such an aggregate, is itself already the result of a political process enacted within that group. While it may be conceivable that in certain quite exceptional cases such common demands or interests embody the identical demands or interests of the members of the group concerned, it is far more common that those members have different demands or interests in mind. In order to have the group as such make demands or determine its interests, some process of reaching agreement and compromise, usually involving a certain amount of struggle and conflict, is required. The differences may be great or small, but anyhow they have to be accommodated, through some process which is essentially political (i.e. that can or should be explained in terms of the scheme discussed). And the case that all members have identical interests, when it may seem as if no political process occurs, can more properly be viewed as a marginal and degenerate case hardly relevant empirically. Now the important thing is that *the behavior of such groups itself being the result of political processes, there is absolutely no guarantee that it will conform to what I and II say.*

Since the theory of integration discussed in 3.3 is largely an elaborated application or specification of the general political theory described in 3.2, the previous critical remarks on the latter also apply to the former – the integration theory is no better than the political theory from which it derives. Furthermore, I have already drawn the attention to some of the more 'technical' defects of the integration theory described (both in 3.3.2 and in 3.3.3). Also, it does not seem necessary or worthwhile to dwell upon the rather obvious imprecisions, vaguenesses, and undecidable issues in the theory. There are some more important issues that merit some brief additional comment.

With regard to the postulates on learning and legitimacy, it should be mentioned that in the form they have been stated they do not allow for the explanation of 'unlearning' and the loss of legitimacy. Nevertheless, in an integration theory one should be able to also account for such 'unlearning' (of allegiance to the national governments, for example) and for the loss of legitimacy of the states' political institutions. Furthermore, postulate XI, in the form stated, sounds somewhat unconvincing. It does not seem very probable that people can come to like everything conceivable in the way it indicates. This suggests that it should be qualified, for example by stipulating that the values or preferences concerned should not be too wide apart. With respect to these postulates (XI and XII), finally, it is to be observed that they, too, refer indiscriminately to individuals and actors consisting of a number of individuals. In view of what I have already said previously on this topic, the validity of this procedure seems doubtful.

Another defect of the theory is that it cavalierly glosses over the problem of the formation of new actors, an important element in the process of integration. That is, it is too readily assumed that new actors will form in a more or less direct and automatic response to the emergence of common interests. However, as Olson in particular has made clear, this assumption entails grave difficulties and cannot generally be simply derived from a postulate on rational behavior (for a discussion of this point I may refer the reader to section 3.2.3).

In view of the limitations of the political conception underlying the theory, as discussed previously, it is not very surprising that the integration theory described here largely ignores the problem of warfare and the application of physical violence with respect to integration. Since it would seem that these have played a more or less important role in many historical cases of integration, ignoring them greatly restricts the scope and applicability of the theory. The more so since integration through warfare and physical violence cannot simply be conceived as an entirely different category; it may be presumed that most empirical cases of integration do or did involve some measure of both typically peaceful processes and the application or threat of physical violence.

Nevertheless, for all its important weaknesses the theory sketched here seems to be plausible enough – as far as it goes. And although it cannot be said to have been tested empirically in a scientifically acceptable way, as has appeared from the several preceding chapters, it equally cannot be denied some empirical backing either. At any rate, it does seem to provide a suitable basis for research; it does at the very least offer a number of research problems that seem to be highly significant.

4. THE PROBLEM OF POLITICAL INTEGRATION - ITS SIGNIFICANCE

The present study was set up as an investigation into what seemed to be a rather special and narrow phenomenon: international political integration. We have ended, in section 3 in particular, with the problem of general political theory, i.e. a theory which deals with the political process as such, and which is not limited to either a domestic or an international setting.

To a fairly large extent this derives from rather general theoretical considerations. The explanation of any political phenomenon whatsoever, however limited its nature may seem to be, raises the problem of general political theory. For such explanation presupposes, applies, or conduces to, a more general political theory from which the phenomenon investigated receives its relevance, meaning, and definition, and which provides the apparatus of postulates and concepts in terms of which to explain it. Thus, to explain voting in parliament presupposes certain notions about individual and group behavior in politics, a conception of governmental and parliamentary institutions, ideas about coalition formation in politics, etc. In the present context it is of only secondary importance that general political theory will often remain implicit rather than expressly so formulated in practice. Whether or not one will actually deal with all the various problems in depth and thus pose the problem of general political theory as such and in full will normally depend upon rather more pragmatic considerations. That is, it will depend upon the availability or non-availability of some pre-existing body of theory which one considers applicable, upon the amount of time and energy available to the investigator, and upon one's ambitions (e.g. whether one intends to do just some explorative research, or to develop and test a strict theory of the phenomenon at issue).

In the case of (international) political integration, however, it soon became clear that no satisfactory analysis was at all possible without at the same time dealing explicitly and in depth with the problem of general political theory. This fact derives from the very fundamental nature of the phenomenon itself. As will have become clear from the preceding text, political integration poses all of the major problems of politics generally in a very direct and immediate fashion – so directly and immediately, indeed, that they cannot properly be ignored or left in implicit form. Thus, the above considerations on the ultimate anchorage of every phenomenon in general theory are reinforced, in the case of political integration, by the nature of the phenomenon itself. Since this phenomenon is often associated with rather narrow research concerns (in particular with those of international or even European integration) it may be useful to enlarge somewhat upon this aspect of the matter.

To begin with, political integration has been seen to represent a quite general phenomenon in that it is neither typically national nor international in kind. It occurs in both settings, and in so far as the theory has been developed at all it applies both to national and to international integration. In fact, as has appeared from chapters three to six, although the authors discussed were concerned primarily with *international* integration, it also became clear that they were unable to establish a clearcut dividing line between it and national integration. In the conception of the phenomenon developed thus far, integration is concerned with a development relevant to any political process whatsoever, namely its institutionalization. And in the light of this conception the distinction between domestic and international politics and integration loses much of such compelling force as it may initially have had. For the differences between the two settings now reduce to differences in the degree to which the political process has become institutionalized. This is as it should be. Taking a longer historical, or wider geographic, view it becomes at once clear that the (Western) national state, too, is the outcome of processes of (initially even *international*) integration, one possible form of the institutionalization of (geographically limited) political processes. These processes cannot be said to have spent themselves, either within actual states or between them. Accordingly it is difficult to see why political integration should be associated restrictively to what is here and now viewed as 'international' politics, thus elevating to theoretical dignity what is after all merely a matter of historical accident. It is an important merit of the above mentioned conception of political integration that it points to the basic continuity between national and international politics and focuses our attention upon a crucial aspect of the political process as such.

Political integration as the institutionalization of a political process is intimately bound up with the perennial problems of war and peace, or, more generally, with the problem of physical violence in politics. As may be recalled from the last section an important element in the definition of the concept is constituted by the limitation of the application of physical violence in the political process (cf. also Max Weber's definition of the 'state' in terms of a monopoly of the application of physical violence; *Weber*, 1925: 28). An increasing incidence of such violence, on the other hand, would represent disintegration. More generally one may say that integration represents a development toward greater stability and reliability of the political process, toward more rule-behavior, toward a political division of labor, and toward a lowering of the costs and risks (violence, warfare!) of the process. Integration, one might say, represents an increasingly 'controlled' political process. But although the connection between the problems of integration and those of physical violence may thus be clear enough, it must be admitted that in the literature discussed here, this aspect of the matter has scarcely been dealt with. To some extent this neglect of the problem of violence might be explained by the fact that the authors concerned have occupied themselves primarily with integration as a *peaceful* process. The problem has been more or less defined away. This, however, it rather unsatisfactory for two interconnected reasons. In the first place, although the *process itself* may well occur in a peaceful fashion, still it *results in* a limitation of political violence. And to explain such limitation does indeed require a theory about the occurrence of violence, whether or not its limitation occurs peacefully. In the second place, to limit oneself to the investigation of peaceful integration processes only would seem to be a rather severe restriction in view of the fact that in so many historical cases of integration (and not only in cases of empires, but also in those of national states) the process has at least been accompanied by violence. Also, by limiting the subject to peaceful integration, one may well lose sight of the role of the means of such violence (such as standing armies) short from actual warfare. Accordingly it is difficult to see how an adequate theory of integration could ignore the problem of physical violence in any of its forms (potential and actual, by armies or police forces, legitimate or illegitimate, etc.).

Another range of problems with which political integration is intimately related is represented by what may be called the 'political order'. That is, integration conceived as the institutionalization of a political process immediately poses the problem of the character or form of such institutionalization. To judge from political history and the actual political landscape, a number of different forms of institutionalization are possible: (colonial) empires, federations, confederations, limited 'functional' organizations such as EEC, hegemonial systems, and, from a somewhat different point of view, in such forms as oligarchy, democracy, totalitarian dictatorships, etc. From the preceding chapters it may have appeared that even the mere problem of finding a classification of such forms has hardly been posed, and that this aspect of the matter, too, has gone largely unnoticed in the literature on integration. Nevertheless, the general problem of integration does indeed immediately raise this problem of the political order, of the 'how' of institutionalization, while it does not seem too far-fetched to expect that the process of integration will be significantly affected by the nature of the institutional set-up which develops.

Thus far I have mainly dealt with a few theoretically important aspects of the problem of integration. What, however, about its 'practical' or empirical significance, its actuality? In the first place it should be realized that if the field should include both processes of integration and of *dis*integration, then it will always be practically relevant in the sense that there will always actually be either integration or disintegration in some political process. Secondly, as has already been pointed out, since integration is concerned both with national and with international political processes, and since processes of state-building are actually taking place in many parts of the world, it being not very reasonable to expect these to be consummated soon, the subject will remain empirically relevant for some time to come. Finally, and most importantly, one may expect integration to proceed even in international life and in the world at large. It will be recalled that integration is generally conceived to be a response to the growing interdependence in various fields of people or political actors generally. Now, to judge from contemporary developments in the fields of economic life, traffic, communications, etc., it would seem that generally such interdependence of all kinds of actors in the world is growing – the world is shrinking in many respects. Also, it does not seem very likely that these developments will be reversed in the forseeable future. Accordingly, granted that the theory is true, at least with respect to the aspect just mentioned, one would expect a general and long-range trend of political integration to occur in the world at large. However, even if true this does not mean that this process will be a quick one, or that it will necessarily occur in a peaceful fashion. For, given the fact that it concerns a rather profound transformation of international political life, and to judge from the actual integrative experiences of the last hundred years or so, one would rather expect integration to be a very slow process. Also, the fact that it will generally result in a decreasing incidence of international warfare is not to say that the process itself will not be accompanied by such warfare. Not only that warfare itself may be an integrative mechanism, i.e. result in integration, but precisely because integration is so important a transformation of political life implying, for one thing, rather fundamental changes in existing interests and 'power' relations, one could hardly expect this to occur without its calamities. Accordingly, the most that one could perhaps say is that there will be a long-range trend toward integration, i.e. that the subject will remain empirically relevant even in international life.

We do not at present know either how the process will actually occur, or what form future international life will take. Thus it is not at all certain that the process will ultimately end up in a giant world-state modelled upon the contemporary nation-state. Such a 'state' would even be rather difficult to conceive even with modern administrative devices. At least a considerable measure of decentralization would have to be introduced. It might even be possible that the political world would come to consist of a large number of separate 'functional' agencies, more or less along the lines of Mitrany's thinking. But then, problems of coordination would inevitably arise thus, perhaps, conducing to a necessity for more general and superordinated agencies or 'government'. There would arise enormous problems of 'representation', problems that are already difficult enough in any contemporary national state, democratically organized or not. Also, while the character of the present-day national state will inevitably change, we do not know how, or in what direction. It is anything but clear that it would necessarily fully disappear from the world stage. At present the theory of integration is so weakly developed that we do not even know what institutional alternatives there are before us.

Integration, so much may have become clear by now, touches some most important aspects of what might be called the 'quality' of political life. It is concerned with the political organization of human life, with the conditions under which politics is, or comes to be, enacted. These considerations open up a somewhat different range of problems than have been dealt with so far: the normative or ethical ones. Briefly, thus far we have merely dealt with the problem of explaining such integration as does actually occur irrespective of the problem whether we like it or not, whether we think the phenomenon ought or ought not to occur. It will be clear, however, that from a more practical point of view these ethical problems are extremely important especially if one wishes to apply the theory to the problem of 'planning' future political developments, or to that of developing an ethically satisfactory alternative. This poses a number of rather difficult philosophical or methodological problems with which I will not deal here (see for a fuller discussion of the subject, *De Vree*, 1970a). Very briefly, the problem is that of developing a different theory, one which is based upon ethical postulates and which is 'tested' not in terms of observables (except for its typically 'descriptive' elements) but in those of other ethical propositions. That is, it is a matter of developing *applied* political theory which, unlike the *descriptive* theories as they have been developed in this book, contain *ethical* propositions, i.e. propositions which say something about what (their author thinks) *ought* or *ought not* to happen, what is *good* or *better* and *bad* or *worse*. While I think such applied political theory both necessary and feasible this does not mean that its formation will be an easy task. For one thing, the purely descriptive theory which is to serve as an important element in such applied theories should be rather highly developed, while it should also be developed in terms which lend themselves to ethical propositions, i.e. which refer to elements in the world that are somehow subject to human control. The theory as developed in the present book hardly qualifies for this purpose. But it does at least have the merit that it provides for the rather precise location of the many problems involved in the phenomenon of integration.

BIBLIOGRAPHY

AKE, Claude, 1967a. *A theory of political integration.* Dorsey Press, Homewood (Ill.).

AKE, Claude, 1967b. Political integration and political stability – a hypothesis. *Wld Polit. 19 (3)*: 486–499.

ALKER Jr., Hayward R., 1969. Supranationalism in the United Nations. In: James N. Rosenau (Ed.), *International politics and foreign policy – a reader in research and theory,* rev. ed., pp. 697–710. Free Press, New York.

ALMOND, Gabriel A., 1960. A functional approach to comparative politics. In: Gabriel A. Almond & James S. Coleman (Ed.), *The politics of the developing areas,* pp. 3–64. Princeton University Press, Princeton (N.J.).

ALMOND, Gabriel A., 1965. A developmental approach to political systems. *Wld Polit. 17 (2)*: 183–214.

ALMOND, Gabriel A. & James S. COLEMAN (Ed.), 1960. *The politics of the developing areas.* Princeton University Press, Princeton (N.J.).

ANDERSON, Stanley V., 1967. *The Nordic Council – a study of Scandinavian regionalism.* University of Washington Press, Seattle/London.

ANGELL, Robert C., 1967. The growth of transnational participation. *J. social Issues 23 (1)*: 108–129.

ANONYMOUS, 1965. Pressiegroepen in de EEG. Europa Instituut, Universiteit van Amsterdam. Europese Monografieën No. 3. Kluwer, Deventer.

ANONYMOUS, 1966a. *International political communities – an anthology.* Doubleday, New York.

ANONYMOUS, 1966b. *Proc. int. Peace Res. Ass.* (Inaugural Conf.). Van Gorcum, Assen.

ANONYMOUS, 1968a. *Besluitvorming in de Europese Gemeenschappen – theorie en praktijk.* Europese Monografieën No. 10. Kluwer, Deventer.

ANONYMOUS, 1968b. *Proc. int. Peace Res. Ass.* (2nd Conf.), 2 vols. Van Gorcum, Assen.

AXLINE, W. Andrew, 1968. *European Community law and organizational development.* Oceana Publications – Dobbs Ferry, New York.

BACHRACH, Peter & Morton S. BARATZ, 1963. Decisions and nondecisions – an analytical framework. *Am. polit. Sci. Rev. 57 (3)*: 632–642.

BARKUN, Michael, 1968. *Law without sanctions – order in primitive societies and the world community.* Yale University Press, New Haven/London.

BARTH, Ernest A. & Stuart D. JOHNSON, 1959. Community power and a typology of social issues. *Social Forces 38 (1)*: 29–32.

BENDIX, Reinhard, 1969. *Nation-building and citizenship – studies of our changing social order.* Doubleday, Garden City (N.Y.).

BERNARD, Stéphan, 1970. *Esquisse d'un modèle de l'intégration européenne.* Institut de Sociologie de l'Université Libre de Bruxelles. (Mimeo.)

BLAU, Peter M., 1964. *Exchange and power in social life.* Wiley, New York, 1967.

BOULDING, Kenneth E., 1962. *Conflict and defense – a general theory.* Harper, New York.

BOULDING, Kenneth E., 1964. Toward a theory of peace. In: Robert Fischer (Ed.), *International conflict and behavioral science – the Craigville papers,* pp. 70–87. Basic Books, New York.

BOULDING, Kenneth E., 1966. Integrative aspects of the international system. *Proc. int. Peace Res. Ass.* (Inaugural Conf.): 27–38. Van Gorcum, Assen.

BRAMS, Steven J., 1966. Transaction flows in the international system. *Am. polit. Sci. Rev. 60 (4)*: 880–898.

BRAMS, Steven J., 1969. The structure of influence relationships in the international system. In: James N. Rosenau (Ed.), *International politics and foreign policy – a reader in research and theory,* pp. 583–599. Free Press, New York.

BUCHANAN, James M. & Gordon TULLOCK, 1962. *The calculus of consent – logical foundations of constitutional democracy.* University of Michigan Press, Ann Arbor (Mich.).

BURGESS, Philip M. & James A. ROBINSON, 1969. Alliances and the theory of collective action – a simulation of coalition processes. In: James N. Rosenau (Ed.), *International politics and foreign policy – a reader in research and theory,* pp. 640–653. Free Press, New York.

BURTON, J.W., 1968. *Systems, states, diplomacy and rules.* University Press, Cambridge.

CHAMBERS, William Nisbet, 1963. *Political parties in a new nation – the American experience, 1776–1809.* Oxford University Press, New York.

COCHRANE, James D., 1969. *The politics of regional integration – the Central American case.* Martinus Nijhoff, The Hague.

CODDINGTON, Alan, 1968. *Theories of the bargaining process.* Allen & Unwin, London.

COHEN, Ronald & John MIDDLETON (Ed.), 1967. *Comparative political systems – studies in the politics of pre-industrial societies.* Natural History Press, Garden City (N.Y.).

COLEMAN, James S., 1960. The political systems of the developing areas. In: Gabriel A. Almond & James S. Coleman (Ed.), *The politics of the developing areas,* pp. 532–576. Princeton University Press, Princeton (N.J.).

Coser, Lewis A., 1967. *Continuities in the study of social conflict.* Free Press, New York.

Cox, Robert W., 1969. The executive head – an essay on leadership in international organization. *Int. Orgn 23 (2):* 205–230.

Dahl, Karl Nandrup, 1968. The role of I.L.O. standards in the global integration process. *J. Peace Res. 5 (4):* 309–351.

Daudt, H., 1962. Sociaal-wetenschappelijke bestudering van politieke verschijnselen. In: H. Daudt et al. (Ed.), *Het conflict als maatschappelijk verschijnsel.* spectrum, Utrecht/Antwerpen. (Dutch.)

Daudt, H. et al. (Ed.), 1962. *Het conflict als maatschappelijk verschijnsel.* Spectrum, Utrecht/Antwerpen. (Dutch.)

Deutsch, Karl W. & William J. Foltz (Ed.), 1963. *Nation-building.* Atherton Press/Prentice Hall, New York/London.

Easton, David, 1953. *The political system – an inquiry into the state of political science.* Knopf, New York, 1960.

Easton, David, 1965. *A systems analysis of political life.* Wiley, New York.

Edwards, Ward & Amos Tversky (Ed.), 1967. *Decision making – selected readings.* Penguin Books.

Eisenstadt, S. N., 1963. *The political systems of empires – the rise and fall of the historical bureaucratic societies.* Free Press of Glencoe, New York.

Elias, Norbert, 1936. *Über den Prozess der Zivilisation – soziogenetische und psychogenetische Untersuchungen,* 2. Bde. Francke, Bern/München, 1969.

Farrell, R. Barry, 1966. *Approaches to comparative and international politics.* Northwestern University Press, Evanston (Ill.).

Fischer, Robert (Ed.), 1964. *International conflict and behavioral science – the Craigville Papers.* Basic Books, New York.

Fischer, William E., 1969. An analysis of the Deutsch sociocausal paradigm of political integration. *Int. Orgn. 23 (2):* 254–290.

Frey, Bruno S., 1970. Die ökonomische Theorie der Politik oder die neue politische Ökonomie – eine Übersicht. *Z. ges. Staatswiss. 126 (1):* 1–23.

Galtung, Johan, 1964. A structural theory of aggression. *J. Peace Res. 1:* 95–119.

Galtung, Johan, 1967a. On the future of the international system. *J. Peace Res. 4:* 305–333.

Galtung, Johan, 1967b. Social position, party identification and foreign policy orientation – a Norwegian case study. In: James N. Rosenau (Ed.), *Domestic sources of foreign policy,* pp. 161–193. Free Press, New York.

Galtung, Johan, 1968a. Small group theory and the theory of international relations – a study in isomorphism. In: Morton A. Kaplan (Ed.), *New approaches to international relations,* pp. 270–302. St. Martin's Press, New York.

Galtung, Johan, 1968b. A structural theory of integration. *J. Peace Res. 5 (4):* 375–395.

Galtung, Johan, 1968c. *Peace research – analysis and recommendations.* Prepared for the Political Committee of the Consultative Assembly of the Council of Europe, Strasbourg.

GALTUNG, Johan, 1968d. Entropy and the general theory of peace. *Proc. int. Peace Res. Ass.* (2nd Conf.), Vol. 2: 3–37. Van Gorcum, Assen.

GALTUNG, Johan, 1969a. Foreign policy opinion as a function of social position. In: James N. Rosenau (Ed.), *International politics and foreign policy – a reader in research and theory,* pp. 551–572. Free Press, New York.

GALTUNG, Johan, 1969b. The social sciences – an essay on polarization and integration. In: Klaus Knorr & James N. Rosenau (Ed.), *Contending approaches to international politics,* pp. 243–285. Princeton University Press, Princeton (N.J.).

GALTUNG, Johan, 1969c. Violence, peace, and peace research. *J. Peace Res. 5 (3):* 167–191.

GREGG, Robert W. (Ed.), 1968. *International organization in the Western hemisphere.* Syracuse University Press, Syracuse (N.Y.).

HAAS, Michael, 1965. A functional approach to international organization. *J. Polit. 27 (3):* 498–517.

HAAS, Michael, 1968a. Societal asymmetries and world peace. *Proc. int. Peace Res. Ass.* (2nd Conf.), Vol. 2: 70–110. Van Gorcum, Assen.

HAAS, Michael, 1968b. Social change and national aggressiveness – 1900–1960. In: J. David Singer (Ed.), *Quantitative international politics – insights and evidence,* pp. 215–244. Free Press, New York.

HANSEN, Roger D., 1967. *Central American regional integration and economic development.* National Planning Association, Washington (D.C.).

HANSEN, Roger D., 1969. Regional integration – reflections on a decade of theoretical efforts. *Wld Polit. 21 (2):* 242–271.

HARSANYI, John C., 1969a. Game theory and the analysis of international conflict. In: James N. Rosenau (Ed.), *International politics and foreign policy – a reader in research and theory,* pp. 370–379. Free Press, New York.

HARSANYI, John C., 1969b. Rational choice models of political behavior vs. functionalist and conformist theories. *Wld Polit. 21 (4):* 513–538.

HAZLEWOOD, Arthur (Ed.), 1967. *African integration and disintegration – case studies in economic and political union.* Oxford University Press, London.

HOBBES, Thomas, 1651. *Leviathan, or the matter, forme, and power, of a commonwealth ecclesiasticall and civill.* Edited by A. R. Waller. University Press, Cambridge, 1904.

HOGAN, Willard N., 1967. *Representative government and European integration.* University of Nebraska Press, Lincoln (Neb.).

HOVLAND, Carl I., Irving L. JANIS & Harold H. KELLY, 1953. *Communication and persuasion – psychological studies of opinion change.* Yale University Press, New Haven 1959.

IKLE, Fred Charles, 1964. *How nations negotiate.* Praeger, New York 1967.

INGLEHART, Ronald, 1967. An end to European integration? *Am. polit. Sci. Rev. 61 (1):* 91–105.

JACOB, Philip E. & Alexine L. ATHERTON, 1965. *The dynamics of international organization – the making of world order.* Dorsey Press, Homewood (Ill.),

JACOB, Philip E. & Henry TEUNE, 1964. The integrative process – guidelines for analysis of the bases of political community. In: Philip E. Jacob & James V. Toscano, *The integration of political communities,* pp. 1–45. Lippincott, Philadelphia.

JACOB, Philip E. & James V. TOSCANO, 1964. *The integration of political communities.* Lippincott, Philadelphia.

KAISER, Karl, 1968. The interaction of regional subsystems – some preliminary notes on recurrent patterns and the role of superpowers. *Wld Polit. 21 (1):* 84–107.

KAPLAN, Harold, 1967. *Urban political systems – a functional analysis of metro Toronto.* Columbia University Press, New York/London.

KAPLAN, Morton A. (Ed.), 1968. *New approaches to international relations.* St. Martin's Press, New York.

KATZ, Daniel, 1967. Group process and social integration – a system analysis of two movements of social protest. *J. social Issues 23 (1):* 3–22.

KAY, David A. (Ed.), 1967. *United Nations political system.* Wiley, New York.

KELMAN, Herbert C., 1969. Patterns of personal involvement in the national system – a social-psychological analysis of political legitimacy. In: James N. Rosenau (Ed.), *International politics and foreign policy – a reader in research and theory,* pp. 276–288. Free Press, New York.

KNORR, Klaus & James N. ROSENAU (Ed.), 1969. *Contending approaches to international politics.* Princeton University Press, Princeton (N.J.).

KUHN, Alfred, 1963. *The study of society – a unified approach.* Irwin/Dorsey Press, Homewood (Ill.).

LANDECKER, Werner S., 1952. Integration and group structure – an area for research. *Social Forces 30 (4):* 394–400.

LANDY, E. A., 1966. *The effectiveness of international supervision – thirty years of I.L.O. experience.* Stevens/Oceana, London/New York.

LASSWELL, Harold D. & Abraham KAPLAN, 1950. *Power and society – a framework for political inquiry.* Yale University Press, New York/London, 1963.

LEFEVER, Ernest W., 1969. State-building in tropical Africa. *Orbis 12 (4):* 984–1003.

LOWI, Theodore J., 1964. American business, public policy – case-studies and political theory. *Wld Polit. 16 (4):* 677–715.

MARK, Max, 1965. *Beyond sovereignty.* Public Affairs Press, Washington (D.C.).

MASTERS, Roger D., 1969. World politics as a primitive political system. In: James N. Rosenau (Ed.), *International politics and foreign policy – a reader in research and theory,* pp. 104–118. Free Press, New York.

MERELMAN, Richard M., 1966. Learning and legitimacy. *Am. polit. Sci. Rev.* *60 (3)*: 548–561.

MERRITT, Richard L., 1963. Nation-building in America – the colonial years. In: Karl W. Deutsch & William J. Foltz (Ed.), *Nation-building*, pp. 56–72. Atherton Press/Prentice Hall, New York/London.

MILBRATH, Lester W., 1967. Interest groups and foreign policy. In: James N. Rosenau (Ed.), *Domestic sources of foreign policy*, pp. 231–251. Free Press, New York.

NEWCOMBE, Alan, 1969. Initiatives and responses in foreign policy. *Peace Res. Rev. 3 (3)*: 1–128.

NEWCOMBE, Hanna, 1967. Alternative approaches to world government. *Peace Res. Rev. 1 (1)*: 1–84.

NORTH, Robert C., 1968. The behavior of nation-states – problems of conflict and integration. In: Morton A. Kaplan (Ed.), *New approaches to international relations*, pp. 303–356. St. Martin's Press, New York.

NORTH, Robert C., Howard E. KOCH Jr. & Dina A. ZINNES, 1960. The integrative functions of conflict. *J. Conflict Resolution 4*: 355–374.

NYE, Joseph S., 1965a. Patterns and catalysts in regional integration. *Int. Orgn 19*: 870–884.

NYE, Joseph S., 1965b. *Pan-Africanism and East African integration.* Harvard University Press, Cambridge (Mass.).

NYE, Joseph S., 1966. East African economic integration. In: *International political communities – an anthology*, pp. 405–436. Doubleday, New York.

NYE, Joseph S., 1967a. Central American regional integration. *Int. Conciliation* 562.

NYE, Joseph S., 1967b. Corruption and political development – a cost-benefit analysis. *Am. polit. Sci. Rev. 61 (2)*: 417–427.

NYE, Joseph S., 1968a. Comparative regional integration – concept and measurement. *Int. Orgn 22 (4)*: 855–880.

NYE, Joseph S. (Ed.), 1968b. International regionalism – readings. Little, Brown & Company, Boston.

NYE, Joseph S., 1969. United States policy toward regional organization. *Int. orgn 23 (3)*: 719–740.

NYE, Joseph S., 1970. *East African integration – a note on measurement.* Geneva, January 1970. (Mimeo.)

OLSON Jr., Mancur, 1965. *The logic of collective action – public goods and the theory of groups.* Harvard University Press, Cambridge (Mass.).

OLSON Jr., Mancur & Richard ZECKHAUSER, 1968. An economic theory of alliances. In: Bruce M. Russett (Ed.), *Economic theories of international politics*, pp. 25–45. Markham, Chicago.

PLISCHKE, Elmer (Ed.), 1964a. *Systems of integrating the international community.* Van Nostrand, Princeton.

PLISCHKE, Elmer, 1964b. International integration – purpose, progress, and prospects. In: Elmer Plischke (Ed.), *Systems of integrating the international community*, pp. 3–26. Van Nostrand, Princeton.

RASER, John R., 1969. Learning and affect in international politics. In: James N. Rosenau (Ed.), *International politics and foreign policy – a reader in research and theory*, pp. 432–441. Free Press, New York.

REINTON, Per Olav, 1967. International structure and international integration – the case of Latin America. *J. Peace Res. 4*: 334–365.

RESCHER, Nicholas, 1969. *Introduction to value theory.* Prentice Hall, Englewood Cliffs (N.J.).

RIKER, William H., 1962. *The theory of political coalitions.* Yale University Press, New Haven/London.

RIKER, William H., 1964. Some ambiguities in the notion of power. *Am. polit. Sci. Rev. 58 (2)*: 341–349.

RIKER, William H. & Donald NIEMI, 1962b. The stability of coalitions on roll calls in the House of Representatives. *Am. polit. Sci. Rev. 56 (1)*: 58–65.

ROSE, Richard, 1969. Dynamic tendencies in the authority of regimes. *Wld Polit. 21 (4)*: 602–628.

ROSENAU, James N., 1966. Pre-theories and theories of foreign policy. In: R. Barry Farrell, *Approaches to comparative and international politics*, pp. 27–92. Northwestern University Press, Evanston (Ill.).

ROSENAU, James N. (Ed.), 1967a. *Domestic sources of foreign policy.* Free Press, New York.

ROSENAU, James N., 1967b. Foreign policy as an issue area. In: James N. Rosenau (Ed.), *Domestic sources of foreign policy*, pp. 11–50. Free Press, New York.

ROSENAU, James N. (Ed.), 1969. *International politics and foreign policy – a reader in research and theory*, rev. ed. Free Press, New York.

RUSSETT, Bruce M., 1963. *Community and contention – Britain and America in the twentieth Century.* MIT Press, Cambridge (Mass.).

RUSSETT, Bruce M., 1967. *International regions and the international system – a study in political ecology.* Rand McNally, Chicago.

RUSSETT, Bruce M., 1968a. Delineating international regions. In: David J. Singer (Ed.), *Quantitative international politics – insight and evidence*, pp. 317–352. Free Press, New York.

RUSSETT, Bruce M., 1968b. Components of an operational theory of international alliance formation. *J. Conflict Resolution 12 (3)*: 285–301.

RUSSETT, Bruce M. (Ed.), 1968c. *Economic theories of international politics.* Markham, Chicago.

RUSSETT, Bruce M., 1969a. Toward a model of competitive international politics. In: James N. Rosenau (Ed.), *International politics and foreign policy – a reader in research and theory*, pp. 119–130. Free Press, New York.

RUSSETT, Bruce M., 1969b. The calculus of deterrence. In: James N. Rosenau (Ed.), *International politics and foreign policy – a reader in research and theory*, pp. 359–369. Free Press, New York.

RUSSETT, Bruce M., 1969c. The ecology of future international politics. In: James N. Rosenau (Ed.), *International politics and foreign policy – a reader in research and theory*, pp. 93–103. Free Press, New York.

SCHELLING, Thomas C., 1960. *The strategy of conflict*. Oxford University Press, New York, 1963.
SCHMITTER, Philippe C., 1969a. Three neo-functional hypotheses about international integration. *Int. Orgn 23 (1)*: 161–166.
SCHMITTER, Philippe C., 1969b. Further notes on operationalizing some variables related to regional integration. *Int. Orgn 23 (2)*: 327–336.
SCOTT, Robert E., Nation-building in Latin America. In: Karl W. Deutsch & William J. Foltz (Ed.), *Nation-building*, pp. 73–83. Atherton Press/Prentice Hall, New York/London.
SEGAL, Aaron, 1966. The integration of developing countries – some thoughts on East Africa and Central America. *J. Common Market Stud. 5 (3)*: 252–282.
SIEGEL, Sidney & Lawrence E. FOURAKER, 1960. *Bargaining and group decision making – experiments in bilateral monopoly*. McGraw-Hill, New York.
SINGER, J. David, 1963. Inter-nation influence – a formal model. *Am. polit. Sci. Rev. 57 (2)*: 420–430.
SINGER, J. David (Ed.), 1968. *Quantitative international politics – insights and evidence*. Free Press, New York.
SNYDER, Louis L., 1968. *The new nationalism*. Cornell University Press, Ithaca (N.Y.).
SPINOZA, Benedict de, 1670–77. *The political works – the Tractatus Theologico-politicus in part and the Tractatus Politicus in full*. Edited and translated with an introduction and notes by A. G. Wernham. Clarendon Press, Oxford, 1958.
STEINER, Jürg, 1969. Nonviolent conflict resolution in democratic systems – Switzerland. *J. Conflict Resolution 13 (3)*: 295–304.
STEVERS, Th.A., 1968. Een economische analyse van het democratisch proces. *Sociale Wet. 11 (1)*: 37–70.
STRAYER, Joseph R., 1963. The historical experience of nation-building in Europe. In: Karl W. Deutsch & William J. Foltz (Ed.), *Nation-building*, pp. 17–26. Atherton Press/Prentice Hall, New York/London.
STREIT, Clarence K., 1939. *Union now – a proposal for a federal union of the democracies of the North Atlantic*. Jonathan Cape, London.

TARLTON, Charles D., 1965. Symmetry and asymmetry as elements of federalism – a theoretical speculation. *J. Polit. 27 (4)*: 861–874.
TAYLOR, Paul, 1968. The concept of community and the European integration process. *J. Common Market Stud. 7 (2)*: 83–101.
TULLOCK, Gordon, 1967. *Toward a mathematics of politics*. University of Michigan Press, Ann Arbor (Mich.).

VAN DYKE, Vernon, 1957. *International politics*. Appleton-Century-Crofts, New York, 1966.

VALKENBURGH, P., 1969. *Anatomie van het conflict – een modeltheoretische benadering.* Samson, Alphen aan de Rijn. (Dutch.)

VREE, J.K. De, 1968a. *Internationale integratie – inleidende opmerkingen.* Amsterdam, mei-juni 1968. (Mimeo; Dutch.)

VREE, J.K. De, 1968b. De wetenschap der politiek – het vraagstuk van een definitie. *Acta polit. 4 (1):* 55–81. (Dutch.)

VREE, J.K. De, 1970a. Opmerkingen over 'theorie' en 'praktijk', *Soc. Wet. 13 (1):* 12–36. (Dutch.)

VREE, J.K. De, 1970b. *Some observation on the theory of political integration.* Amsterdam, march 1970. (Mimeo.)

WALLERSTEIN, Immanuel, 1967. *Africa, the politics of unity – an analysis of a contemporary social movement.* Random House, New York.

WATTS, R.L., 1966. *New federations – experiments in the Commonwealth.* Clarendon Press, Oxford.

WEBER, Max, 1925. *Grundriss der Sozialökonomik. 3. Abt. Wirtschaft und Gesellschaft,* 2. vermehrte Aufl. Mohr, Tübingen.

WEINER, Myron, 1965. Political integration and political development. *Ann. Am. Acad. polit. social Sci. 358:* 52–64.

WEISSBERG, Robert, 1969. Nationalism, integration, and French and German elites. *Int. Orgn 23 (2):* 337–347.

WHEARE, K.C., 1963. *Federal government,* 4th ed. Oxford University Press, London (1st ed. 1946).

WILDAVSKY, Aaron B., 1962. The analysis of issue-contexts in the study of decision making. *J. Polit. 24 (4):* 717–732.

WILSON, David A., 1963. Nation-building and revolutionary war. In: Karl W. Deutsch & William J. Foltz (Ed.), *Nation-building,* pp. 84–94. Atherton Press/Prentice Hall, New York/London.

YALEM, Ronald J., 1965. *Regionalism and world order.* Public Affairs Press, Washington (D.C.).

YOUNG, Oran R., 1968a. *The politics of force-bargaining during international crises.* Princeton University Press, Princeton (N.J.).

YOUNG, Oran R., 1968b. The United Nations and the international system. *Int. Orgn 23 (4):* 902–922.

APPENDIX TO SECTION 3: LIST OF POSTULATES

I   A demand is supported by an actor to the extent that it agrees with the substance of his own demands or interests.

II   A decision is supported by an actor to the extent that it agrees with the substance of his own demands or interests.

III   The decisions that will actually be taken at some moment are those which are supported by a stronger coalition than any of the relevant alternative decisions.

IV   Actors will make demands if and to the extent that the behavior of the other actors in the collectivity concerned is important to them for the realization of their own goals.

V-1   The more frequently an actor interacts with other actors the more important will be the behavior of these latter for the realization of that actor's goals.

V-2   For any actor, the behavior of other actors with whom he interacts is the more (less) important for the realization of his goals, the more (less) highly preferred the goals involved in those interactions are by the actor.

VI   The more similar actors are with respect to their goals, values, and preferences, the greater the likelihood that they will make similar demands.

VII   The significance of support, its magnitude, or the strength of a supporting coalition increases as the number of individuals involved increases.

VIII The more physical, economic, intellectual, moral, organizational, or propagandistic resources an actor or coalition of actors commands, the greater the significance of its support.

IX   The greater an actor's or coalition's access, i.e., the closer it is to actual decision-makers, the greater the significance of its support.

X   Support is the more significant, the more resources are invested in it.

XI   The longer an actor is made to behave in a particular fashion, the greater the likelihood that he will actually prefer this behavior.

XII   The more often some behavior or relationship has led to, or contributed to, the realization of an actor's interests, the greater the likelihood that the actor will think it right and proper.

INDEX

Eisenstadt, 18, 343, **352**, 355
Elazar, 29
Elias, 352
Etzioni, 1, 3, 16, 225 ff., 270, 318, 344, 349, 354, 365
European Coal and Steel Community (ECSC), 131, 141, 269
European Communities, 1, 10, 26
European Economic Community (EEC), 145, 269, 270, 276, 292, 299, 373

Fabian Society, 39
Federalism, 18, 22, 27 ff.
Feyerabend, 81, 83
Fieldhouse, 18
Fischer, 33
Foerster, 23, 24, 25, 38
Fourastié, 58
France, 24
Frank, 68
Freeman, 20
Freund, 58
Frey, 67
Friedrich, 29, 31, 32, 33, 88, 235
Frohock, 60
Functionalism, 18, 22, 37 ff., 106

Galtung, 16, 333, 335, 336, 346, 351, 352, 361
Gaulle, de, 142, 143, 189, 234
Greece, 19, 20
Groot, de, 80, 83, 86, 87
Guild socialism, 38

Haas, 1, 3, 16, 38, 43, 88, 106 ff., 167, 186, 187, 196, 197, 205, 218, 219, 239, 242, 266, 269, 270, 273, 274, 277, 282, 287, 310, 311, 322, 323, 332, 338, 340, 347, 350, 352, 355
Habsburg Empire, 19
Hanseatic League, 19
Harsanyi, 331
Hempel, 69, 72, 73, 75, 80, 81, 84, 86
Hitler, 363, 367
Hobbes, 40, 334

Hoffmann, 85
Hovland, 348

Industrial revolution, 8
Industrial committees, 149
International Labor Organization (ILO), 38, 107, 141, 145, 147, 148, 149, 150, 154, 155, 156
Internationalism, 18, 22 ff.
International Telegraphic Union, 9

Jacob, 335, 336
Johnson, Dr., 56
Johnson, Stuart D., 339

Kaiser, 163
Kant, 25
Kaplan, Abraham, 183, 232, 280
Kaplan, Morton A., 88, 89, 339
Kotarbiński, 76
Kuhn, 67, 88, 89, 91, 348
Krech, 60

Landecker, 346
Lasswell, 183, 232, 280
Latin America, 108
Latin American Free Trade Association (LAFTA), 1
League of Nations, 39
Leinfellner, 66, 75, 81, 86
Lewis, 59, 63, 65, 87
Liberalism, 38
Lindberg, 1, 3, 16, 88, 269 ff., 318, 322, 329, 344, 352
Locke, 40
Louisiana, 19
Lowi, 277, 339

Macedonia Empire, 20
Marc, 29, 30, 36
Marin, 25
Mark, 33
Marxism, 38
Masters, 333
Maxwell, 60, 81, 82